SIGNIFICANT CASES IN CRIMINAL PROCEDURE

SIGNIFICANT CASES IN
CRIMINAL PROCEDURE

SECOND EDITION

Craig Hemmens
Missouri State University

Alan Thompson
The University of Southern Mississippi

Lisa S. Nored
The University of Southern Mississippi

OXFORD
UNIVERSITY PRESS

Oxford University Press is a department of the University of Oxford. It furthers the University's objective of excellence in research, scholarship, and education by publishing worldwide.

Oxford   New York
Auckland   Cape Town   Dar es Salaam   Hong Kong   Karachi
Kuala Lumpur   Madrid   Melbourne   Mexico City   Nairobi
New Delhi   Shanghai   Taipei   Toronto

With offices in
Argentina   Austria   Brazil   Chile   Czech Republic   France   Greece
Guatemala   Hungary   Italy   Japan   Poland   Portugal   Singapore
South Korea   Switzerland   Thailand   Turkey   Ukraine   Vietnam

For titles covered by Section 112 of the US Higher Education Opportunity Act, please visit www.oup.com/us/he for the latest information about pricing and alternate formats.

Published by Oxford University Press.
198 Madison Avenue, New York, NY 10016
www.oup.com

Library of Congress Cataloging-in-Publication Data

Hemmens, Craig.
   Significant cases in criminal procedure / Craig Hemmens, Missouri State University; Alan Thompson, The University of Southern Mississippi; Lisa S. Nored, The University of Southern Mississippi.
      pages cm.—(Criminal justice case briefs)
   Includes bibliographical references and index.
   ISBN 978-0-19-995791-0 (pbk.: alk. paper)
1. Searches and seizures—United States—Cases.   2. Criminal procedure—United States—Cases.
3. Criminal justice, Administration of—United States—Cases.
I. Thompson, Alan, 1968-   II. Nored, Lisa S.   III. Title.
KF9630.H46 2013
345.73'0522—dc23   2012045166

CONTENTS

PREFACE

This book is intended to serve as a supplement to an undergraduate criminal justice textbook on search and seizure and interrogations, or, as it is better known in law schools, "criminal procedure." It may also be used by a graduate student in criminal justice or a law-school student struggling to understand the law while wading through the myriad (and often contradictory) opinions contained in the typical law-school casebook.

While nothing substitutes for reading the original case opinion, the reality is that only those with a passion for the subject and plenty of time can afford to always go first to the source. This book is intended to assist those who are trying to read the original opinion, and to provide more detail than can be contained in a typical textbook.

The book is divided into sections that mirror the typical criminal justice textbook and law-school casebook approach to the subject, so that students and instructors can easily refer to related cases. All the significant U.S. Supreme Court cases are included, through the 2011–2012 term.

Each case brief follows the same basic format: Facts, Issue, Holding, Rationale, Case Excerpt, and Case Significance. The *Facts* section includes the relevant facts of the case that led to the eventual Supreme Court decision, as well as a brief explanation of the decisions in the lower courts. The *Issue* is the question presented to the Supreme Court for its ruling. The *Holding* is the result, the decision by the Supreme Court. The *Rationale* section contains the explanation of the Supreme Court for its decision. The *Case Excerpt* section provides some of the language from the court's opinion. The *Case Significance* section contains a discussion of why the case matters to criminal justice.

We hope that this book is of use to instructors and students seeking to understand the often-arcane world of criminal procedure. We welcome any comments or suggestions that readers have.

ACKNOWLEDGMENTS

Craig Hemmens would like to thank Mary, Emily, and Amber for their love and support.

Alan Thompson would like to thank his wife Leslie and colleagues at The University of Southern Mississippi for their continued support and enduring friendship.

Lisa S. Nored would like to extend her heartfelt thanks to Grayson Langan for her continued assistance and insight, and to her boys, Hunter, Holden, Hayden, and Hayes, who always tolerate the intrusion of her work.

The authors wish to extend their sincere thanks to Sarah Calabi at Oxford University Press for her support of this project and her willingness to go the extra mile to make it happen. The authors would also like to thank Richard Beck at Oxford University Press for his assistance and Wendy Lee Walker for making our writing readable.

The authors would also like to thank the reviewers who helped shape this book:

First edition: John S. Dempsey, Suffolk Community College; Robert A. Harvie, St. Martin's College; Raymond G. Kessler, Sul Ross State University; Patrick Mueller, Stephen F. Austin State University; Jim Ruiz, Pennsylvania State University–Harrisburg; Lawrence C. Trostle, University of Alaska–Anchorage; Marian Williams, Bowling Green State University.

The authors would also like to thank the following reviewers, who provided invaluable feedback:

- Gretchen H. Choe, University of North Texas at Dallas
- Sue Carter Collins, Georgia State University
- Jacinta M. Gau, University of Central Florida
- Jo-Ann Della Giustina, Bridgewater State University
- Stephane J. Kirven, Sacred Heart University

TABLE OF CASES

CASE HOLDINGS

CHAPTER ONE: THE EXCLUSIONARY RULE

WEEKS v. UNITED STATES, **232 U.S. 383 (1914):** Evidence seized in violation of the Fourth Amendment by federal law enforcement officers is not admissible in a federal criminal trial.

ROCHIN v. CALIFORNIA, **342 U.S. 165 (1952):** Evidence obtained as the result of a search that "shocks the conscience" is inadmissible in a criminal trial because the search violates the due process clause of the Fourteenth Amendment.

MAPP v. OHIO, **367 U.S. 643 (1961):** The exclusionary rule applies to all state criminal trials.

WONG SUN v. UNITED STATES, **371 U.S. 471 (1963):** Evidence obtained indirectly as a result of an illegal search by the police (known as "fruit of the poisonous tree") is excluded from a criminal trial unless the taint of the illegal search is subsequently purged by the police.

NIX v. WILLIAMS, **467 U.S. 431 (1984):** If police can demonstrate that evidence they obtained illegally would inevitably have been obtained through lawful means, that evidence may be admitted at a criminal trial.

UNITED STATES v. LEON, **468 U.S. 897 (1984):** Evidence seized by officers who act in good-faith reliance on a search warrant that is later declared invalid may be admitted at a criminal trial.

MASSACHUSETTS v. SHEPPARD, **468 U.S. 981 (1984):** Evidence seized by officers who act in good-faith reliance on a search warrant that is later declared invalid may be admitted at a criminal trial.

MINNESOTA v. OLSON, **495 U.S. 91 (1990):** A warrantless, nonconsensual entry of a residence to arrest an overnight guest, without an exigent circumstance, violates the Fourth Amendment.

ARIZONA v. EVANS, **514 U.S. 1 (1995):** Evidence seized in violation of the Fourth Amendment, where the violation was the result of erroneous information received from court employees, is admissible in a criminal trial.

HERRING v. UNITED STATES, **555 U.S. 135 (2009):** If an arrest and search is conducted based upon a negligent error by a police clerk who believed, in good faith, that a current outstanding warrant existed for the individual but that warrant was actually recalled, the exclusionary rule will not mandate that evidence not be admitted at trial.

DAVIS v. UNITED STATES, **— U.S. — (2011):** The good-faith exception to the exclusionary rule will apply in cases where law enforcement conducts a lawful search authorized by precedent at the time but is subsequently found to be unconstitutional in a later, separate case.

CHAPTER TWO: WHAT CONSTITUTES PROBABLE CAUSE?

BECK v. OHIO, **379 U.S. 89 (1964):** Probable cause to arrest exists when the police have reasonably trustworthy information that would warrant a person of "reasonable caution" to believe a crime is taking place or has taken place.

DRAPER v. UNITED STATES, **358 U.S. 307 (1959):** Information supplied by an informant that is later corroborated by the police can establish probable cause to arrest.

ILLINOIS v. GATES, **462 U.S. 213 (1983):** A totality-of-circumstances analysis is required for the purpose of determining whether information supplied by an informant constitutes probable cause to search.

ILLINOIS v. CABALLES, **543 U.S. 405 (2005):** The use of a narcotics-detection dog during a traffic stop, which is not deliberately prolonged, is not an improper search under the Fourth Amendment because this conduct does not compromise any legitimate interest in privacy.

CHAPTER THREE: STOP AND FRISK

TERRY v. OHIO, **392 U.S. 1 (1968):** The police may stop and frisk individuals with reasonable suspicion that criminal activity is afoot.

ADAMS v. WILLIAMS, **407 U.S. 143 (1972):** A police officer may conduct a stop and frisk based on information provided by a reliable informant.

UNITED STATES v. HENSLEY, **469 U.S. 221 (1985):** The police may conduct an investigative stop of an individual who is the subject of a "wanted" flyer.

UNITED STATES v. SOKOLOW, **490 U.S. 1 (1989):** It is not a violation of the Fourth Amendment to stop someone based on a "drug courier profile," provided that reasonable suspicion exists.

ALABAMA v. WHITE, **496 U.S. 325 (1990):** An anonymous tip, corroborated by the police, creates "reasonable suspicion" to justify a stop and frisk.

MINNESOTA v. DICKERSON, **508 U.S. 366 (1993):** The police may seize contraband detected through the sense of touch during a protective pat-down search only if the contraband is immediately apparent and no manipulation takes place.

FLORIDA v. J. L., **529 U.S. 266 (2000):** The Fourth Amendment does not authorize police to undertake a warrantless frisk based solely upon an anonymous tip.

ILLINOIS v. WARDLOW, **528 U.S. 119 (2000):** An individual's sudden flight from a high-crime area creates reasonable suspicion, justifying a stop and frisk.

ARIZONA v. JOHNSON, **555 U.S. 323 (2009):** Officers who conduct routine traffic stops may perform a pat down of a driver and any passengers upon reasonable suspicion that they may be armed and dangerous.

CHAPTER FOUR: WHEN HAS A SEIZURE OCCURRED?

SCHMERBER v. CALIFORNIA, **384 U.S. 757 (1966):** The warrantless "seizure" of one's blood is constitutional.

MICHIGAN v. CHESTERNUT, **486 U.S. 567 (1988):** Following a person does not constitute a seizure within the meaning of the Fourth Amendment.

BROWER v. COUNTY OF INYO, **489 U.S. 593 (1989):** A roadblock used by the police to stop a fleeing felon constitutes a seizure within the meaning of the Fourth Amendment.

CALIFORNIA v. HODARI D., **499 U.S. 621 (1991):** A Fourth Amendment seizure of a person does not take place unless the suspect submits to the officer or the officer uses physical force to apprehend the suspect.

FLORIDA v. BOSTICK, **501 U.S. 429 (1991):** The appropriate test for determining whether a person on a bus is seized is whether a reasonable passenger would feel free to decline officers' requests or otherwise terminate the encounter.

BOND v. UNITED STATES, **529 U.S. 334 (2000):** It is a violation of the Fourth Amendment for police officers, without any suspicion, to physically manipulate bus passengers' luggage.

KYLLO v. UNITED STATES, **533 U.S. 27 (2001):** It is a violation of the Fourth Amendment for the police to scan, without a warrant, the details of a home with a device that is not in general public use.

ILLINOIS v. MCARTHUR, **531 U.S. 326 (2001):** An officer's refusal to let a person into his or her residence, knowing that the person will destroy evidence therein, does not violate the Fourth Amendment.

HIIBEL v. NEVADA, **542 U.S. 177 (2004):** In a decision that dismayed privacy rights advocates and pleased law enforcement, a divided Supreme Court upheld a state statute requiring persons detained on the basis of reasonable suspicion to identify themselves when requested to do so by a police officer.

MUEHLER v. MENA, **544 U.S. 93 (2005):** Occupants of places to be searched may be detained during the search and reasonable force may be used to effectuate that detention. If the initial search is valid, no additional justification is needed to inquire about identity or immigration status.

BRENDLIN v. CALIFORNIA, **551 U.S. 249 (2007):** For purposes of the Fourth Amendment, a passenger is "seized" during a traffic stop, because a reasonable person in that situation would not feel free to leave.

CHAPTER FIVE: **ARREST**

UNITED STATES v. WATSON, **423 U.S. 411 (1976):** A warrantless arrest in a public place is constitutional, so long as the police have probable cause.

DUNAWAY v. NEW YORK, **442 U.S. 200 (1979):** A person cannot be seized and transported to a police station without probable cause.

PAYTON v. NEW YORK, **445 U.S. 573 (1980):** Absent exigent circumstances, it is unconstitutional to make a warrantless entry into a private place for the purpose of effecting an arrest.

WELSH v. WISCONSIN, **466 U.S. 740 (1984):** The Fourth Amendment does not permit the warrantless arrest of a person in a private residence when the arrestable offense is not jailable.

UNITED STATES v. ALVAREZ-MACHAIN, **504 U.S. 655 (1992):** A foreigner can be forcibly abducted from his or her country of origin and brought to the United States for trial, provided the abduction does not violate any treaties.

ATWATER v. CITY OF LAGO VISTA, **532 U.S. 318 (2001):** It is not a violation of the Fourth Amendment to arrest a person for an offense that carries no jail term.

CHAPTER SIX: **STANDARDS FOR THE USE OF FORCE**

TENNESSEE v. GARNER, **471 U.S. 1 (1985):** It is a violation of the Fourth Amendment for the police to use deadly force to apprehend an unarmed fleeing felon.

GRAHAM v. CONNOR, **490 U.S. 396 (1989):** Use of force claims against the police must be judged from a Fourth Amendment objective reasonableness standpoint.

SCOTT v. HARRIS, **550 U.S. 372 (2007):** A police officer's attempt to terminate a dangerous high-speed car chase that threatens the lives of innocent bystanders does not violate the Fourth Amendment, even when it places the fleeing motorist at risk of serious injury or death.

CHAPTER SEVEN: **SEARCHES WITH WARRANTS**

COOLIDGE v. NEW HAMPSHIRE, **403 U.S. 443 (1971):** Attorneys general cannot issue search warrants because they are not considered "neutral and detached magistrates."

ZURCHER v. STANFORD DAILY, **436 U.S. 547 (1978):** A warrant can be issued for the search of premises controlled by an innocent third party, provided that probable cause is present.

MINCEY v. ARIZONA, **437 U.S. 385 (1978):** If no exigent circumstances exist, a warrant must be obtained to search a homicide scene.

STEAGALD v. UNITED STATES, **451 U.S. 204 (1981):** Police officers can search the home of a third party for a person for whom they have an arrest warrant, but a separate search warrant must be obtained.

MICHIGAN v. SUMMERS, **452 U.S. 692 (1981):** A warrant carries with it the authority to detain residents of houses to be searched pursuant to a valid warrant.

MARYLAND v. GARRISON, **480 U.S. 79 (1987):** Evidence is admissible when officers mistakenly and in good faith execute a search warrant at a location not authorized in the warrant.

CALIFORNIA v. GREENWOOD, **486 U.S. 35 (1988):** Items placed in the trash for collection on a public street may be searched without a warrant or probable cause.

MINNESOTA v. CARTER, **525 U.S. 83 (1998):** A person who is in another's apartment with consent and for the purpose of doing business does not enjoy an expectation of privacy.

GROH v. RAMIREZ, **540 U.S. 551 (2004):** The particularity requirement of the Fourth Amendment is violated when the warrant itself fails to identify the person or things the petitioner intends to seize.

UNITED STATES v. JONES, **132 S.Ct. 945 (2012):** The attachment of a Global Positioning System (GPS) tracking device to an individual's vehicle, and subsequent use of that device to monitor the vehicle's movements on public streets, constitutes a search within the meaning of the Fourth Amendment.

CHAPTER EIGHT: **THE KNOCK AND ANNOUNCE RULE**

WILSON v. ARKANSAS, **514 U.S. 927 (1995):** Unless exigent circumstances exist, the Fourth Amendment's reasonableness clause requires that officers knock and announce their presence when serving search or arrest warrants.

RICHARDS v. WISCONSIN, **520 U.S. 385 (1997):** The Fourth Amendment does not permit a blanket exception to the knock and announce requirement for felony drug warrants.

UNITED STATES v. BANKS, **540 U.S. 31 (2003):** There is no set time period that police must wait before entering a dwelling after they knock and announce; what is a reasonable time period depends on the totality of the circumstances facing the police when they seek entry.

HUDSON v. MICHIGAN, **547 U.S. 586 (2006):** Applying the exclusionary rule to violations of the knock and announce rule is not the most effective means of enforcing the knock and announce rule.

CHAPTER NINE: SEARCH INCIDENT TO ARREST

WARDEN v. HAYDEN, **387 U.S. 294 (1967):** The prohibition on the seizure of items of only evidential value and allowing seizure of instrumentalities, fruits, or contraband is no longer accepted as being required by the Fourth Amendment.

CHIMEL v. CALIFORNIA, **395 U.S. 752 (1969):** The police may search the area within the immediate control of an arrestee in order to discover any weapons or to prevent the destruction of evidence.

VALE v. LOUISIANA, **399 U.S. 30 (1970):** The police may not conduct a warrantless search of a suspect's home when the suspect is arrested outside the home and exigent circumstances are not present.

UNITED STATES v. ROBINSON, **414 U.S. 218 (1973):** A police officer may conduct a full search of an arrestee, even when the officer does not fear for his or her safety.

UNITED STATES v. EDWARDS, **415 U.S. 800 (1974):** A search incident to arrest can take place several hours after the arrest.

MARYLAND v. BUIE, **494 U.S. 325 (1990):** A police officer can conduct a warrantless "protective sweep" of an area where a suspect is arrested.

VIRGINIA v. MOORE, **553 U.S. 164 (2006):** Warrantless arrests for crimes committed in the presence of an arresting officer are reasonable under the Constitution, and while states are free to regulate such arrests however they desire, state restrictions do not alter Fourth Amendment protection.

ARIZONA v. GANT, **556 U.S. 332 (2009):** A search incident to arrest involving a vehicle may not be conducted once the arrestee has been secured and is no longer a potential threat to officers or able to destroy evidence, unless the search is for evidence related to the crime of arrest.

CHAPTER TEN: CONSENT SEARCHES

STONER v. CALIFORNIA, **376 U.S. 483 (1964):** A hotel clerk may not give valid consent to search a hotel room rented to a criminal suspect.

BUMPER v. NORTH CAROLINA, **391 U.S. 543 (1968):** Consent obtained by police officers who obtain that consent by lying about the existence of a search warrant is not valid.

SCHNECKLOTH v. BUSTAMONTE, **412 U.S. 218 (1973):** Knowledge of the right to refuse consent is only one of the circumstances to be considered in determining whether a consent search is voluntary.

FLORIDA v. ROYER, **460 U.S. 491 (1983):** Consent to search is not valid if it is obtained by the police during a seizure that was not based on probable cause.

ILLINOIS v. RODRIGUEZ, **497 U.S. 177 (1990):** The police may enter a home without a warrant based upon the consent of a third party whom the police, at the time of entry, reasonably believe to possess common authority over the premises, but who in fact does not.

FLORIDA v. JIMENO, **500 U.S. 248 (1991):** Consent to search a car includes consent to search closed containers located within the car.

UNITED STATES v. DRAYTON ET AL., **536 U.S. 194 (2002):** The police may randomly approach individuals and ask for consent to search their luggage or personal belongings absent any indication that criminal activity is afoot.

GEORGIA v. RANDOLPH, **547 U.S. 103 (2006):** When a physically present inhabitant gives express refusal to a police search of his or her home, the consent of another occupant is invalid, unless there are exigent circumstances.

CHAPTER ELEVEN: PLAIN VIEW SEARCHES

TEXAS V. BROWN, **460 U.S. 730 (1983):** It need not be immediately apparent that evidence is contraband for the plain view doctrine to apply; only probable cause is necessary.

ARIZONA V. HICKS, **480 U.S. 321 (1987):** A plain view seizure requires probable cause that the item to be seized is contraband.

HORTON V. CALIFORNIA, **496 U.S. 128 (1990):** Inadvertence is not a requirement of the plain view doctrine.

CHAPTER TWELVE: **OPEN FIELDS SEARCHES**

OLIVER v. UNITED STATES, **466 U.S. 170 (1984):** The open fields doctrine applies outside the curtilage of a home, even when the property owner takes steps to exclude the public.

CALIFORNIA v. CIRAOLO, **476 U.S. 207 (1986):** The Fourth Amendment is not violated by the naked-eye aerial observation of areas within the curtilage.

UNITED STATES v. DUNN, **480 U.S. 294 (1987):** A barn located fifty yards from a house and surrounded by a fence is not within the curtilage of the residence and is therefore not protected by the Fourth Amendment.

CHAPTER THIRTEEN: **VEHICLE SEARCHES**

CARROLL v. UNITED STATES, **267 U.S. 132 (1925):** Police are authorized to undertake a warrantless roadside search of a vehicle if probable cause exists that evidence of criminal activity contained therein will be lost or destroyed if time is taken to secure a warrant.

CHAMBERS v. MARONEY, **399 U.S. 42 (1970):** The warrantless search of a vehicle that has been transported to a police station does not violate the Fourth Amendment so long as officers have probable cause to believe that it contains evidence of criminal activity.

DELAWARE v. PROUSE, **440 U.S. 648 (1979):** Except in situations where there is at least articulable and reasonable suspicion that a motorist is unlicensed or that a vehicle is unregistered, or that either the vehicle or occupants are subject to seizure for some violation of law, stopping a car solely for purposes of checking the driver's license and registration is unreasonable under the Fourth Amendment. In other words, the police may not make random traffic stops for purposes of checking a driver's license or vehicle registration in the absence of some violation of law.

NEW YORK v. BELTON, **453 U.S. 454 (1981):** Officers may search the passenger compartment of a vehicle and its contents incident to a lawful arrest. Not only may they look inside the glove compartment and other storage receptacles, but they may also examine any other closed containers even if there is a low probability that incriminating evidence will be discovered.

UNITED STATES v. ROSS, **456 U.S. 798 (1982):** Officers may open closed containers found during a warrantless vehicle search so long as they have probable cause to believe that contraband may be found therein.

MICHIGAN v. LONG, **463 U.S. 1032 (1983):** A protective search of a vehicle's passenger compartment for weapons is reasonable under the principles articulated in *Terry v. Ohio.*

CALIFORNIA v. CARNEY, **471 U.S. 386 (1985):** A motor home that is being used on the public roadways in a manner other than as a residence or dwelling qualifies as an automobile for purposes of conducting a warrantless search under established Fourth Amendment standards.

FLORIDA v. WELLS, **495 U.S. 1 (1990):** Evidence that is found within a closed container should be excluded in cases where the officer's discretion to look therein was not narrowly guided by agency policy.

CALIFORNIA v. ACEVEDO, **500 U.S. 565 (1991):** Police officers are authorized to search any container found within a vehicle without having to first secure a warrant so long as they have probable cause to believe that it holds contraband or other evidence of criminal activity.

OHIO v. ROBINETTE, **519 U.S. 33 (1996):** Police officers are not required under the Fourth Amendment to inform a motorist that he or she is free to leave before requesting consent to search a vehicle.

PENNSYLVANIA v. LABRON, **518 U.S. 938 (1996):** The very fact that a vehicle is mobile creates an exigent circumstance precluding the need for officers to first obtain a warrant before searching a vehicle that has been lawfully stopped. In other words, officers are not required to secure a warrant before searching a vehicle so long as they have solid probable cause to believe that incriminating evidence may be found therein.

WHREN v. UNITED STATES, **517 U.S. 806 (1996):** Pretextual traffic stops are constitutional so long as an officer has probable cause to believe that a traffic violation or some other offense has occurred.

MARYLAND v. WILSON, **519 U.S. 408 (1997):** Police officers may direct any and all passengers to exit and remain outside of a vehicle that has been lawfully stopped.

KNOWLES v. IOWA, **525 U.S. 113 (1998):** The full search of a vehicle incident to a traffic stop in which the officer issues a citation rather than arresting the motorist violates the Fourth Amendment.

WYOMING v. HOUGHTON, **526 U.S. 295 (1999):** Where officers have probable cause to conduct a warrantless vehicle search, they are also authorized to search a passenger's personal belongings (i.e., purse, bag, or other such receptacle) where there exists the possibility that contraband may be contained therein.

MARYLAND v. PRINGLE, **540 U.S. 366 (2003):** The passenger of a car can be charged with possession of contraband absent a specific showing that the object(s) belonged to him or her.

ILLINOIS v. LIDSTER, **540 U.S. 419 (2004):** The manner in which the police conducted the checkpoint stop did not violate the Fourth Amendment.

CHAPTER FOURTEEN: **REGULATORY SEARCHES**

SOUTH DAKOTA v. OPPERMAN, **428 U.S. 364 (1976):** A warrantless, suspicionless inventory search of an impounded vehicle does not violate the Fourth Amendment, but the search must follow standard operating procedures.

ILLINOIS v. LAFAYETTE, **462 U.S. 640 (1983):** The police may search an arrestee, including his or her personal items, as part of a routine inventory incident to booking and jailing.

CAMARA v. MUNICIPAL COURT, **387 U.S. 523 (1967):** The Fourth Amendment bars prosecution of persons who refuse to permit warrantless code inspections of their personal residences.

NEW YORK v. BURGER, **482 U.S. 691 (1987):** Inspections of vehicle junkyards fall within the "closely regulated business" exception to the Fourth Amendment's warrant requirement.

UNITED STATES v. MARTINEZ-FUERTE, **428 U.S. 543 (1976):** Roadblocks near international borders for the purpose of detecting illegal aliens do not violate the Fourth Amendment.

MICHIGAN DEPARTMENT OF STATE POLICE v. SITZ, **496 U.S. 444 (1990):** Warrantless, suspicionless highway sobriety checkpoints do not violate the Fourth Amendment.

CITY OF INDIANAPOLIS v. EDMOND, **531 U.S. 32 (2000):** Suspicionless vehicle checkpoints for detecting illegal drugs violate the Fourth Amendment.

NEW JERSEY v. T.L.O., **469 U.S. 325 (1985):** School officials do not need a warrant or probable cause for a school disciplinary search.

O'CONNOR v. ORTEGA, **480 U.S. 709 (1987):** Government employees enjoy Fourth Amendment protection in their offices.

VERNONIA SCHOOL DISTRICT 47J v. ACTON, **515 U.S. 646 (1995):** Random, suspicionless drug tests of school athletes do not violate the Fourth Amendment.

FERGUSON v. CHARLESTON, **523 U.S. 67 (2001):** The Fourth Amendment is violated when hospital personnel, working with the police, test pregnant mothers for drug use without their consent.

BOARD OF EDUCATION OF INDEPENDENT SCHOOL DISTRICT v. EARLS, **536 U.S. 822 (2002):** Random, suspicionless drug tests of students who participate in extracurricular activities do not violate the Fourth Amendment.

GRIFFIN v. WISCONSIN, **483 U.S. 868 (1987):** Probationers can be forced to submit to warrantless searches of their residences.

UNITED STATES v. KNIGHTS, **534 U.S. 112 (2001):** Evidence seized from the warrantless search of a probationer's apartment is admissible under the Fourth Amendment when the search is legally authorized by the terms of probation.

BRIGHAM CITY v. STUART, **547 U.S. 398 (2006):** Under the exigent circumstance exception to the Fourth Amendment, police officers are authorized to enter a residence in the interest of protecting the welfare of a person when there exists an objectively reasonable basis for believing that person may be in peril.

ONTARIO v. QUON, **560 U.S. — (2010):** Because the search of Quon's text messages was reasonable, petitioners did not violate respondent's Fourth Amendment rights.

KENTUCKY v. KING, **— U.S. — (2011):** An exigent circumstance that is created by police officers does not justify entry and search under existing exceptions to the Fourth Amendment.

CHAPTER FIFTEEN: **ELECTRONIC SURVEILLANCE**

OLMSTEAD v. UNITED STATES, **277 U.S. 438 (1928):** Electronic eavesdropping (i.e., wiretapping) does not constitute a search within the meaning of the Fourth Amendment unless a physical intrusion or trespass into a protected area occurs.

BERGER v. NEW YORK, **388 U.S. 41 (1967):** Electronic eavesdropping constitutes a search, which, in the absence of clearly limited guidelines regarding the information sought and how it is to be "returned," violates the Fourth Amendment prohibition against unreasonable searches and seizures.

KATZ v. UNITED STATES, **389 U.S. 347 (1967):** Despite the fact that a telephone booth exists in public, individuals who make use of it possess a reasonable expectation of privacy. Thus, any electronic monitoring of the phone constitutes a search. No physical intrusion needs to occur in order for the Fourth Amendment to be triggered.

UNITED STATES v. KARO, **468 U.S. 705 (1984):** The warrantless monitoring of a homing device inside a private residence violates the Fourth Amendment.

UNITED STATES V. JONES, — U.S. — **(2012):** The Government's attachment of the GPS device to the vehicle, and its use of that device to monitor the vehicle's movements, constitutes a search under the Fourth Amendment.

CHAPTER SIXTEEN: **PRETRIAL IDENTIFICATION PROCEDURES**

UNITED STATES v. WADE, **388 U.S. 218 (1967):** The Fifth Amendment does not prohibit the state from requiring a defendant to participate in a postindictment lineup conducted for identification purposes. However, the Sixth Amendment requires the presence of counsel during such procedures, given their critical nature. Any identification testimony derived from a postindictment lineup procedure in which a defendant was denied the right to counsel violates the Sixth Amendment and is thus inadmissible at trial.

KIRBY v. ILLINOIS, **406 U.S. 682 (1972):** The Sixth Amendment does not require that a suspect's attorney be present for any preindictment lineups conducted by the police for identification purposes.

MANSON v. BRATHWAITE, **432 U.S. 98 (1977):** The Fourteenth Amendment does not require the automatic exclusion of testimony based upon a police officer's identification of the defendant, even if it was obtained as the result of a procedure that may have been unnecessarily suggestive.

UNITED STATES v. CREWS, **445 U.S. 463 (1980):** An in-court identification of a suspect by a witness is admissible even if the identification is the result of an illegal arrest when the witness's independent recollections of the suspect antedated the unlawful arrest.

PERRY v. NEW HAMPSHIRE, — U.S. — **(2012):** The due process clause does not require a preliminary judicial inquiry into the reliability of eyewitness identification when the identification was not procured under unnecessarily suggestive circumstances arranged by law enforcement.

CHAPTER SEVENTEEN: **RIGHT TO COUNSEL**

POWELL ET AL. v. ALABAMA, **287 U.S. 45 (1932):** The denial of legal counsel in a capital case constitutes a violation of due process under the Fourteenth Amendment.

GIDEON v. WAINWRIGHT, **372 U.S. 335 (1963):** The Sixth Amendment requires the appointment of legal counsel to represent an indigent defendant facing prosecution on state felony charges.

ESCOBEDO v. ILLINOIS, **378 U.S. 478 (1964):** The police must allow a suspect to speak with an attorney if one is requested during a custodial interrogation.

MASSIAH v. UNITED STATES, **377 U.S. 201 (1964):** The Sixth Amendment prohibits the police from surreptitiously obtaining incriminating statements from a suspect who has previously been charged with a crime and retained an attorney.

UNITED STATES v. HENRY, **447 U.S. 264 (1980):** The government cannot enlist the assistance of a jailhouse informant for purposes of gathering incriminating information from a criminal defendant.

ROTHGERY v. GILLESPIE COUNTY, **554 U.S. 191 (2008):** A criminal defendant's initial appearance before a magistrate judge, where he learns the charge against him and his liberty is subject to restriction, marks the initiation of adversary judicial proceedings that trigger attachment of the Sixth Amendment right to counsel.

KANSAS v. VENTRIS, **556 U.S. — (2009):** Incriminating statements obtained in violation of the Sixth Amendment right to counsel may be used to impeach the testimony of the defendant. Such statements cannot be used to prove guilt, however.

MONTEJO v. LOUISIANA, **556 U.S. 778 (2009):** The Supreme Court explicitly overruled *Michigan v.*

Jackson, stating that it had proved unworkable and that there were sufficient safeguards of the right to counsel in place without the additional complexity that the rule added.

CHAPTER EIGHTEEN: THE DEVELOPMENT AND SCOPE OF THE MIRANDA WARNINGS

BROWN v. MISSISSIPPI, **297 U.S. 278 (1936):** Confessions that are obtained by way of physical torture, coercion, or brutality on the part of law enforcement officials are not admissible at trial under the Fourteenth Amendment's due process clause.

MIRANDA v. ARIZONA, **384 U.S. 436 (1966):** The police must inform a suspect of his or her constitutional right to legal representation and protection from self-incrimination during custodial interrogation. Any incriminating statements obtained in violation of these rights are inadmissible at trial.

EDWARDS v. ARIZONA, **451 U.S. 477 (1981):** Officers may not reinitiate contact with a suspect who has previously invoked the right to remain silent and have the assistance of counsel during custodial interrogation. In other words, once a suspect states that he or she desires legal representation during custodial interrogation, the questioning must stop immediately and may not resume until the request has been satisfied, even if only to inquire whether or not the individual has had a change of mind and wants to confess.

SOUTH DAKOTA v. NEVILLE, **459 U.S. 553 (1983):** Admission into evidence of a DWI defendant's refusal to take a blood-alcohol test does not violate the Fifth Amendment right to avoid self-incrimination. The failure of an officer to inform a DWI suspect that refusal to take a blood-alcohol test may be introduced at trial does not constitute a violation of due process.

BERKEMER v. MCCARTY, **468 U.S. 420 (1984):** The roadside questioning of a motorist who is detained pursuant to a lawful traffic stop does not constitute a custodial interrogation. Consequently, officers are not required to inform traffic violators of their *Miranda* rights.

NEW YORK v. QUARLES, **467 U.S. 649 (1984):** The concern for public safety clearly outweighs strict adherence to the principles of *Miranda*.

OREGON v. ELSTAD, **470 U.S. 298 (1985):** A confession that is properly obtained subsequent to an unsolicited and unwarned statement is not automatically rendered inadmissible under the Fifth Amendment.

COLORADO v. CONNELLY, **479 U.S. 157 (1986):** A suspect who is lacking a fully rational state of mind may validly waive his or her *Miranda* rights and, in the absence of any coercive police behavior, any incriminating statements are admissible under state rules of evidence.

COLORADO v. SPRING, **479 U.S. 564 (1987):** The police are not required to provide suspects with advance notice of all possible topics of interrogation in order for a waiver of *Miranda* rights to be valid. In other words, the police do not have to tell a suspect which specific crime(s) they intend to ask questions about.

PATTERSON v. ILLINOIS, **487 U.S. 285 (1988):** A suspect who has been properly advised of his or her *Miranda* rights during postindictment questioning is deemed to have also been sufficiently informed of the accompanying Sixth Amendment right to counsel. A valid waiver of the *Miranda* rights simultaneously implicates both the Fifth Amendment right to remain silent as well as the Sixth Amendment right to counsel.

ARIZONA v. ROBERSON, **486 U.S. 675 (1988):** The Supreme Court held that the previously established *Edwards* rule prohibits officers from initiating repeated interrogations of a suspect once he or she has invoked the Fifth Amendment right to counsel even if the subsequent interrogation focuses on an altogether separate offense.

DUCKWORTH v. EAGAN, **492 U.S. 195 (1989):** It is not necessary for the *Miranda* warnings to be presented or recited exactly as they appeared in the original case.

MINNICK v. MISSISSIPPI, **498 U.S. 146 (1990):** When, during the course of custodial interrogation, a suspect asks for counsel, all questioning must immediately cease and may not resume until such time as counsel is present in the room.

PENNSYLVANIA v. MUNIZ, **496 U.S. 582 (1990):** Not only may the police ask routine questions of DWI suspects during booking procedures, but they are also allowed to videotape the responses without having to first inform the arrestee of his or her *Miranda* rights.

ARIZONA v. FULMINANTE, **499 U.S. 279 (1991):** The "harmless error" doctrine is applicable to cases involving the improper admission of an involuntary confession at trial.

MCNEIL v. WISCONSIN, **501 U.S. 171 (1991):** A request for assistance of counsel at a bail hearing does not constitute an invocation of the Fifth Amendment right to counsel under *Miranda* for other uncharged offenses.

DAVIS v. UNITED STATES, **512 U.S. 452 (1994):** Authorities may continue to question a suspect who has knowingly and voluntarily waived his or her *Miranda* rights until such time as he or she clearly asks for assistance of counsel.

MISSOURI v. SEIBERT, **542 U.S. 600 (2004):** The two-step technique of questioning a suspect first, then warning him or her, then questioning again, violates the Fifth Amendment.

UNITED STATES v. PATANE, **542 U.S. 360 (2004):** A failure to provide a suspect with the *Miranda* warning does not automatically require the suppression of physical evidence that is the product of an otherwise voluntary statement.

FLORIDA v. POWELL, **559 U.S. — (2010):** The police department's effort to warn incoming arrestees of their *Miranda* rights was not constitutionally flawed simply because it failed to specifically inform them that they have the right to have an attorney physically present during questioning.

MARYLAND v. SHATZER, **559 U.S. — (2010):** The *Edwards* rule does not apply where a significant amount of time (more than 14 days) has elapsed.

BERGHUIS v. THOMPKINS, **560 U.S. — (2010):** A suspect must verbally indicate a desire to remain silent in order to invoke the protections afforded by *Miranda*.

J.D.B. v. NORTH CAROLINA, **564 U.S. — (2011):** Given J.D.B.'s age (13), he was in custody and therefore entitled to the protections afforded by *Miranda* and its progeny.

CHAPTER NINETEEN: WHAT CONSTITUTES INTER-ROGATION?

BREWER v. WILLIAMS, **430 U.S. 387 (1977):** Officers are prohibited from appealing to a suspect's moral or religious beliefs for purposes of soliciting incriminating statements in the absence of legal representation.

RHODE ISLAND v. INNIS, **446 U.S. 291 (1980):** The conversation between the two officers did not constitute an interrogation or its functional equivalent as the suspect was not directly involved in the exchange. Therefore, no Sixth Amendment right was either implicated or violated.

ARIZONA v. MAURO, **481 U.S. 520 (1987):** The self-incrimination privilege of the Fifth Amendment does not forbid the introduction of incriminating statements made by a suspect to his or her spouse in the presence of a police officer, especially in instances where the suspect was not subjected to any compelling influences, psychological ploys, or direct questioning generally characteristic of custodial interrogation or its functional equivalent.

CHAPTER TWENTY: CIVIL LIABILITY

MONROE v. PAPE, **365 U.S. 167 (1961):** 42 U.S.C. Section 1983 can serve as a cause of action against police officers who misuse their authority.

MONELL v. DEPARTMENT OF SOCIAL SERVICES OF NEW YORK, **436 U.S. 658 (1978):** Local units of government can be held liable under 42 U.S.C. Section 1983 only when the constitutional violation is sanctioned by official municipal policy or custom.

OWEN v. CITY OF INDEPENDENCE, **445 U.S. 622 (1980):** Municipalities can be held liable under 42 U.S.C. Section 1983 and cannot assert a good-faith defense.

MALLEY v. BRIGGS, **475 U.S. 335 (1986):** Individual police officers are entitled to only qualified immunity under Section 1983.

CITY OF CANTON v. HARRIS, **489 U.S. 378 (1989):** Inadequate training can lead to municipal liability under Section 1983, but only if it amounts to deliberate indifference.

WILL v. MICHIGAN DEPARTMENT OF STATE POLICE, **491 U.S. 58 (1989):** Neither states nor state officials, acting in their official capacity, can be sued under Section 1983.

BOARD OF THE COUNTY COMMISSIONERS OF BRYAN COUNTY v. BROWN, **520 U.S. 397 (1997):** A county cannot be held liable under Section 1983 for a single hiring decision.

MCMILLIAN v. MONROE COUNTY, **520 U.S. 781 (1997):** Whether a sheriff is a representative of the county or of the state is determined by the state's constitution, laws, or regulations.

COUNTY OF SACRAMENTO v. LEWIS, **523 U.S. 833 (1998):** A police officer will not be held liable for a substantive due process violation unless his or her conduct "shocks the conscience."

SAUCIER v. KATZ, **533 U.S. 194 (2001):** The questions of whether excessive force is used and whether qualified immunity should be granted are to be kept separate and not fused into a single inquiry.

TOWN OF CASTLE ROCK, COLORADO v. GONZALES, **545 U.S. 748 (2005):** Respondent, Gonzales, did not have a protected property interest in the enforcement of the restraining order under Colorado law.

PEARSON v. CALLAHAN, **555 U.S. — (2010):** The *Saucier* procedure should not be regarded as an inflexible requirement and petitioners are entitled to qualified immunity on the ground that it was not clearly established at the time of the search that their conduct was unconstitutional.

INTRODUCTION

THE SUPREME COURT AND THE POLICE

All democratic societies question the level of authority over the individual citizen granted to the state. Social contract theory posits that, by choosing to live among others, individuals give up some of their liberty and permit the state to intervene in their lives. But how much? And in what manner? These questions are particularly relevant when the police, in the investigation of criminal activity, interfere with the liberty interests of citizens. While the criminal law sets forth the appropriate code of conduct for all citizens, criminal procedure comprises the rules governing the manner in which the state may go about depriving an individual of liberty. Criminal procedure includes when and in what manner law enforcement may detain, arrest, or search a person. It also includes when and how police may interrogate criminal suspects and conduct identification procedures.

Balancing the rights of the individual and the authority of the police is a difficult, but crucial, process. Packer (1964) asserts that there are two competing models of the criminal justice system: due process and crime control. The due process model is concerned primarily with protection of individual privacy. It emphasizes the importance of the formal legal process as a means of ensuring that mistakes are kept to a minimum and operates on the presumption of innocence. In contrast, the crime control model is primarily concerned with the reduction of crime and the protection of public order. It emphasizes the use of discretion and police power as a means of quickly and efficiently investigating and screening cases, and operates on the presumption of guilt. Criminal procedure

law attempts to balance the differing goals of these two models, but it is a zero–sum game. Granting the police greater power to investigate crime means reducing individual liberty and privacy. Conversely, increasing individual rights may result in suspects who are factually guilty going free because the state is unable to prove legal guilt beyond a reasonable doubt, the burden of proof in criminal cases.

The U.S. Constitution, including the Bill of Rights and the Fourteenth Amendment, is the legal foundation for most criminal procedure decisions. The Bill of Rights sets forth 23 individual rights, and the Fourteenth Amendment guarantees of due process and equal protection have been interpreted by the U.S. Supreme Court to incorporate much of the Bill of Rights against state action. Originally, the Bill of Rights was conceived as applying only to the federal government, but during the twentieth century the Supreme Court has interpreted the due process clause of the Fourteenth Amendment to incorporate many of the individual rights contained in the Bill of Rights. Incorporation means that the individual right (such as the Fourth Amendment right to be free from unreasonable searches and seizures) is included in the Fourteenth Amendment's guarantees of due process and equal protection. Rights incorporated in the Fourteenth Amendment are those the Court has deemed "fundamental." These rights are applied against the states and include most of the criminal procedure-related provisions of the Fourth, Fifth, Sixth, and Eighth Amendments.

Other sources for criminal procedure law are state constitutions and federal and state statutes. States are free to provide more individual rights than the federal Constitution but cannot abridge any federal Constitutional rights. In the past, states were seen as somewhat less protective of the rights of criminal suspects. However, in recent years a number of state courts have interpreted their state constitutions as providing greater limitations on what the police may do. Consequently, criminal defendants may be accorded more rights and protections by state courts than by the U.S. Supreme Court.

As most criminal procedure law is derived from the provisions of the Bill of Rights, in particular the Fourth, Fifth, and Sixth Amendments, courts are frequently called upon to interpret the meaning of these Amendments and to apply them to current fact situations. For example, the Fifth Amendment prohibits compelling a person to testify against himself, but does requiring an individual to take a breathalyzer test or give a blood sample constitute testimony when the results may be used to prosecute him at trial? The Fourth Amendment prohibits the unreasonable seizure and search of persons, places, and effects, but what is an "effect"? And what is "unreasonable"? Courts must answer these questions to determine when police officers have exceeded the scope of their authority, either intentionally or unintentionally. The U.S. Supreme Court has the final word on the constitutionality of any state action challenged as a violation of a constitutional right. Consequently, much of criminal procedure law is based on Supreme Court decisions. As courts decide only the case before them and do not issue policy directives, criminal procedure law has developed fitfully, on a case-by-case basis. Much of criminal procedure law has been written in the past 50 years since the Supreme Court began to apply the provisions of the Bill of Rights to the states, who conduct the bulk of criminal investigation and prosecution.

REFERENCES

Abrahamson, S.S. (1985). "Criminal Law and State Constitutions: The Emergence of State Constitutional Law." *Texas Law Review* 63: 1141.

Amar, A.R. (1994). "Fourth Amendment First Principles." *Harvard Law Review* 107: 757.

Caplan, G.M. (1985). "Questioning Miranda." *Vanderbilt Law Review* 38: 1417.

Cuddihy, W. (1990). "The Fourth Amendment: Origins and Original Meaning." Claremont, CA. Unpublished doctoral dissertation.

Grano, J.D. (1974). "Kirby, Biggers and Ash: Do Any Constitutional Safeguards Remain Against the Danger of Convicting the Innocent?" *Michigan Law Review* 72: 717.

Hemmens, C. (1997). "The Police, the Fourth Amendment, and Unannounced Entry: *Wilson v. Arkansas.*" *Criminal Law Bulletin* 33(1): 29.

Hemmens, C., and J.R. Maahs. (1996). "Reason to Believe: When Does Detention End and a Consensual Encounter Begin? An Analysis of *Ohio v. Robinette.*" *Ohio Northern Law Review* 23(2): 309.

Hemmens, C., R.V. del Carmen, and K.E. Scarborough. (1997). "Grave Doubts About 'Reasonable Doubt': Confusion in State and Federal Courts." *Journal of Criminal Justice* 25(3): 231.

LaFave, W.R. (1996). *Search and Seizure: A Treatise on the Fourth Amendment* (3rd edition). Minneapolis, MN: West.

Loewy, A.H. (1989). "Police-Obtained Evidence and the Constitution: Distinguishing Unconstitutionally Obtained Evidence from Unconstitutionally Used Evidence." *Michigan Law Review* 87: 907.

Mertens, W.J., and S. Wasserstrom. (1981). "The Good Faith Exception to the Exclusionary Rule: Deregulating the Police and Derailing the Law." *Georgetown Law Journal* 70: 365.

Packer, H. (1964). "Two Models of the Criminal Process." *University of Pennsylvania Law Review* 113: 1.

Schulhofer, S.J. (1987). "Reconsidering Miranda." *University of Chicago Law Review* 54: 435.

Slobogin, C., and J.E. Schumacher. (1993). "Reasonable Expectations of Privacy and Autonomy in Fourth Amendment Cases: An Empirical Look at 'Understandings Recognized and Permitted By Society.' " *Duke Law Journal* 42: 727.

Stuntz, W.J. (1992). "Implicit Bargains, Government Power, and the Fourth Amendment." *Stanford Law Review* 44: 553.

CHAPTER ONE

THE EXCLUSIONARY RULE

WEEKS v. UNITED STATES, *232 U.S. 383 (1914)*

ROCHIN v. CALIFORNIA, *342 U.S. 165 (1952)*

MAPP v. OHIO, *367 U.S. 643 (1961)*

WONG SUN v. UNITED STATES, *371 U.S. 471 (1963)*

NIX v. WILLIAMS, *467 U.S. 431 (1984)*

UNITED STATES v. LEON, *468 U.S. 897 (1984)*

MASSACHUSETTS v. SHEPPARD, *468 U.S. 981 (1984)*

MINNESOTA v. OLSON, *495 U.S. 91 (1990)*

ARIZONA v. EVANS, *514 U.S. 1 (1995)*

HERRING v. UNITED STATES, *555 U.S. 135 (2009)*

DAVIS v. UNITED STATES, *—U.S.—(2011)*

INTRODUCTION

The exclusionary rule provides that evidence obtained by law enforcement officers in violation of the Fourth Amendment guarantee against unreasonable searches and seizures is not admissible in a criminal trial to prove guilt. The primary purpose of the exclusionary rule is to deter police misconduct. While some proponents argue that the rule emanates from the Constitution, the Supreme Court has indicated that it is merely a judicially created remedy for violations of the Fourth Amendment.

The exclusionary rule is perhaps the most controversial legal issue in criminal justice. Application of the rule may lead to the exclusion of important evidence and the acquittal of persons who are factually, if not legally, guilty. Consequently, the exclusionary rule has been the subject of intense debate. Proponents argue it is the only effective means of protecting individual rights from police misconduct, while critics decry the exclusion from trial of relevant evidence. Despite calls for its abolition and shifts in the composition of the Supreme Court, the exclusionary rule remains entrenched in American jurisprudence. But while the rule has survived, it has not gone unscathed. Supreme Court decisions over the years have limited the scope of the rule and created several exceptions.

The Supreme Court first addressed the issue of the admissibility of illegally obtained evidence in 1886, when it held in *Boyd v. United States,* 116 U.S. 616, that the forced disclosure of papers amounting to evidence of crimes violated the constitutional right of the defendant against unreasonable search and seizure, so such items were inadmissible in court proceedings. In 1914 the Supreme Court held in *Weeks v. United States* that evidence illegally obtained by federal law enforcement officers was not admissible in a federal criminal trial. At the time the Fourth Amendment did not apply to the states, only the federal government. Because the *Weeks* decision applied only against the federal government, state law enforcement officers were still free to seize evidence illegally without fear of exclusion in state criminal proceedings. In addition, evidence seized illegally by state police could be turned over to federal law enforcement officers for use in federal prosecutions, as long as federal officers were not directly involved in the illegal seizure. This was known as the "silver platter" doctrine because illegally seized evidence could be turned over to federal law enforcement officers "as if on a silver platter" (LaFave and Israel 1992). In 1960, in *Elkins v. United States,* 364 U.S. 206, the Court put an end to this practice, prohibiting the introduction of illegally seized evidence in federal prosecutions regardless of whether the illegality was committed by state or federal agents.

In 1949, in *Wolf v. Colorado*, 338 U.S. 25, the Supreme Court applied the Fourth Amendment to the states, incorporating it into the due process clause of the Fourteenth Amendment. However, the Court refused to mandate the remedy of the exclusionary rule. Just three years later the Court modified its position somewhat, holding in *Rochin v. California* that evidence seized in a manner that "shocked the conscience" must be excluded as violative of due process. Exactly what type of conduct shocked the conscience was left to be determined on a case-by-case basis. The exclusionary rule thus became applicable to state criminal proceedings, but its application was uneven.

Finally, in 1961, in *Mapp v. Ohio*, the Court took the step it failed to in *Wolf* and explicitly applied the remedy of the exclusionary rule to the states. The Court did so because it acknowledged the states had failed to provide an adequate alternative remedy for violations of the Fourth Amendment. While there was language in *Mapp* that suggested the exclusionary rule originated from the Constitution and was not merely a judicially created remedy, subsequent decisions indicate the Court views the rule not as part of the Constitution, but rather as a means of enforcing the Fourth Amendment prohibition against unreasonable searches and seizures.

The Supreme Court in *Mapp* stated that the exclusionary rule serves at least two purposes: the deterrence of police misconduct and the protection of judicial integrity. In recent years, however, the Court has focused almost entirely upon the deterrence of police misconduct, leading to the creation of several exceptions to the rule. The Court has also held that the exclusionary rule does not apply to a variety of proceedings other than the criminal trial.

In 1984, the Court held in *Massachusetts v. Sheppard* that evidence obtained by the police acting in good faith on a search warrant issued by a neutral and detached magistrate that is ultimately found to be invalid may nonetheless be admitted at trial. The Court stressed that the primary rationale for the exclusionary rule—deterrence of police misconduct—did not warrant exclusion of evidence obtained by police who act reasonably and in good-faith reliance upon the actions of a judge. By "good faith," the Court meant the police are unaware that the warrant is invalid.

The Court emphasized that the good-faith exception did not apply to errors made by the police, even if the errors were entirely inadvertent. The exception applies only to situations where the police relied on others who, it later turns out, made a mistake. Subsequent cases reiterated this point. In 1995, in *Arizona v. Evans*, the Court refused to apply the exclusionary rule to evidence seized by a police officer who acted in reliance on a computer entry, made by a court clerk, that was later found to be in error. In contrast to its earlier holding in *Massachusetts v. Sheppard*, the Court, in *Herring v. United States* (2009), held that mistakes by police personnel would not result in the imposition of the exclusionary rule. Later, in *Davis v. United States* (2011), the Court held that the exclusionary rule should not result in the suppression of evidence by police who acted in good faith and in conformity with existing precedent.

The Court has also established the "inevitable discovery" exception to the exclusionary rule. This exception, developed in *Nix v. Williams*, permits the use at trial of evidence illegally obtained by the police if they can demonstrate that they would have discovered the evidence anyway by legal means. The burden is on the police to prove they would in fact have discovered the evidence lawfully. Police have only infrequently been able to establish this exception.

The Court has been reluctant to extend the reach of the exclusionary rule to proceedings other than criminal trials. The Court has consistently refused to apply the exclusionary rule to evidence seized by private parties, if they are not acting in concert with or at the behest of the police. The rule does not apply to evidence presented to the grand jury. An unlawful arrest does not bar prosecution of the arrestee, as the exclusionary rule is an evidentiary rule rather than a rule of jurisdictional limitation. The rule is inapplicable in both civil tax assessment proceedings and civil deportation proceedings. The exclusionary rule does not apply to parole revocation hearings.

The Court has also been reluctant to apply the exclusionary rule to aspects of the criminal trial that are not directly related to the determination of guilt. Thus, illegally obtained evidence may be used to impeach a defendant's testimony or to determine the appropriate sentence for a convicted defendant.

REFERENCES

Amar, A.R. (1997). *The Constitution and Criminal Procedure*. New Haven, CT: Yale University Press.

Cole, D. (1999). *No Equal Justice*. New York: The New Press.

Decker, J.F. (1992). *Revolution to the Right: Criminal Procedure Jurisprudence During the Burger-Rehnquist Court Era.* New York: Garland.

LaFave, W.R., and J.H. Israel. (1992). *Criminal Procedure* (2nd ed.). Minneapolis, MN: West Publishing.

WEEKS v. UNITED STATES
232 U.S. 383 (1914)

FACTS
Weeks was arrested by a police officer without a warrant at the Union Station in Kansas City, Missouri, where he was employed by an express company. Other police officers had gone to the Weeks' house, and being told by a neighbor where the key was kept, found it and entered the house. They searched Weeks' room and took possession of various papers and articles found there, which were afterwards turned over to the U.S. Marshal. Later the same day police officers returned with the marshal, who thought he might find additional evidence, and, being admitted by someone in the house, probably a boarder, the marshal searched Weeks' room and carried away certain letters and envelopes found in the drawer of a chiffonier. Neither the marshal nor the police officer had a search warrant. Weeks was convicted of unlawful use of the mail, and the U.S. Supreme Court granted certiorari.

ISSUE
Is evidence that is illegally seized by the police admissible at trial?

HOLDING
No. The letters in question were taken from the house of the accused by an official of the United States, acting under color of his office, in direct violation of the constitutional rights of the defendant.

RATIONALE
"The right of the court to deal with papers and documents in the possession of the district attorney and other officers of the court, and subject to its authority, was recognized in an earlier case. That papers wrongfully seized should be turned over to the accused has been frequently recognized in the early as well as later decisions of the courts. In holding them and permitting their use upon the trial, we think prejudicial error was committed. As to the papers and property seized by the policemen, it does not appear that they acted under any claim of Federal authority such as would make the amendment applicable to such unauthorized seizures.... What remedies the defendant may have against them we need not inquire, as the Fourth Amendment is not directed to individual misconduct of such officials. Its limitations reach the Federal government and its agencies."

CASE EXCERPT
"He acted without sanction of law, doubtless prompted by the desire to bring further proof to the aid of the Government, and under color of his office undertook to make a seizure of private papers in direct violation of the constitutional prohibition against such action. Under such circumstances, without sworn information and particular description, not even an order of court would have justified such procedure, much less was it within the authority of the United States Marshal to thus invade the house and privacy of the accused."

CASE SIGNIFICANCE
This case established the exclusionary rule and applied it to the actions of federal law enforcement officers. The Supreme Court stopped short of applying the rule to state law enforcement officers, however, as the Court at this time had not yet incorporated the Fourth Amendment into the due process clause of the Fourteenth Amendment.

ROCHIN v. CALIFORNIA
342 U.S. 165 (1952)

FACTS
Having "some information" that Rochin was selling narcotics, three police officers entered his home and forced their way into the bedroom where Rochin and his wife were standing. When he was asked by the police about two capsules lying on the bedside table, Rochin put them in his mouth. After an unsuccessful struggle to extract them by force, the officers took Rochin to a hospital, where an emetic was forced into his stomach against his will. He vomited two capsules, which were found to contain morphine. These were admitted in evidence over his objection and he was convicted in a state court of violating a state law forbidding possession of morphine. The U.S. Supreme Court then granted certiorari.

ROCHIN v. CALIFORNIA *(cont.)*

ISSUE

Did the actions of the officers violate the limitations that the due process clause of the Fourteenth Amendment imposes on the conduct of criminal proceedings by the states?

HOLDING

Yes. The methods used by the police violated the due process clause of the Fourteenth Amendment.

RATIONALE

"Due process of law, as a historic and generative principle, precludes defining, and thereby confining, these standards of conduct more precisely than to say that convictions cannot be brought about by methods that offend 'a sense of justice.' It would be a stultification of the responsibility which the course of constitutional history has cast upon this Court to hold that in order to convict a man the police cannot extract by force what is in his mind but can extract what is in his stomach. To attempt in this case to distinguish what lawyers call 'real evidence' from verbal evidence is to ignore the reasons for excluding coerced confessions. Use of involuntary verbal confessions in State criminal trials is constitutionally obnoxious not only because of their unreliability. They are inadmissible under the Due Process Clause even though statements contained in them may be independently established as true. Coerced confessions offend the community's sense of fair play and decency. So here, to sanction the brutal conduct which naturally enough was condemned by the court whose judgment is before us, would be to afford brutality the cloak of law. Nothing would be more calculated to discredit law and thereby to brutalize the temper of a society."

CASE EXCERPT

"This is conduct that shocks the conscience. Illegally breaking into the privacy of the petitioner, the struggle to open his mouth and remove what was there, the forcible extraction of his stomach's contents—this course of proceeding by agents of government to obtain evidence is bound to offend even hardened sensibilities. They are methods too close to the rack and the screw to permit of constitutional differentiation."

CASE SIGNIFICANCE

In this case the Supreme Court chose not to apply the federal exclusionary rule against the states (this was not done until *Mapp v. Ohio* in 1961) but to rely on the due process clause to overturn the conviction. The end result is the same. Today the evidence would be excluded through application of the exclusionary rule.

MAPP v. OHIO
367 U.S. 643 (1961)

FACTS

Cleveland police officers arrived at Mapp's home and sought consent to search it for a bombing suspect. When she refused consent, officers showed Mapp a piece of paper that they claimed was a search warrant. Mapp took this piece of paper and placed it in her bosom. A struggle ensued in which the officers recovered the piece of paper and as a result of which they handcuffed appellant because she had been "belligerent" in resisting their official rescue of the "warrant" from her person. Mapp was then forcibly taken upstairs to her bedroom, where the officers searched a dresser, a chest of drawers, a closet, and some suitcases. They also looked into a photo album and through personal papers belonging to her. The search spread to the rest of the home. Police officers eventually found several drawings of nude individuals and charged Mapp with possession of obscene materials. At the trial no search warrant was produced by the prosecution, nor was the failure to produce one explained or accounted for. Mapp was convicted of possession of obscene materials; she appealed, and the Supreme Court granted certiorari.

ISSUE

Should the evidence found in Mapp's home have been inadmissible at trial, thereby making the Fourth Amendment enforceable upon the states based on the due process clause of the Fourteenth Amendment?

HOLDING

Yes. All evidence obtained by searches and seizures in violation of the federal Constitution is inadmissible in a criminal trial in a state court.

RATIONALE

"Since the Fourth Amendment's right of privacy has been declared enforceable against the States through the Due Process Clause of the Fourteenth, it is enforceable against them by the same sanction of exclusion as is used against the Federal Government. Were it otherwise, then just as without the *Weeks* rule the assurance against unreasonable federal searches and seizures would be 'a form of words,' valueless and undeserving of mention in a perpetual charter of inestimable human liberties, so too, without that rule the freedom from state invasions of privacy would be so ephemeral and so neatly severed from its conceptual nexus with the freedom from all brutish means of coercing evidence as not to merit this Court's high regard as a freedom 'implicit in the concept of ordered liberty.'"

CASE EXCERPT

"Moreover, our holding that the exclusionary rule is an essential part of both the Fourth and Fourteenth Amendments is not only the logical dictate of prior cases, but it also makes very good sense. There is no war between the Constitution and common sense. Presently, a federal prosecutor may make no use of evidence illegally seized, but a State's attorney across the street may, although he supposedly is operating under the enforceable prohibitions of the same Amendment. Thus the State, by admitting evidence unlawfully seized, serves to encourage disobedience to the Federal Constitution which it is bound to uphold."

CASE SIGNIFICANCE

This ruling basically overturned the decision in *Wolf v. Colorado* (1949), which left a shortcut to conviction open to the state, which, according to the Court, "tends to destroy the entire system of constitutional restraints on which the liberties of the people rest." This ruling imposed the exclusionary rule (*Weeks v. United States*) upon the states.

WONG SUN v. UNITED STATES

371 U.S. 471 (1963)

FACTS

Petitioners were convicted of fraudulent and knowing transportation and concealment of illegally imported heroin, in violation of 21 U.S.C. 174. Although the court of appeals held that the arrests of both petitioners without warrants were illegal, because they were not based on "probable cause" within the meaning of the Fourth Amendment nor "reasonable grounds" within the meaning of the Narcotics Control Act of 1956, it affirmed their convictions, notwithstanding

the admission in evidence over their timely objections of (1) statements made orally by petitioner Toy in his bedroom at the time of his arrest; (2) heroin surrendered to the agents by a third party as a result of those statements; and (3) unsigned statements made by each petitioner several days after his arrest, and after being lawfully arraigned and released on his own recognizance. The court of appeals held that these items were not the fruits of the illegal arrests and, therefore, were properly admitted in evidence. The U.S. Supreme Court then granted certiorari.

ISSUE

Was the court of appeals incorrect in its holding that these items were not the fruits of illegal arrests and, therefore, admissible in court?

HOLDING

Yes. The court of appeals was incorrect. Evidence obtained indirectly as a result of an unlawful arrest or search is not admissible.

RATIONALE

"There was neither reasonable grounds nor probable cause for Toy's arrest, since the information upon which it was based was too vague and came from too untested a source to accept it as probable cause for the issuance of an arrest warrant; and this defect was not cured by the fact that Toy fled when a supposed customer at his door early in the morning revealed that he was a narcotics agent. In view of the fact that, after his unlawful arrest, petitioner Wong Sun had been lawfully arraigned and released on his own recognizance and had returned voluntarily several days later when he made his unsigned statement, the connection between his unlawful arrest and the making of that statement was so attenuated that the unsigned statement was not the fruit of the unlawful arrest and, therefore, it was properly admitted in evidence.... The statements made by Toy in his bedroom at the time of his unlawful arrest were the fruits of the agents' unlawful action, and they should have been excluded from evidence. The narcotics taken from a third party as a result of statements made by Toy at the time of his arrest were likewise fruits of the unlawful arrest, and they should not have been admitted as evidence against Toy.... The seizure of the narcotics admitted in evidence invaded no right of privacy of person or premises, which would entitle Wong Sun to object to its use at his trial."

WONG SUN v. UNITED STATES *(cont.)*

CASE EXCERPT

"We need not hold that all evidence is 'fruit of the poisonous tree' simply because it would not have come to light but for the illegal actions of the police. Rather, the more apt question in such a case is whether, granting establishment of the primary illegality, the evidence to which instant objection is made has been come at by exploitation of that illegality or instead by means sufficiently distinguishable to be purged of the primary taint."

CASE SIGNIFICANCE

This case dealt with the "purged taint" exception to the exclusionary rule. Under the exclusionary rule, evidence seized in violation of the Fourth Amendment is excluded from evidence. Under the purged taint exception, however, if the prosecution can demonstrate that evidence was obtained in a manner unrelated to the illegal police activity, it may be admitted.

NIX v. WILLIAMS

467 U.S. 431 (1984)

FACTS

Following the disappearance of a 10-year-old girl in Des Moines, Iowa, Williams was arrested and arraigned in Davenport, Iowa. The police informed Williams' counsel that they would drive Williams back to Des Moines without questioning him, but during the trip one of the officers began a conversation with Williams that ultimately resulted in his making incriminating statements and directing the officers to the child's body. A systematic search of the area that was being conducted with the aid of 200 volunteers and that had been initiated before Williams made the incriminating statements was terminated when Williams guided police to the body. Before trial in an Iowa state court for first-degree murder, the court denied Williams' motion to suppress evidence of the body and all related evidence, including the body's condition as shown by an autopsy, Williams having contended that such evidence was the fruit of his illegally obtained statements made during the automobile ride. Williams was convicted, and the Iowa Supreme Court affirmed, but later federal court habeas corpus proceedings ultimately resulted in the Supreme Court holding that the police had obtained Williams' incriminating statements through interrogation in

violation of his Sixth Amendment right to counsel. However, it was noted that even though the statements could not be admitted at a second trial, evidence of the body's location and condition might be admissible on the theory that the body would have been discovered even if the incriminating statements had not been elicited from Williams. At Williams' second state court trial, his incriminating statements were not offered in evidence, nor did the prosecution seek to show that Williams had directed the police to the child's body. However, evidence concerning the body's location and condition was admitted, the court having concluded that the state had proved that if the search had continued the body would have been discovered within a short time in essentially the same condition as it was actually found. Williams was again convicted of first-degree murder, and the Iowa Supreme Court affirmed. In subsequent habeas corpus proceedings, the federal district court, denying relief, also concluded that the body inevitably would have been found. However, the court of appeals reversed, holding that—even assuming that there is an inevitable discovery exception to the exclusionary rule—the state had not met the exception's requirement that it be proved that the police did not act in bad faith. The U.S. Supreme Court then granted certiorari.

ISSUE

Was the body admissible at trial under the inevitable discovery exception to the exclusionary rule?

HOLDING

Yes. The evidence pertaining to the discovery and condition of the victim's body was properly admitted at Williams' second trial on the grounds that it would ultimately or inevitably have been discovered even if no violation of any constitutional provision had taken place.

RATIONALE

The core rationale for extending the exclusionary rule to evidence that is the fruit of unlawful police conduct is that such course is needed to deter police from violations of constitutional and statutory protections notwithstanding the high social cost of letting obviously guilty persons go unpunished. On this rationale, the prosecution is not to be put in a better position than it would have been in if no illegality had transpired. By contrast, the independent source doctrine—allowing admission of evidence that has been discovered by means wholly independent of any constitutional violation—rests on the rationale that society's interest in deterring unlawful police conduct and the public interest in having juries receive all probative evidence of a crime are properly balanced by putting the police in the same, not a worse, position that they would have been in if no police error or misconduct had occurred. Although the independent source doctrine does not apply here, its rationale is wholly consistent with and justifies adoption of the ultimate or inevitable discovery exception to the exclusionary rule. If the prosecution can establish by a preponderance of the evidence that the information ultimately or inevitably would have been discovered by lawful means—here the volunteers' search—then the deterrence rationale has so little basis that the evidence should be received. Under the inevitable discovery exception, the prosecution is not required to prove the absence of bad faith, since such a requirement would result in withholding from juries relevant and undoubted truth that would have been available to police absent any unlawful police activity. This would put the police in a worse position than they would have been in if no unlawful conduct had transpired and would fail to take into account the enormous societal cost of excluding evidence in the search for truth in the administration of justice. Significant disincentives to obtaining evidence illegally—including the possibility of departmental discipline and civil liability—lessen the likelihood that the ultimate or inevitable discovery exception will promote police misconduct. The record here supports the finding that the search party ultimately or inevitably would have discovered the victim's body. The evidence clearly shows that the searchers were approaching the actual location of the body, that the search would have been resumed had Williams not led the police to the body, and that the body inevitably would have been found.

CASE EXCERPT
"When the challenged evidence has an independent source, exclusion of such evidence would put the police in a worse position than they would have been in absent any error or violation. There is a functional similarity between these two doctrines in that exclusion of evidence that would inevitably have been discovered would also put the government in a worse position, because the police would have obtained that evidence if no misconduct had taken place. Thus, while the independent source exception would not justify admission of evidence in this case, its rationale is wholly consistent with and justifies our adoption of the ultimate or inevitable discovery exception to the exclusionary rule."

CASE SIGNIFICANCE
This case was an example of the "inevitable discovery" exception to the exclusionary rule. This exception is rarely used, as it is difficult to prove except in cases such as this one, where the police are searching for something at the time that the constitutional violation takes place.

UNITED STATES v. LEON
468 U.S. 897 (1984)

FACTS
Acting on the basis of information obtained from a confidential informant, officers of the Burbank (California) Police Department initiated a drug-trafficking investigation involving surveillance of Leon's activities. Based on an affidavit summarizing the police officers' observations, a search warrant for three residences and several automobiles was obtained. The search warrant application was reviewed by several deputy district attorneys and a judge. Ensuing searches produced large quantities of drugs and other evidence. Leon was indicted for several federal drug offenses and filed motions to suppress the evidence seized pursuant to the warrant. The district court granted the motions in part, concluding that the affidavit was insufficient to establish probable cause. Although recognizing that the police had acted in good faith, the court rejected the government's suggestion that the Fourth Amendment exclusionary rule should not apply where evidence is seized in reasonable, good-faith reliance on a search warrant. The court of appeals affirmed, also refusing the government's invitation to recognize a good-faith exception to the exclusionary rule. The U.S. Supreme Court then granted certiorari.

ISSUE
Should the Fourth Amendment exclusionary rule be applied to evidence gathered by law enforcement officers acting in good faith on a warrant later deemed to be invalid?

HOLDING
No. The Fourth Amendment exclusionary rule should not be applied so as to bar the use in the prosecution's

UNITED STATES v. LEON (*cont.*)

case in chief of evidence obtained by officers acting in reasonable reliance on a search warrant issued by a detached and neutral magistrate but ultimately found to be invalid.

RATIONALE

"An examination of the Fourth Amendment's origin and purposes makes clear that the use of fruits of a past unlawful search or seizure works no new Fourth Amendment wrong. The question whether the exclusionary sanction is appropriately imposed in a particular case as a judicially created remedy to safeguard Fourth Amendment rights through its deterrent effect, must be resolved by weighing the costs and benefits of preventing the use in the prosecution's case in chief of inherently trustworthy tangible evidence. Indiscriminate application of the exclusionary rule—impeding the criminal justice system's truth-finding function and allowing some guilty defendants to go free—may well generate disrespect for the law and the administration of justice. Application of the exclusionary rule should continue where a Fourth Amendment violation has been substantial and deliberate, but the balancing approach that has evolved in determining whether the rule should be applied in a variety of contexts—including criminal trials—suggests that the rule should be modified to permit the introduction of evidence obtained by officers reasonably relying on a warrant issued by a detached and neutral magistrate. The deference accorded to a magistrate's finding of probable cause for the issuance of a warrant does not preclude inquiry into the knowing or reckless falsity of the affidavit on which that determination was based, and the courts must also insist that the magistrate purport to perform his neutral and detached function and not serve merely as a rubber stamp for the police. Moreover, reviewing courts will not defer to a warrant based on an affidavit that does not provide the magistrate with a substantial basis for determining the existence of probable cause. However, the exclusionary rule is designed to deter police misconduct rather than to punish the errors of judges and magistrates. Admitting evidence obtained pursuant to a warrant while at the same time declaring that the warrant was somehow defective will not reduce judicial officers' professional incentives to comply with the Fourth Amendment, encourage them to repeat their mistakes, or lead to the granting of all colorable warrant requests. Even assuming that the exclusionary rule effectively deters some police misconduct and

provides incentives for the law enforcement profession as a whole to conduct itself in accord with the Fourth Amendment, it cannot be expected, and should not be applied, to deter objectively reasonable law enforcement activity. In the ordinary case, an officer cannot be expected to question the magistrate's probable-cause determination or his judgment that the form of the warrant is technically sufficient. Once the warrant issues, there is literally nothing more the policeman can do in seeking to comply with the law, and penalizing the officer for the magistrate's error, rather than his own, cannot logically contribute to the deterrence of Fourth Amendment violations. A police officer's reliance on the magistrate's probable-cause determination and on the technical sufficiency of the warrant he issues must be objectively reasonable. Suppression remains an appropriate remedy if the magistrate or judge in issuing a warrant was misled by information in an affidavit that the affiant knew was false or would have known was false except for his reckless disregard of the truth, or if the issuing magistrate wholly abandoned his detached and neutral judicial role. Nor would an officer manifest objective good faith in relying on a warrant based on an affidavit so lacking in indicia of probable cause as to render official belief in its existence entirely unreasonable. Finally, depending on the circumstances of the particular case, a warrant may be so facially deficient—i.e., in failing to particularize the place to be searched or the things to be seized—that the executing officers cannot reasonably presume it to be valid."

CASE EXCERPT

"As yet, we have not recognized any form of good-faith exception to the Fourth Amendment exclusionary rule. But the balancing approach that has evolved during the years of experience with the rule provides strong support for the modification currently urged upon us…our evaluation of the costs and benefits of suppressing reliable physical evidence seized by officers reasonably relying on a warrant issued by a detached and neutral magistrate leads to the conclusion that such evidence should be admissible in the prosecution's case in chief."

CASE SIGNIFICANCE

This case, and *Massachusetts v. Sheppard*, decided the same day, are very important because they create the so-called "good-faith" exception to the exclusionary rule. This exception allows the introduction at trial of evidence that was seized in violation of the Fourth

Amendment, so long as it can be shown that the police were unaware of the violation and relied in good faith on the actions of others—in this instance, a judge who issued the search warrant. It is important to recognize that the good-faith exception does not apply when the police knowingly or mistakenly violate the Fourth Amendment.

MASSACHUSETTS v. SHEPPARD
468 U.S. 981 (1984)

FACTS
On the basis of evidence gathered in the investigation of a homicide in the Roxbury section of Boston, a police detective drafted an affidavit to support an application for an arrest warrant and a search warrant authorizing the search of Sheppard's residence. The affidavit stated that the police wished to search for certain described items, including the victim's clothing and a blunt instrument that might have been used on the victim. The affidavit was reviewed and approved by the district attorney. Because it was Sunday, the local court was closed, and the police had a difficult time finding a warrant application form. The detective finally found a warrant form previously used in another district to search for controlled substances. After making some changes in the form, the detective presented it and the affidavit to a judge at his residence, informing him that the warrant form might need to be further changed. Concluding that the affidavit established probable cause to search Sheppard's residence and telling the detective that the necessary changes in the warrant form would be made, the judge made some changes, but did not change the substantive portion, which continued to authorize a search for controlled substances; nor did he alter the form so as to incorporate the affidavit. The judge then signed the warrant and returned it and the affidavit to the detective, informing him that the warrant was sufficient authority in form and content to carry out the requested search. The ensuing search of Sheppard's residence by the detective and other police officers was limited to the items listed in the affidavit, and several incriminating pieces of evidence were discovered. Thereafter, Sheppard was charged with first-degree murder. At a pretrial suppression hearing, the trial judge ruled that while the warrant was defective in that it did not particularly describe the items to be seized, the incriminating evidence could be admitted because the police had acted in good faith in executing

what they reasonably thought was a valid warrant. At the subsequent trial, Sheppard was convicted. The Massachusetts Supreme Judicial Court held that the evidence should have been suppressed, and the U.S. Supreme Court granted certiorari.

ISSUE
Should evidence obtained based on a search warrant that is invalid because of a mistake made by a judge be excluded from trial?

HOLDING
No. Federal law does not require the exclusion of the disputed evidence when the police are not responsible for the error and act in "good faith" in executing the warrant.

RATIONALE
"The exclusionary rule should not be applied when the officer conducting the search acted in objectively reasonable reliance on a warrant issued by a detached and neutral magistrate that subsequently is determined to be invalid. Here, there was an objectively reasonable basis for the officers' mistaken belief that the warrant authorized the search they conducted. The officers took every step that could reasonably be expected of them. At the point where the judge returned the affidavit and warrant to the detective, a reasonable police officer would have concluded, as the detective did, that the warrant authorized a search for the materials outlined in the affidavit. A police officer is not required to disbelieve a judge who has just advised him that the warrant he possesses authorizes him to conduct the search he has requested.

"An error of constitutional dimensions may have been committed with respect to the issuance of the warrant in this case, but it was the judge, not the police officer, who made the critical mistake."

CASE EXCERPT
"Suppressing evidence because the judge failed to make all the necessary clerical corrections despite his assurances that such changes would be made will not serve the deterrent function that the exclusionary rule was designed to achieve. Accordingly, federal law does not require the exclusion of the disputed evidence in this case."

CASE SIGNIFICANCE
This case and *United States v. Leon,* decided the same day, were very important because they created the

MASSACHUSETTS v. SHEPPARD *(cont.)*

so-called "good-faith" exception to the exclusionary rule. This exception allows the introduction at trial of evidence that was seized in violation of the Fourth Amendment, so long as it can be shown that the police were unaware of the violation and relied in good faith on the actions of others—in this instance, a judge who issued the search warrant. It is important to recognize the good-faith exception does not apply when the police knowingly or mistakenly violate the Fourth Amendment.

MINNESOTA v. OLSON
495 U.S. 91 (1990)

FACTS

Police suspected Olson of being the driver of the getaway car used in a robbery–murder. After recovering the murder weapon and arresting the suspected murderer, they surrounded the home of two women with whom they believed Olson had been staying, based on an anonymous tip. When police telephoned the home and told one of the women that Olson should come out, a male voice was heard saying, "Tell them I left." Without seeking permission and with weapons drawn, the officers entered the home, found Olson hiding in a closet, and arrested him. Shortly thereafter, he made an incriminating statement, which the trial court refused to suppress. He was convicted of murder, armed robbery, and assault. The Minnesota Supreme Court reversed, ruling that Olson had a sufficient interest in the women's home to challenge the legality of his warrantless arrest, that the arrest was illegal because there were no exigent circumstances to justify warrantless entry, and that his statement was tainted and should have been suppressed. The U.S. Supreme Court then granted certiorari.

ISSUE

May police officers lawfully make a warrantless, nonconsensual entry without an exigent circumstance?

HOLDING

No. The arrest violated Olson's Fourth Amendment rights. An overnight guest has a reasonable expectation of privacy.

RATIONALE

"Olson's status as an overnight guest is alone sufficient to show that he had an expectation of privacy in the home that society is prepared to recognize as reasonable. The distinctions relied on by the State between this case and *Jones*—that there the overnight guest was left alone and had a key to the premises with which he could come and go and admit and exclude others— are not legally determinative. All citizens share the expectation that hosts will more likely than not respect their guests' privacy interests even if the guests have no legal interest in the premises and do not have the legal authority to determine who may enter the household. There were no exigent circumstances justifying the warrantless entry: An entry may be justified by hot pursuit of a fleeing felon, the imminent destruction of evidence, the need to prevent a suspect's escape, or the risk of danger to the police or others; but, in the absence of hot pursuit, there must be at least probable cause to believe that one or more of the other factors was present and, in assessing the risk of danger, the gravity of the crime and likelihood that the suspect is armed should be considered."

CASE EXCERPT

"To hold that an overnight guest has a legitimate expectation of privacy in his host's home merely recognizes the everyday expectations of privacy that we all share. Staying overnight in another's home is a longstanding social custom…From the overnight guest's perspective, he seeks shelter in another's home precisely because it provides him with privacy, a place where he and his possessions will not be disturbed by anyone but his host and those his host allows inside."

CASE SIGNIFICANCE

This case clearly established that police officers may not enter the home of a third party to arrest a visitor unless they have consent to enter or there exists some exigent circumstance that justifies not obtaining a search warrant. An overnight guest is presumed to have a reasonable expectation of privacy while he or she is a guest in another's home.

ARIZONA v. EVANS
514 U.S. 1 (1995)

FACTS

Evans was arrested by Phoenix police during a routine traffic stop when a patrol car's computer indicated that there was an outstanding misdemeanor warrant for his arrest. A subsequent search of his car revealed a bag of marijuana, and he was charged with possession. Evans moved to suppress the marijuana as the fruit of an unlawful arrest, since the misdemeanor warrant had been quashed before his arrest. The trial court granted the motion, but the court of appeals reversed on the ground that the exclusionary rule's purpose would not be served by excluding evidence obtained because of an error by employees not directly associated with the arresting officers or their police department. In reversing, the Arizona Supreme Court rejected the distinction between clerical errors committed by law enforcement personnel and similar mistakes by court employees and predicted that the exclusionary rule's application would serve to improve the efficiency of criminal justice system record-keepers. The U.S. Supreme Court then granted certiorari.

ISSUE
Must evidence that has been seized illegally but in good faith, based on a clerical error unknown to the arresting officer, be suppressed in accordance with the exclusionary rule?

HOLDING
No. The exclusionary rule does not require suppression of evidence seized in violation of the Fourth Amendment where the erroneous information resulted from clerical errors of court employees.

RATIONALE
"The exclusionary rule is a judicially created remedy designed to safeguard against future violations of Fourth Amendment rights through its deterrent effect. However, the issue of exclusion is separate from whether the Amendment has been violated. The Amendment does not expressly preclude the use of evidence obtained in violation of its commands, and exclusion is appropriate only where the rule's remedial objectives are thought most efficaciously served. The same framework that this Court used in *United States v. Leon* to determine that there was no sound reason to apply the exclusionary rule as a means of deterring misconduct on the part of judicial officers responsible for issuing search warrants applies in this case. The exclusionary rule was historically designed as a means of deterring police misconduct, not mistakes by court employees. In addition, Evans offers no evidence that court employees are inclined to ignore or subvert the Fourth Amendment or that lawlessness among these actors requires application of the extreme sanction of

exclusion. In fact, the Justice Court Clerk testified that this type of error occurred only once every three or four years. Finally, there is no basis for believing that application of the exclusionary rule will have a significant effect on the court employees responsible for informing the police that a warrant has been quashed.

CASE EXCERPT
"If court employees were responsible for the erroneous computer record, the exclusion of evidence at trial would not sufficiently deter future errors so as to warrant such a severe sanction…Because court clerks are not adjuncts to the law enforcement team engaged in the often competitive enterprise of ferreting out crime, they have no stake in the outcome of particular criminal prosecutions."

CASE SIGNIFICANCE
This case is important because it extends the "good-faith" exception to the exclusionary rule to cover errors by court employees. The Supreme Court has been unwilling to extend the exclusionary rule beyond its original parameters, instead creating exceptions for situations where a warrant is deemed invalid because of a mistake made by someone other than the police officer.

HERRING v. UNITED STATES
555 U.S. 135 (2009)

FACTS
In 2004, Herring drove to the Coffee County, Alabama, Sheriff's Department to retrieve some personal items from an impounded vehicle. When a deputy sheriff learned that Herring was at the impound lot, he asked the department's warrant clerk to find out if there were any outstanding arrest warrants for Herring. The clerk determined there was an outstanding warrant from a neighboring county. The deputy sheriff arrested Herring as he was driving away, and a search of Herring and his truck incident to the arrest turned up methamphetamine in Herring's pocket and a pistol under the front seat of his truck. Shortly after the arrest and search, the clerk discovered the arrest warrant had been recalled. Herring was indicted on charges of possessing methamphetamine and being a felon in possession of a firearm. He moved to suppress the evidence, arguing that because the arrest warrant on which the officer relied had been withdrawn, the searches did not take place incident to a lawful arrest.

HERRING v. UNITED STATES *(cont.)*

The district court denied Herring's motion, holding that application of the exclusionary rule would not deter future mistakes, as the arresting officer had acted on a good-faith belief that the warrant was valid and had found the evidence before learning the warrant had been recalled. Herring was convicted. On appeal, the Eleventh Circuit affirmed, stating that while the searches were unlawful, whether the evidence obtained through those searches must be suppressed was a separate question. The court of appeals acknowledged that the police were negligent, but that the exclusionary rule would not deter in these situations and the benefits of applying the rule outweighed the cost. The court noted that the exclusionary sanction would not be levied against the department which was guilty of negligent record-keeping, but instead against a different department in another county that was entirely innocent of any wrongdoing.

ISSUE

If an arrest and search is conducted based upon a negligent error by a police clerk who believed a current outstanding warrant existed for the individual but was actually recalled, can that evidence potentially be admitted at trial?

HOLDING

Yes. The Supreme Court held that a negligent error by a police clerk does not necessarily require exclusion of the evidence obtained.

RATIONALE

In *Arizona v. Evans* (1995), the Supreme Court held the exclusionary rule did not apply to evidence seized incident to an arrest that was unlawful under the Fourth Amendment because it was based on erroneous information negligently provided by a court employee. The question before the Court here was whether the exclusionary rule applies when the erroneous information was negligently provided by law enforcement personnel. In this case, the majority asserted that the *Evans* decision had not addressed the applicability of the good-faith exception to police mistakes. Significantly, while the facts of the case involve a clerical error by the police, the language of the opinion does not limit the holding to clerical errors. It applies fully to negligence by police officers in their day-to-day determination whether there is probable cause to conduct a search. If the officer is merely negligent in

concluding he has probable cause to conduct a search or make an arrest, the exclusionary rule does not apply to whatever evidence he finds.

CASE EXCERPT

"We do not suggest that all recordkeeping errors by the police are immune from the exclusionary rule. In this case, however, the conduct at issue was not so objectively culpable as to require exclusion…If the police have been shown to be reckless in maintaining a warrant system, or to have knowingly made false entries to lay the groundwork for future false arrests, exclusion would certainly be justified under our cases should such misconduct cause a Fourth Amendment violation."

CASE SIGNIFICANCE

This marks the first time the Court has applied the good-faith exception to mistakes made by police officers rather than to mistakes made by others that police officers relied upon in good faith. The one limitation on the Court's opinion is the Court's statement that its rule applies to police conduct "attenuated from the arrest," whatever that means.

DAVIS v. UNITED STATES
—U.S.—(2011)

FACTS

In 2007, prior to the *Gant* decision, Davis was a passenger in a vehicle that was pulled over in a routine traffic stop. The driver of the vehicle was subsequently arrested for driving while intoxicated, and Davis was also arrested for providing the police with a false name. Both the driver and Davis were handcuffed and secured in the back of squad cars. After having secured Davis and the driver, police searched the interior of the detained vehicle and found a gun in Davis' jacket, which was in the vehicle. Davis was charged with being a felon in possession of a firearm. Davis sought to suppress the firearm. Davis admitted that the search complied with existing Eleventh Circuit precedent that adhered to *Belton*, and that the court was obliged to follow that precedent, but asserted his Fourteenth Amendment right to raise the issue on appeal. While Davis' appeal was pending, the Supreme Court decided *Gant*. In *New York v. Belton* (1981), the Supreme Court created a "bright-line rule" for when police officers may search a vehicle after making a custodial arrest: when an officer has made a lawful custodial arrest of the occupant of an automobile, the officer may, as part of the arrest, search the passenger compartment of that automobile. This rule stood largely unmodified by the Court until *Arizona v. Gant* (2009). In this case, the Court held that the *Belton* exception to the search warrant requirement did not apply to situations where the arrestee has been removed from the vehicle and secured.

ISSUE
When law enforcement conducts a lawful search authorized by precedent at the time (*New York v. Belton*) but is subsequently found to be unconstitutional in a later, separate case (*Arizona v. Gant*), can the government successfully argue the search is valid using the good-faith exception to the exclusionary rule?

HOLDING
Yes. The search of the vehicle in this case occurred two years before the *Gant* decision was rendered. The purpose of the exclusionary rule is to deter law enforcement from violating citizens' constitutional rights. However, at the time, the officers were unaware of the future rulings of the Supreme Court. As such, "searches conducted in objectively reasonable reliance on binding appellate precedent are not subject to the exclusionary rule."

RATIONALE
The Supreme Court held that at the time of the search the officer was adhering to established precedent regulating searches and applied the good-faith exception to the exclusionary rule. The purpose of the exclusionary rule is to deter future Fourth Amendment violations. Before the exclusionary rule is applied a cost–benefit analysis must be conducted, and for evidence to be excluded from trial "the deterrence benefits of suppression must outweigh its heavy costs."

When officers conduct a search in good faith on established precedent, even if the search is later found to be unconstitutional, the evidence gathered in that search should be admitted as the police were obeying the law as it was then understood and thus acting in good faith.

CASE EXCERPT
"Under our exclusionary-rule precedents, this acknowledged absence of police culpability dooms Davis's claim. Police practices trigger the harsh sanction of exclusion only when they are deliberate enough to yield 'meaningful' deterrence, and culpable enough to be 'worth the price paid by the justice system.' The conduct of the officers here was neither of these things... The police acted in strict compliance with binding precedent, and their behavior was not wrongful. Unless the exclusionary rule is to become a strict-liability regime, it can have no application in this case."

CASE SIGNIFICANCE
This case is significant because it solidified that the primary purpose of the exclusionary rule is to deter all types of law enforcement misconduct, whether negligent, reckless, or intentional. As such, this case reaffirms the good-faith exception to the exclusionary rule. When officers make a mistake that is objectively reasonable, they are not culpable. This includes actions that at the time are valid but later are overruled by precedent. Applying new requirements by the Supreme Court for the exclusionary rule to previous cases would create a number of problems related to retroactivity. Also, it is worth noting that both Justice Kagan and Justice Sotomayor agreed with Justice Alito—their support of this continued diminution of the exclusionary rule does not bode well for its continued existence.

DISCUSSION QUESTIONS

1. What justification did the Supreme Court provide for imposing the exclusionary rule on the states in *Mapp v. Ohio*?
2. What is the primary purpose of the exclusionary rule, according to the Supreme Court?
3. What are some of the exceptions to the exclusionary rule?
4. Is the exclusionary rule based on a particular provision of the Constitution or Bill of Rights?
5. To what areas of criminal justice has the Supreme Court refused to apply the exclusionary rule?
6. Why does the court allow evidence that was improperly obtained, but obtained in good faith, by the agents of government into a criminal trial?
7. What distinguishes the inevitable discovery exception from the independent source exception?
8. What types of conduct by police might require the imposition of the exclusionary rule?
9. Should overnight guests have an expectation of privacy in the home of another?
10. What actions in *Rochin v. California* "shocked the conscience" of the Court?

CHAPTER TWO

WHAT CONSTITUTES PROBABLE CAUSE?

BECK v. OHIO, *379 U.S. 89 (1964)*

DRAPER v. UNITED STATES, *358 U.S. 307 (1959)*

ILLINOIS v. GATES, *462 U.S. 213 (1983)*

ILLINOIS v. CABALLES, *543 U.S. 405 (2005)*

INTRODUCTION

In principle, *probable cause* means the same thing regardless of the conduct in which the police engage. It has been defined by the Supreme Court as more than bare suspicion; it exists when "the facts and circumstances within [the officers'] knowledge and of which they [have] reasonably trustworthy information [are] sufficient to warrant a prudent man in believing that the [suspect] had committed or was committing an offense" (*Beck v. Ohio*).

These are legal definitions of little use to those on the front lines. A more practical definition of probable cause is more than 50 percent certainty. It lies somewhere below absolute certainty and proof beyond a reasonable doubt (the latter of which is necessary to obtain a criminal conviction), and somewhere above a hunch or reasonable suspicion (the latter of which is required to conduct a stop and frisk).

The notion of a "prudent man" means that courts consider what the average "person on the street" would believe, not what a person who has received special training in the identification and apprehension of law breakers (police officer, judge, etc.) would believe. This is not to say, however, that the experience of a police officer must take a back seat to the probable cause determination.

Probable cause is always required in the following scenarios: (1) arrests with warrants; (2) arrests without warrants; (3) searches and seizures of property with warrants; and (4) searches and seizures of property without warrants. When warrants are required, the probable cause determination is made by the magistrate charged with issuing the warrant; when warrants are not used, the police officer makes the probable cause determination. Generally "probable cause can be obtained from police radio bulletins, tips from 'good citizen' informers who have happened by chance to see criminal activity, reports from victims, anonymous tips, and tips from 'habitual' informers who mingle with people in the underworld and who themselves may [even] be criminals. Probable cause can be based on various combinations of these sources" (Miles et al. 1988–89, 6:4).

When the police make *arrests,* the probable cause determination concerns whether an offense has been committed and whether the suspect did, in fact, commit the offense. In the case of a search, however, the probable cause issue concerns whether the items to be seized are connected with criminal activity and whether they can be found in the place to be searched. This means, then, that the courts sometimes treat the probable cause requirement differently depending on the conduct the police engage in.

One point needs to be underscored: Probable cause to search does not necessarily create probable cause to arrest, and, alternatively, probable cause to arrest does not necessarily create probable cause to search. With regard to the latter point, consider this hypothetical: Police officers pursue a drug suspect into her residence and, based an a hot pursuit exigency, arrest her in her living room. Assuming probable cause was in place to pursue the suspect, the police do not possess unfettered latitude once in the house to search the place top to bottom. The courts have placed restrictions on what can be done in a situation such as this—that is, on how far the police can go with a search following (incident to) arrest. We will cover searches incident to arrest in a later chapter, but this example illustrates that the ingredients in the probable cause recipe are not always the same for arrests as they are for searches.

REFERENCE

Miles, J.G., Jr., D.B. Richardson, and A.E. Scudellari. (1988–1989). *The Law Officer's Pocket Manual.* Washington, D.C.: Bureau of National Affairs.

BECK v. OHIO
379 U.S. 89 (1964)

FACTS
On the afternoon of November 10, 1961, William Beck was driving his car near East 115th Street and Beulah Avenue in Cleveland, Ohio. City police officers confronted him, identified themselves, and ordered him to pull over to the curb. The officers possessed neither an arrest warrant nor a search warrant. Placing him under arrest, they searched his car but found nothing of interest. They then took him to a nearby police station, where they searched his person and found an envelope containing a number of clearing house slips. Beck was charged in the Cleveland Municipal Court with possession of clearing house slips in violation of a state criminal statute. He filed a motion to suppress the clearing house slips in question, arguing that the police had obtained them by means of an unreasonable search and seizure in violation of the Fourth and Fourteenth Amendments.

ISSUE
Were the arrest and subsequent search in violation of the Fourth Amendment?

HOLDING
Yes. Police have probable cause to arrest when they have reasonably trustworthy information that would warrant a person of "reasonable caution" to believe a crime is taking place or has taken place.

RATIONALE
"Whether an arrest without warrant is constitutionally valid depends upon whether, at the moment the arrest was made, the officer had probable cause to make it, that is, whether at that moment the facts and circumstances within his knowledge and of which he had reasonably trustworthy information were sufficient to warrant a prudent man in believing that the suspect had committed or was committing an offense."

CASE EXCERPT
"Beyond that, the arresting officer who testified said no more than that someone (he did not say who) had told him something (he did not say what) about the petitioner. We do not hold that the officer's knowledge of the petitioner's physical appearance and previous record was either inadmissible or entirely irrelevant upon the issue of probable cause. But to hold knowledge of either or both of these facts constituted probable cause would be to hold that anyone with a previous criminal record could be arrested at will."

CASE SIGNIFICANCE
This case is significant because the Court announced one of its most often cited definitions of probable cause, based on the "prudent man." *Beck* can be understood as requiring police officers to show probable cause based on what a reasonable person, not a single individual, would believe. While the officers in *Beck* may have thought, individually, that they had probable cause to stop the vehicle, the Court noted that a "prudent man," or reasonable person, would not have.

DRAPER v. UNITED STATES
358 U.S. 307 (1959)

FACTS
A federal narcotics agent was notified by a paid informer who had supplied reliable information in the past that Draper was selling drugs. The informant also notified the agent that Draper had gone to Chicago to obtain more drugs and that he would be returning on a train carrying a tan bag that would contain the narcotics. Finally, the informant described what clothes Draper would be wearing and mentioned that he would be walking quickly after exiting the train. The agent observed a man fitting the description given by

DRAPER v. UNITED STATES *(cont.)*

the informant. Without a warrant, Draper was arrested. He was searched and drugs were found. Draper was convicted at trial despite his motion to suppress the evidence.

ISSUE

Can information provided by an informant that is later corroborated by a law enforcement officer establish probable cause to arrest?

HOLDING

Yes. So long as an informant's tip "is reasonably corroborated by other matters within the officer's knowledge," the tip can be considered credible for purposes of establishing probable cause to arrest.

RATIONALE

The informant had supplied reliable information in the past. Also, the agent took steps to verify the information supplied by the informant. When the information provided by the informant was found to be accurate, the officer had probable cause to arrest Draper.

CASE EXCERPT

"Hereford may have been hearsay to Marsh, but coming from one employed for that purpose and whose information had always been found accurate and reliable, it is clear that Marsh would have been derelict in his duties had he not pursued it…And surely, with every other bit of Hereford's information being thus personally verified, Marsh had 'reasonable grounds' to believe that the remaining unverified bit of Hereford's information—that Draper would have the heroin with him—was likewise true."

CASE SIGNIFICANCE

Draper essentially permitted reliance on hearsay for purposes of establishing probable cause to arrest. Ordinarily hearsay is not admissible in a criminal trial. However, the Supreme Court appears not to have a problem with hearsay in the probable cause context, as long as law enforcement officers corroborate what was said. This case was also controversial because even though the informant supplied information that proved to be accurate, nothing the agent observed prior to Draper's arrest was itself incriminating. It is important to realize that *Draper* dealt with arrests, not searches, so it basically stands alone.

ILLINOIS v. GATES

462 U.S. 213 (1983)

FACTS

In mid-1978, the Bloomingdale, Illinois, Police Department received an anonymous letter informing them that Gates and his wife made a living selling drugs, that they bought most of their drugs in Florida, and that on a certain date Gates would be driving back from Florida with a car full of drugs. A police officer obtained Gates' address and set forth to corroborate the various details (there were others) set forth in the anonymous letter. The officer found that Gates had flown down to Florida, stayed the night in a hotel, and driven north the next day in a car with Illinois license plates. The letter and the information resulting from the officer's investigation were set forth in an affidavit in support of a search warrant. A search warrant was issued. Officers serving the warrant found drugs in Gates' house and car. He was arrested and charged with violating state drug laws, and the U.S. Supreme Court granted certiorari.

ISSUE

Does an anonymous letter containing no information as to the informant's reliability and basis of knowledge coupled with corroboration by a police officer provide probable cause for obtaining a search warrant?

HOLDING

Yes. The two-pronged *Aguilar* test, requiring that police officers demonstrate informants' reliability and basis of knowledge, is abandoned in favor of a "totality of circumstances" analysis. A deficiency in one prong can be satisfied by a strong showing in the other.

RATIONALE

"We conclude that it is wiser to abandon the 'two-pronged test' established by our decisions in *Aguilar* and *Spinelli*. In its place we reaffirm the totality-of-circumstances analysis that traditionally has informed probable cause determinations.…The task of the issuing magistrate is simply to make a practical, common-sense decision whether, given all the circumstances set forth in the affidavit before him, including the 'veracity' and 'basis of knowledge' of persons supplying hearsay information, there is a fair probability that contraband or evidence of a crime will be found in a particular place."

CASE EXCERPT

"The direction taken by decisions following *Spinelli* poorly serves 'the most basic function of any government'…The strictures that inevitably accompany the 'two-pronged test' cannot avoid seriously impeding the task of law enforcement. If, as the Illinois Supreme Court apparently thought, that test must be rigorously applied in every case, anonymous tips seldom would be of greatly diminished value in police work. Ordinary citizens, like ordinary witnesses, generally do not provide extensive recitations of the basis of their everyday observations."

CASE SIGNIFICANCE

Gates is significant because it simplifies the probable cause analysis. If a police officer cannot adequately demonstrate an informant's reliability but can demonstrate the informant's basis of knowledge with a strong showing, then probable cause can be established. The reverse is also true: a weak showing in the "basis of knowledge" prong can be counteracted by a strong showing as to the informant's past reliability.

ILLINOS v. CABALLES

543 U.S. 405 (2005)

FACTS

Caballes was driving down the highway when he was pulled over by Illinois State Trooper Gillette for speeding. Within only 10 minutes, the following actions took place. The officer reported the stop to the police dispatcher, which was overheard by an Illinois State Police Drug Interdiction Team member, Officer Graham, who immediately drove to the scene of the traffic stop with his narcotics-detection dog. When Graham approached the scene, Gillette was in the process of writing Caballes a warning ticket, while Caballes was sitting in Gillette's vehicle. Graham noticed Caballes' car was on the side of the road and decided to walk the narcotics dog around the vehicle. The dog alerted Graham to the trunk of the car and both officers opened the trunk, where they then discovered marijuana. Caballes was arrested and later convicted.

ISSUE

When an individual is lawfully detained during a traffic stop, does the admission of evidence inadvertently discovered by a drug-detection dog that

is led around the vehicle without probable cause of the presence of illegal drugs violate the Fourth Amendment?

HOLDING

No. The Court held the use of a narcotics-detection dog during a traffic stop, which is not deliberately prolonged, is not an improper search under the Fourth Amendment because this conduct does not "compromise any legitimate interest in privacy."

RATIONALE

The Court explains when a seizure for a minor traffic stop is intentionally prolonged beyond the time an officer could reasonably complete the necessary requirements, that seizure may become unlawful. However, in this case the events happened quickly and the Court accepts the state court's finding that the time taken by Officer Gillette was entirely reasonable. As such, the question turns to whether "the use of the dog converted the citizen-police encounter from a lawful traffic stop into a drug investigation" that lacked probable cause. The Court rejects this analysis by explaining when conduct by law enforcement does not "compromise any legitimate interest in privacy," it does not violate the Fourth Amendment. In the case of narcotic-detection dogs during a lawful traffic stop, the legitimate privacy interests are not implicated because the dog "discloses only the presence or absence of narcotics, a contraband item."

CASE EXCERPT

"In this case, the dog sniff was performed on the exterior of the respondent's car while he was lawfully seized for a traffic violation. Any intrusion on respondent's privacy expectations does not rise to the level of a constitutionally cognizant infringement."

CASE SIGNIFICANCE

This case is significant because it clarifies the meaning of legitimate privacy interests. In the majority opinion, Justice Stevens distinguishes this case from their decision in *Kyllo v. United States*, 533 US. 27 (2001), where the Court found the use of a thermal-imaging device to detect whether marijuana was being grown in a private home violated the Fourth Amendment. Specifically, the use of the thermal-imaging device to look inside one's home detects both lawful and unlawful activity. For example, law enforcement could

ILLINOS v. CABALLES *(cont.)*

determine "at what hour each night the lady of the house takes her daily sauna and bath." In contrast, the narcotics-detection dog in the case does not detect lawful activity. The dog can only alert law enforcement to "the location of a substance that no individual has any right to possess."

DISCUSSION QUESTIONS

1. Discuss sources of information that would lead an officer to conclude that probable cause to *arrest* is present.
2. Discuss sources of information that would lead an officer to conclude that probable cause to *search* is present.
3. What does probable cause mean from a practical standpoint? That is, explain probable cause in simple, nonlegal terminology that could be understood by anyone.
4. What happens if probable cause to arrest or search is not present? Are the available remedies (e.g., exclusionary rule, civil liability) sufficient?
5. Our criminal justice system requires proof beyond a reasonable doubt for a finding of guilty in a criminal trial. Probable cause is a substantially lower standard. What explanations can you offer for this apparent discrepancy?
6. Was the Supreme Court's decision in *Illinois v. Gates* a smart one? Who benefits most from the Court's decision in that case?
7. Describe the difference between the rule created in *Aguilar v. Texas* and the test developed in *Spinelli v. United States*.
8. Do you agree with the holding of *Illinois v. Caballes*? Explain why or why not.
9. Should the existence of probable cause be evaluated from an objective or subjective perspective?
10. Should informants' tips serve as a basis to establish probable cause? Is this good public policy? Why or why not?

CHAPTER THREE

STOP AND FRISK

TERRY v. OHIO, *392 U.S. 1 (1968)*

ADAMS v. WILLIAMS, *407 U.S. 143 (1972)*

UNITED STATES v. HENSLEY, *469 U.S. 221 (1985)*

UNITED STATES v. SOKOLOW, *490 U.S. 1 (1989)*

ALABAMA v. WHITE, *496 U.S. 325 (1990)*

MINNESOTA v. DICKERSON, *508 U.S. 366 (1993)*

FLORIDA v. J. L., *529 U.S. 266 (2000)*

ILLINOIS v. WARDLOW, *528 U.S. 119 (2000)*

ARIZONA v. JOHNSON, *555 U.S. 323 (2009)*

INTRODUCTION

As we have seen, probable cause is required to justify a search or seizure within the meaning of the Fourth Amendment. But much police activity does not reach the level of intrusion that occurs when a search or seizure is carried out. For example, the police routinely have to confront people on the street or pull over automobiles in order to question them or enforce traffic laws. If probable cause were required under such circumstances, there would be very little the police could do in terms of investigating suspicious activity.

Recognizing that these "lesser intrusions" are essential to the police mission, the Supreme Court in *Terry v. Ohio* established a different level of justification for such activities. The standard the Court created was "reasonable suspicion," something below probable cause but above a hunch. *Terry* dealt with so-called "stop and frisk" activities, but reasonable suspicion as a standard of justification also permeates other arenas of criminal procedure (traffic stops, for example—see *Arizona v. Johnson*).

In *Terry* an officer's attention was drawn to two men on a street corner who appeared to the officer to be "casing" a store for a robbery. The officer approached the men and asked them to identify themselves. The officer then proceeded to pat the men down and found a gun on each man. The men were placed under arrest.

They tried to suppress the guns, but the Supreme Court eventually held the officer's actions valid in the interest of "effective crime prevention and detection." Balancing an intrusion that was arguably less serious than a search with the interests of society in apprehending law breakers, the Court held that a lower standard than probable cause was required because "street encounters between citizens and police officers are incredibly rich in diversity."

There is no clear definition of "reasonable suspicion," just as there is no clear definition of probable cause. As a level of justification lying below probable cause, then, reasonable suspicion is "considerably less than proof of wrongdoing by a preponderance of evidence" (*United States v. Sokolow*) but more than an unparticularized hunch. Recently, the Supreme Court held that the appropriate standard for determining whether reasonable suspicion exists is one that focuses on the totality of circumstances. Also, the Supreme Court agrees that substantial deference should be given to trained police officers in deciding when reasonable suspicion is present.

Like probable cause, reasonable suspicion can be based on a number of different sources, including informants. But because the reasonable suspicion standard falls below probable cause on the justification scale, less information is required. In *Adams v.*

Williams, for example, the Supreme Court held that reasonable suspicion may be based on an anonymous telephone tip so long as the police are able to corroborate certain details released by the informant. In a similar case, *Alabama v. White,* the Supreme Court observed: "Reasonable suspicion is a less demanding standard than probable cause not only in the sense that reasonable suspicion can be established with information that is different but also in the sense that reasonable suspicion can arise from information that is less reliable than that required to show probable cause." But anonymous tips alone are insufficient for establishing reasonable suspicion (*Florida v. J. L.*).

In *United States v. Hensley,* the Supreme Court unanimously held that the reasonable suspicion standard is satisfied when the police rely on "wanted" flyers, even flyers from other jurisdictions. A restriction on this ruling was that the flyer, regardless of its place of origin, be based on articulable facts that connect the suspect to criminal activity. The Court in *Hensley* also had to decide whether a stop based on reasonable suspicion of *prior* criminal activity was permissible under the Fourth Amendment's reasonableness standard. All decisions up to that point dealt with suspected criminal activity immediately before the officer's arrival or criminal activity likely to have occurred but for the officer's arrival. In *Hensley* the police stopped a man 12 days after the commission of a robbery for which he was suspected. The Court upheld the police's action and stated that it "would not only hinder the investigation, but might also enable the suspect to flee in the interim and to remain at large."

One of the Supreme Court's most recent decisions concerning reasonable suspicion is *Illinois v. Wardlow.* In that case Chicago police officers were patrolling an area known for narcotics traffic. Upon seeing the officers, Wardlow ran and was chased down by the police. He was caught and patted down. The officers found a Colt .38 pistol and arrested him. Wardlow appealed his conviction, arguing that the stop and frisk was illegal because the officers did not have reasonable suspicion. The Court disagreed with his arguing, noting that "a location's characteristics are relevant in determining whether the circumstances are sufficiently suspicious to warrant further investigation." In addition, the Court noted that "it was Wardlow's unprovoked flight that aroused the officers' suspicion" and that "nervous, evasive behavior is another pertinent factor in determining reasonable suspicion, and headlong flight is the consummate act of evasion." Thus, in the Court's

view, the officers did have reasonable suspicion to stop and frisk Wardlow.

So far we have focused almost exclusively on the definition of reasonable suspicion. Other Supreme Court cases, however, deal with restrictions concerning stops and frisks themselves. These restrictions focus on (1) how far the police can "go" in terms of frisking someone and (2) how long stops can take. Concerning the first of these restrictions, *Minnesota v. Dickerson* informs us that the police may seize contraband detected through the sense of touch during a protective pat-down search only if the contraband is immediately apparent and no manipulation takes place. Thus, frisks are truly limited to "pat downs." As for the time involved in a stop, the Supreme Court's decision in *United States v. Sharpe* was that a 40-minute detention for the purpose of a limited investigation does not violate the Fourth Amendment, provided that reasonable suspicion is present. In fact, the Court has upheld stops that last substantially longer, even as much as several hours.

In *Arizona v. Johnson,* the Court clarified its previous holdings in *Mimms, Wilson,* and *Brendlin,* concluding that officers who conduct routine traffic stops may perform a pat down of a driver and any passengers upon reasonable suspicion that they may be armed and dangerous.

TERRY v. OHIO
392 U.S. 1 (1968)

FACTS
A Cleveland detective (McFadden) on a downtown beat he had been patrolling for many years observed two strangers (Terry and another man, Chilton) on a street corner. He saw them proceed alternately back and forth along an identical route, pausing to stare in the same store window, which they did for a total of about 24 times. Each completion of the route was followed by a conference between the two on a corner, at one of which they were joined by a third man (Katz), who left swiftly. Suspecting the two men of "casing a job, a stick-up," the officer followed them and saw them rejoin the third man a couple of blocks away in front of a store. The officer approached the three, identified himself as a policeman, and asked their names. The men "mumbled something," whereupon McFadden spun petitioner around, patted down his outside clothing, and found in his overcoat pocket, but was unable to remove, a pistol. The officer ordered the three into

the store. He removed petitioner's overcoat, took out a revolver, and ordered the three to face the wall with their hands raised. He patted down the outer clothing of Chilton and Katz and seized a revolver from Chilton's outside overcoat pocket. He did not put his hands under the outer garments of Katz (since he discovered nothing in his pat down that might have been a weapon) or under petitioner's or Chilton's outer garments until he felt the guns. The three were taken to the police station. Petitioner and Chilton were charged with carrying concealed weapons. The defense moved to suppress the weapons. The court denied the motion to suppress and admitted the weapons into evidence. The court distinguished between an investigatory "stop" and an arrest, and between a "frisk" of the outer clothing for weapons and a full-blown search for evidence of crime. Terry and Chilton were found guilty, an intermediate appellate court affirmed, and the state supreme court dismissed the appeal on the ground that "no substantial constitutional question" was involved. The U.S. Supreme Court then granted certiorari.

ISSUE

May a police officer conduct a stop and frisk based on reasonable suspicion?

HOLDING

Yes. A police officer who has "reasonable suspicion" of criminal activity may briefly stop an individual and question him, and if the officer fears for his safety, he may conduct a pat-down search of the outer clothing of the suspect.

RATIONALE

"Where a reasonably prudent officer is warranted in the circumstances of a given case in believing that his safety or that of others is endangered, he may make a reasonable search for weapons of the person believed by him to be armed and dangerous regardless of whether he has probable cause to arrest that individual for a crime or the absolute certainty that the individual is armed. Though the police must whenever practicable secure a warrant to make a search and seizure, that procedure cannot be followed where swift action based upon on-the-spot observations of the officer on the beat is required. The reasonableness of any particular search and seizure must be assessed in light of the particular circumstances against the standard of whether a man of reasonable caution is warranted in believing that the action taken was appropriate. The officer here

was performing a legitimate function of investigating suspicious conduct when he decided to approach petitioner and his companions. An officer justified in believing that an individual whose suspicious behavior he is investigating at close range is armed may, to neutralize the threat of physical harm, take necessary measures to determine whether that person is carrying a weapon. A search for weapons in the absence of probable cause to arrest must be strictly circumscribed by the exigencies of the situation. An officer may make an intrusion short of arrest where he has reasonable apprehension of danger before being possessed of information justifying arrest. The officer's protective seizure of petitioner and his companions, and the limited search which he made, were reasonable, both at their inception and as conducted. The actions of petitioner and his companions were consistent with the officer's hypothesis that they were contemplating a daylight robbery and were armed. The officer's search was confined to what was minimally necessary to determine whether the men were armed, and the intrusion, which was made for the sole purpose of protecting himself and others nearby, was confined to ascertaining the presence of weapons."

CASE EXCERPT

"The distinctions of classical 'stop-and-frisk' theory thus serve to divert attention from the central inquiry under the Fourth Amendment—the reasonableness in all the circumstances of the particular governmental invasion of a citizen's personal security. 'Search' and 'seizure' are not talismans. We therefore reject the notions that the Fourth Amendment does not come into play at all as a limitation upon police conduct if the officers stop short of something called a 'technical arrest' or a 'full-blown search'... And in determining whether the seizure and search were 'unreasonable' our inquiry is a dual one—whether the officer's action was justified at its inception, and whether it was reasonably related in scope to the circumstances which justified the interference in the first place."

CASE SIGNIFICANCE

This case is very important, for it authorized police to conduct a "stop and frisk," or investigative detention. This may be done on less than probable cause—all the police need is "reasonable suspicion." While a stop is a seizure, and a frisk is a search, both may be conducted with less evidence than that required for an arrest or a full search. This decision, handed down by the often

TERRY v. OHIO *(cont.)*

vilified "liberal" Warren Court, was actually a major victory for police officers, as it gives them tremendous authority to investigate possible criminal activity.

ADAMS v. WILLIAMS
407 U.S. 143 (1972)

FACTS
Acting on a tip supplied moments earlier by a reliable informant known to him, a police officer asked Adams to open his car door. Adams responded by instead rolling down the car window, at which point the officer reached into the car and found a loaded handgun (which had not been visible from the outside) in Adams' waistband, precisely where the informant had said it would be. Adams was arrested for unlawful possession of a handgun. A search incident to the arrest disclosed heroin on Adams' person (as the informant had also reported), as well as other weapons in the car. Adams was convicted and sentenced to prison. His petition for federal habeas corpus relief was denied by the district court. The court of appeals reversed, holding that the evidence that had been used in the trial resulting in Williams' conviction had been obtained by an unlawful search. The U.S. Supreme Court then granted certiorari.

ISSUE
May a police officer conduct a stop and frisk based on information provided by a reliable informant?

HOLDING
Yes. As *Terry v. Ohio* recognizes, a policeman making a reasonable investigatory stop may conduct a limited protective search for concealed weapons when he has reason to believe that the suspect is armed and dangerous. Additionally, a stop and frisk based on information not personally observed by a police officer is reasonable under the Fourth Amendment.

RATIONALE
The Supreme Court "rejects Williams' argument that reasonable cause for a stop and frisk can only be based on the officer's personal observation, rather than on information supplied by another person. Informants' tips, like all other clues and evidence coming to a policeman on the scene, may vary greatly in their value and reliability. One simple rule will not cover every situation. Some tips, completely lacking in indicia of reliability, would either warrant no police response or require further investigation before a forcible stop of a suspect would be authorized. But in some situations—for example, when the victim of a street crime seeks immediate police aid and gives a description of his assailant, or when a credible informant warns of a specific impending crime—the subtleties of the hearsay rule should not thwart an appropriate police response."

CASE EXCERPT
"Probable cause does not require the same type of specific evidence of each element of the offense as would be needed to support a conviction. Rather, the court will evaluate generally the circumstances at the time of the arrest to decide if the officer had probable cause for his action."

CASE SIGNIFICANCE
This case extended the availability of the stop and frisk procedure to situations where a police officer obtains information from an informant rather than from personal observation (as was the case in *Terry v. Ohio*). This was a logical extension of the stop and frisk doctrine, since an arrest, which requires probable cause, may also be made based on information obtained from a reliable informant.

UNITED STATES v. HENSLEY
469 U.S. 221 (1985)

FACTS
Following an armed robbery in the Cincinnati suburb of St. Bernard, Ohio, a St. Bernard police officer, on the basis of information obtained from an informant that Hensley had driven the getaway car during the robbery, issued a "wanted flyer" to other police departments in the area. The flyer stated that Hensley was wanted for investigation of the robbery, described him and the date and location of the robbery, and asked the other departments to pick him up and hold him for the St. Bernard police. Subsequently, on the basis of the flyer and after inquiring without success as to whether a warrant was outstanding for Hensley's arrest, police officers from Covington, Kentucky, another Cincinnati suburb, stopped an automobile that Hensley was seen driving. One of the officers recognized a passenger in the car as a convicted felon and, upon observing a

revolver butt protruding from underneath that passenger's seat, arrested him. After a search of the car uncovered other handguns, Hensley was also arrested. Hensley was then indicted on the federal charge of being a convicted felon in possession of firearms. He moved to suppress the handguns from evidence on the grounds that the Covington police had stopped him in violation of the Fourth Amendment. The federal district court denied Hensley's motion, and he was convicted. The court of appeals reversed, holding that the stop of Hensley's car was improper because the crime being investigated was not imminent or ongoing, but rather was already completed, that the "wanted" flyer was insufficient to create a reasonable suspicion that Hensley had committed a crime, and that therefore his conviction rested on evidence obtained through an illegal arrest. The U.S. Supreme Court granted certiorari.

ISSUE

May the police conduct an investigative stop of an individual who is the subject of a "wanted" flyer?

HOLDING

Yes. The ability to briefly stop that person, ask questions, or check identification in the absence of probable cause promotes the strong government interest in solving crimes and bringing offenders to justice.

RATIONALE

"Restraining police action until after probable cause is obtained would not only hinder the investigation but might also enable the suspect to flee and remain at large. The law enforcement interests at stake in these circumstances outweigh the individual's interest to be free of a stop and detention that is no more extensive than permissible in the investigation of imminent or ongoing crimes. When police have a reasonable suspicion, grounded in specific and articulable facts, that a person they encounter was involved in or is wanted in connection with a completed felony, then a *Terry* stop may be made to investigate that suspicion. If a "wanted flyer" has been issued on the basis of articulable facts supporting a reasonable suspicion that the person wanted has committed an offense, then reliance on that flyer justifies a stop to check identification, to pose questions, or to detain the person briefly while attempting to obtain further information. It is the objective reading of the flyer that determines whether police officers from a department other than the one that issued the flyer can defensibly act in reliance on it. Assuming that the police make a *Terry* stop in objective reliance on a flyer, the evidence uncovered in the course of the stop is admissible if the police who issued the flyer possessed a reasonable suspicion justifying the stop, and if the stop that occurred was not significantly more intrusive than would have been permitted the issuing department. Under the above principles, the investigatory stop of Hensley was reasonable under the Fourth Amendment, and therefore the evidence discovered during the stop was admissible. The justification for a stop did not evaporate when the armed robbery was completed. Hensley was reasonably suspected of involvement in a felony and was at large from the time the suspicion arose until the stop by the Covington police. A brief stop and detention at the earliest opportunity after the suspicion arose was fully consistent with Fourth Amendment principles. The flyer issued by the St. Bernard police, objectively read and supported by a reasonable suspicion on the part of the issuing department, justified the length and intrusiveness of the stop and detention that occurred."

CASE EXCERPT

"We need not and do not decide today whether *Terry* stops to investigate all past crimes, however serious, are permitted. It is enough to say that, if police have a reasonable suspicion, grounded in specific and articulable facts, that a person they encounter was involved in or is wanted in connection with a completed felony, then a *Terry* stop may be made to investigate that suspicion."

CASE SIGNIFICANCE

This case extended the reach of the stop and frisk procedure to situations where a police officer has not observed suspicious conduct but has it on good authority that an individual is a criminal suspect. *Terry* allowed a stop and frisk on reasonable suspicion; in this case the Supreme Court allowed a police officer to treat a "wanted" flyer or bulletin as sufficient information to create "reasonable suspicion."

UNITED STATES v. SOKOLOW

490 U.S. 1 (1989)

FACTS

Sokolow was stopped in Honolulu International Airport by Drug Enforcement Administration agents. There were several reasons why the agents stopped

UNITED STATES v. SOKOLOW *(cont.)*

Sokolow: (1) he paid $2,100 for two plane tickets from a roll of $20 bills; (2) he traveled under a name that did not match the name under which his telephone number was listed; (3) his destination was Miami, a city known for its illegal drug traffic; (4) he stayed in Miami for only 48 hours, despite the fact that a round-trip flight from Miami to Honolulu takes approximately 20 hours; (5) he appeared nervous while moving about the terminal; and (6) he did not check any luggage. The agents found 1,063 grams of cocaine in his carry-on luggage and Sokolow was convicted of drug possession. The case later came before the U.S. Supreme Court.

ISSUE

Was there reasonable suspicion to stop Sokolow based on a "drug-courier profile"?

HOLDING

Yes. The circumstances in this case established reasonable suspicion that Sokolow was transporting illegal drugs. Accordingly, the stop was justified based on the *Terry* exception to the Fourth Amendment's probable cause requirement.

RATIONALE

Paying $2,100 in cash for two airplane tickets is out of the ordinary, and it is even more out of the ordinary to pay that sum from a roll of $20 bills containing nearly twice that amount of cash. Most business travelers, we feel confident, purchase airline tickets by credit card or check so as to have a record for tax or business purposes, and few vacationers carry with them thousands of dollars in $20 bills. We also think the agents had a reasonable ground to believe that respondent was traveling under an alias; the evidence was by no means conclusive, but it was sufficient to warrant consideration. While a trip from Honolulu to Miami, standing alone, is not a cause for any sort of suspicion, here there was more: surely few residents of Honolulu travel from that city for 20 hours to spend 48 hours in Miami during the month of July. "Any one of these factors is not by itself proof of any illegal conduct and is quite consistent with innocent travel. But we think taken together they amount to reasonable suspicion. . . . The reasonableness of the officer's decision to stop a suspect does not turn on the availability of less intrusive investigatory techniques." Such a rule would unduly hamper the police's ability to make swift, on-the-spot decisions—here, respondent was about to get into a taxicab—and it would require courts to indulge in unrealistic second-guessing.

CASE EXCERPT

"A court sitting to determine the existence of reasonable suspicion must require the agent to articulate the factors leading to that conclusion, but the fact that these factors may be set forth in a 'profile' does not somehow detract from their evidentiary significance as seen by a trained agent."

CASE SIGNIFICANCE

Sokolow is significant because it addressed whether "drug-courier profiles" can be used to establish reasonable suspicion to conduct a *Terry* stop. It is important to understand, however, that the Court did not decide on the constitutionality of drug-courier profiling. Instead, it was concerned with whether the facts as set forth in this case created reasonable suspicion to stop. As indicated in the Court's reasoning, it did not matter whether Sokolow's actions fit a "profile," only that the actions provided sufficient justification to conduct a stop.

ALABAMA v. WHITE
496 U.S. 325 (1990)

FACTS

Police received an anonymous telephone tip that White would be leaving a particular apartment at a particular time in a particular vehicle, that she would be going to a particular motel, and that she would be in possession of cocaine. They immediately proceeded to the apartment building, saw a vehicle matching the caller's description, observed White as she left the building and entered the vehicle, and followed her along the most direct route to the motel, stopping her vehicle just short of the motel. A consensual search of the vehicle revealed marijuana and, after White was arrested, cocaine was found in her purse. The Court of Criminal Appeals of Alabama reversed her conviction on possession charges, holding that the trial court should have suppressed the marijuana and cocaine because the officers did not have the reasonable suspicion necessary under *Terry v. Ohio* to justify the investigatory stop of the vehicle. The U.S. Supreme Court granted certiorari.

ISSUE

Does an anonymous tip, corroborated by the police, create "reasonable suspicion" to justify a stop and frisk?

HOLDING

Yes. The anonymous tip, as corroborated by independent police work, exhibited sufficient indicia of reliability to provide reasonable suspicion to make the investigatory stop.

RATIONALE

"Under *Adams v. Williams,* an informant's tip may carry sufficient 'indicia of reliability' to justify a *Terry* stop even though it may be insufficient to support an arrest or search warrant. Moreover, *Illinois v. Gates* adopted a 'totality-of-the-circumstances' approach to determining whether an informant's tip establishes probable cause, whereby the informant's veracity, reliability, and basis of knowledge are highly relevant. These factors are also relevant in the reasonable-suspicion context, although allowance must be made in applying them for the lesser showing required to meet that standard. Standing alone, the tip here is completely lacking in the necessary indicia of reliability, since it provides virtually nothing from which one might conclude that the caller is honest or his information reliable and gives no indication of the basis for his predictions regarding White's criminal activities. However, although it is a close question, the totality of the circumstances demonstrates that significant aspects of the informant's story were sufficiently corroborated by the police to furnish reasonable suspicion. Although not every detail mentioned by the tipster was verified—e.g., the name of the woman leaving the apartment building or the precise apartment from which she left—the officers did corroborate that a woman left the building and got into the described vehicle. Given the fact that they proceeded to the building immediately after the call and that White emerged not too long thereafter, it also appears that her departure was within the time frame predicted by the caller. Moreover, since her four-mile route was the most direct way to the motel, but nevertheless involved several turns, the caller's prediction of her destination was significantly corroborated even though she was stopped before she reached the motel. Furthermore, the fact that the caller was able to predict her future behavior demonstrates a special familiarity with her affairs. Thus, there was reason to believe that the caller was honest and well informed, and to impart some degree of reliability to his allegation that White was engaged in criminal activity."

CASE EXCERPT

"Reasonable suspicion, like probable cause, is dependent upon both the content of information possessed by police and its degree of reliability. Both factors—quantity and quality—are considered in the 'totality of the circumstances—the whole picture'…if a tip has a relatively low degree of reliability, more information will be required to establish the requisite quantum of suspicion than would be required if the tip were more reliable."

CASE SIGNIFICANCE

This case stood for the proposition that the amount and quality of information necessary to establish "reasonable suspicion" is not as high as that required for "probable cause."

MINNESOTA v. DICKERSON
508 U.S. 366 (1993)

FACTS

Based upon Dickerson's seemingly evasive actions when approached by police officers and the fact that he had just left a building known for cocaine traffic, the officers decided to investigate further. They stopped and frisked Dickerson. The pat-down search revealed no weapons, but the officer conducting it testified that he felt a small lump in Dickerson's jacket pocket that he believed to be a lump of crack cocaine upon examining it with his fingers, whereupon he reached into the pocket and retrieved a small bag of cocaine. The state trial court denied Dickerson's motion to suppress the cocaine, and he was found guilty of possession of a controlled substance. The Minnesota Court of Appeals reversed. In affirming, the state supreme court held that both the stop and the frisk of Dickerson were valid under *Terry v. Ohio,* but found the seizure of the cocaine to be unconstitutional. Refusing to enlarge the "plain-view" exception to the Fourth Amendment's warrant requirement, the court appeared to adopt a categorical rule barring the seizure of any contraband detected by an officer through the sense of touch during a pat-down search. The U.S. Supreme Court then granted certiorari.

ISSUE

Was the officer's manipulation of the crack cocaine in the suspect's pocket permissible under *Terry*?

MINNESOTA v. DICKERSON (cont.)

HOLDING

No. The police may seize contraband detected through the sense of touch during a protective pat-down search only if the contraband is immediately apparent and no manipulation takes place.

RATIONALE

"*Terry* permits a brief stop of a person whose suspicious conduct leads an officer to conclude, in light of his experience, that criminal activity may be afoot, and a pat-down search of the person for weapons when the officer is justified in believing that the person may be armed and presently dangerous. This protective search—permitted without a warrant and on the basis of reasonable suspicion less than probable cause—is not meant to discover evidence of crime, but must be strictly limited to that which is necessary for the discovery of weapons, which might be used to harm the officer or others. If the protective search goes beyond what is necessary to determine if the suspect is armed, it is no longer valid under *Terry,* and its fruits will be suppressed. In *Michigan v. Long*, the seizure of contraband other than weapons during a lawful *Terry* search was justified by reference to the Court's cases under the 'plain view' doctrine. That doctrine—which permits police to seize an object without a warrant if they are lawfully in a position to view it, if its incriminating character is immediately apparent, and if they have a lawful right of access to it—has an obvious application by analogy to cases in which an officer discovers contraband through the sense of touch during an otherwise lawful search. Thus, if an officer lawfully pats down a suspect's outer clothing and feels an object whose contour or mass makes its identity immediately apparent, there has been no invasion of the suspect's privacy beyond that already authorized by the officer's search for weapons. The officer who conducted the search was not acting within the lawful bounds marked by *Terry* at the time he gained probable cause to believe that the lump in Dickerson's jacket was contraband. The officer never thought that the lump was a weapon, but did not immediately recognize it as cocaine. Rather, he determined that it was contraband only after he squeezed, slid, and otherwise manipulated the pocket's contents. While *Terry* entitled him to place his hands on Dickerson's jacket and to feel the lump in the pocket, his continued exploration of the pocket after he concluded that it contained no weapon was unrelated to the sole justification for the search under *Terry*. Because this further search was constitutionally invalid, the seizure of the cocaine that followed is likewise unconstitutional."

CASE EXCERPT

"If a police officer lawfully pats down a suspect's outer clothing and feels an object whose contour or mass makes its identity immediately apparent, there has been no invasion of the suspect's privacy beyond that already authorized by the officer's search for weapons; if the object is contraband, its warrantless seizure would be justified by the same practical considerations that inhere in the plain-view context."

CASE SIGNIFICANCE

This case is significant because it made clear the limitations of the frisk portion of the stop and frisk procedure. The frisk is permitted only for officer safety, and officers are barred from removing items they feel during the frisk that they know are not weapons. The Court does leave the door slightly open, however—if an officer can demonstrate that he felt an item that he knew immediately, without any additional manipulation, was contraband, then he could seize it. Some lower courts have allowed such seizures, while others have not.

FLORIDA v. J. L.
529 U.S. 266 (2000)

FACTS

Miami-Dade police received an anonymous tip that a young black man wearing a plaid shirt standing at a particular bus stop was carrying a gun. Upon arriving at the specified location, officers observed an individual matching the description provided by the caller. A frisk was conducted and a weapon was recovered from the pocket of "J. L.," who was then arrested on charges of carrying a concealed firearm without a permit as well as underage possession of a firearm. The trial court granted J. L.'s motion to suppress, but an intermediate appellate court reversed. The Florida Supreme Court held that the search was unlawful and the U.S. Supreme Court granted certiorari.

ISSUE

Does the Fourth Amendment authorize police to undertake a warrantless frisk based solely upon an anonymous tip?

HOLDING

No. An anonymous tip that a person is carrying a gun is insufficient to justify a warrantless stop and frisk in the absence of further information that criminal activity is afoot.

RATIONALE

"In *Terry v. Ohio* (1968), the Supreme Court granted police officers authority under the Fourth Amendment to conduct limited warrantless frisks in situations where there exists reason to believe that criminal activity may be afoot and that an individual is armed and dangerous. This authority is limited insofar as the officer must be acting upon information or suspicious behavior that has been observed firsthand. In the present case the officers themselves did not observe any suspicious behavior but, instead, relied upon information provided by an anonymous caller whose reputation for giving reliable information was unverifiable. Although the tipster accurately described J. L.'s appearance and whereabouts, the Court nonetheless rejected the State's request for a broader interpretation and application of the *Terry* standard. In essence, the Court reasoned that although an anonymous tip may accurately describe an individual's appearance and location, this limited information does not adequately justify a warrantless stop and frisk of that person."

CASE EXCERPT

"[A]n automatic firearm exception to our established reliability analysis would rove too far. Such an exception would enable any person seeking to harass another to set in motion an intrusive, embarrassing police search of the targeted person simply by placing an anonymous call falsely reporting the target's unlawful carriage of a gun."

CASE SIGNIFICANCE

This case is important because it established the rule of law that police officers cannot conduct a *Terry* stop and frisk based solely on anonymous information that a particular individual may be armed with a weapon. When the police receive information of this type it must first be corroborated by their own observation and experience before being acted upon. Although responding officers will understandably be eager to act upon such tips, it is instead suggested that they take a moment to observe the suspect firsthand in order to (1) establish whether or not criminal activity is afoot and (2) determine the reasonable likelihood that the individual is actually armed and dangerous. If officers act immediately upon uncorroborated information provided by an anonymous tipster, the resulting stop and frisk will be deemed violative of the Fourth Amendment and any incriminating evidence that is seized will be rendered inadmissible. Just because a tipster has accurately described an individual's location and physical characteristics (e.g., race, height, weight, clothing, etc.), this information does not constitute prima facie evidence that criminal activity is afoot or that the person is actually armed and dangerous. Instead, officers are required by the ruling in this case to independently verify such information through visual observation buttressed by their past experiences in similar situations.

ILLINOIS v. WARDLOW
528 U.S. 119 (2000)

FACTS

Chicago police officers converged upon a neighborhood with a reputation for high crime and open-air drug transactions. Two officers observed Wardlow immediately flee the area on foot and, upon catching up to him, seized a firearm unlawfully in his possession. A motion to suppress was denied and Wardlow was convicted on charges of unlawful use of a weapon by a felon. A state appellate court reversed on grounds that the arresting officer lacked reasonable suspicion for the detention as required by *Terry v. Ohio*. The state supreme court affirmed on the basis that Wardlow's flight from the area was, in and of itself, not enough to justify the ensuing stop and frisk. The U.S. Supreme Court then granted certiorari.

ISSUE

Does an individual's sudden flight from a high-crime area create reasonable suspicion justifying a *Terry* stop and frisk?

HOLDING

Yes. An individual's unprovoked flight from a high-crime area, taken in combination with other factors such as characteristics of the location and nervous or evasive behavior, is enough to create reasonable suspicion authorizing the police to undertake a *Terry* stop and frisk.

RATIONALE

The Supreme Court ruled that there was no violation of Wardlow's Fourth Amendment rights. Cases such as

ILLINOIS v. WARDLOW (cont.)

this are governed by the rule established in *Terry v. Ohio* requiring officers to first develop reasonable suspicion that criminal activity is afoot and that an individual may be armed and dangerous before initiating a stop and frisk. "The fact that Wardlow immediately fled the area upon becoming aware of a police presence does not in and of itself satisfy this standard. However, when taken in conjunction with other factors such as an individual's nervous/evasive behavior and the neighborhood's reputation for drug-related activity, a brief detention such as that which Wardlow experienced may be justified. Once stopped, officers are authorized to conduct a limited frisk of the individual to ensure their own safety as well as that of others." In other words, while immediate flight from an area does not in and of itself indicate that criminal activity is afoot, officers are reasonably justified in the detention of an individual for purposes of making such a determination. If no evidence of unlawful behavior is discovered, then the individual must be allowed to go on his or her way.

CASE EXCERPT

"Headlong flight—wherever it occurs—is the consummate act of evasion: It is not necessarily indicative of wrongdoing, but it is certainly suggestive of such. In reviewing the propriety of an officer's conduct, courts do not have available empirical studies dealing with inferences drawn from suspicious behavior, and we cannot reasonably demand scientific certainty from judges or law enforcement officers where none exists. Thus, the determination of reasonable suspicion must be based on commonsense judgments and inferences about human behavior."

CASE SIGNIFICANCE

This case addressed the longstanding question of whether or not officers are authorized to stop an individual who has done nothing more than flee the area upon becoming aware of their presence. While flight alone does not automatically justify detention, an individual may be lawfully stopped when such evasive activity occurs in light of an officer's firsthand knowledge about criminal activity patterns within a given neighborhood. Thus, if an officer knows that a given area has a history of open-air drug transactions (or other forms of criminal activity) and an individual is observed fleeing the vicinity upon becoming aware of a police presence, the officer is justified in making an investigative *Terry* stop for purposes of determining

whether or not criminal activity is afoot. During the course of this stop a limited frisk of the individual may also be undertaken for purposes of ensuring officer safety. If no weapons or evidence of criminal activity are discovered, then the individual must immediately be released and allowed to go on his or her way.

ARIZONA v. JOHNSON
555 U.S. 323 (2009)

FACTS

Johnson was a passenger in a car stopped by members of the Arizona state police gang task force near Tucson after the vehicle's registration was found to be suspended due to an underlying insurance issue. Under Arizona law, the offense was a civil infraction for which the driver could receive a citation. While the basis for the stop was a minor traffic violation, officers also questioned the occupants of the car about recent gang activity in the area. This conversation led the officers to believe Johnson was a member of the Crips, a street gang with a reputation for being violent and armed. The officer observed that Johnson was wearing a blue bandana, was from an area where the Crips were prevalent, and had a scanner on him. An officer asked Johnson to step out of the car to continue the conversation; he complied and was immediately patted down for weapons. During the frisk a weapon and drugs were found on Johnson, and he was arrested and subsequently convicted on the weapons charge. On appeal, Johnson argued that the evidence discovered during the frisk should be suppressed because the officers did not have probable cause to believe he was involved in criminal activity or to search him. The Arizona appellate courts found that Johnson was not ordered out of the car because officers feared for their safety, but simply because they wanted to speak with him. Since the officers did not fear for their safety, they had no authority to conduct a frisk.

ISSUE

May officers who conduct routine traffic stops perform a pat down of a driver and any passengers upon reasonable suspicion that they may be armed and dangerous?

HOLDING

Yes. Officers who conduct routine traffic stops may perform a pat down of a driver and any passengers upon reasonable suspicion that they may be armed and dangerous.

RATIONALE

A lawful roadside stop begins when a vehicle is pulled over for investigation of a traffic violation. The temporary seizure of driver and passengers ordinarily continues, and remains reasonable, for the duration of the stop. Normally, the stop ends when the police have no further need to control the scene and inform the driver and passengers they are free to leave. An officer's inquiries into matters unrelated to the justification for the traffic stop, this Court has made plain, do not convert the encounter into something other than a lawful seizure, so long as those inquiries do not measurably extend the duration of the stop. A traffic stop of a car communicates to a reasonable passenger that he or she is not free to terminate the encounter with the police and move about at will. Nothing occurred in this case that would have conveyed to Johnson that, prior to the frisk, the traffic stop had ended or that he was otherwise free "to depart without police permission." Officer Trevizo surely was not constitutionally required to give Johnson an opportunity to depart the scene after he exited the vehicle without first ensuring that, in so doing, she was not permitting a dangerous person to get behind her. Since Johnson was lawfully detained, the police could frisk him so long as they had reason to believe he was armed and dangerous; the fact that police believed Johnson was a member of a street gang with a reputation for violence was sufficient.

CASE EXCERPT

"'[C]onsensual' is an 'unrealistic' characterization of the Trevizo-Johnson interaction. '[T]he encounter… took place within minutes of the stop'; the patdown followed 'within mere moments' of Johnson's exit from the vehicle; beyond genuine debate, the point at which Johnson could have felt free to leave had not yet occurred."

CASE SIGNIFICANCE

Johnson is important because it clarified the authority of the police during traffic stops, consistent with the Fourth Amendment, to conduct a pat down of drivers and passengers whom they have reasonable suspicion to believe may be armed and dangerous. In *Johnson*, the Court synthesized the previous holdings in *Mimms*, *Wilson*, and *Brendlin*, thus clarifying the use of *Terry*-type pat downs during traffic stops. The *Johnson* decision allows police to engage in pat downs that will, in turn, better protect the safety of officers during traffic stops, which are often a dangerous point of contact for officers.

DISCUSSION QUESTIONS

1. Do you agree with the Supreme Court's decision in *Terry*?
2. Presumably, a person who is not "stopped" is free to leave. If a person is confronted by a police officer, and not technically stopped, is that person truly free to leave?
3. Has the Supreme Court expanded on or chipped away at *Terry*? How so?
4. Do you agree with the practice of drug-courier profiling? Why or why not?
5. Identify as many factors as you can that would give a police officer reasonable suspicion to conduct a stop.
6. What makes traffic stops potentially dangerous situations for police officers?
7. What might lead a police officer to believe a geographical area is associated with gang activity, as in *Arizona v. Johnson*?
8. Should wanted flyers suffice as a basis for reasonable suspicion? How will the police officer know the information contained in the flyer is accurate?
9. What fact(s) might give a police officer reason to believe that an individual is armed and dangerous?
10. What is the difference between probable cause and reasonable suspicion? Is the difference a qualitative or quantitative one?

CHAPTER FOUR

WHEN HAS A SEIZURE OCCURRED?

SCHMERBER V. CALIFORNIA, *384 U.S. 757 (1966)*

MICHIGAN v. CHESTERNUT, *486 U.S. 567 (1988)*

BROWER v. COUNTY OF INYO, *489 U.S. 593 (1989)*

CALIFORNIA v. HODARI D., *499 U.S. 621 (1991)*

FLORIDA v. BOSTICK, *501 U.S. 429 (1991)*

BOND v. UNITED STATES, *529 U.S. 334 (2000)*

KYLLO v. UNITED STATES, *533 U.S. 27 (2001)*

ILLINOIS v. MCARTHUR, *531 U.S. 326 (2001)*

HIIBEL v. NEVADA, *542 U.S. 177 (2004)*

MUEHLER v. MENA, *544 U.S. 93 (2005)*

BRENDLIN v. CALIFORNIA, *551 U.S. 249 (2007)*

INTRODUCTION

The Fourth Amendment is implicated when a search or seizure occurs. That is, whenever a person or piece of property is "seized," the Fourth Amendment applies. The definition of seizure has a very specific meaning in criminal procedure. Nothing has to be physically grasped for a seizure to take place. Indeed, even when police stop short of actually touching a person, their actions can still constitute a seizure. At the other extreme, though, there are certain things the police can do to inconvenience people without triggering the Fourth Amendment. It is important to distinguish between two types of seizures: (1) seizures of property and (2) seizures of persons.

As the Supreme Court declared in *United States v. Jacobsen*, 466 U.S. 109 (1984), a seizure of tangible property occurs "when there is some meaningful interference with an individual's possessory interest in that property." In determining whether a piece of property is seized, courts often refer to people's "actual" or "constructive" possession. A piece of property is in a person's actual possession if the person is physically holding or grasping it. Constructive possession, by comparison, refers to possession of property without physical contact (e.g., a bag that is next to a person on the ground, but not in his or her hands). A piece of property is "seized," therefore, if the police remove it from a person's actual or constructive possession, such as when they take a person's luggage at an airport and move it to another room to be searched.

Seizure of a person occurs when a police officer, by means of physical force or show of authority, intentionally restrains an individual's liberty in such a manner that a reasonable person would believe that he or she is not free to leave. Another way of understanding a Fourth Amendment seizure is by asking a question: Would a reasonable person believe that he or she is free to decline the officer's requests or otherwise terminate the encounter? In general, a "no" answer means a seizure has occurred. However, in a recent case, *Florida v. Bostick,* the Supreme Court stated that the appropriate test for determining whether a person—in that case, a person on a bus—is seized is whether a reasonable passenger would feel free to decline the officer's requests or otherwise terminate the encounter.

The seizure of a person does not have to be physical for the Fourth Amendment to be implicated. For example, a seizure can occur when a police officer simply questions a person. The Supreme Court stated in *Terry v. Ohio,* 392 U.S. 1 (1968), that "[N]ot all personal intercourse between policemen and citizens involves 'seizures' of persons" (p. 20, n. 16), but a seizure *does* occur when the officer's conduct in conjunction with questioning would convince a reasonable person that he or she is not free to leave.

A seizure can also occur in pursuit, even if the person sought by the police is never caught, although it is not always clear whether a pursuit constitutes a seizure. This is important because if the pursuit of a suspect is *not* a seizure, then the police may lawfully chase people without justification and, if the person discards anything during the chase, the police may lawfully seize the item because the Fourth Amendment does not apply. In fact, as the Supreme Court noted in *California v. Hodari D.,* when an officer chases a suspect but does not lay hands on him or her, a seizure does not occur until the suspect submits to police authority.

In *Hodari D.* a police officer chased a suspect on foot. The officer did not have justification to stop or arrest the suspect. The suspect discarded an item during the chase, which the officer stopped to pick up. The Supreme Court upheld the officer's action because the suspect was still in flight at the time the officer picked up the object. The Supreme Court did state in *Hodari D.,* however, that a seizure *does* occur the instant a police officer lays hands on a suspect during a chase, even if the suspect is able to break away from the officer's grasp. Relying heavily on the holding in *Hodari D.,* the Court, in *Brendlin v. California* (2007), held that a passenger in a vehicle is "seized" during a traffic stop, because a reasonable person in that situation would not feel free to leave.

The definitions of seizure offered thus far are general. The cases discussed throughout this chapter, however, offer some more specific definitions and address whether certain types of seizures can be considered constitutional. Concerning the definition of a seizure, the ruling from *Michigan v. Chesternut* states that following a person does not constitute a seizure within the meaning of the Fourth Amendment. Alternatively, the Supreme Court held in *Brower v. County of Inyo* that a roadblock used by the police to stop a fleeing felon constitutes a seizure within the meaning of the Fourth Amendment.

As to the appropriateness of certain seizures, we discuss the following cases. For example, in *Schmerber v. California,* the Supreme Court held that the warrantless "seizure" of blood is constitutional. In *Bond v.*

United States, the Court held that it is a violation of the Fourth Amendment for police officers, without any suspicion, to physically manipulate bus passengers' luggage. Finally, in *Illinois v. McArthur,* the Court held that an officer's refusal to let a person into his or her residence, knowing that the person will destroy evidence therein, does not violate the Fourth Amendment.

In *Hiibel v. Nevada* (2004), the Court concluded that a "stop and identify" statute that required that an individual provide a name only did not violate the Fourth Amendment. Further, such a request in cases where an officer is not acting pursuant to a state statute do not violate the Fourth Amendment.

In *Muehler v. Mena* (2005), the Court addressed the use of detention of occupants while a search warrant is executed. In upholding the detention, the Court also approved the use of a reasonable amount of force, such as the use of handcuffs, to ensure officer safety.

SCHMERBER v. CALIFORNIA
384 U.S. 757 (1966)

FACTS
Schmerber was arrested for driving under the influence of alcohol while he was in the hospital receiving treatment for injuries he suffered during an accident. A blood sample was taken by a doctor at the request of one of the police officers. The blood was drawn over Schmerber's protest, as well as his attorney's. The blood sample indicated intoxication and was admitted against Schmerber at trial. He was convicted of driving under the influence. He objected to admission of the evidence, arguing that the Fifth and Fourteenth Amendments had been violated when the blood sample was taken, and the U.S. Supreme Court granted certiorari.

ISSUE
Did the warrantless "seizure" of Schmerber's blood violate his constitutional rights?

HOLDING
No. Drawing blood from a criminal suspect without his or her consent does not violate the Constitution as long as it is done by trained medical professionals.

SCHMERBER v. CALIFORNIA *(cont.)*

RATIONALE

"*Breithaupt* was also a case in which police officers caused blood to be withdrawn from the driver of an automobile involved in an accident, and in which there was ample justification for the officer's conclusion that the driver was under the influence of alcohol. There, as here, the extraction was made by a physician in a simple, medically acceptable manner in a hospital environment. There, however, the driver was unconscious at the time the blood was withdrawn and hence had no opportunity to object to the procedure. We affirmed the conviction there resulting from the use of the test in evidence, holding that under such circumstances the withdrawal did not offend 'that "sense of justice" of which we spoke in *Rochin v. California.*' *Breithaupt* thus requires the rejection of petitioner's due process argument, and nothing in the circumstances of this case or in supervening events persuades us that this aspect of *Breithaupt* should be overruled."

CASE EXCERPT

"The officer in the present case, however, might reasonably have believed that he was confronted with an emergency, in which the delay necessary to obtain a warrant, under the circumstances, threatened the destruction of evidence. We are told that the percentage of alcohol in the blood begins to diminish shortly after drinking stops, as the body functions to eliminate it from the system ... Similarly, we are satisfied that the test chosen to measure petitioner's blood-alcohol level was a reasonable one ... Such tests are a commonplace in these days of periodic physical examination."

CASE SIGNIFICANCE

This case is significant not just because it permitted warrantless "seizures" of blood based on exigent circumstances (i.e., the fact that the alcohol in Schmerber's blood would "disappear" in time) but because it addressed several other important constitutional issues. The Court stated that seizure of blood, a type of real or physical evidence, does not violate the Fifth Amendment's self-incrimination clause because it is not testimonial evidence. Schmerber also argued that his right to counsel was denied, but the Court stated that because he wasn't yet charged with a crime, the Sixth Amendment did not apply. Finally, the Court held that Schmerber's due process rights were not

violated because of the manner by which the blood was extracted.

MICHIGAN v. CHESTERNUT
486 U.S. 567 (1988)

FACTS

Four officers on patrol in a marked squad car observed a car pull over to the curb. A man emerged from the car and approached Chesternut, who was standing on the street corner. When Chesternut saw the patrol car nearing the corner where he stood, he turned and began to run away. The patrol car followed Chesternut, driving alongside him as he ran down the sidewalk. The officers observed Chesternut pull several packets out of his pocket and throw them away. Officers stopped to examine the items Chesternut had discarded and determined that they were codeine pills. Chesternut was arrested for possession of narcotics. At a preliminary hearing, he argued that the officer's conduct prior to disposal of the packets was a search and that the evidence should be excluded. The U.S. Supreme Court granted certiorari.

ISSUE

Does the act of following a person constitute a seizure within the meaning of the Fourth Amendment?

HOLDING

No. The appropriate test for determining whether a person is seized within the meaning of the Fourth Amendment is whether a reasonable person, viewing all the circumstances in their totality, would conclude that he or she is not free to leave.

RATIONALE

"The test provides that the police can be said to have seized an individual 'only if, in view of all the circumstances surrounding the incident, a reasonable person would have believed that he was not free to leave.' ... Applying the Court's test to the facts of this case, we conclude that Chesternut was not seized by the police before he discarded the packets containing the controlled substance. Although Officer Peltier referred to the police conduct as a 'chase,' and the magistrate who originally dismissed the complaint was impressed by this description, the characterization is not enough, standing alone, to implicate Fourth Amendment protections. ... [T]he police conduct involved here would not have communicated to the reasonable person an attempt to capture or otherwise intrude upon Chesternut's freedom of movement. The record does not reflect that the police activated a siren or flashers; or that they commanded Chesternut to halt, or displayed any weapons; or that they operated the car in an aggressive manner to block Chesternut's course or otherwise control the direction or speed of his movement."

CASE EXCERPT

"Contrary to respondent's assertion that a chase necessarily communicates that detention is intended and imminent, the police conduct involved here would not have communicated to the reasonable person an attempt to capture or otherwise intrude upon respondent's freedom of movement. While the very presence of a police car driving parallel to a running pedestrian could be somewhat intimidating, this kind of police presence does not, standing alone, constitute a seizure."

CASE SIGNIFICANCE

This case is significant because it addressed the issue of when a person is considered "seized" by the police. The actions in this case are different from the typical stop and frisk or arrest situation because the police followed alongside Chesternut and did not actually chase him. Since the police in this case did not block Chesternut's path or otherwise engage in actions that would suggest he was not free to leave, the Court concluded that a seizure did not take place. Accordingly, the Fourth Amendment was not implicated. You may be wondering about Chesternut's subsequent arrest. It was deemed constitutional because the police developed probable cause to arrest after stopping to pick up the packets and determining that they contained contraband. Had the police not stopped to pick up the packets and proceeded directly to the arrest stage, their actions would have been considered unconstitutional, because probable cause was developed only after determining what was in the packets.

BROWER v. COUNTY OF INYO
489 U.S. 593 (1989)

FACTS

Brower stole a car and eluded the police in a high-speed chase that took place over a 20-mile stretch.

Accordingly, police parked an 18-wheeler truck and trailer across both lanes of the highway on which Brower was traveling, blocking his path. They also pointed the headlights of their police cars in Brower's direction, which was intended to blind him. Brower crashed into the roadblock and was killed. Brower's family and estate brought a Section 1983 civil lawsuit against the police, alleging that the roadblock violated Brower's Fourth Amendment right to be free from unreasonable seizures.

ISSUE

Is a roadblock used by the police to block a fleeing suspect considered a seizure within the meaning of the Fourth Amendment?

HOLDING

Yes. A Fourth Amendment seizure occurs where there is a "governmental termination of freedom of movement through means intentionally applied."

RATIONALE

"Consistent with the language, history, and judicial construction of the Fourth Amendment, a seizure occurs when governmental termination of a person's movement is effected through means intentionally applied. Because the complaint alleges that Brower was stopped by the instrumentality set in motion or put in place to stop him, it states a claim of Fourth Amendment 'seizure.' "

CASE EXCERPT

"In determining whether the means that terminates the freedom of movement is the very means that the government intended we cannot draw too fine a line... We think it enough for a seizure that a person be stopped by the very instrumentality set in motion or put in place in order to achieve that result. It was enough here, therefore, that Brower was meant to be stopped by the physical obstacle of the roadblock—and that he was so stopped."

CASE SIGNIFICANCE

This case is important not because of the constitutionality of the police action, but because it addressed the definition of a seizure. The Court held that what the police did in Brower was "seize" him within the meaning of the Fourth Amendment. As such, constitutional protections applied. The Court remanded the case back to the court of appeals to determine whether the

BROWER v. COUNTY OF INYO *(cont.)*

district court erred in concluding that the roadblock was reasonable. If the lower court decided that the roadblock was reasonable, then the officers would not be held civilly liable. This case is an example of one of the many minute issues the Supreme Court considers. As far as criminal procedure goes, the Supreme Court is responsible for deciding constitutional questions, not questions of guilt, innocence, liability, and so forth. Those decisions are left to the lower courts.

CALIFORNIA v. HODARI D.
499 U.S. 621 (1991)

FACTS
Officers McColgin and Pertoso were on patrol in a high-crime area of Oakland, California. They wore street clothes but were also wearing jackets with the word "Police" across the front and back. When they turned around a corner, they observed approximately four youths surrounding a small red car parked near the curb. When the youths saw the officers approaching, they ran. Hodari and another youth ran west through an alley; the others fled south. The red car also headed south at high speed. The officers gave chase. Hodari emerged from the alley and, just as Officer Petoso almost caught up to him, he threw away what appeared to be a small rock. Shortly thereafter, Officer Petoso overtook Hodari, handcuffed him, and radioed for assistance. A search incident to arrest turned up $130 in cash. The "rock" that Hodari threw away turned out to be crack cocaine. Hodari argued that at the time of the chase he had been "seized," and that the cocaine was inadmissible because the officers lacked reasonable suspicion at that point.

ISSUE
Does a seizure occur when, while an officer is giving chase, a person tosses away contraband?

HOLDING
No. A seizure does not occur when a suspect flees from an officer and the officer applies no physical force. If a suspect submits to a police officer and/or the officer applies physical force, the suspect is seized within the meaning of the Fourth Amendment.

RATIONALE
"To say that an arrest is effected by the slightest application of physical force, despite the arrestee's escape, is

not to say that for Fourth Amendment purposes there is a continuing arrest during the period of fugitivity. If, for example, Pertoso [the officer] had laid his hands upon Hodari to arrest him, but Hodari had broken away and had then cast away the cocaine, it would hardly be realistic to say that disclosure had been made during the course of an arrest. The present case, however, is even one step further removed. It does not involve the application of any physical force; Hodari was untouched by Officer Pertoso at the time he discarded the cocaine. His defense relies instead upon the proposition that a seizure occurs 'when the officer, by means of physical force or show of authority, has in some way restrained the liberty of a citizen.' Hodari contends that Pertoso's pursuit qualified as a 'show of authority' calling upon Hodari to halt. The narrow question before us is whether, with respect to a show of authority as with respect to application of physical force, a seizure occurs even though the subject does not yield. We hold that it does not."

CASE EXCERPT
"The word 'seizure' readily bears the meaning of a laying on of hands or application of physical force to restrain movement, even when it is ultimately unsuccessful. ('She seized the purse-snatcher, but he broke out of her grasp.') It does not remotely apply, however, to the prospect of a policeman yelling 'Stop, in the name of the law!' at a fleeing form that continues to flee. That is no seizure."

CASE SIGNIFICANCE
This case considered yet another narrow area with regard to investigative stops and arrests. Hodari argued that prior to the point that he discarded the cocaine, a seizure had taken place, requiring at least reasonable suspicion. Had the Court ruled in Hodari's favor, then the police would not be able to chase suspicious individuals without justification. Fortunately for the law enforcement community, the Court held that it is permissible to chase suspicious individuals (who do not submit to police authority and where physical force is not used); however, for any subsequent intrusions such as a frisk or an arrest to be constitutional, appropriate justification must first be in place. Justification was present in this case because when Hodari discarded the contraband, the officer had probable cause to arrest, not to mention reasonable suspicion to stop. If Hodari eluded the police and was not arrested, but the cocaine was nevertheless seized, it would be admissible against

Hodari (assuming he was eventually found) under the abandonment doctrine.

FLORIDA v. BOSTICK
501 U.S. 429 (1991)

FACTS
Pursuant to a routine police drug interdiction effort intended to uncover drug trafficking, two police officers boarded a bus and questioned the passengers. Without any suspicion, they asked the defendant, Bostick, for his ticket and identification, then they asked to search his luggage, advising him of his right to refuse consent. Bostick consented to the search and cocaine was found in his luggage. He later sought suppression of the drugs, arguing that they had been improperly seized.

ISSUE
Did the Florida Supreme Court err in adopting a *per se* rule that every encounter on a bus is a seizure?

HOLDING
Yes. The appropriate test for determining when a seizure takes place is whether, taking into account all of the circumstances surrounding the encounter, a reasonable passenger would feel free to decline the officers' requests or terminate the encounter.

RATIONALE
"Our cases make it clear that a seizure does not occur simply because a police officer approaches an individual and asks a few questions. So long as a reasonable person would feel free 'to disregard the police and go about his business,' the encounter is consensual and no reasonable suspicion is required. The encounter will not trigger Fourth Amendment scrutiny unless it loses its consensual nature."

CASE EXCERPT
"The Florida Supreme Court…adopted a *per se* rule prohibiting the police from randomly boarding buses as a means of drug interdiction. The state court erred, however, in focusing on whether Bostick was 'free to leave' rather than on the principle that those words were intended to capture…When the person is seated on a bus and has no desire to leave, the degree to which a reasonable person would feel that he or she could leave is not an accurate measure of the coercive effect of the encounter."

CASE SIGNIFICANCE
This case is important because it helped clarify the somewhat muddy definition of seizure. It led to a somewhat different test than that announced in *Chesternut*. In *Chesternut* the appropriate test for determining whether a seizure took place was whether a reasonable person would believe he or she was free to leave. Relying on this definition, Bostick argued that he was not free to leave because the officers blocked his path and the bus was about to depart. The Florida Supreme Court agreed with this argument. However, the Supreme Court stated that the Florida court used the wrong test. Justice O'Connor, who wrote the Court's opinion, observed that Bostick would not have felt free to leave even if the police had not been there, given the imminent departure of the bus. Accordingly, the Supreme Court remanded the case back to the Florida court to determine whether, consistent with the new definition, a seizure actually took place.

BOND v. UNITED STATES
529 U.S. 334 (2000)

FACTS
Bond was a passenger on a Greyhound bus that left California bound for Little Rock, Arkansas. The bus stopped, as required, at the Border Patrol checkpoint at Sierra Blanca, Texas. Agent Cantu boarded the bus to check the immigration status of all the passengers. After he concluded that all of the passengers were lawfully in the United States, he walked toward the front of the bus. On the way, he squeezed the soft luggage that passengers had placed in the overhead storage racks above the seats. As Cantu inspected the luggage above Bond's seat, he noticed that it contained a "brick-like" object. Bond claimed ownership of the bag and allowed Cantu to open it. Upon opening the bag, Cantu discovered a "brick" of methamphetamine. Bond was arrested, indicted, and convicted, despite his motion to exclude the drugs. The U.S. Supreme Court then granted certiorari.

ISSUE
Can a law enforcement officer engage in a suspicionless physical manipulation of a bus passenger's luggage?

HOLDING
No. It is a violation of the Fourth Amendment for law enforcement officials to, without suspicion, physically manipulate bus passengers' luggage.

BOND v. UNITED STATES *(cont.)*

RATIONALE

"Our Fourth Amendment analysis embraces two questions. First, we ask whether the individual, by his conduct, has exhibited an actual expectation of privacy; that is, whether he has shown that 'he [sought] to preserve [something] as private....' Here, petitioner sought to preserve privacy by using an opaque bag and placing that bag directly above his seat. Second, we inquire whether the individual's expectation of privacy is 'one that society is prepared to recognize as reasonable....' When a bus passenger places a bag in an overhead bin, he expects that other passengers or bus employees may move it for one reason or another. Thus, a bus passenger clearly expects that his bag may be handled. He does not expect that other passengers or bus employees will, as a matter of course, feel the bag in an exploratory manner. But this is exactly what the agent did here. We therefore hold that the agent's physical manipulation of petitioner's bag violated the Fourth Amendment."

CASE EXCERPT

"Physically invasive inspection is simply more intrusive than purely visual inspection. For example, in *Terry v. Ohio* we stated that a 'careful [tactile] exploration of the outer surfaces of a person's clothing all over his or her body' is a 'serious intrusion upon the sanctity of the person, which may inflict great indignity and arouse strong resentment, and is not to be undertaken lightly.' Although Agent Cantu did not 'frisk' petitioner's person, he did conduct a probing tactile examination of petitioner's carry-on luggage. Obviously, petitioner's bag was not part of his person. But travelers are particularly concerned about their carry-on luggage; they generally use it to transport personal items that, for whatever reason, they prefer to keep close at hand. Here, petitioner concedes that, by placing his bag in the overhead compartment, he could expect that it would be exposed to certain kinds of touching and handling. But petitioner argues that Agent Cantu's physical manipulation of his luggage 'far exceeded the casual contact [petitioner] could have expected from other passengers.'"

CASE SIGNIFICANCE

This case straddled the line separating searches from frisks. Regardless, the Supreme Court has never permitted "physical manipulation" of luggage, people's clothing, or other items with anything less than prob-

able cause. Here, the officer had no suspicion at all. The evidence was excluded. This case was a prime example of the exclusionary rule in operation. It was also a case that "fired up" critics of the exclusionary rule. Evidence belonging to a clearly guilty criminal was declared inadmissible, which probably means that Bond's conviction will be overturned.

KYLLO v. UNITED STATES
533 U.S. 27 (2001)

FACTS

In 1991, a special agent with the Department of Interior, Bureau of Land Management, began to suspect that Kyllo was cultivating marijuana in his Florence, Oregon, triplex. To confirm his suspicions, the agent enlisted the help of the Oregon National Guard and used an Agema Termovision to scan the triplex. The scan was conducted from a vehicle parked on a public street and indicated that the roof of Kyllo's garage, as well as a side wall of his residence, were radiating more heat than neighboring homes. Based on the scan, tips from informants, evidence that Kyllo's wife had previously been arrested for drug offenses, and subpoenaed utility bills, a search warrant was issued. The warrant was executed and agents found 100 marijuana plants in Kyllo's home. Kyllo was indicted and then convicted in federal court following a plea agreement. Prior to his conviction, he argued that the thermal evidence should be excluded. The U.S. Supreme Court then granted certiorari.

ISSUE

Is it a violation of the Fourth Amendment for the government, without probable cause or a warrant, to use devices not in general public use to view details of a home?

HOLDING

Yes. It is a violation of the Fourth Amendment for the government, without a probable cause and a warrant, to use devices not in general public use to view details of a home.

RATIONALE

While the government argued that the thermal imager used in *Kyllo* did not result in "physical penetration" of the exterior walls and, as such, did not reveal any "intimate details" concerning what was happening in

Kyllo's residence, the Court stated that the absence of physical intrusion could no longer "foreclose further Fourth Amendment inquiry." And, according to the Court, "in the home, our cases show, all details are intimate details, because the entire area is held safe from prying government eyes…how warm—or even how relatively warm—Kyllo was heating his residence" is an intimate detail.

CASE EXCERPT

"We have said that the Fourth Amendment draws 'a firm line at the entrance to the house.' That line, we think, must be not only firm but also bright—which requires clear specification of those methods of surveillance that require a warrant. While it is certainly possible to conclude from the videotape of the thermal imaging that occurred in this case that no 'significant' compromise of the homeowner's privacy has occurred, we must take the long view, from the original meaning of the Fourth Amendment forward."

CASE SIGNIFICANCE

This case is important because it placed significant restrictions on law enforcement's ability to rely on thermal imaging scans. Prior to *Kyllo,* in most jurisdictions the police could scan people's residences for excessive heat and then, with additional corroboration, use the information to obtain a search warrant. Now, in light of *Kyllo,* the police cannot legally use thermal imagers to scan people's homes without first obtaining a warrant based on probable cause. Thus, the Court in *Kyllo* was not directly concerned with the constitutionality of the thermal imaging scan, but rather with whether such a scan constitutes a search within the meaning of the Fourth Amendment. It held that thermal imaging scans are searches that must be supported by probable cause. To some critics, this decision seriously hampers law enforcement's ability to detect indoor marijuana-growing operations.

ILLINOIS v. MCARTHUR

531 U.S. 326 (2001)

FACTS

Police officers accompanying a woman to the trailer where she lived were informed that her husband had a quantity of marijuana hidden therein. The officers asked the man for permission to search the trailer but were denied entry. While one of the officers left to secure a search warrant, the other officer refused to allow McArthur reentry into his residence. When the officer returned with a warrant, a search was initiated and a small quantity of marijuana was found. McArthur was arrested and charged with misdemeanor possession. The trial court accepted a motion to suppress based upon McArthur's claim that the evidence was the fruit of an unlawful seizure, namely the officers' refusal to let him reenter the trailer unaccompanied so that he could "have destroyed the marijuana." A state appellate court affirmed and the state supreme court denied the prosecution's request for leave to appeal; the U.S. Supreme Court then granted certiorari.

ISSUE

Did the refusal to allow McArthur reentry into his residence knowing that he would likely destroy evidence of criminal activity contained therein violate the Fourth Amendment seizure clause?

HOLDING

No. The brief seizure of McArthur's residence and the officer's refusal to allow him reentry did not violate the Fourth Amendment's seizure clause.

RATIONALE

The Fourth Amendment requires the issuance of a warrant based upon probable cause before a search and/or seizure may be undertaken. There are, however, a number and variety of judicially created exceptions to the warrant clause. One such exception is that of exigency. The Court has long held that suspects do not have a constitutional right to destroy evidence of their involvement in criminal activity. Where time and circumstance preclude the police from obtaining a warrant, a narrowly limited search may be undertaken in the interest of preventing the imminent destruction of evidence. The facts of this case met such criteria. Had McArthur been allowed to reenter the residence, he would have surely destroyed the marijuana hidden therein before the police could return with a warrant. Knowing this, the police temporarily "seized" the residence from his possession. Because of the exigent circumstances and law enforcement interest at stake, combined with the brevity of the seizure, no Fourth Amendment violation was deemed to have occurred.

CASE EXCERPT

"The police officers in this case had probable cause to believe that a home contained contraband, which

ILLINOIS v. MCARTHUR *(cont.)*

was evidence of a crime. They reasonably believed that the home's resident, if left free of any restraint, would destroy that evidence. And they imposed a restraint that was both limited and tailored reasonably to secure law enforcement needs while protecting privacy interests. In our view, the restraint met the Fourth Amendment's demands."

CASE SIGNIFICANCE

This case gave the police authority to refuse an individual entry into a dwelling (or part of a dwelling) if there is reason to believe that once inside he or she will attempt to destroy evidence of criminal activity. In effect, the police are briefly "seizing" the dwelling (or part thereof, such as a room) until such time as a warrant can be secured. It is important to note, however, that the Court did not specify how long such a seizure may last.

HIIBEL v. NEVADA
542 U.S. 177 (2004)

FACTS

A sheriff's deputy responded to a call from a witness who indicated that a male had assaulted a female in a pickup truck on a certain road. A deputy was dispatched to the scene, where he found a truck matching the description provided by the caller. A woman was sitting inside the truck and a man, who appeared to be intoxicated, was standing beside it. The deputy approached the man, explained why he was there, and asked him for identification. The man refused to provide any identification, became agitated, and insisted he had done nothing wrong. The deputy explained that he wanted to find out who the man was and what he was doing there. The deputy made several requests for identification, all of which were refused. The man then began to taunt the deputy and told the deputy to arrest him. After several more failed attempts to get the man to identify himself (there were eleven attempts altogether), the deputy arrested the man. Hiibel was charged with obstruction of police authority for failing to provide an officer with his name, in violation of a Nevada statute that requires persons detained on the basis of reasonable suspicion (i.e., a *Terry* stop) to identify themselves. He was tried, convicted, and fined $250. The U.S. Supreme Court granted certiorari after his conviction was affirmed.

ISSUE

Can an individual who has been lawfully detained be required to provide his or her identity to an officer pursuant to a state "stop and identify" statute?

HOLDING

Yes. A stop and identify statute does not violate the Fourth or Fifth Amendment. Individuals who have been lawfully detained may be required to provide their name to a police officer upon request. Because there was no real danger of incrimination by revelation of a name, there is no violation of the Fifth Amendment, which is concerned only with the compulsory revelation of potentially "incriminating" information.

RATIONALE

While the Fourth Amendment does not compel a suspect to answer any questions directed at him by a police officer, including questions regarding his identity, a state "stop and identify" statute (such as existed here and as exists in about half the states) does not run afoul of the Fourth Amendment. This is because the statute at issue here required a suspect to identify himself *only* if he were properly detained on the basis of reasonable suspicion. There was no requirement that someone identify himself or herself if the officer lacked at least reasonable suspicion. Under the reasonable suspicion standard, a law enforcement officer's actions are deemed reasonable if the Court, after balancing the interests of the government against the privacy intrusion, determines that the officer's conduct is reasonable. Here, the deputy had an interest in determining what had happened and had reasonable suspicion to detain and question Hiibel in an effort to determine what had happened.

The Court also rejected Hiibel's Fifth Amendment claim, noting that providing one's name in this situation did not constitute incrimination, and that the Fifth Amendment protected only against compelled testimony. Hiibel had no reason to believe that his name would in any way serve to incriminate him; thus, he could be compelled to identify himself.

CASE EXCERPT

"The principles of *Terry* permit a State to require a suspect to disclose his name in the course of a *Terry* stop. The reasonableness of a seizure under the Fourth Amendment is determined by balancing its intrusion on the individual's Fourth Amendment interests against its promotion of legitimate government interests. The Nevada statute satisfies that standard. The request for identity has an immediate relation to the purpose, rationale, and practical demands of a *Terry* stop. The threat of criminal sanction helps ensure that the request for identity does not become a legal nullity."

CASE SIGNIFICANCE

The *Hiibel* decision is important because it clarifies the constitutionality of a statue "stop and identify" statute under both the Fourth and Fifth Amendments. Moreover, this decision holds that a police request for an individual to identify himself or herself does not violate the Fourth Amendment in cases where there the officer is not acting pursuant to a state "stop and identify" statute.

MUEHLER v. MENA
544 U.S. 93 (2005)

FACTS

Based on information gleaned from the investigation of a gang-related drive-by shooting, petitioners Muehler and Brill had reason to believe at least one member of a gang—the West Side Locos—lived at 1363 Patricia Avenue. They also suspected that the individual was armed and dangerous, since he had recently been involved in the drive-by shooting. As a result, Muehler obtained a search warrant for that address that authorized a broad search of the house and premises for, among other things, deadly weapons and evidence of gang membership. In light of the high degree of risk involved in searching a house suspected of housing at least one, and perhaps multiple, armed gang members, a Special Weapons and Tactics (SWAT) team was used to secure the residence and grounds before the search. At the time of the search, Mena was asleep in her bed when the officers entered her bedroom and placed her in handcuffs at gunpoint. Three other individuals found on the property were also handcuffed. The SWAT team then took the individuals and Mena into a converted garage, which contained several beds and some other bedroom furniture. While the search proceeded, one or two officers guarded the four detainees, who were allowed to move around the garage but remained in handcuffs. Aware that the West Side Locos gang was composed primarily of illegal immigrants, the officers had notified the Immigration and Naturalization Service (INS) that they would be conducting the search, and an INS officer accompanied the officers executing the warrant. During their detention in the garage, an officer asked for each detainee's name, date of birth, place of birth, and immigration status. The INS officer later asked the detainees for their immigration documentation. Mena's status as a permanent resident was confirmed by her papers.

The search of the premises yielded a .22-caliber handgun with .22-caliber ammunition, a box of .25-caliber ammunition, several baseball bats with gang writing, various additional gang paraphernalia, and a bag of marijuana. Before the officers left the area, Mena was released.

In a Section 1983 suit against the officers, Mena alleged that she was detained "for an unreasonable time and in an unreasonable manner" in violation of the Fourth Amendment. In addition, she claimed that the warrant and its execution were overbroad, that the officers failed to comply with the "knock and announce" rule, and that the officers had needlessly destroyed property during the search. The officers moved for summary judgment, asserting that they were entitled to qualified immunity, but the District Court denied their motion. The Court of Appeals affirmed that denial, except for Mena's claim that the warrant was overbroad; on this claim the Court of Appeals held that the officers were entitled to qualified immunity. After a trial, a jury, pursuant to a special verdict form, found that Officers Muehler and Brill violated Mena's right to be free from unreasonable seizures by detaining her both with force greater than that which was reasonable and for a longer period than that which was reasonable. The jury awarded Mena $10,000 in actual damages and $20,000 in punitive damages against each petitioner for a total of $60,000.

ISSUE

Did the two- to three-hour detention of Mena, an occupant of a home being searched, with the use of handcuffs and questioning about her immigration status, violate the Fourth Amendment?

HOLDING

No. Occupants of places to be searched may be detained during the search and reasonable force may be used to effectuate that detention. If the initial search is valid, no additional justification is needed to inquire about identity or immigration status.

RATIONALE

"Inherent in *Summers*' authorization to detain an occupant of the place to be searched is the authority

MUEHLER v. MENA *(cont.)*

to use reasonable force to effectuate the detention. Indeed, *Summers* itself stressed that the risk of harm to officers and occupants is minimized "if the officers routinely exercise unquestioned command of the situation." The officers' use of force in the form of handcuffs to effectuate Mena's detention in the garage, as well as the detention of the three other occupants, was reasonable because the governmental interests outweigh the marginal intrusion. The imposition of correctly applied handcuffs on Mena, who was already being lawfully detained during a search of the house, was undoubtedly a separate intrusion in addition to detention in the converted garage. The detention was thus more intrusive than that which we upheld in *Summers*."

But this was no ordinary search. The governmental interests in not only detaining, but using handcuffs, are at their maximum when, as here, a warrant authorizes a search for weapons and a wanted gang member resides on the premises. In such inherently dangerous situations, the use of handcuffs minimizes the risk of harm to both officers and occupants. Though this safety risk inherent in executing a search warrant for weapons was sufficient to justify the use of handcuffs, the need to detain multiple occupants made the use of handcuffs all the more reasonable. Mena argues that, even if the use of handcuffs to detain her in the garage was reasonable as an initial matter, the duration of the use of handcuffs made the detention unreasonable. The duration of a detention can, of course, affect the balance of interests under *Graham*. However, the 2- to 3-hour detention in handcuffs in this case does not outweigh the government's continuing safety interests. As we have noted, this case involved the detention of four detainees by two officers during a search of a gang house for dangerous weapons. We conclude that the detention of Mena in handcuffs during the search was reasonable.

Mena also challenged questioning by officers regarding her immigration status. Because…the initial *Summers* detention was lawful; the Court of Appeals did not find that the questioning extended the time Mena was detained. Thus no additional Fourth Amendment justification for inquiring about Mena's immigration status was required.

CASE EXCERPT

"An officer's authority to detain incident to a search is categorical; it does not depend on the quantum of proof justifying detention or the extent of the intrusion to be imposed by the seizure. Thus, Mena's detention for the duration of the search was reasonable under *Summers* because a warrant existed to search 1363 Patricia Avenue and she was an occupant of that address at the time of the search. Inherent in *Summers'* authorization to detain an occupant of the place to be searched is the authority to use reasonable force to effectuate the detention."

CASE SIGNIFICANCE

In *Mena*, the Court reaffirmed the ability of police to detain occupants when a search is being conducted pursuant to *Michigan v. Summers* (1981). While the ability of the police to detain Mena was clear under the Court's previous holding in *Summers,* the Court also addressed the use of handcuffs to carry out the detention. In approving this practice, the Court furthered the safety interests of law enforcement in carrying out a search warrant. Moreover, the Court upheld the inquiry regarding Mena's immigration status during the search.

BRENDLIN v. CALIFORNIA
551 U.S. 249 (2007)

FACTS

A police officer on routine traffic patrol noticed a vehicle with expired registration. Dispatch confirmed that the owner had applied for and was awaiting delivery of new tags. The officer observed a valid temporary permit in the rear window authorizing the vehicle to be driven but nonetheless pulled the car over to investigate further. Upon approaching the car, the officer recognized the passenger as Brendlin, whom he believed had an arrest warrant out for a parole violation. Officer Brokenbrough returned to his vehicle and verified that there was an arrest warrant for Brendlin. He returned to the car, ordered Brendlin out, arrested him, and searched him and the passenger compartment of the car incident to the arrest. After police discovered marijuana and materials used to manufacture methamphetamine, Brendlin was charged with a variety of drug crimes based on the evidence seized during his arrest for the parole violation. He sought to have the evidence suppressed, arguing that his Fourth Amendment rights were violated when the officer stopped the car without probable cause or even reasonable belief that a crime had occurred (the *Terry* standard). Brendlin claimed that when the car was initially stopped, he, a passenger in the car, was seized along with the driver. The trial court denied his suppression motion, and he pled guilty to manufacturing methamphetamine and was sentenced to four years in prison.

On appeal, the California Court of Appeals reversed the trial court and ordered the evidence suppressed as the fruit of a Fourth Amendment violation—in this case, the unjustified stop of the car, which constituted a seizure of the driver (who yielded to a show of the officer's authority by pulling over, per *Hodari D.*) and any passengers, since a passenger would not feel free to leave (per *Mendenhall*). The California Supreme Court then reversed the Court of Appeals and upheld the trial court's denial of Brendlin's suppression motion, by a 4–3 vote. The California Supreme Court acknowledged the traffic stop was unjustified but determined that Brendlin, as a mere passenger, was not "seized" when the car was initially pulled over, but instead was seized only at the moment Officer Brokenbrough arrested him for the parole violation. Seeking relief, Brendlin appealed to the U.S. Supreme Court.

ISSUE
Is a passenger in a vehicle subject to a traffic stop "seized" or "detained" for purposes of the Fourth Amendment, thus allowing the passenger to contest the legality of the traffic stop and claim the protections of the Fourth Amendment and the exclusionary rule?

HOLDING
Yes. A passenger is "seized" during a traffic stop because a reasonable person in that situation would not feel free to leave.

RATIONALE
The Court unanimously held that "a traffic stop necessarily curtails the travel a passenger has chosen just as much as it halts the driver." Therefore, a reasonable person who is a passenger in a vehicle during a traffic stop would not feel free to leave. "Brendlin was seized from the moment the driver's car came to a halt on the side of the road." The California Supreme Court should not have used *Hodari D.* to analyze when a seizure took place, as its test is appropriate only for those circumstances where there is not a clear submission to authority on the part of the suspect. *Hodari D.* was not seized when the officer shouted "stop" because *Hodari D. did not stop*. Here, when the police officer asserted his authority to stop the car (by turning on his flashing lights), the driver clearly submitted to his authority by pulling her car off the road and stopping.

CASE EXCERPT
"A traffic stop necessarily curtails the travel a passenger has chosen just as much as it halts the driver, diverting both from the stream of traffic to the side of the road, and the police activity that normally amounts to intrusion on 'privacy and personal security' does not normally (and did not here) distinguish between passenger and driver. An officer who orders one particular car to pull over acts with an implicit claim of right based on fault of some sort, and a sensible person would not expect a police officer to allow people to come and go freely from the physical focal point of an investigation into faulty behavior or wrongdoing. If the likely wrongdoing is not the driving, the passenger will reasonably feel subject to suspicion owing to close association; but even when the wrongdoing is only bad driving, the passenger will expect to be subject to some scrutiny, and his attempt to leave the scene would be so obviously likely to prompt an objection from the officer that no passenger would feel free to leave in the first place."

CASE SIGNIFICANCE
This case clarifies what most commentators thought was already pretty clear—that when a police officer conducts a traffic stop, he or she "seizes" (for purposes of the Fourth Amendment and the exclusionary rule) not only the driver but the passengers as well, even though the probable cause/reasonable belief that justifies the traffic stop may be limited to the driver's conduct. This is based on the Supreme Court standard for when a seizure occurs—when a reasonable person would not feel free to leave. Additionally, the decision, while extending the protections of the Fourth Amendment to passengers, also extends the power of the police to the passengers—since they are "seized" during the traffic stop, passengers can be treated similar to drivers (e.g., ordered in/out of the vehicle, asked for identification, etc.).

DISCUSSION QUESTIONS

1. Identify the various types of seizures that come under the protection of the Fourth Amendment.
2. Was the Court's decision in *California v. Hodari D.* a reasonable one? In other words, was the Supreme Court correct in stating that seizures occur only when someone submits to police authority or is the target of some degree of physical force?
3. In *Brower v. County of Inyo* the Supreme Court declared that a police roadblock constitutes a seizure

within the meaning of the Fourth Amendment. Should a person who is fleeing the police enjoy Fourth Amendment protection? Does the *Brower* decision in any way interfere with the police's ability to set up roadblocks to apprehend fleeing suspects?

4. In *Bond v. United States* the police searched a bus passenger's luggage and found contraband, but the evidence was ruled inadmissible. This case illustrates the controversy surrounding the exclusionary rule. Was it an appropriate decision to effectively let the defendant off because of police actions?

5. *Schmerber v. California* dealt with the warrantless "seizure" of the blood of a suspected drunk driver.

To what extent is this decision relevant today, with the advent of breathalyzers and video cameras in police cars?

6. What is the standard for establishing that a person has been "seized"?

7. What is the standard for establishing that property has been "seized"?

8. What are exigent circumstances? Give three examples that may be considered to be "exigent."

9. Compare and contrast actual and constructive possession.

10. Give two examples when an individual may not feel that he or she is free to leave during an encounter with police.

CHAPTER FIVE

ARREST

UNITED STATES v. WATSON, *423 U.S. 411 (1976)*

DUNAWAY v. NEW YORK, *442 U.S. 200 (1979)*

PAYTON v. NEW YORK, *445 U.S. 573 (1980)*

WELSH v. WISCONSIN, *466 U.S. 740 (1984)*

UNITED STATES v. ALVAREZ-MACHAIN, *504 U.S. 655 (1992)*

ATWATER v. CITY OF LAGO VISTA, *532 U.S. 318 (2001)*

INTRODUCTION

Students of criminal procedure often become confused when instructors toss around terms like "seizure," "stop," and "arrest" without elaborating on each term's distinct meaning. Think of *stops* and *arrests* as being different types of seizures. Additionally, think of both types of *seizures* as falling on a sliding scale of seriousness: an arrest is the most intrusive and a stop is the next most intrusive. In one sense, distinguishing between an arrest and a lesser type of intrusion is easy. For example, when a suspect is handcuffed, placed in the back of a patrol car, and driven to the police station for booking, an arrest has clearly occurred. Alternatively, if a person is accosted by a single police officer and asked general questions about suspected involvement in a crime, an arrest has not occurred. However, there are many police–citizen encounters that fall between these two extremes. A stop can evolve into an arrest if the circumstances are just so. A seizure short of a formal arrest may be so intrusive as to constitute a *de facto* arrest, in which case probable cause, rather than reasonable suspicion, would be required to make the encounter constitutional.

Generally, the courts will weigh (1) the duration of a stop and (2) the degree of intrusion in assessing whether a stop evolves into an arrest. Sometimes the courts also refer to the officers' intentions and the manner in which the stop takes place. For example, in *Dunaway v. New York,* the Supreme Court ruled that stationhouse detentions required probable cause. In that case, police

officers took a man into custody during the course of a robbery/murder investigation. They read Dunaway his *Miranda* warnings and subjected him to questioning—without probable cause. The Supreme Court reversed Dunaway's subsequent conviction. Again, the Court did not decide on the arrest issue, but it did declare that custodial interrogation such as that in *Dunaway* must be supported by probable cause.

Notwithstanding the distinctions between arrests and lesser intrusions such as stops, it is also important to consider (1) the location where police make arrests and (2) whether warrants are required for doing so. For example, *United States v. Watson* instructs us that arrests made in public places do not require warrants. Even if the arrestable offense is not a serious one, the police can still make warrantless arrests in public. For example, in *Atwater v. City of Lago Vista,* the Supreme Court declared that the police can arrest people for seatbelt violations and, by extension, other nonjailable offenses.

People enjoy substantial Fourth Amendment protection when the police effect arrests in private places. In particular, according to the Supreme Court's decision in *Payton v. New York,* it is unconstitutional for the police to make warrantless arrests of individuals in private places. Only if exigent (i.e., emergency) circumstances exist, such as the potential for the destruction of evidence, can the police make warrantless arrests in private places. In *Welsh v. Wisconsin,* the Court has also held that the police cannot enter people's homes without warrants to make arrests for nonjailable offenses. (Note that *Welsh* dealt with an arrest in a private place and is to be distinguished from *Atwater*.)

One important arrest case deals with arrests made in other jurisdictions than that where the arrestee was to be tried. In *United States v. Alvarez-Machain*, the Court upheld the abduction of an individual from another country to be brought back to the United States for trial. A key qualifier to that decision, however, was that the abduction did not violate any extradition treaties.

UNITED STATES v. WATSON

423 U.S. 411 (1976)

FACTS

An informant, Khoury, phoned a postal inspector and informed him that Watson was in possession of a stolen credit card. On five to ten previous occasions Khoury had provided the inspector with reliable information on postal inspection matters, some involving Watson. Later the same day Khoury delivered the card to the inspector. On learning that Watson had agreed to furnish additional cards, the inspector asked Khoury to arrange to meet with Watson. Watson canceled that engagement, but on another day, Khoury met with Watson at a restaurant. Khoury had been instructed that if Watson had additional stolen credit cards, Khoury was to give a designated signal. The signal was given, the officers closed in, and Watson was arrested. A search incident to arrest revealed that Watson had no credit cards on his person, so the inspector asked if he could look inside Watson's car, which was standing within view. Watson said, "Go ahead," and repeated these words when the inspector cautioned that "[i]f I find anything, it is going to go against you." The inspector entered the car and found under the floor mat an envelope containing two credit cards in the names of other persons. These cards were the basis for two counts of a four-count indictment charging Watson with possessing stolen mail. The U.S. Supreme Court granted certiorari.

ISSUE

Is a warrantless arrest in a public place constitutional, so long as the police have probable cause?

HOLDING

Yes. Police officers may arrest people in public places, even if there is time to obtain a warrant, so long as probable cause is in place in advance.

RATIONALE

"The usual rule is that a police officer may arrest without a warrant one believed by the officer upon reasonable cause to have been guilty of a felony.... Just last term, while recognizing that maximum protection of individual rights could be assured by requiring a magistrate's review of the factual justification prior to any arrest, we stated that 'such a requirement would constitute an intolerable handicap for legitimate law enforcement' and noted that the Court 'has never invalidated an arrest supported by probable cause solely because the officers failed to secure a warrant.'"

CASE EXCERPT

"Law enforcement officers may find it wise to seek arrest warrants where practicable to do so, and their judgments about probable cause may be more readily accepted where backed by a warrant issued by a magistrate. But we decline to transform this judicial preference into a constitutional rule when the judgment of the Nation and Congress has for so long been to authorize warrantless public arrests on probable cause rather than to encumber criminal prosecutions with endless litigation with respect to the existence of exigent circumstances, whether it was practicable to get a warrant, whether the suspect was about to flee, and the like."

CASE SIGNIFICANCE

The Supreme Court has repeatedly stated that warrantless arrests under exigent circumstances conform to Fourth Amendment requirements, so long as probable cause is in place *a priori*. An arrest in a public place is basically one of these exigencies; suspects would obviously flee if the police were required to first obtain a warrant before making the arrest. Even if there is time to obtain a warrant, the Court stated that officers need not obtain one. *Watson* therefore gave the police considerable latitude in terms of making arrests. Arrests in public places coupled with probable cause conform to the strictures of the Fourth Amendment.

DUNAWAY v. NEW YORK

442 U.S. 200 (1979)

FACTS

An informant stated that Dunaway was involved in the killing of a pizza restaurant owner. The informant was questioned, but the information he provided did not give the police probable cause for a warrant to arrest Dunaway. The police only had reasonable suspicion that Dunaway was involved in the killing. Detectives therefore asked patrol officers to pick up Dunaway and bring him to the stationhouse for questioning. Dunaway was taken into custody at a neighbor's house. He was then transported to the police station, placed in an interrogation room, and advised of his *Miranda* rights. He waived his right to counsel and made incriminating statements. The U.S. Supreme Court granted certiorari.

ISSUE

May a person be seized and transported to a police station for interrogation based only on reasonable suspicion?

HOLDING

No. Stationhouse detentions during which interrogation takes place must be supported by probable cause. Taking a person into custody against his or her will for the purpose of interrogation requires probable cause. Even if no formal arrest is made, the act of taking one into custody still requires probable cause.

RATIONALE

"The detention of petitioner was in important respects indistinguishable from a traditional arrest. Petitioner was not questioned briefly where he was found [as a *Terry* stop would permit]. Instead, he was taken from a neighbor's home to a police car, transported to a police station, and placed in an interrogation room. He was never informed that he was 'free to go'; indeed, he would have been physically restrained if he had refused to accompany the officer or had tried to escape their custody. The application of the Fourth Amendment's requirement of probable cause does not depend on whether an intrusion of this magnitude is termed an 'arrest' under state law. The mere facts that petitioner was not told he was under arrest, was not 'booked,' and would not have had an arrest recorded if the interrogation had proved fruitless, while not insignificant for all purposes, obviously do not make petitioner's seizure even roughly analogous to the narrowly defined intrusions involved in *Terry* and its progeny."

CASE EXCERPT

"The application of the Fourth Amendment's requirement of probable cause does not depend on whether an intrusion of this magnitude is termed an 'arrest' under state law... Indeed, any 'exception' that could cover a seizure as intrusive as that in this case would threaten to swallow the general rule that Fourth Amendment seizures are 'reasonable' only if based on probable cause."

CASE SIGNIFICANCE

This case addressed the gray area between an investigative stop and a full-blown arrest. Had police simply accosted Dunaway and questioned him, then the Fourth Amendment probably would not have been violated. However, when they took Dunaway into custody, from within another person's dwelling no less, they should have had probable cause. Probable cause was required even though Dunaway was never formally placed under arrest. The actions in this case amounted to a "*de facto* arrest," a seizure almost identical to a traditional arrest. It also does not matter that Dunaway was advised of his *Miranda* rights. His statements were considered "fruit of the poisonous tree" because they were arrived at via an unconstitutional seizure.

PAYTON v. NEW YORK

445 U.S. 573 (1980)

FACTS

Two days after the murder of a gas station attendant, New York detectives had assembled evidence sufficient to establish probable cause to believe that Payton had committed the murder. They broke into his apartment to arrest him without first obtaining a warrant. Payton was not there but was found later. While the officers were in the apartment, however, a shell casing, which was in plain view, was seized and used against Payton at his murder trial. The U.S. Supreme Court granted certiorari.

ISSUE

Absent exigent circumstances, is a warrantless entry for the purpose of making an arrest constitutional?

HOLDING

No. The constitutional protection granted to the individual's interest in the privacy of his own home applies equally to a warrantless entry for the purpose of arresting a resident of the house. Unless exigent circumstances are present, it is unconstitutional to make a warrantless entry into a private place for the purpose of effecting an arrest.

PAYTON v. NEW YORK *(cont.)*

RATIONALE

"In terms that apply equally to seizures of property and to seizures of persons, the Fourth Amendment has drawn a firm line at the entrance to the house. Absent exigent circumstances, that threshold may not reasonably be crossed without a warrant."

CASE EXCERPT

"A greater burden is placed…on officials who enter a home or dwelling without consent. Freedom from intrusion into the home or dwelling is the archetype of the privacy protection secured by the Fourth Amendment…The constitutional protection afforded to the individual's interest in the privacy of his own home is equally applicable to a warrantless entry for the purpose of arresting a resident of the house; for it is inherent in such an entry that a search for the suspect may be required before he can be apprehended. An entry to arrest and an entry to search for and to seize property implicate the same interest in preserving the privacy and the sanctity of the home, and justify the same level of constitutional protection."

CASE SIGNIFICANCE

This case reinforced the notion that people have a high expectation of privacy in their homes. The police must now obtain a warrant to arrest a person in a private place. Exceptions to this requirement exist, however. "Hot pursuit," an exigency, permits warrantless entry. Also, if there is probable cause to believe a suspect may pose a danger to other individuals, destroy evidence, or flee if not apprehended immediately, a warrantless entry is permissible.

WELSH v. WISCONSIN

466 U.S. 740 (1984)

FACTS

At about 9 p.m. on a rainy night a person witnessed a car being driven erratically. After veering back and forth, the car swerved off the road and came to a stop in an open field. The car was not damaged and the driver was not injured. The witness pulled behind the car in order to prevent it from being driven on the road. The police were called, but the driver of the vehicle walked away prior to their arrival. A check of the vehicle's registration showed that Welsh, the owner, lived within a short distance of where the car

had been abandoned. The police proceeded to Welsh's residence, entered it, and arrested him in his bedroom. At the time of this case Wisconsin law considered driving while intoxicated, the offense for which Welsh was arrested, a noncriminal violation punishable by a maximum fine of $200. The U.S. Supreme Court granted certiorari.

ISSUE

Does the Fourth Amendment permit the warrantless arrest of a suspect in a private dwelling, when the arrestable offense is not jailable?

HOLDING

No. The warrantless nighttime entry of a person's home to make an arrest for a nonjailable offense violates the Fourth Amendment.

RATIONALE

"Our hesitation in finding exigent circumstances, especially when warrantless arrests in the home are at issue, is especially appropriate when the underlying offense for which there is probable cause to arrest is relatively minor. Before agents of the government may invade the sanctity of the home, the burden is on the government to demonstrate exigent circumstances that overcome the presumption of unreasonableness that attaches to all warrantless home entries. When the government's interest is only to arrest for a minor offense, that presumption of unreasonableness is difficult to rebut, and the government usually should be allowed to make such arrests only with a warrant issued upon probable cause by a neutral and detached magistrate….We therefore conclude that the common-sense approach utilized by most lower courts is required by the Fourth Amendment prohibition on 'unreasonable searches and seizures,' and hold that an important factor to be considered when determining whether an exigency exists is the gravity of the underlying offense for which the arrest is being made."

CASE EXCERPT

"It is axiomatic that the physical entry of the home is the chief evil against which the wording of the Fourth Amendment is directed…Consistently with these long-recognized principles, the Court decided in *Payton v. New York* that warrantless felony arrests in the home are prohibited by the Fourth Amendment, absent probable cause and exigent circumstances."

CASE SIGNIFICANCE

Warrantless entry into the home is unconstitutional absent probable cause *and* exigent circumstances. The police had probable cause to enter Welsh's home, but the Supreme Court declared that minor offenses do not create a sufficient exigency such that warrantless entry should be sanctioned. Thus, not only should the police consider possible flight, destruction of evidence, or harm to others, but the seriousness of the underlying offense as well.

UNITED STATES v. ALVAREZ-MACHAIN
504 U.S. 655 (1992)

FACTS

Alvarez-Machain was a citizen and resident of Mexico. However, he was indicted in the United States for his participation in the kidnapping and murder of a Drug Enforcement Administration agent, Enrique Camarena-Salazar. Alvarez-Machain was abducted by U.S. authorities at his place of employment in Guadalajara, Mexico. He was then flown to El Paso, Texas, where he was arrested by DEA agents. He claimed at trial that the district court that was to try his case lacked jurisdiction because his abduction was in violation of an extradition treaty between the United States and Mexico.

ISSUE

Can a foreigner be forcibly abducted from his or her country of origin and brought to the United States for trial, provided the abduction does not violate any treaties?

HOLDING

Yes. The abduction of a foreigner that is not in violation of a treaty does not deprive a U.S. court of jurisdiction over the foreigner's criminal trial, even if the abduction is over the other country's protest.

RATIONALE

"This Court has never departed from the rule announced in *Ker v. Illinois* ... that the power of a court to try a person for crime is not impaired by the fact that he had been brought within the court's jurisdiction by reason of a 'forcible abduction.' No persuasive reasons are newly presented to justify overruling this line of cases. They rest on the sound basis that due process of law is satisfied when one present in court is convicted of [a] crime after having been fairly apprised of the charges against him and after a fair trial in accordance with constitutional procedural safeguards. There is nothing in the Constitution that requires a court to permit a guilty person rightfully convicted to escape justice because he was brought to trial against his will."

CASE EXCERPT

"The language of the Treaty, in the context of its history, does not support the proposition that the Treaty prohibits abductions outside of its terms ... to infer from this Treaty and its terms that it prohibits all means of gaining the presence of an individual outside of its terms goes beyond established precedent and practice ... to imply from the terms of this Treaty that it prohibits obtaining the presence of an individual by means outside of the procedures the Treaty establishes requires a much larger inferential leap ... The fact of respondent's forcible abduction does not therefore prohibit his trial in a court in the United States for violations of the criminal laws of the United States."

CASE SIGNIFICANCE

The Court stated that "[n]either the [extradition] treaty's language nor the history of negotiations and practice under it supports the proposition that it prohibits abductions outside its terms." This decision is therefore important because it permits authorities to forcibly abduct criminal defendants from other countries, assuming the abduction does not violate a treaty. This decision extended *Frisbie v. Collins* beyond the U.S. border.

ATWATER v. CITY OF LAGO VISTA
532 U.S. 318 (2001)

FACTS

A Texas police officer on traffic patrol observed Atwater and her two young children driving without their seatbelts. Failure to wear a seatbelt is a misdemeanor in Texas, punishable by a maximum $50 fine. Failure to wear a seatbelt is known as a citation-only offense, because it carries no possibility of incarceration. Nevertheless, the officer arrested Atwater. The officer's actions were authorized by Texas law, which holds that peace officers can arrest and cite for all offenses, even nonjailable ones. Atwater posted bail shortly after arrest and eventually pled no contest to

ATWATER v. CITY OF LAGO VISTA *(cont.)*

the seatbelt violation. She then brought a Section 1983 lawsuit against the officer and his employer, alleging that the arrest violated her Fourth Amendment right to be free from unreasonable seizures.

ISSUE

Is it a violation of the Fourth Amendment to arrest a person for an offense that carries no jail term?

HOLDING

No. It is reasonable for a police officer with probable cause to believe a crime has been committed in his presence to make an arrest for a minor criminal offense. The Fourth Amendment permits arrest for offenses that carry no jail term.

RATIONALE

"Atwater has cited no particular evidence that those who framed and ratified the Fourth Amendment sought to limit peace officers' warrantless misdemeanor arrest authority to instances of actual breach of the peace, and the Court's review of framing-era documentary history has likewise failed to reveal any such design. Nor is there in any of the modern historical accounts of the Fourth Amendment's adoption any substantial indication that the Framers intended such a restriction. Indeed, to the extent the modern histories address the issue, their conclusions are to the contrary. The evidence of actual practice also counsels against Atwater's position. During the period leading up to and surrounding the framing of the Bill of Rights, colonial and state legislatures, like Parliament before them, regularly authorized local officers to make warrantless misdemeanor arrests without a breach of the peace condition. That the Fourth Amendment did not originally apply to the States does not make state practice irrelevant in unearthing the Amendment's original meaning. A number of state constitutional search-and-seizure provisions served as models for the Fourth Amendment, and the fact that many of the original States with such constitutional limitations continued to grant their officers broad warrantless misdemeanor arrest authority undermines Atwater's position."

CASE EXCERPT

"Atwater's arrest satisfied constitutional requirements. There is no dispute that Officer Turek had probable cause to believe that Atwater had committed a crime in his presence. She admits that neither she nor her children were wearing seatbelts…Turek was accordingly authorized (not required, but authorized) to make a custodial arrest without balancing costs and benefits or determining whether or not Atwater's arrest was in some sense necessary."

CASE SIGNIFICANCE

In many ways this case is both significant and insignificant. It is significant because it granted wide latitude to law enforcement in terms of making arrests for minor offenses. On the other hand, it is doubtful that many police officers will now decide to start arresting people for minor, nonjailable offenses. Importantly, the offense in *Atwater,* even though fairly minor, was criminal. The Supreme Court did not address the constitutionality of arrests for noncriminal offenses; for example, in most states exceeding the posted speed limit (within reason) is not a criminal offense, but rather a violation.

DISCUSSION QUESTIONS

1. *Atwater* gave police the authority to arrest people for seatbelt violations and other nonjailable offenses. Is this decision likely to affect the police profession in a noticeable way? That is, are police officers now more likely to arrest people for seatbelt violations?

2. Discuss examples of exigent circumstances that would permit police to make warrantless arrests in private places.

3. What factors help the courts distinguish between an arrest and a lesser intrusion such as a *Terry* stop?

4. What is the requisite justification for a constitutionally valid arrest? What happens if that justification is not present? (At least two remedies are conceivable.)

5. Based on your assessment of the cases covered in this chapter, has the Supreme Court been more "friendly" to the police or to criminals? That is, which group (police or criminals) has had the largest number of cases decided in its favor?

6. Should American courts allow trials of individuals who are "abducted" from a foreign country? Why or why not?

7. Why are warrantless arrests allowed to be made in public places?

8. Should exigent circumstances be an exception to the warrant requirement? Why or why not?

CHAPTER SIX

STANDARDS FOR THE USE OF FORCE

TENNESSEE v. GARNER, *471 U.S. 1 (1985)*

GRAHAM v. CONNOR, *490 U.S. 396 (1989)*

SCOTT v. HARRIS, *550 U.S. 372 (2007)*

INTRODUCTION

Almost every state has a law or regulation concerning police use of force. The American Law Institute adopted just one such regulation, which resembles many others in place around the country. Section 120.7 states that a police officer "may use such force as is reasonably necessary to effect the arrest, to enter premises to effect the arrest, or to prevent the escape from custody of an arrested person." Further, deadly force is authorized when the crime in question is a felony and when such force "creates no substantial risk to innocent persons" and the officer "reasonably believes" that there is a "substantial risk" that the fleeing felon will inflict harm on other people or police officers.

In *Tennessee v. Garner,* the Supreme Court adopted a rule similar to the American Law Institute's formulation. *Garner* involved the shooting death of a young, unarmed fleeing felon. The result was the leading Supreme Court precedent concerning the use of deadly force to apprehend fleeing felons. The *Garner* decision declared unconstitutional a Tennessee statute that authorized police officers who give notice of the intent to arrest to "use all the necessary means to effect the arrest" if the suspect flees or resists.

The Court ruled that deadly force may be used when (1) it is necessary to prevent the suspect's escape and (2) the officer has probable cause to believe the suspect poses a serious threat of death or serious physical injury to other people or police officers. One would think that the Supreme Court would be unanimous in a decision such as this, but three justices dissented, noting

that the statute struck down by the majority "assist[s] the police in apprehending suspected perpetrators of serious crimes and provide[s] notice that a lawful police order to stop and submit to arrest may not be ignored with impunity."

Four years after *Garner,* the Supreme Court decided the landmark case of *Graham v. Connor,* which set the standard for nondeadly force. The Court declared emphatically that all claims involving allegations of excessive force against police officers must be analyzed under the Fourth Amendment's reasonableness requirement. Further, the Court adopted an "objective reasonableness" test to decide when excessive force is used. This requires focusing on what a *reasonable* police officer would do "without regard to [the officer's] underlying intent or motivation." In helping to decide what a reasonable police officer would do, the Court looked to three factors: (1) the severity of the crime, (2) whether the suspect poses a threat, and (3) whether the suspect is resisting and/or attempting to flee the scene. Courts must, in focusing on these three factors, allow "for the fact that police officers are often forced to make split-second judgments—about the amount of force that is necessary in a particular situation." Generally, then, if the crime in question is a serious one and the suspect is dangerous and resists arrest, the suspect will have difficulty succeeding with an excessive force claim.

Incidentally, both the *Garner* and *Graham* decisions resulted from Section 1983 lawsuits. Garner's surviving family members and Graham himself both sued on the grounds that their constitutional rights had been violated. Unlike many of the cases this book focuses on, which involve evidence of crimes (weapons, drugs, confessions, etc.), *Garner* and *Graham* did not focus on how evidence was obtained, because there was none. The only remedy available to Garner's family and Graham was civil litigation.

TENNESSEE v. GARNER
471 U.S. 1 (1985)

FACTS
Memphis police officers responded to a prowler call. When they arrived at the scene, a woman was standing on her porch pointing toward the adjacent house. She said "they" were breaking in next door. One officer went behind the adjacent house. He heard a door slam and observed Garner, 15, running across the back yard. He stopped at a six-foot-high chain-link fence located at the edge of the yard. The officer's flashlight illuminated Garner's face and hands. There was no sign of a weapon. The officer yelled, "Police, halt," and took steps toward Garner as he was beginning to climb the fence. The officer was convinced that Garner would escape if he made it over the fence. As such, the officer shot Garner. He died from a gunshot wound to the back of the head. The officer was acting under Tennessee state law, which stated that "if, after notice of the intention to arrest the defendant, he either flee[s] or forcibly resist[s], the officer may use all the necessary means to effect the arrest." Garner's family brought a Section 1983 lawsuit, alleging that Garner's seizure violated the Fourth Amendment.

ISSUE
Is it a violation of the Fourth Amendment for police to use deadly force to apprehend a fleeing felon who poses no apparent threat to others?

HOLDING
Yes. It is a violation of the Fourth Amendment for police to use deadly force on a nonviolent fleeing felon, unless there is probable cause to believe that the suspect poses a significant threat of death or serious injury to the officer or others.

RATIONALE
The Court felt that the constitution prohibited the use of deadly force to apprehend a suspect poses no immediate threat to the officer and no threat to others. While

allowing a suspect to escape is of course an unfortunate outcome, the alternative—killing—a suspect who is not clearly dangerous—is unacceptable.

CASE EXCERPT
"The use of deadly force to prevent the escape of all felony suspects, whatever the circumstances, is constitutionally unreasonable. It is not better that all felony suspects die than that they escape. Where the suspect poses no immediate threat to the officer and no threat to others, the harm resulting from failing to apprehend him does not justify the use of deadly force to do so. It is no doubt unfortunate when a suspect who is in sight escapes, but the fact that the police arrive a little late or are a little slower afoot does not always justify killing the suspect. A police officer may not seize an unarmed, nondangerous suspect by shooting him dead."

CASE SIGNIFICANCE
This is the most significant Supreme Court case addressing deadly force to date, as it placed restrictions on when the police can use deadly force to apprehend fleeing felons. Deadly force is now permissible only when, after warning the suspect, the officer has probable cause that serious harm or injury will befall other individuals. It is worth mentioning that *Garner* probably did not alter police practice in all jurisdictions around the country. At issue in the case was the constitutionality of Tennessee's statute. Other states maintained, and continue to maintain, restrictive statutes governing the use of deadly force. The same applies to police departments around the country; many adopted restrictive deadly force policies well before the Court's decision in *Garner*.

GRAHAM v. CONNOR
490 U.S. 396 (1989)

FACTS
Graham, a diabetic, asked a friend to drive him to a nearby convenience store so he could purchase some orange juice to counteract an insulin reaction. There were too many people in line at the store, so he left and asked to be driven to his friend's house. Officer Connor of the Charlotte (NC) Police Department became suspicious in light of Graham's quick entry into and exit from the convenience store. The officer followed the car and stopped it. The driver explained that Graham was having an insulin reaction, but the officer ordered

both men out of the car while he determined what happened in the store. Other officers arrived and handcuffed Graham. They ignored his attempts to explain what happened. Graham sustained several injuries during the encounter, but was eventually released. He brought a Section 1983 lawsuit against the police, alleging that the officers applied excessive force.

ISSUE
Can police officers be held liable under the Fourth Amendment for excessive force and, if so, what standard should be used?

HOLDING
Yes. The appropriate standard is objective reasonableness under the Fourth Amendment.

RATIONALE
"The 'reasonableness' of a particular use of force must be judged from the perspective of a reasonable officer on the scene, rather than with the 20/20 vision of hindsight. The Fourth Amendment is not violated by an arrest based on probable cause, even though the wrong person is arrested, nor by the mistaken execution of a valid search warrant on the wrong premises. With respect to a claim of excessive force, the same standard of reasonableness at the moment applies: 'Not every push or shove, even if it may later seem unnecessary in the peace of a judge's chamber,' violates the Fourth Amendment. The calculus of reasonableness must embody allowance for the fact that police officers are often forced to make split-second judgments—in circumstances that are tense, uncertain, and rapidly evolving—about the amount of force that is necessary in a particular situation."

CASE EXCERPT
The Court held that the reasonableness of a police officer's actions, including the use of deadly force, must be judged not from the perspective of hindsight or in the abstract, but by what a reasonable officer on the scene.

CASE SIGNIFICANCE
Graham is the leading Supreme Court case dealing with excessive force. It cleared up any past ambiguities as to the appropriate constitutional standard by which to judge excessive force claims. Now, when a plaintiff alleges that a police officer violated his or her Fourth Amendment rights, he or she must show that the officer acted in an objectively unreasonable fashion—that

is, "without regard to [the officer's] underlying intent or motivation."

SCOTT v. HARRIS
550 U.S. 372 (2007)

FACTS
In 2001, a Georgia county deputy clocked Harris's vehicle at 73 miles per hour on a highway with a 55-mile-per-hour speed limit. The deputy activated his blue flashing lights, indicating that respondent should pull over. Instead, Harris drove off, initiating a chase at speeds exceeding 85 miles per hour. Deputy Timothy Scott joined the chase, along with other officers. During the chase Scott took over as the lead pursuit vehicle. He decided to attempt to terminate the episode by bumping the rear of Harris's vehicle. As a result, Harris lost control of his vehicle and crashed. Harris suffered significant injuries as a result of the crash and was rendered a quadriplegic. He filed a Section 1983 lawsuit, alleging Scott violated the Fourth Amendment by using excessive force to apprehend him.

ISSUE
Can an officer take actions that place a fleeing motorist at risk of serious injury or death in order to stop the motorist's flight from endangering the lives of innocent bystanders?

HOLDING
Yes. A police officer's attempt to terminate a dangerous high-speed car chase that threatens the lives of innocent bystanders does not violate the Fourth Amendment, even when it places the fleeing motorist at risk of serious injury or death.

RATIONALE
In an 8–1 decision authored by Justice Scalia, the Court held that the police officer's actions did not violate the Reasonableness Clause of the Fourth Amendment, even though these actions placed the lives of innocent bystanders at risk. The Court emphasized that the suspect had created the risk of harm by virtue of his behavior in attempting to evade the police. .

CASE EXCERPT
"A police officer's attempt to terminate a dangerous high-speed car chase that threatens the lives of innocent bystanders does not violate the Fourth

SCOTT v. HARRIS *(cont.)*

Amendment, even when it places the fleeing motorist at risk of serious injury or death."

CASE SIGNIFICANCE

This case is significant because it clarifies when police may engage in high speed pursuits, and when the police may use deadly force to end a high speed pursuit in an effort to protect the public form possible harm by the fleeing suspect.

DISCUSSION QUESTIONS

1. *Garner* and *Graham* set fairly strict standards for the use of deadly and nondeadly force. To what extent do these standards directly affect law enforcement officers?

2. Besides *Garner* and *Graham,* what other documents, cases, laws, and standards govern the use of force in the law enforcement profession?

3. Why do you suppose the Supreme Court chose the Fourth Amendment's reasonableness standard as the appropriate one for evaluating claims of unconstitutional force by the police?

4. *Graham* applies to the police, not corrections officers. The Supreme Court has announced that the Eighth Amendment should be used to judge claims of unconstitutional force by corrections officers. Moreover, the Court has declared that corrections officers cannot be held liable for Eighth Amendment violations unless their conduct is malicious and sadistic (see *Hudson v. McMillian,* 503 U.S. 1 [1992]). Why do you suppose a higher standard has been adopted for corrections officers?

5. What can be done to combat excessive force?

CHAPTER SEVEN

SEARCHES WITH WARRANTS

INTRODUCTION

Search warrants have three essential components: (1) they must be issued by a neutral and detached magistrate, (2) probable cause is required, and (3) they need to conform to the Fourth Amendment's particularity requirement. Some attention also needs to be given to the procedures for serving search warrants as well as to when search warrants are required and how they are to be issued. Each of these topics is addressed in the paragraphs that follow.

Most judges are considered neutral and detached. Even so, the Supreme Court has focused, in a number of cases, on this first critical warrant requirement. For example, in *Coolidge v. New Hampshire,* the Court declared that a state attorney general cannot issue a search warrant. State attorneys general are chief prosecutors and thus inclined to side with law enforcement officers.

There have even been some cases where the Court has focused on the extent to which judges can be viewed as neutral and detached. For example, in *Lo-Ji Sales, Inc. v. New York,* 442 U.S. 319 (1979), a magistrate issued a warrant for two "obscene" items, but he also authorized the police to seize any other items that he might find obscene upon examination of the location to be searched. The magistrate then accompanied the officers on the search, discovered items he deemed to be obscene, and added them to the initial warrant.

The items were then admitted into evidence against the defendants. The Supreme Court declared that the magistrate was not acting in a neutral and detached capacity: "he was not acting as a judicial officer but as an adjunct law-enforcement officer." Also, if a magistrate has a financial interest in the issuance of warrants, he or she cannot be considered neutral and detached.

Probable cause was discussed in Chapter Two, and we do not need to revisit its definition here. However, it is important to point out that, as a component of a valid search warrant, probable cause is required. The probable cause showing in a search warrant is twofold: the officer applying for the search warrant must show probable cause that the items to be seized are (1) connected with criminal activity and (2) in the location to be searched.

The particularity requirement for search warrants is twofold. First, the warrant must specify the place to be searched. Next, the warrant must specify the items to be seized. The reason for this particularity requirement stems from the Framers' concerns with so-called "general warrants." General warrants, which were issued by the English Crown, permitted basically limitless searches for evidence of treason.

Contrary to popular belief, search warrants do not need to state with absolute precision the place to be searched. It "is enough if the description is such that the officer with a search warrant can, with reasonable effort, ascertain and identify the place intended" (*Steele v. United States,* 267 U.S. 498 [1925]). However, the items mentioned in the warrant should be described with sufficient specificity that a reasonable officer would know where to look for them. In *Groh v. Ramirez,* the Court reinforced the particularity requirement and the need to specify the person or items to be seized in the warrant. In *Groh,* the Court held that the fact that the items were specified in the affidavit did not satisfy the particularity requirement and therefore the warrant violated the Fourth Amendment. Moreover, approval of the application for a warrant by a judicial officer does not shield law enforcement officers from civil liability where the Fourth Amendment is not satisfied.

In situations where the warrant incorrectly specifies the place to be searched, the courts will focus on the reasonableness of the officers' mistake. For example, in *Maryland v. Garrison,* police officers obtained a warrant to search the person of Lawrence McWebb and the premises known as 2036 Park Avenue, third-floor apartment. They believed that McWebb's apartment occupied the entire third floor when, in fact, there were two apartments on that floor—one of which belonged to Garrison. The Court held that the warrant was valid because it was based on information by a trusted informant and because the police inquired with the local utility company and were given the impression that there was only one apartment on the third floor. As for the items to be seized, the warrant must clearly specify what the police wish to seize.

Next, there are several important requirements concerning the service of search warrants. One of these requirements, known as the knock and announce rule, is discussed in Chapter Eight. Aside from the knock and announce rule, two cases are important. First, the police may also detain people as needed while serving a search warrant (*Michigan v. Summers*). According to the Court, "a warrant to search for contraband founded on probable cause implicitly carries with it the limited authority to detain the occupants of the premises while a proper search is conducted." Second, in *Steagald v. United States,* the Supreme Court responded to Justice Marshall's concern that while an arrest warrant may protect a person "from an unreasonable seizure, it [does] absolutely nothing to protect [a third party's] privacy interest in being free from an unreasonable invasion and search of his home." Accordingly, the Court decided that in such situations the police must obtain not only an arrest warrant for the person they seek, but a *separate* warrant to search a third-party residence for the arrestee.

Two additional cases that we consider in this chapter deal with the issuance of search warrants. First, in *Zurcher v. Stanford Daily,* the Supreme Court held that a warrant can be issued for the search of premises controlled by an innocent third party, provided that probable cause is present. Next, in *Mincey v. Arizona,* the Court held that if no exigent circumstances exist, a warrant must be obtained to search the scene of a homicide.

COOLIDGE v. NEW HAMPSHIRE
403 U.S. 443 (1971)

FACTS
Pamela Mason, a 14-year-old girl, left her home in Manchester, New Hampshire, during a bad snowstorm, apparently because she was called away for a babysitting job. Her body was found several days later near a busy highway. She had been murdered. Coolidge was questioned and asked to take a lie detector test. Detectives also interviewed Coolidge's wife while her husband was at the police station taking the lie detector test. The wife produced four guns and clothing that she thought her husband was wearing on the night of the murder. Coolidge was held in a jail cell overnight on an unrelated charge and released the next day. Two weeks later the attorney general, who was also a justice of the peace, issued a warrant authorizing the police to search Coolidge's car. Incriminating evidence was found in the trunk.

ISSUE
Can a warrant be issued by a member of the executive branch of government?

HOLDING
No. The warrant issued by the attorney general, the state's chief investigator and prosecutor, was invalid because it was not issued by a neutral and detached magistrate.

RATIONALE
One of the most basic premises of the Fourth Amendment is the requirement that warrants may be issued only by a "neutral and detached magistrate." This requirement works to ensure that there is a clear

delineation between the role of the police and the judiciary in criminal cases. In *Coolidge*, the warrant was issued by the chief government enforcement agent who was acting as a justice of the peace pursuant to New Hampshire law. Such a practice violates the fundamental tenets of the Fourth Amendment and the notions of due process as set forth in the Fourteenth Amendment. In affirming the need for an independent judicial officer to review police requests for warrants, the Court held that "The security of one's privacy against arbitrary intrusion by the police—which is at the core of the Fourth Amendment—is basic to a free society." *Coolidge*, 403 U.S. at 453 (*quoting Wolf v. Colorado*, 338 U.S. 25 (1949)). The Court further held "that prosecutors and policemen simply cannot be asked to maintain the requisite neutrality with regard to their own investigations—the 'competitive enterprise' that must rightly engage their single-minded attention." *Coolidge*, 402 U.S. at 450. To sanction a practice such as that in *Coolidge* would be tantamount to approving searches without a warrant at all.

CASE EXCERPT

"The classic statement of the policy underlying the warrant requirement of the Fourth Amendment is that of Mr. Justice Jackson, writing for the Court in *Johnson v. United States,* 333 U.S. at 10: 'The point of the Fourth Amendment, which often is not grasped by zealous officers, is not that it denies law enforcement the support of the usual inferences which reasonable men draw from evidence. Its protection consists in requiring that those inferences be drawn by a neutral and detached magistrate instead of being judged by the officer engaged in the often competitive enterprise of ferreting out crime. Any assumption that evidence sufficient to support a magistrate's disinterested determination to issue a search warrant will justify the officer in making a search without a warrant would reduce the Amendment to a nullity and leave the people's homes secure only in the discretion of police officers.' "

CASE SIGNIFICANCE

The Fourth Amendment expressly requires that warrants be issued by a neutral and detached magistrate. For some years, however, the Supreme Court did not decide who is to be considered neutral and detached. This case resolved the issue; attorneys general and other employees of the executive branch of government are not considered neutral and detached for purposes of the Fourth Amendment. Even members

of the judicial branch can be considered not neutral and detached. If, for example, a judge receives a fee for each warrant issued, the warrant will be invalid under the Fourth Amendment (see *Connally v. Georgia*, 429 U.S. 245 (1977)).

ZURCHER v. STANFORD DAILY
436 U.S. 547 (1978)

FACTS
On Friday, April 9, 1971, officers of the Palo Alto Police Department and the Santa Clara County Sheriff's Department responded to a call from the director of the Stanford University Hospital requesting the removal of several demonstrators who had seized control of the hospital's offices and occupied them for nearly 24 hours. Several officers were injured while attempting to interrupt the demonstration. The next day, the Sunday edition of the *Stanford Daily* printed several pictures of the violent confrontation. The day after that, the district attorney secured a warrant to search the *Stanford Daily*'s offices for the pictures in question, so that the police could identify the people responsible for injuring police officers during the confrontation. The *Stanford Daily* was an innocent third party, as the warrant did not implicate the newspaper. A thorough search took place but no evidence other than the published photos was found. The paper brought a lawsuit against the police, arguing that a subpoena *duces tecum* should have been utilized to obtain the photos instead of a search. The U.S. Supreme Court granted certiorari.

ISSUE
May a search warrant be issued to search premises controlled by innocent third parties who are suspected of having evidence of a crime?

HOLDING
Yes. Searches with warrants of property belonging to third parties are permissible, so long as probable cause is in place and all other Fourth Amendment warrant requirements are followed.

RATIONALE
"The critical element in a reasonable search is not that the owner of the property is suspected of a crime but that there is reasonable cause to believe that the specific 'things' to be searched for and seized are located on

ZURCHER v. STANFORD DAILY *(cont.)*

the property in which entry is sought....Aware of the long struggle between Crown and press and desiring to curb unjustified official intrusions, the Framers took the enormously important step of subjecting searches to the test of reasonableness and to the general rule requiring search warrants issued by neutral magistrates. They nevertheless did not forbid warrants where the press was involved, did not require special showings that subpoenas would be impractical, and did not insist that the owner of the place to be searched, if connected with the press, must be shown to be implicated in the offense being investigated. Further, the prior cases do no more than insist that the courts apply the warrant requirement with particular exactitude when the First Amendment interest would be endangered by the search. As we see it, no more than this is required where the warrant requested is for the seizure of criminal evidence reasonably believed to be on the premises occupied by a newspaper. Properly administered, the preconditions for a warrant—probable cause, specificity with respect to the place to be searched and the things to be seized, and overall reasonableness—should afford sufficient protection against the harms that are assertedly threatened by warrants for searching newspaper offices."

CASE EXCERPT

"Under existing law, valid warrants may be issued to search any property, whether or not occupied by a third party, at which there is probable cause to believe that fruits, instrumentalities, or evidence of a crime will be found. Nothing on the face of the Amendment suggests that a third-party search warrant should not normally issue. The Warrant Clause speaks of search warrants issued on 'probable cause' and 'particularly describing the place to be searched, and the persons or things to be seized.' In situations where the State does not seek to seize 'persons' but only those 'things' which there is probable cause to believe are located on the place to be searched, there is no apparent basis in the language of the Amendment for also imposing the requirements for a valid arrest—probable cause to believe that the third party is implicated in the crime."

CASE SIGNIFICANCE

This case is significant because it clarified the authority of law enforcement officials to search for evidence of crimes. A search need not be addressed at a particular person's dwelling. Instead, the focus now is on where the evidence to be seized is located. If such evidence is located in a third-party dwelling, the Fourth Amendment does not prohibit a search in such a location, so long as probable cause and a warrant are in place prior to the search. In most circumstances, though, searches of the type described in *Zurcher* should be limited to contraband, the fruits of crime, or the instrumentalities of crime.

MINCEY v. ARIZONA
437 U.S. 385 (1978)

FACTS

Undercover officer Headricks purchased heroin from Mincey in his apartment. Later that day, Headricks returned with several other plainclothes police officers and a deputy district attorney. The apartment door was opened by Hodgman, a friend of Mincey. Headricks slipped inside and then went into the bedroom. Hodgman unsuccessfully attempted to shut the door before any of the other officers could gain entry. Shots were fired in the bedroom and Officer Headricks emerged and collapsed on the floor. When officers entered the bedroom, they found Mincey on the floor, shot and barely conscious. Homicide detectives learned of the incident and responded to the house 10 minutes after the shooting. They took charge of the crime scene and began a search of the premises and the collection of evidence. The search lasted four days. No warrant was obtained. Headricks died later in the hospital. The U.S. Supreme Court later granted certiorari.

ISSUE

Is a search warrant required to search the scene of a homicide?

HOLDING

Yes. If no exigent circumstances exist, a warrant must be obtained to search a murder scene despite the nature of the crime. The Court declined to endorse an additional exception to the warrant requirement when the search involves a crime scene.

RATIONALE

"The Fourth Amendment proscribes all unreasonable searches and seizures, and it is a cardinal principle that 'searches conducted outside judicial process, without prior approval by judge or magistrate, are per se unreasonable under the Fourth Amendment—subject only to a few specifically established and well-delineated exceptions.' The Arizona Supreme Court did not hold that the search of the petitioner's apartment fell within any of the exceptions to the warrant requirement previously recognized by this Court, but rather that the search of a homicide scene should be recognized as an additional exception."

CASE EXCERPT

"Except for the fact that the offense under investigation was a homicide, there were no exigent circumstances in this case. There was no indication that evidence would be lost, destroyed, or removed during the time required to obtain a search warrant. Indeed, the police guard at the apartment minimized that possibility. And there is no suggestion that a search warrant could not easily and conveniently have been obtained. We decline to hold that the seriousness of the offense under investigation itself creates exigent circumstances of the kind that under the Fourth Amendment justify a warrantless search."

CASE SIGNIFICANCE

This case is important because, according to the Court, "the seriousness of the offense under investigation did not itself create exigent circumstances of the kind that under the Fourth Amendment justify a warrantless search, where there is no indication that evidence would be lost, destroyed, or removed during the time required to obtain a search warrant and there is no suggestion that a warrant could not easily and conveniently have been obtained." In other words, murder scenes do not create "exigent circumstances," which generally permit warrantless searches.

STEAGALD v. UNITED STATES
451 U.S. 204 (1981)

FACTS

An informant provided the DEA with the phone number where Lyons, a federal fugitive, could be reached over the next 24 hours. An address that corresponded to the number was obtained from the phone company and two days later, agents drove to the address to search for Lyons. There was an outstanding arrest warrant for Lyons. Gaultney and Steagald were observed outside the house. Officers approached them with guns drawn, frisked them, and demanded identification. When agents went to the front door of the address where

Lyons was thought to be, Gaultney's wife answered the door and told the agents that she was alone in the house. She was detained by one agent while another searched the house. Lyons was not found, but a substance that appeared to be cocaine was observed in plain view. The agent in charge sent someone to obtain a search warrant for the premises. Meanwhile, the search continued and additional incriminating evidence was found. The U.S. Supreme Court granted certiorari.

ISSUE

Without a separate *search* warrant, can police officers search the home of a third party for a person for whom they have an *arrest* warrant?

HOLDING

No. An arrest warrant is valid only for an arrest in a suspect's place of residence or in a public place, not in a third-party dwelling. A separate search warrant must also be obtained before arrest warrants can be served in third-party dwellings.

RATIONALE

"Whether the arrest warrant issued in this case adequately safeguarded the interests protected by the Fourth Amendment depends upon what the warrant authorized the agents to do. To be sure, the warrant embodied a judicial finding that there was probable cause to believe that Ricky Lyons had committed a felony, and the warrant therefore authorized the officers to seize Lyons. However, the agents sought to do more than use the warrant to arrest Lyons in a public place or in his home; instead, they relied on the warrant as legal authority to enter the home of a third person based on their belief that Ricky Lyons might be a guest there. Regardless of how reasonable this belief might have been, it was never subjected to the detached scrutiny of a judicial officer. Thus, while the warrant in this case may have protected Lyons from an unreasonable seizure, it did absolutely nothing to protect petitioner's privacy interest in being free from an unreasonable invasion and search of his home. Instead, petitioner's only protection from an illegal entry and search was the agent's personal determination of probable cause. In the absence of exigent circumstances, we have consistently held that such judicially untested determinations are not reliable enough to justify an entry into a person's home to arrest him without a warrant, or a search of a home for objects in the absence of a search warrant. We see no reason to depart from this settled

STEAGALD v. UNITED STATES *(cont.)*
course when the search of a home is for a person rather than an object."

CASE EXCERPT

"Since warrantless searches of a home are impermissible absent consent or exigent circumstances, we conclude that the instant search violated the Fourth Amendment."

CASE SIGNIFICANCE

This case is significant because it placed restrictions on the service of arrest warrants. Arrest warrants can only be served in one of two places: (1) public areas and (2) the suspect's place of residence. Following *Steagald,* a separate search warrant must be obtained when the search for a suspect will include third-party dwellings. This assumes, however, that no exigent circumstances are present. Had the police in *Steagald* been able to show that Lyons would have escaped had they waited for a search warrant, the search would have been upheld.

MICHIGAN v. SUMMERS
452 U.S. 692 (1981)

FACTS

Summers descended the front stairs of his house and was confronted by Detroit police officers who were there to execute a search warrant to look for narcotics. The officers requested Summers' assistance in gaining entry and detained him while the search was conducted. Narcotics were found in the basement and Summers was arrested. A search incident to arrest also revealed that narcotics were in his coat pocket. The U.S. Supreme Court granted certiorari.

ISSUE

Do police have authority to detain residents of a house that is to be searched pursuant to a valid warrant?

HOLDING

Yes. A warrant carries with it the authority to detain residents of houses to be searched pursuant to a valid warrant.

RATIONALE

In assessing the justification for the detention of an occupant of premises being searched for contraband pursuant to a valid warrant, both the law enforcement interest and the nature of the "articulable facts" supporting the detention are relevant. Most obvious is the legitimate law enforcement interest in preventing flight in the event that incriminating evidence is found. Less obvious, but sometimes of greater importance, is the interest in minimizing the risk of harm to the officers. Although no special danger to the police is suggested by the evidence in this record, the execution of a warrant to search for narcotics is the kind of transaction that may give rise to sudden violence or frantic efforts to conceal or destroy evidence. The risk of harm to both the police and the occupants is minimized if the officers routinely exercise unquestioned command of the situation. Finally, the orderly completion of the search may be facilitated if the occupants of the premises are present. Their self-interest may induce them to open locked doors or locked containers to avoid the use of force that is not only damaging to property but may also delay the completion of the task at hand.

CASE EXCERPT

"The existence of a search warrant, however, also provides an objective justification for the detention. A judicial officer has determined that police have probable cause to believe that someone in the home is committing a crime. Thus, a neutral magistrate rather than an officer in the field has made the critical determination that the police should be given a special authorization to thrust themselves into the privacy of a home. The connection of an occupant to that home gives the police officer an easily identifiable and certain basis for determining that suspicion of criminal activity justifies a detention of that occupant."

CASE SIGNIFICANCE

This case is significant because it enhanced the authority of the police when executing a search warrant. However, the key to this case is that it dealt with the detention of the person whose residence was to be searched. With regard to the detention of third parties who may be at the scene, the Supreme Court has been much more restrictive. In *Ybarra v. Illinois,* 444 U.S. 85 (1979), the Court refused to sanction the pat-down search of a patron of a bar that was about to be searched pursuant to valid warrant. The Court did not sanction the pat down because the state was unable to provide any articulable suspicion that Ybarra, a patron of the bar, was a threat to the officers who were there to serve the search warrant.

MARYLAND v. GARRISON

480 U.S. 79 (1987)

FACTS

Baltimore police officers obtained and executed a warrant to search the person of Lawrence McWebb and the "premises known as 2036 Park Avenue third floor apartment." The police reasonably believed that there was only one apartment on the third floor, but in fact there were two. The warrant was mistakenly served in Garrison's apartment. Police found heroin, and Garrison was convicted for possession of a controlled substance. The U.S. Supreme Court granted certiorari.

ISSUE

Is evidence admissible when officers mistakenly and in good faith execute a search warrant at a location not authorized in the warrant?

HOLDING

Yes. A warrant that lacks particularity with regard to the place to be searched is valid if it is served in good faith.

RATIONALE

"Plainly, if the officers had known, or even if they should have known, that there were two separate dwelling units on the third floor of 2036 Park Avenue, they would have been obligated to exclude Garrison's apartment from the scope of the requested warrant. But we must judge the constitutionality of their conduct in light of the information available to them at the time they acted. Those items of evidence that emerge after the warrant is issued have no bearing on whether or not a warrant was validly issued. Just as the discovery of contraband cannot validate a warrant invalid when issued, so is it equally clear that the discovery of facts demonstrating that a valid warrant was unnecessarily broad does not retroactively invalidate the warrant. The validity of the warrant must be assessed on the basis of the information that the officers disclosed, or had a duty to discover and to disclose, to the issuing magistrate. On the basis of that information, we agree with the conclusion of all three Maryland courts that the warrant, insofar as it authorized a search that turned out to be ambiguous in scope, was valid when it issued."

CASE EXCERPT

"The officers' conduct and the limits of the search were based on the information available as the search proceeded. While the purposes justifying a police search strictly limit the permissible extent of the search, the Court has also recognized the need to allow some latitude for honest mistakes that are made by officers in the dangerous and difficult process of making arrests and executing search warrants."

CASE SIGNIFICANCE

The Fourth Amendment requires that no warrants shall issue without, among other things, describing the place to be searched and the persons or things to be seized. This is known as the "particularity requirement." Search warrants satisfy the particularity requirement with a valid address and a description of the items to be seized. The warrant in *Garrison* was deficient in terms of the place to be searched; that is, the address was incomplete. Nevertheless, the Supreme Court applied the good faith doctrine. In its reasoning, the Court stated that there was a reasonable effort on the part of the officers to determine the address of the location to be searched. Had they not taken these steps and, instead, sought a "general warrant" to search multiple dwellings, the evidence would not have been admissible.

CALIFORNIA v. GREENWOOD

486 U.S. 35 (1988)

FACTS

In early 1984, Investigator Stracner of the Laguna Beach Police Department learned that a suspect had informed a federal drug-enforcement agent that a truck filled with illegal narcotics was going to Greenwood's residence. A neighbor had also complained that many vehicles had stopped at Greenwood's house for short periods of time during the night. Stracner placed Greenwood's house under surveillance and confirmed that several vehicles came and went late at night. She asked the neighborhood's trash collector to pick up the garbage bags in front of Greenwood's house and turn them over to her. A search of the garbage bags revealed evidence of narcotics use. Information from the garbage search was used in an affidavit for a search warrant. A warrant was issued and served, and drugs were found. Greenwood was arrested and charged. Additional complaints came in about narcotics use at Greenwood's house. The garbage was searched for a second time and, again, evidence of narcotics use was found and Greenwood was arrested again. The U.S. Supreme Court granted certiorari.

CALIFORNIA v. GREENWOOD (cont.)

ISSUE

Can items placed in the trash for collection on a public street be searched without a warrant or probable cause?

HOLDING

Yes. Trash left for collection in an area open to the public is considered abandoned. No expectation of privacy exists in garbage left in opaque bags outside the curtilage of a home.

RATIONALE

"The warrantless search and seizure of the garbage bags left at the Greenwood house would violate the Fourth Amendment only if the Greenwoods manifested a subjective expectation of privacy in their garbage that society accepts as objectively reasonable.... It may well be that the Greenwoods did not expect that the contents of their garbage bags would become known to the police or other members of the public. An expectation of privacy does not give rise to Fourth Amendment protection, however, unless society is prepared to accept that expectation as objectively reasonable."

CASE EXCERPT

"We conclude that the Greenwoods exposed their garbage to the public sufficiently to defeat their claim to Fourth Amendment protection. It is common knowledge that plastic garbage bags left on or at the side of a public street are readily accessible to animals, children, scavengers, snoops, and other members of the public. Moreover, respondents placed their refuse at the curb for the express purpose of conveying it to a third party, the trash collector, who might himself have sorted through respondents' trash or permitted others, such as the police, to do so. Accordingly, having deposited their garbage in an area particularly suited for public inspection and, in a manner of speaking, public consumption, for the express purpose of having strangers take it, respondents could have had no reasonable expectation of privacy in the inculpatory items that they discarded."

CASE SIGNIFICANCE

This case is significant because it reinforced the distinction between looking for evidence of a crime and engaging in "searches" within the meaning of the Fourth Amendment. In this case, the Court said that a search did not take place because there is no expectation of privacy in garbage placed on a public street for removal. The Court effectively said that garbage left for removal is "abandoned." Nothing prohibits law enforcement officials from examining, even without any justification, abandoned property.

MINNESOTA v. CARTER
525 U.S. 83 (1998)

FACTS

Based on information supplied by an informant, a police officer went to an apartment where narcotics violations were presumably taking place. The officer observed through the ground-floor window people putting white powder into bags. When Carter and an accomplice, Johns, left the apartment, they were stopped by the police in their car. Officers observed a handgun in the car and arrested both men. A search of the automobile incident to arrest revealed drugs and drug paraphernalia. The officers then obtained an arrest warrant and returned to the apartment to arrest Thompson, the lessee. A search of the apartment revealed additional drugs. The officers later learned that Carter and Johns visited Thompson's apartment from another city and that they were there for only a short time for the purpose of packaging drugs. Certiorari was granted by the U.S. Supreme Court.

ISSUE

Does a person who is in another's apartment with consent and for the purpose of doing business enjoy an expectation of privacy?

HOLDING

No. A person who is in another's dwelling with consent and there to do business does not enjoy a reasonable expectation of privacy.

RATIONALE

"Respondents here were obviously not overnight guests, but were essentially present for a business transaction and were only in the home for a matter of hours. There is no suggestion that they had a previous relationship with Thompson, or that there was any other purpose to their visit. Nor was there anything similar to the overnight guest relationship in *Olson* to suggest a degree of acceptance into the household. While the apartment was a dwelling for Thompson, it was for these respondents simply a place to do business."

CASE EXCERPT

"But the extent to which the Fourth Amendment protects people may depend upon where those people are. We have held that capacity to claim the protection of the Fourth Amendment depends...upon whether the person who claims the protection of the Amendment has a legitimate expectation of privacy in the invaded place. The text of the Amendment suggests that its protections extend only to people in 'their' houses. But we have held that in some circumstances a person may have a legitimate expectation of privacy in the house of someone else."

CASE SIGNIFICANCE

The Supreme Court has stated that overnight guests enjoy an expectation of privacy in third-party dwellings. In this case, however, the guests were there for a short time and only to do business. The Court held that they did not enjoy an expectation of privacy. This decision is important because the defendants argued that the officers' actions were unconstitutional because they engaged in an unjustified search, thereby violating their Fourth Amendment rights. The Court stated that the Fourth Amendment was never implicated because even though the officers were government actors (one requirement for a Fourth Amendment search to take place), the defendants did not enjoy an expectation of privacy in the apartment (the second requirement for a search).

GROH v. RAMIREZ
540 U.S. 551 (2004)

FACTS

Based on a tip from a concerned citizen concerning the presence of weapons on the Ramirez ranch, an ATF agent applied for a search warrant. The agent prepared and signed an application for a warrant to search the ranch that stated that the search was for "any automatic firearms or parts to automatic weapons, destructive devices to include but not limited to grenades, grenade launchers, rocket launchers, and any and all receipts pertaining to the purchase or manufacture of automatic weapons or explosive devices or launchers." The agent supported the application with a detailed affidavit that set forth the basis for his belief that the listed items were concealed on the ranch. The application and the affidavit were presented to a federal magistrate, along with a completed warrant form,

and the warrant was issued. Although the application particularly described the place to be searched and the contraband petitioner expected to find, the warrant itself was less specific; it failed to identify any of the items that petitioner intended to seize. In the portion of the form that called for a description of the "person or property" to be seized, petitioner typed a description of respondents' two-story blue house rather than the alleged stockpile of firearms. The warrant did not incorporate by reference the itemized list contained in the application. The warrant recited that the magistrate was satisfied the affidavit established probable cause to believe that contraband was concealed on the premises, and that sufficient grounds existed for the warrant's issuance.

Following a search on the Ramirez property, no weapons or explosives were found. No criminal charges were filed. Thereafter, the Ramirez family filed suit against the agent for violation of their constitutional rights pursuant to Section 1983.

ISSUE

Is the particularity requirement of the Fourth Amendment violated when the warrant itself fails to identify the person or things sought?

HOLDING

Yes. The Fourth Amendment is violated when the warrant itself fails to identify the person or things the petitioner intends to seize.

RATIONALE

"This warrant did not simply omit a few items from a list of many to be seized, or misdescribe a few of several items. Nor did it make what fairly could be characterized as a mere technical mistake or typographical error. Rather, in the space set aside for a description of the items to be seized, the warrant stated that the items consisted of a 'single dwelling residence...blue in color.' In other words, the warrant did not describe the items to be seized at all. In this respect the warrant was so obviously deficient that we must regard the search as 'warrantless' within the meaning of our case law. 'We are not dealing with formalities.' Because "'the right of a man to retreat into his own home and there be free from unreasonable governmental intrusion'" stands "'[a]t the very core' of the Fourth Amendment," our cases have firmly established the "'basic principle of the Fourth Amendment that searches and seizures inside a home without a warrant are presumptively

GROH v. RAMIREZ *(cont.)*

unreasonable." Thus, 'absent exigent circumstances, a warrantless entry to search for weapons or contraband is unconstitutional even when a felony has been committed and there is probable cause to believe that incriminating evidence will be found within.'"

CASE EXCERPT
"The mere fact that the magistrate issued a warrant does not necessarily establish that he agreed that the scope of the search should be as broad as the affiant's request. Even though petitioner acted with restraint in conducting the search, the inescapable fact is that this restraint was imposed by the agents themselves, not by a judicial officer. It is incumbent on the officer executing a search warrant to ensure the search is lawfully authorized and lawfully conducted. Because petitioner did not have in his possession a warrant particularly describing the things he intended to seize, proceeding with the search was clearly unreasonable under the Fourth Amendment."

CASE SIGNIFICANCE
This case serves to underscore the Court's unwillingness to make exceptions to the core requirements of the Fourth Amendment. Further, it reinforces the expectation that the individual seeking the warrant will not be entitled to qualified immunity when omissions such as those in this case occur. As such, law enforcement officers or other government agents must work diligently to ensure that all Fourth Amendment requirements are followed. Failure to do so may subject the officer or agent to civil liability. This case serves to remove any expectation that the fact that the warrant is approved by a judicial officer will insulate the officer from liability.

UNITED STATES v. JONES
132 S.Ct. 945 (2012)

FACTS
Jones was suspected of trafficking in narcotics by a joint FBI and Metropolitan Police Department task force. Officers employed various investigative techniques, including visual surveillance of the nightclub that Jones operated, installation of a camera focused on the front door of the club, and a pen register and wiretap covering Jones's cellular phone. Based on information obtained from their investigation, a warrant was sought to authorize the use of an electronic tracking device on the Jeep Grand Cherokee registered to Jones's wife. A warrant was issued authorizing installation of the device in the District of Columbia within ten days. On day eleven, agents installed a GPS tracking device on the undercarriage of the Jeep while it was parked in a public parking lot in Maryland. The vehicle was tracked by the government for twenty-eight days.

ISSUE
Does the attachment of a GPS tracking device to an individual's vehicle, and subsequent use of that device to monitor the vehicle's movements on public streets, constitute a search or seizure within the meaning of the Fourth Amendment?

HOLDING
Yes. The installation of the GPS to gather information from a vehicle did constitute a search for purposes of the Fourth Amendment.

RATIONALE
"Our later cases, of course, have deviated from that exclusively property-based approach. In *Katz v. United States*, 389 U.S. 347 (1967), we said that 'the Fourth Amendment protects people, not places,' and found a violation in attachment of an eavesdropping device to a public telephone booth. Our later cases have applied the analysis of Justice Harlan's concurrence in that case, which said that a violation occurs when government officers violate a person's 'reasonable expectation of privacy.' The Government contends that no search occurred here, since Jones had no 'reasonable expectation of privacy' in the area of the Jeep accessed by Government agents (its underbody) and in the locations of the Jeep on the public roads, which were visible to all. But we need not address the Government's contentions, because Jones's Fourth Amendment rights do not rise or fall with the *Katz* formulation. At bottom, we must 'assur[e] preservation of that degree of privacy against government that existed when the Fourth Amendment was adopted.' *Kyllo*, supra, at 34, 121 S. Ct. 2038, 150 L. Ed. 2d 94. As explained, for most of our history the Fourth Amendment was understood to embody a particular concern for government trespass upon the areas ('persons, houses, papers, and effects') it enumerates. *Katz* did not repudiate that understanding. Less than two years later the Court upheld defendants' contention that the Government could not introduce against them conversations between

other people obtained by warrantless placement of electronic surveillance devices in their homes. The opinion rejected the dissent's contention that there was no Fourth Amendment violation 'unless the conversational privacy of the homeowner himself is invaded.' *Alderman v. United States,* 394 U.S. 165, 176, 89 S. Ct. 961, 22 L. Ed. 2d 176 (1969). '[W]e [do not] believe that *Katz,* by holding that the Fourth Amendment protects persons and their private conversations, was intended to withdraw any of the protection which the Amendment extends to the home.' "

CASE EXCERPT

"It is important to be clear about what occurred in this case: The Government physically occupied private property for the purpose of obtaining information. We have no doubt that such a physical intrusion would have been considered a 'search' within the meaning of the Fourth Amendment when it was adopted."

CASE SIGNIFICANCE

This case provides useful guidance regarding the application of Fourth Amendment principles to the use of modern technological devices for police investigations. The Court clarifies in its holding the shift from the purely property-based analysis under the Fourth Amendment to the modern "reasonable expectation of privacy" approach and how the same applies to the use of certain technology. Due to increased use of technology in the commission and investigation of crimes, the *Jones* decision will certainly have an impact on a growing number of cases.

DISCUSSION QUESTIONS

1. Identify several officials who cannot be considered neutral and detached for purposes of the Fourth Amendment.
2. Is it possible for the police to manipulate the Fourth Amendment's particularity requirement to their benefit?
3. The Fourth Amendment clearly lists the requirements for a valid warrant, yet the Supreme Court has authorized several varieties of warrantless searches and seizures. Why do you suppose this is?
4. Name three exceptions to the warrant requirement.
5. What is an anticipatory search warrant? When may this type of warrant be useful?
6. Where do people have a "reasonable expectation of privacy"? What does this concept require?
7. Name the three essential components of a search warrant.
8. Explain the concept of probable cause.
9. Why should police be able to detain occupants of a residence when executing a search warrant?
10. Should there be a "good faith" exception for law enforcement when serving a warrant? Why or why not?

CHAPTER EIGHT

THE KNOCK AND ANNOUNCE RULE

WILSON v. ARKANSAS, *514 U.S. 927 (1995)*

RICHARDS v. WISCONSIN, *520 U.S. 385 (1997)*

UNITED STATES v. BANKS, *540 U.S. 31 (2003)*

HUDSON v. MICHIGAN, *547 U.S. 586 (2006)*

INTRODUCTION

At common law, the police were entitled to break into a house to make an arrest after announcing their presence as well as the reason for being there. Nowadays, the method of entry the police can use to serve warrants (arrest and search) is usually set forth in legislation. With regard to federal law enforcement, for example, 18 U.S.C. Section 3109 states that an officer "may break open any outer or inner door or window of a house…to execute a search warrant, if, after notice of his authority and purpose, he is refused admittance."

Almost without exception the law requires that police officers announce their presence and state their authority (e.g., "Police officers, search warrant!"). There are several reasons for this: (1) it helps avoid needless destruction of property; (2) it helps prevent violence resulting from unnecessary surprise; and (3) it helps preserve people's dignity and privacy. Of course, there are certain situations where these reasons for a "knock and announce" requirement do not serve their intended purposes. The second reason can work against its intention; requiring police to announce their presence may increase the possibility of violence rather than reducing it. What, then, are the criteria for determining when a knock and announce is not required? It is useful to turn to Supreme Court precedent to answer this question.

One of the first cases where the Court addressed the constitutionality of the common law knock and announce requirement was *Wilson v. Arkansas*. The Supreme Court ruled that the officers *were* required to follow the knock and announce requirement when serving warrants.

The Supreme Court later clarified its position in the case of *Richards v. Wisconsin*. There, the Court held that police can dispense with the knock and announce requirement if they have *reasonable suspicion* that such a requirement "would be dangerous or futile, or that it would inhibit the effective investigation of the crime by, for example, allowing the destruction of evidence." Basically, then, if the police have reasonable suspicion to believe that exigent circumstances are present, it is not always necessary that they knock on the door and announce their presence.

WILSON v. ARKANSAS
514 U.S. 927 (1995)

FACTS

Wilson engaged in several narcotics transactions with a police informant over a period of several months. Based on these transactions, police officers obtained an arrest warrant for Wilson and a search warrant for her home. Once they arrived at Wilson's residence, the officers identified themselves and stated that they had a warrant as they entered the home through an unlocked door. The officers found several incriminating items. Wilson sought suppression of the evidence on the grounds that the officers did not follow the common law practice of knocking and announcing their presence.

ISSUE

In the absence of exigent circumstances, does the Fourth Amendment's reasonableness clause require that officers "knock and announce" their presence during the service of warrants?

HOLDING

Yes. Unless exigent circumstances exist, the Fourth Amendment's reasonableness clause requires that officers knock and announce their presence when serving search or arrest warrants.

RATIONALE

"An examination of the common law of search and seizure...leaves no doubt that the reasonableness of a search of a dwelling may depend in part on whether law enforcement officers announce their presence and authority prior to entering....Our own cases have acknowledged that the common-law principle of announcement is embedded in Anglo-American law, but we have never squarely held that this principle is an element of the reasonableness inquiry under the Fourth Amendment. We now so hold."

CASE EXCERPT

"For now, we leave to the lower courts the task of determining the circumstances under which an unannounced entry is reasonable under the Fourth Amendment. We simply hold that although a search or seizure of a dwelling might be constitutionally defective if police officers enter without prior announcement, law enforcement interests may also establish the reasonableness of an unannounced entry."

CASE SIGNIFICANCE

This case was intended to restrict law enforcement officers from forcibly entering people's residences to serve warrants when doing so is not necessary. It also reinforced the importance of privacy interests in the home. However, if the threat of physical violence exists, if evidence is likely to be destroyed, or if the suspect is likely to escape, then announcement is not necessary. It would be unreasonable to require officers to place their lives in danger, or risk losing evidence or the suspect, by always announcing their presence during the service of warrants.

RICHARDS v. WISCONSIN

520 U.S. 385 (1997)

FACTS

Officers obtained a warrant to search Richards' hotel room for drugs and drug paraphernalia. The officers' request for a no-knock warrant was denied by the judge. When attempting to serve the warrant, one officer knocked on Richards' door and identified himself as a maintenance worker. Richards then saw one of the uniformed officers and slammed the door. At that point, the officers identified themselves and forcibly entered the unit. A search revealed incriminating evidence. An officer later justified the no-knock entry on the grounds that "police officers are never required to knock and announce when executing a search warrant in a felony drug investigation because of the special circumstances of today's drug culture." The case later came before the U.S. Supreme Court.

ISSUE

Does the Fourth Amendment permit a blanket exception to the common law knock and announce requirement for felony drug warrants?

HOLDING

No. The Fourth Amendment does not permit a blanket exception to the knock and announce requirement for felony drug warrants. Instead, the police must have reasonable suspicion—determined on a case-by-case basis—that knocking and announcing their presence "would be dangerous or futile, or that it would inhibit the effective investigation of the crime by, for example, allowing the destruction of evidence."

RATIONALE

"[T]he fact that felony drug investigations may frequently present circumstances warranting a no-knock entry cannot remove from the neutral scrutiny of a reviewing court the reasonableness of the police decision not to knock and announce in a particular case. Instead, in each case, it is the duty of a court confronted with the question to determine whether the facts and circumstances of the particular entry justified dispensing with the knock-and-announce requirement....In order to justify a 'no knock' entry, the police must have reasonable suspicion that knocking and announcing their presence, under the particular circumstances,

RICHARDS v. WISCONSIN (cont.)

would be dangerous or futile, or that it would inhibit the effective investigation of the crime by, for example, allowing the destruction of evidence."

CASE EXCERPT

"In order to justify a no-knock entry, the police must have a reasonable suspicion that knocking and announcing their presence, under the particular circumstances, would be dangerous or futile, or that it would inhibit the effective investigation of the crime by, for example, allowing the destruction of evidence. This standard—as opposed to a probable-cause requirement—strikes the appropriate balance between the legitimate law enforcement concerns at issue in the execution of search warrants and the individual privacy interests affected by no-knock entries."

CASE SIGNIFICANCE

This case offered some clarification to the Court's decision in *Wilson v. Arkansas. Wilson* held that the police are required to knock and announce their presence when serving warrants, but that there are numerous exceptions to the rule. In *Richards,* the Court emphatically stated that there are no *blanket* exceptions, and that each situation must be viewed individually. However, Justice Brennan's dissent in *Ker v. California,* 374 U.S. 23 (1963), a case decided some years earlier, offered some useful guidelines that, arguably, are still in place today: "[T]he Fourth Amendment is violated by an unannounced police intrusion into a private home, with or without an arrest warrant, except (1) where the persons within already know of the officers' authority and purpose, or (2) where the officers are justified in the belief that persons within are in imminent peril of bodily harm, or (3) where those within, made aware of the presence of someone outside (because, for example, there has been a knock at the door), are then engaged in activity which justifies the officers in their belief that an escape or the destruction of evidence is being attempted."

UNITED STATES v. BANKS

540 U.S. 31 (2003)

FACTS

Las Vegas police and FBI agents arrived at LaShawn Banks' apartment to execute a search warrant for drugs. The officers identified themselves, stated their purpose, and demanded immediate entry. After waiting between 15 and 20 seconds without hearing a sound from within the apartment, the officers broke down the front door with a battering ram and entered, finding Banks naked and dripping water in the hallway. He had apparently been taking a shower when the officers arrived and demanded entry. Banks claimed that he did not hear the knock and announcement, but had heard the officers' forced entry. The officers executed the search warrant, finding a large quantity of cocaine and drug paraphernalia. Banks was arrested and the contraband seized.

Prior to trial, the District Court denied Banks' motion to suppress the seized evidence and statements he made to the police. Banks then pled guilty and was sentenced to slightly more than eleven years in prison. He then appealed the District Court's denial of his suppression motion. The Ninth Circuit Court of Appeals reversed the District Court and ordered the evidence suppressed. The Court of Appeals noted that the Fourth Amendment required the police to act "reasonably" in executing a search warrant, and that part of the reasonableness inquiry included determining what constituted a "reasonable" waiting period before forcible entry was permitted. The Ninth Circuit panel created four categories of entries and a list of factors to be considered in assessing reasonableness. The Ninth Circuit next asserted that because the officers in *Banks* had not been explicitly denied entrance, they were required to delay their forcible entrance for a "sufficient period of time." The Court of Appeals concluded the police did not wait a sufficient period of time before entering Banks' apartment, and ordered the evidence suppressed.

The Ninth Circuit decision was in conflict with decisions in several other circuits, all of which had held that a waiting period of approximately twenty seconds was sufficient. Citing this conflict among the circuits, the government sought certiorari from the U.S. Supreme Court.

ISSUE

Is a fifteen- to twenty-second wait prior to forcible entry reasonable under the totality of the circumstances?

HOLDING

Yes. There is no set time period; what is reasonable depends on the totality of the circumstances facing the police when they seek entry.

RATIONALE

The Court acknowledged that while "this call is a close one," the police were justified in not waiting any longer or waiting for an explicit refusal before breaking down the door to Banks' apartment. This was because the police had a search warrant for drugs, which are easily and quickly destroyed. The exigent circumstance of the possible destruction of evidence justified not waiting any longer. The case might well be different if the items in the search warrant were different: "Police seeking a stolen piano may be able to spend more time to make sure they really need the battering ram." The court, by noting the Fourth Amendment and its lack of specifics regarding formalities when serving a warrant, proceeded to utilize a totality-of-the-circumstances approach to determining reasonableness.

CASE EXCERPT

"[A] general reasonableness analysis threatens to distort the 'totality of the circumstances' approach and "terms like significant amount of time, and an even more substantial amount of time, tell very little."

CASE SIGNIFICANCE

The Supreme Court in *Ramirez* rejected the Ninth Circuit's attempt to graft a requirement onto the general reasonableness requirement that when property is destroyed during the execution of a search warrant, there must be a showing of heightened exigency. The Supreme Court made it clear they perceived the Ninth Circuit's four-part matrix as nothing more than an attempt to resurrect an approach the Supreme Court rejected in *Ramirez*.

HUDSON v. MICHIGAN
547 U.S. 586 (2006)

FACTS

Police obtained a warrant authorizing a search for drugs and firearms at the home of Booker Hudson. When the police arrived to execute the warrant, they announced their presence but waited only a short time—perhaps "three to five seconds"—before turning the knob of the unlocked front door and entering Hudson's home. Large quantities of drugs were found. A loaded gun was lodged between the cushion and armrest of the chair in which he was sitting. Hudson was charged under Michigan law with unlawful drug and firearm possession. Hudson moved to suppress all the seized evidence,

arguing that the premature entry violated his Fourth Amendment rights. The Michigan trial court granted his motion. On interlocutory review, the Michigan Court of Appeals reversed, relying on Michigan Supreme Court cases holding that suppression is inappropriate when entry is made pursuant to warrant but without properly knocking and announcing the police presence. The Michigan Supreme Court denied leave to appeal, and Hudson was convicted of drug possession. He renewed his Fourth Amendment claim on appeal, but the Court of Appeals rejected it and affirmed the conviction. The Michigan Supreme Court again declined review, and the U.S. Supreme Court granted certiorari.

ISSUE

Does violation of the knock and announce rule require the suppression of all evidence found in the search, per the exclusionary rule?

HOLDING

No. Applying the exclusionary rule to violations of the knock and announce rule is not the most effective means of enforcing the knock and announce rule.

RATIONALE

The cost of applying the exclusionary rule to violations of the knock and announce rule are too great, and the exclusionary rule should not be used in such situations when there are more effective and less costly (to effective law enforcement) means of enforcing the Fourth Amendment. Such violations can be enforced through police training and discipline, and through lawsuits brought by aggrieved citizens. Applying the exclusionary rule to knock and announce violations would have little or no deterrent effect.

CASE EXCERPT

"What the knock-and-announce rule has never protected, however, is one's interest in preventing the government from seeing or taking evidence described in a warrant. Since the interests that *were* violated in this case have nothing to do with the seizure of the evidence, the exclusionary rule is inapplicable."

CASE SIGNIFICANCE

This case is significant because it has the effect of limiting the ability of persons to exclude evidence seized in violation of the knock and announce rule. Thus, after several cases in which the Supreme Court held that the knock and announce rule and its common

HUDSON v. MICHIGAN *(cont.)*
law exceptions were part of the Fourth Amendment, the Court essentially gutted the rule by taking away the most effective means of enforcing it, the exclusionary rule.

DISCUSSION QUESTIONS

1. Is the knock and announce rule too rigid?
2. Should the police be able to dispense with the knock and announce rule on more occasions?
3. Identify circumstances when it is not practical to knock and announce.
4. Identify circumstances when a knock and announce requirement is critical.
5. What are the possible consequences of either sticking with or dispensing with the knock and announce requirement?

CHAPTER NINE

SEARCH INCIDENT TO ARREST

WARDEN v. HAYDEN, *387 U.S. 294 (1967)*

CHIMEL v. CALIFORNIA, *395 U.S. 752 (1969)*

VALE v. LOUISIANA, *399 U.S. 30 (1970)*

UNITED STATES v. ROBINSON, *414 U.S. 218 (1973)*

UNITED STATES v. EDWARDS, *415 U.S. 800 (1974)*

MARYLAND v. BUIE, *494 U.S. 325 (1990)*

VIRGINIA v. MOORE, *553 U.S. 164 (2006)*

ARIZONA v. GANT, *556 U.S. 332 (2009)*

INTRODUCTION

Imagine a situation where a police officer with probable cause arrests a suspect, who then reaches into his pocket. Imagine further what would go through the police officer's mind as he or she observes this behavior. Such is the reasoning behind the "search incident to arrest" exception to the Fourth Amendment's warrant requirement. The logic for permitting police officers to engage in a search of a suspect incident to arrest (i.e., following an arrest) is that it would be impractical—even dangerous—to wait for a warrant.

The leading case in the area of incident searches is *Chimel v. California.* As the Supreme Court stated, a search incident to arrest is permitted "to remove any weapons that the [arrestee] might seek to use in order to resist arrest or effect his escape" and to "seize any evidence on the arrestee's person in order to prevent its concealment or destruction."

The most basic requirement concerning searches incident to arrest—one that often goes overlooked—is that the arrest must be lawful. When the arrest itself is not lawful (i.e., when it is not based on probable cause), any search that follows is unlawful. Another important threshold issue with regard to searches incident to arrest concerns the nature of the offense. Courts have grappled with whether a search should be permitted when the offense on which the arrest is based is not serious. Because the rationale of the exception is officer safety, then is officer safety likely to be compromised

when a minor as opposed to a serious offense justifies the arrest?

Two important Supreme Court cases have sought to answer these questions. First, in *United States v. Robinson,* the Court reversed a lower court's decision that only a pat down of the suspect's outer clothing was permissible following an arrest for driving with a revoked license. And in a companion case to *Robinson, Gustafson v. Florida,* 414 U.S. 260 (1973), the Court upheld the search of a suspect after his arrest for failure to have his driver's license.

The Supreme Court offered two reasons for its opinions in *Robinson* and *Gustafson.* First, according to Chief Justice Rehnquist, "[i]t is scarcely open to doubt that the danger to an officer is far greater in the case of the extended exposure which follows the taking of a suspect into custody and transporting him to the police station than in the case of the relatively fleeting contact resulting from the typical *Terry* stop." Second, the Court believed a bright-line rule was in order given the stakes involved: "A police officer's determination as to how and where to search the person of a suspect whom he has arrested is necessarily a quick *ad hoc* judgment which the Fourth Amendment does not require to be broken down in each instance into an analysis of each step in the search" (*United States v. Robinson*).

Generally, a search incident to arrest should take place close in time to the arrest. However, in *United States*

v. *Edwards*, the Supreme Court—in a 5–4 decision—upheld the warrantless search and seizure of an arrestee's clothing ten hours after his arrest, while he was in jail. The Court noted that "searches and seizures that could be made on the spot at the time of arrest may legally be conducted later when the accused arrives at the place of detention." The Court did point out, however, that the taking of Edwards' clothing at the time of the arrest would have been impractical because it "was late at night[,] no substitute clothing was then available for Edwards to wear, and it would certainly have been unreasonable for the police to have stripped respondent of his clothing and left him exposed in his cell throughout the night." Thus, the *Edwards* decision established the rule that noncontemporaneous searches incident to arrest are permissible when (1) an immediate search is nearly impossible and (2) the exigency still exists at the time of the later search.

The Supreme Court has also restricted the scope of searches incident to arrest. Returning to *Chimel v. California*, the Supreme Court created the so-called "arm-span rule." In the Court's words, a search incident to arrest is limited to the area "within [the] immediate control" of the person arrested—that is, "the area from within which he might have obtained either a weapon or something that could have been used as evidence against him."

The cases discussed thus far have focused narrowly on the scope of the incident search exception with reference to the arrestee. What if another person *besides* the arrestee poses a threat to the police? This concern has led to several exceptions to the arm-span rule, to which we now turn.

First, in *Maryland v. Buie*, the Supreme Court expanded the scope of the incident search in two ways. It held that the police may, as part of a search incident to arrest, look in areas immediately adjoining the place of arrest for other persons who might attack the officers; no justification is required. The key, however, is that such a search occurs incident to arrest. Next, the Court held that at any point up to the time the arrest is completed, the police may engage in a "protective sweep" (i.e., "a cursory visual inspection of those places in which a person might be hiding"), but reasonable suspicion must exist for such a sweep to be justified. Thus, no justification is required *after* arrest, but reasonable suspicion is required to engage in a sweep up to the point of the arrest.

Aside from the possible danger to police officers from "confederates" is the potential for such third

parties to engage in the destruction of evidence. Only one Supreme Court case appears to address this issue: *Vale v. Louisiana*. In that case, police had warrants authorizing the arrest of the defendant. While engaged in surveillance of the house, the officers observed the defendant come out of the house and engage in what appeared to be a drug sale. They arrested the defendant outside the home, but then went back inside the house and searched it, according to the officers because two of the defendant's relatives had arrived at the house in the meantime and could have destroyed evidence. *Vale* was actually a case concerning exigent circumstances, and the Court reversed the Louisiana Supreme Court's decision that upheld the search, but the Court's opinion was not particularly instructive. It stated in relevant part that there is "no reason, so far as anything before us appears, to suppose that it was impracticable for [the officers] to obtain a search warrant as well," but did not expressly state that related searches would always be unconstitutional.

WARDEN v. HAYDEN
387 U.S. 294 (1967)

FACTS

The police were informed that an armed robbery had occurred and that the suspect, Hayden, had thereafter entered a certain house. Minutes later they arrived there and were told by Hayden's wife that she had no objection to their searching the house. Certain officers arrested Hayden in an upstairs bedroom when it became clear he was the only man in the house. Others simultaneously searched the first floor and cellar. One found weapons in a flush tank; another, looking "for a man or the money," found in a washing machine clothing of the type the suspect was said to have worn. Ammunition was also found. These items were admitted into evidence without objection at Hayden's trial, which resulted in his conviction. After unsuccessful state court proceedings, Hayden sought and was denied habeas corpus relief in district court. The court of appeals found the search lawful, but reversed on the ground that the clothing seized during the search was immune from seizure, being of "evidential value only." The U.S. Supreme Court granted certiorari.

ISSUE

Is there, under the Fourth Amendment, a distinction between merely evidentiary materials—which may not be seized either under the authority of a search warrant or during the course of a search incident to arrest—and those objects that may validly be seized, including the instrumentalities and means by which a crime is committed, the fruits of crime such as stolen property, weapons by which escape of the person arrested might be effected, and property the possession of which is a crime?

HOLDING

No. The distinction prohibiting seizure of items of only evidential value and allowing seizure of instrumentalities, fruits, or contraband is no longer accepted as being required by the Fourth Amendment.

RATIONALE

"There is no rational distinction between a search for 'mere evidence' and one for an 'instrumentality' in terms of the privacy which is safeguarded by the Fourth Amendment; nor does the language of the Amendment itself make such a distinction. The clothing items involved here are not 'testimonial' or 'communicative' and their introduction did not compel Hayden to become a witness against himself in violation of the Fifth Amendment. The premise that property interests control government's search and seizure rights, on which *Gouled v. United States* partly rested, is no longer controlling as the Fourth Amendment's principal object is the protection of privacy, not property. The related premise of *Gouled* that government may not seize evidence for the purpose of proving crime has also been discredited. The Fourth Amendment does not bar a search for that purpose provided that there is probable cause, as there was here, for the belief that the evidence sought will aid in a particular apprehension or conviction."

CASE EXCERPT

"The remedy of suppression, moreover, which made possible protection of privacy from unreasonable searches without regard to proof of a superior property interest, likewise provides the procedural device necessary for allowing otherwise permissible searches and seizures conducted solely to obtain evidence of crime. For just as the suppression of evidence does not entail a declaration of superior property interest in the person aggrieved, thereby enabling him to suppress evidence unlawfully seized despite his inability to demonstrate such an interest (as with fruits, instrumentalities, contraband), the refusal to suppress evidence carries no

declaration of superior property interest in the State, and should thereby enable the State to introduce evidence lawfully seized despite its inability to demonstrate such an interest."

CASE SIGNIFICANCE

This case stood for two propositions: (1) that a warrant is not required if probable cause and exigent circumstances exist and (2) that there is no distinction between types of evidence.

CHIMEL v. CALIFORNIA

395 U.S. 752 (1969)

FACTS

Police officers armed with an arrest warrant, but not a search warrant, were admitted to Chimel's home by his wife, where they awaited his arrival. When he entered he was arrested. Although he denied the officers' request to "look around," they nonetheless conducted a search of the entire house "on the basis of the lawful arrest." At Chimel's trial on burglary charges, items taken from his home were admitted over objection that they had been unconstitutionally seized. His conviction was affirmed by the California appellate courts, which held that the search was justified as incident to a valid arrest. The U.S. Supreme Court granted certiorari.

ISSUE

May police officers search the area surrounding an arrestee incident to a lawful arrest?

HOLDING

Yes. Police may search the area within the immediate control of an arrestee, in order to discover any weapons or to prevent the destruction of evidence.

RATIONALE

An arresting officer may search the arrestee's person to discover and remove weapons and to seize evidence to prevent its concealment or destruction, and may search the area "within the immediate control" of the person arrested, meaning the area from which he might gain possession of a weapon or destructible evidence. For the routine search of rooms other than that in which an arrest occurs, or for searching desk drawers or other closed or concealed areas in that room itself, absent well-recognized exceptions,

CHIMEL v. CALIFORNIA *(cont.)*

a search warrant is required. While the reasonableness of a search incident to arrest depends upon "the facts and circumstances—the total atmosphere of the case," those facts and circumstances must be viewed in the light of established Fourth Amendment principles, and the only reasoned distinction is one between (1) a search of the person arrested and the area within his reach and (2) more extensive searches. The scope of the search here was unreasonable under the Fourth and Fourteenth Amendments, as it went beyond petitioner's person and the area from within which he might have obtained a weapon or something that could have been used as evidence against him, and there was no constitutional justification, in the absence of a search warrant, for extending the search beyond that area.

CASE EXCERPT

"Application of sound Fourth Amendment principles to the facts of this case produces a clear result. The search here went far beyond the petitioner's person and the area from within which he might have obtained either a weapon or something that could have been used as evidence against him. There was no constitutional justification, in the absence of a search warrant, for extending the search beyond that area. The scope of the search was, therefore, 'unreasonable' under the Fourth and Fourteenth Amendments and the petitioner's conviction cannot stand."

CASE SIGNIFICANCE

This case made it clear that the police may not only search a person when making an arrest, but may also search an area surrounding the arrestee—what the court termed the "area of immediate control," and which other courts have described as the "lunge area." This extension of the search incident exception is based on the same rationale: to allow officers to protect themselves from harm and to prevent the possible destruction of evidence.

VALE v. LOUISIANA
399 U.S. 30 (1970)

FACTS

Police officers, possessing warrants for Vale's arrest, were watching the house where he resided. They observed what they suspected was an exchange of narcotics between a known addict and Vale outside the

house, after Vale had gone into the house and brought something out to the addict. They arrested Vale at the front steps and announced that they would then search his house incident to his arrest. A search of the then-unoccupied house disclosed narcotics in a bedroom. The Louisiana Supreme Court, affirming Vale's conviction for possessing heroin, held that the search did not violate the Fourth Amendment, as it occurred "in the immediate vicinity of the arrest" and was "substantially contemporaneous therewith." The U.S. Supreme Court then granted certiorari.

ISSUE

May the police conduct a warrantless search of a suspect's home when the suspect is arrested outside the home and there are no exigent circumstances present?

HOLDING

No. The warrantless search of appellant's house violated the Fourth Amendment.

RATIONALE

"Even under *Chimel v. California,* holding that the warrantless search of a house can be justified as incident to a lawful arrest, there is no precedent of this Court to sustain the validity of this search. If a search of a house is to be upheld as incident to an arrest, the arrest must take place inside the house. A warrantless search of a dwelling is constitutionally valid only in 'a few specifically established and well-delineated exceptions,' and the search cannot be justified solely because narcotics, which are easily destroyed, are involved."

CASE EXCERPT

"The difficulty is that the two arrest warrants on which the Court seems to rely so heavily were not issued because of any present misconduct of Vale's; they were issued because the bond had been increased for an earlier narcotics charge then pending against Vale. When the police came to arrest Vale, they knew only that his bond had been increased. There is nothing in the record to indicate that, absent the increased bond, there would have been probable cause for an arrest, much less a search."

CASE SIGNIFICANCE

This case limited the "search incident to arrest" exception somewhat. Police may not use the exception to conduct a search of a residence if the suspect is arrested outside the residence.

UNITED STATES v. ROBINSON
414 U.S. 218 (1973)

FACTS
Robinson was arrested for driving while his license was revoked. In accordance with prescribed procedures, the arresting officer made a search of Robinson's person, in the course of which he found in a coat pocket a cigarette package containing heroin. Robinson was charged with and convicted of drug possession. The court of appeals reversed on the ground that the heroin had been obtained as a result of a search in violation of the Fourth Amendment, and the U.S. Supreme Court granted certiorari.

ISSUE
May a police officer conduct a full search of an arrestee, even though he does not fear for his safety?

HOLDING
Yes. In the case of a lawful custodial arrest, a full search of the person is not only an exception to the warrant requirement of the Fourth Amendment but is also a "reasonable" search under that Amendment.

RATIONALE
"A search incident to a valid arrest is not limited to a frisk of the suspect's outer clothing and removal of such weapons as the arresting officer may, as a result of such frisk, reasonably believe and ascertain that the suspect has in his possession, and the absence of probable fruits or further evidence of the particular crime for which the arrest is made does not narrow the standards applicable to such a search. A custodial arrest of a suspect based on probable cause is a reasonable intrusion under the Fourth Amendment and a search incident to the arrest requires no additional justification, such as the probability in a particular arrest situation that weapons or evidence would in fact be found upon the suspect's person; and whether or not there was present one of the reasons supporting the authority for a search of the person incident to a lawful arrest need not be litigated in each case. Since the custodial arrest here gave rise to the authority to search, it is immaterial that the arresting officer did not fear Robinson or suspect that he was armed."

CASE EXCERPT
"Nor are we inclined, on the basis of what seems to us to be a rather speculative judgment, to qualify the breadth of the general authority to search incident to a lawful custodial arrest on an assumption that persons arrested for the offense of driving while their licenses have been revoked are less likely to possess dangerous weapons than are those arrested for other crimes. It is scarcely open to doubt that the danger to an officer is far greater in the case of the extended exposure which follows the taking of a suspect into custody and transporting him to the police station than in the case of the relatively fleeting contact resulting from the typical *Terry*-type stop. This is an adequate basis for treating all custodial arrests alike for purposes of search justification."

CASE SIGNIFICANCE
This case stands for the proposition that the police may always conduct a full body search when making an arrest. Prior to this decision, many lower courts allowed a full search only if the police officer feared for his safety. Now, any time a police officer takes a person into custody, for any offense, the officer may conduct a full body search.

UNITED STATES v. EDWARDS
415 U.S. 800 (1974)

FACTS
Edwards was arrested shortly after 11 p.m. and taken to jail. The next morning, a warrantless seizure was made of his clothing and over his objection at his later trial, which resulted in conviction, was used as evidence. The court of appeals reversed, holding that the court held that the warrantless seizure of Edwards' clothing "after the administrative process and the mechanics of the arrest [had] come to a halt" was unconstitutional. The U.S. Supreme Court granted certiorari.

ISSUE
Did the warrantless search of Edwards' clothing several hours after his seizure and while he was in custody violate the Fourth Amendment?

HOLDING
No. The search and seizure of Edwards' clothing did not violate the Fourth Amendment.

RATIONALE
"Once an accused has been lawfully arrested and is in custody, the effects in his possession at the place of

UNITED STATES v. EDWARDS *(cont.)*

detention that were subject to search at the time and place of arrest may lawfully be searched and seized without a warrant even after a substantial time lapse between the arrest and later administrative processing, on the one hand, and the taking of the property for use as evidence, on the other."

CASE EXCERPT

"[I]t seems to us that the normal processes incident to arrest and custody had not been completed when Edwards was placed in his cell on the night of May 31. With or without probable cause, the authorities were entitled at that point not only to search Edwards' clothing but also to take it from him and keep it in official custody. The police were also entitled to take from Edwards any evidence of the crime in his immediate possession, including his clothing…This was and is a normal incident of a custodial arrest, and reasonable delay in effectuating it does not change the fact that Edwards was no more imposed upon than he could have been at the time and place of the arrest or immediately upon arrival at the place of detention."

CASE SIGNIFICANCE

This case is important because it gave police the authority to conduct a search incident to arrest at some point after the arrest—there is no requirement that the search be "contemporaneous" with the arrest. This was a significant expansion of the search incident exception, which was originally created to protect officers making an arrest. Extending the time period for the search seems to run counter to the rationale for the exception but relieves police officers from having to do the search right away or not at all.

MARYLAND v. BUIE
494 U.S. 325 (1990)

FACTS

Following an armed robbery by two men, one of whom was wearing a red running suit, several police officers obtained arrest warrants for Buie and his suspected accomplice and executed the arrest warrant for Buie at his house. After Buie was arrested upon emerging from the basement, one of the officers entered the basement "in case there was someone else" there and seized a red running suit lying in plain view. The trial court denied Buie's motion to suppress the running suit, the suit was

introduced into evidence, and Buie was convicted of armed robbery and a weapons offense. The intermediate appellate court affirmed the denial of the suppression motion, but the state supreme court reversed, ruling that the running suit was inadmissible because the officer who conducted the "protective sweep" of the basement did not have probable cause to believe that a serious and demonstrable potentiality for danger existed when he searched the basement. The U.S. Supreme Court then granted certiorari.

ISSUE

May a police officer conduct a warrantless "protective sweep" of the area where a suspect is arrested?

HOLDING

Yes. The Fourth Amendment permits a limited protective sweep in conjunction with an in-home arrest when the searching officer possesses a reasonable belief based on specific and articulable facts that the area to be swept harbors an individual posing a danger to those present during the arrest.

RATIONALE

"In holding that, respectively, an on-the-street 'frisk' and a roadside search of an automobile's passenger compartment were reasonable despite the absence of a warrant or probable cause, *Terry v. Ohio* and *Michigan v. Long* balanced the Fourth Amendment interests of the persons with whom they were dealing against the immediate interests of the police in protecting themselves from the danger posed by hidden weapons. Here, the police had an analogous interest in taking steps to assure themselves that Buie's house was not harboring other persons who were dangerous and who could unexpectedly launch an attack, and the fact that Buie had an expectation of privacy in rooms that were not examined by the police prior to the arrest does not mean that such rooms were immune from entry. No warrant was required, and as an incident to the arrest the officers could, as a precautionary matter and without probable cause or reasonable suspicion, look in closets and other spaces immediately adjoining the place of arrest from which an attack could be launched. Beyond that, however, just as in *Terry* and *Long,* there must be articulable facts which, taken together with the rational inferences from those facts, would warrant a reasonably prudent officer in believing that the area to be swept harbors an individual posing a danger. Such a protective sweep is not a full search of the premises, but may extend only to a cursory inspection of those spaces where a person may be found. The sweep lasts no longer than is necessary to dispel the reasonable suspicion of danger and in any event no longer than it takes to complete the arrest and depart the premises."

CASE EXCERPT

"Such a protective sweep, aimed at protecting the arresting officers, if justified by the circumstances, is nevertheless not a full search of the premises, but may extend only to a cursory inspection of those spaces where a person may be found. The sweep lasts no longer than is necessary to dispel the reasonable suspicion of danger and in any event no longer than it takes to complete the arrest and depart the premises."

CASE SIGNIFICANCE

This case allowed police officers to conduct a limited protective sweep of the premises when they make an arrest, but only if they can articulate the facts that indicate they may be in danger. In addition, searches are limited to possible hiding spots and must be of short duration.

VIRGINIA v. MOORE

553 U.S. 164 (2006)

FACTS

Moore was arrested for the misdemeanor offense of driving with a suspended license. Moore was not searched immediately by the officers after his arrest, but following a consent search of his hotel room, the officers searched his person and found that he was carrying 16 grams of crack cocaine and $516 in cash. Virginia law required the officers to have issued Moore a summons rather than arrested him for the offense of driving with a suspended license. Because his arrest for the traffic offense violated state law, Moore challenged the subsequent search and argued that it violated the Fourth Amendment. Moore was charged with possessing cocaine with the intent to distribute it in violation of Virginia law and filed a motion to suppress the evidence. The trial court denied the motion to suppress; Moore was convicted and sentenced to a term of five years. Moore appealed his conviction and the Virginia Supreme Court reversed, holding "that since the arresting officers should have issued Moore a citation under state law, and the Fourth Amendment does not permit search incident to citation, the arrest search

violated the Fourth Amendment." The U.S. Supreme Court granted certiorari.

ISSUE

Does a search incident to an arrest that violated state law require that the evidence seized be suppressed?

HOLDING

No. The Court held that warrantless arrests for crimes committed in the presence of an arresting officer are reasonable under the Constitution, and that while states are free to regulate such arrests however they desire, state restrictions do not alter Fourth Amendment protection.

RATIONALE

"We reaffirm against a novel challenge what we have signaled for more than half a century. When officers have probable cause to believe that a person has committed a crime in their presence, the Fourth Amendment permits them to make an arrest, and to search the suspect in order to safeguard evidence and ensure their own safety. In a long line of cases, we have said that when an officer has probable cause to believe a person committed even a minor crime in his presence, the balancing of private and public interests is not in doubt. The arrest is constitutionally reasonable. Our decisions counsel against changing this calculus when a State chooses to protect privacy beyond the level that the Fourth Amendment requires. We have treated additional protections exclusively as matters of state law."

CASE EXCERPT

"A State is free to prefer one search-and-seizure policy among the range of constitutionally permissible options, but its choice of a more restrictive option does not render the less restrictive ones unreasonable, and hence unconstitutional. If we concluded otherwise, we would often frustrate rather than further state policy. Virginia chooses to protect individual privacy and dignity more than the Fourth Amendment requires, but it also chooses not to attach to violations of its arrest rules the potent remedies that federal courts have applied to Fourth Amendment violations."

CASE SIGNIFICANCE

This case is important because it clarifies the role of state law when evaluating Fourth Amendment challenges to searches incident to arrest. Despite state law, the Court did not alter the relevant inquiry under

VIRGINIA v. MOORE *(cont.)*
the Fourth Amendment for purposes of determining whether the evidence was required to be excluded.

ARIZONA v. GANT

556 U.S. 332 (2009)

FACTS

Gant was arrested for driving with a suspended license after he drove up to the scene of a drug arrest, parked, and exited his vehicle. Officers handcuffed him and placed him in the backseat of the patrol car, and then searched his car, discovering drugs and a weapon. He was convicted but on appeal sought to have the evidence seized during the search of his car suppressed, on the ground that it was conducted without a warrant or probable cause. Under *Chimel v. California* (1969), police may conduct a search incident to arrest of the arrestee and the area of the arrestee's immediate control to prevent the destruction of evidence and for officer safety. Under *New York v. Belton* (1981), when someone in a vehicle is being arrested, the area of immediate control is defined as the passenger compartment of the vehicle, and it may be searched even if the driver is secured in a police vehicle. The Arizona Supreme Court reversed his conviction, holding that a search incident to arrest exception does not apply when an arrestee has been secured.

ISSUE

May the police conduct a search of a vehicle once the suspect has been secured?

HOLDING

No. A search incident to arrest involving a vehicle may not be conducted once the arrestee has been secured and is no longer a potential threat to officers or able to destroy evidence, unless the search is for evidence related to the crime of arrest.

RATIONALE

"The underlying reasons that justify the search incident exception (prevention of evidence destruction and officer safety) are not present when the arrestee is secured. The arrest here was for driving with a suspended license, and no evidence related to that offense could be uncovered during a search. The majority acknowledged that most lower courts had interpreted *Belton* as allowing a search of a vehicle incident to

arrest whenever there was an arrest of an occupant of the vehicle, but the Court insisted that this was a misinterpretation of *Belton*. Under this broad reading of *Belton*, a vehicle search would be authorized incident to every arrest of a recent occupant notwithstanding that in most cases the vehicle's passenger compartment will not be within the arrestee's reach at the time of the search. To read *Belton* as authorizing a vehicle search incident to every recent occupant's arrest would thus untether the rule from the justifications underlying the *Chimel* exception—a result clearly incompatible with our statement in *Belton* that it 'in no way alters the fundamental principles established in the *Chimel* case regarding the basic scope of searches incident to lawful custodial arrests.' Accordingly, we reject this reading of *Belton* and hold that the *Chimel* rationale authorizes police to search a vehicle incident to a recent occupant's arrest only when the arrestee is unsecured and within reaching distance of the passenger compartment at the time of the search. Although it does not follow from *Chimel*, we also conclude that circumstances unique to the vehicle context justify a search incident to a lawful arrest when it is "reasonable to believe evidence relevant to the crime of arrest might be found in the vehicle.""

CASE EXCERPT

"A rule that gives police the power to conduct such a search whenever an individual is caught committing a traffic offense, when there is no basis for believing evidence of the offense might be found in the vehicle, creates a serious and recurring threat to the privacy of countless individuals. Indeed, the character of that threat implicates the central concern underlying the Fourth Amendment—the concern about giving police officers unbridled discretion to rummage at will among a person's private effects."

CASE SIGNIFICANCE

The *Gant* decision is an important step in the evolution of the search incident to arrest exception. In *Gant*, the Court accepted the invitation to review the *Belton* decision and its implementation in the lower courts. A broad interpretation of *Belton* was common practice, thus allowing police to search vehicles and passenger compartments even in cases when the arrestee was secured. Following *Gant*, such practice can no longer be sustained, and therefore, absent the existence of another exception to the warrant requirement, those searches are deemed unreasonable and unconstitutional. *Gant*, therefore, is important because it clarifies *Belton*, limits the scope of search incident to arrest involving vehicles, and provides guidance to police regarding the scope of their authority in these situations.

DISCUSSION QUESTIONS

1. How large should an arrestee's "grabbing area" be?
2. Is it possible that the police could manipulate a protective sweep to their advantage?
3. What are the requirements for a search incident to arrest?
4. Identify reasons for the search incident to arrest exception to the Fourth Amendment's warrant requirement.
5. Provide an example of an unconstitutional search incident to arrest.
6. What was the rationale of the court in *Vale v. Louisiana* (1970)?
7. Why does the court allow more liberal search policies once an individual has been placed within a detention?
8. Does the opinion in *Virginia v. Moore* diminish the authority of the states? Why or why not?
9. Compare and contrast the holdings in *New York v. Belton* (see Chapter Thirteen) and *Arizona v. Gant*.
10. Why would a state prohibit arrests for certain offenses as in *Virginia v. Moore*?

CHAPTER TEN

CONSENT SEARCHES

STONER v. CALIFORNIA, *376 U.S. 483 (1964)*

BUMPER v. NORTH CAROLINA, *391 U.S. 543 (1968)*

SCHNECKLOTH v. BUSTAMONTE, *412 U.S. 218 (1973)*

FLORIDA v. ROYER, *460 U.S. 491 (1983)*

ILLINOIS v. RODRIGUEZ, *497 U.S. 177 (1990)*

FLORIDA v. JIMENO, *500 U.S. 248 (1991)*

UNITED STATES v. DRAYTON ET AL., *536 U.S. 194 (2002)*

GEORGIA v. RANDOLPH, *547 U.S. 103 (2006)*

INTRODUCTION

There is one clear-cut situation where absolutely no justification is required for the police to engage in a search. This situation is consent. When a person consents to a search, neither probable cause nor reasonable suspicion is necessary. Consent searches are still bound by the Fourth Amendment, but they begin following someone's waiver of his or her Fourth Amendment rights.

Cases involving consensual searches can be placed into three categories. Consensual searches must be voluntary, so several cases have focused on the meaning of this term. Other cases have defined the scope of consent searches, and still others have focused on exactly whether third-party individuals can give consent in order to subject another person's private effects to a search.

The general rule is that validly obtained consent justifies a warrantless search with or without probable cause. However, for consent to be valid it must be voluntary. If consent is the result of duress or coercion, then any evidence obtained as a result will be inadmissible. When does duress or coercion take place? There is no clear answer to this question. Instead, the Court has opted for a "totality of circumstances" test.

Importantly, consent to search may be valid even if the consenting party is unaware of the fact that he or she can refuse consent (*Schneckloth v. Bustamonte*).

As the Court stated in *Ohio v. Robinette,* 519 U.S. 33 (1996), "just as it 'would be thoroughly impractical to impose on the normal consent search the detailed requirements of an effective warning,' so too would it be unrealistic to require police officers to always inform detainees that they are free to go before a consent to search may be deemed involuntary." Likewise, nothing prohibits authorities from randomly approaching individuals and asking for consent to search, even without suspicion that criminal activity is afoot (*United States v. Drayton et al.*). Consent must be voluntary, however.

Importantly, while a consent search need not be based on probable cause or any other standard of justification, if consent is obtained following an unlawful seizure, then it will not be considered valid. Such was the decision reached in *Florida v. Royer*. There, the Supreme Court held that because Royer "was being illegally detained when he consented to the search of his luggage,...the consent was tainted by the illegality and was ineffective to justify the search."

The scope of a consent search is limited to the terms of the consent. In other words, the person giving consent "calls the shots." This was the decision reached in the case of *Florida v. Jimeno*. For example, if a person says "you may look around," this does not necessarily mean the police can look *anywhere* for evidence of criminal activity.

A handful of Supreme Court cases have focused on whether third parties can give consent to have another person's property searched (e.g., a landlord consenting to have a tenant's apartment searched, parents consenting to have their child's room searched, etc.). As far as the immediate family is concerned, the general rule is that wives and husbands can give consent to have their partners' property searched and parents can give consent to have their children's property searched, but children cannot give consent to have their parents' property searched. The reason children cannot give consent is that they are considered "incompetent" to give voluntary consent, given their age. By contrast, landlords cannot give consent to search property rented to another person (*Stoner v. California*). However, in a case involving co-occupants (*Georgia v. Randolph* [2006]), the Supreme Court held that "when a physically present inhabitant gives express refusal to a police search of their home, the consent of another occupant is invalid, unless there are exigent circumstances."

More confusing is the situation of a roommate, former girlfriend, friend, or extended family member. Two important Supreme Court cases are relevant here. First, third-party consent can be given if (1) the third-party individual possesses "common authority" over the area to be searched and (2) the nonconsenting party (e.g., the roommate) is not present (*United States v. Matlock*, 415 U.S. 164 [1974]). According to the Court, "common authority" rests on "mutual use of the property by persons generally having joint access or control for most purposes." Thus, a third party could give consent to have a shared bathroom searched but not to have her roommate's bedroom searched. What happens, however, if the nonconsenting party is present and affirmatively objects to the search? The courts are divided on this issue.

There are some cut-and-dried situations where two people possess common authority over a particular area, but what happens when it is not clear to officers at the scene whether common authority exists? In response to this question, the Supreme Court has held that warrantless entry of private premises by police officers is valid if based on the "apparent authority" doctrine. In other words, a warrantless entry of a residence is valid if it is based on the consent of a person whom the police reasonably believe has authority to grant consent, even if their beliefs are erroneous (*Illinois v. Rodriguez*). The test for reasonableness in this situation, according to the Court, is: "[W]ould the facts available to the officer at the moment [of the entry]…warrant a man of reasonable caution in the belief that the consenting party had authority over the premises?" *Rodriguez* involved consent given by a former girlfriend who possessed apparent authority to grant consent because she still had a key to her ex-boyfriend's apartment.

STONER v. CALIFORNIA
376 U.S. 483 (1964)

FACTS
Police investigating the armed robbery of a grocery store found several items that led them to suspect Stoner was the robber. They tracked him to a hotel where, without a search or arrest warrant, they entered and searched Stoner's room in his absence, having been given access to and consent to search by a hotel clerk. There they found evidence associated with the crime. Stoner was arrested two days later in another state and, following a trial in which the articles were used as evidence, was convicted. He appealed, and the U.S. Supreme Court granted certiorari.

ISSUE
May a hotel clerk give valid consent to search a hotel room rented to a criminal suspect?

HOLDING
No. A hotel guest is entitled to the constitutional protection against unreasonable searches and seizures. The hotel clerk had no authority to permit the room search and the police had no basis to believe that petitioner had authorized the clerk to permit the search.

RATIONALE
"It is true that when a person engages a hotel room he undoubtedly gives 'implied or express permission' to 'such persons as maids, janitors or repairmen' to enter his room 'in the performance of their duties.' But the conduct of the night clerk and the police in the present case was of an entirely different order."

CASE EXCERPT
"It is important to bear in mind that it was the petitioner's constitutional right which was at stake here, and not the night clerk's nor the hotel's. It was a right, therefore, which only the petitioner could waive by word or deed, either directly or through an agent. It is true that the night clerk clearly and unambiguously

STONER v. CALIFORNIA *(cont.)*

consented to the search. But there is nothing in the record to indicate that the police had any basis whatsoever to believe that the night clerk had been authorized by the petitioner to permit the police to search the petitioner's room."

CASE SIGNIFICANCE

This case made it clear that a hotel guest has a reasonable expectation of privacy in his or her hotel room, even though he or she does not own it and hotel staff may enter it for purposes related to the operation of the hotel. Consent to allow hotel staff into the room does not eliminate the reasonable expectation of privacy.

BUMPER v. NORTH CAROLINA
391 U.S. 543 (1968)

FACTS

Four police officers appeared at Bumper's home, announced that they had a search warrant, and were told by the owner, Bumper's grandmother, to "go ahead." In fact, the officers did not have a search warrant. The search turned up evidence implicating Bumper in a rape. At the hearing on a motion to suppress, which was denied, the prosecutor stated that he did not rely on a warrant to justify the search, but on the consent of the grandmother. Bumper was convicted, and the state supreme court affirmed. The U.S. Supreme Court granted certiorari.

ISSUE

Is consent obtained by police officers who lie about the existence of a search warrant valid?

HOLDING

No. A search cannot be justified as lawful on the basis of consent when that "consent" has been given only after the official conducting the search has asserted that he possesses a warrant; such consent is not voluntary, and consent must be voluntary.

RATIONALE

"When a prosecutor seeks to rely upon consent to justify the lawfulness of a search, he has the burden of proving that the consent was, in fact, freely and voluntarily given. This burden cannot be discharged by showing no more than acquiescence to a claim of lawful authority. A search conducted in reliance upon a

warrant cannot later be justified on the basis of consent if it turns out that the warrant was invalid. The result can be no different when it turns out that the State does not even attempt to rely upon the validity of the warrant, or fails to show that there was, in fact, any warrant at all."

CASE EXCERPT

"When a law enforcement officer claims authority to search a home under a warrant, he announces in effect that the occupant has no right to resist the search. The situation is instinct with coercion—albeit colorably lawful coercion. Where there is coercion there cannot be consent."

CASE SIGNIFICANCE

This case established the requirement that police officers not mislead suspects about the existence of a search warrant in an attempt to gain consent to search. Consent obtained in such a fashion is deemed involuntary, and thus invalid. Left unanswered by the Supreme Court in this case was whether consent obtained by an officer who merely threatens to obtain a search warrant is valid. Lower courts are split on this issue.

SCHNECKLOTH v. BUSTAMONTE
412 U.S. 218 (1973)

FACTS

A police officer on routine patrol stopped a car with Bustamonte and five others in it for having a headlight and license plate light out. During a consent search, evidence was discovered that was used to convict Bustamonte of unlawfully possessing a check. In a habeas corpus proceeding, the court of appeals, reversing the district court, held that the prosecution had failed to prove that consent to the search had been made with the understanding that it could freely be withheld. The U.S. Supreme Court granted certiorari.

ISSUE

Must the state prove that the individual giving consent to a search knows he or she has the right to withhold consent?

HOLDING

No. When the subject of a search is not in custody and the state would justify a search on the basis of his consent, the Fourth and Fourteenth Amendments require that it demonstrate that the consent was in fact voluntary; voluntariness is to be determined from the totality of the surrounding circumstances. While knowledge of a right to refuse consent is a factor to be taken into account, the state need not prove that whoever gave permission to search knew that he or she had a right to withhold his or her consent.

RATIONALE

"In determining whether a defendant's will was overborne in a particular case, the Court has assessed the totality of all the surrounding circumstances—both the characteristics of the accused and the details of the interrogation. Some of the factors taken into account have included the youth of the accused, his lack of education, or his low intelligence, the lack of any advice to the accused of his constitutional rights, the length of detention, the repeated and prolonged nature of the questioning, and the use of physical punishment such as the deprivation of food or sleep. The Court determined the factual circumstances surrounding the confession, assessed the psychological impact on the accused, and evaluated the legal significance of how the accused reacted.

"The significant fact of all of the Court's past decisions on this subject is that none of them turned on the presence or absence of a single controlling criterion; each reflected a careful scrutiny of all the surrounding circumstances. In none of them did the Court rule that the Due Process Clause required the prosecution to prove as part of its initial burden that the defendant knew he had a right to refuse to answer the questions that were put. While the state of the accused's mind, and the failure of the police to advise the accused of his rights, were certainly factors to be evaluated in assessing the 'voluntariness' of an accused's responses, they were not in and of themselves determinative."

CASE EXCERPT

"There is a vast difference between those rights that protect a fair criminal trial and the rights guaranteed under the Fourth Amendment. Nothing, either in the purposes behind requiring a 'knowing' and 'intelligent' waiver of trial rights, or in the practical application of such a requirement suggests that it ought to be extended to the constitutional guarantee against unreasonable searches and seizures."

CASE SIGNIFICANCE

This case clarified the requirements for obtaining consent to conduct a search. Where the Supreme Court requires, under *Miranda v. Arizona,* 384 U.S. 436 (1966) that a suspect in custody be advised of his right to remain silent before the police may lawfully interrogate him, there is no such requirement that police advise a suspect of his right to refuse consent to a search when seeking such consent. Thus the Court has created a hierarchy of protection of individual rights—a suspect must be informed of his Fifth and Sixth Amendment rights before police may proceed with a custodial interrogation, but a suspect need not be informed of his Fourth Amendment rights before police seek a waiver of those rights.

FLORIDA v. ROYER

460 U.S. 491 (1983)

FACTS

After purchasing a one-way airline ticket to New York City at Miami International Airport under an assumed name and checking his two suitcases bearing identification tags with the same assumed name, Royer went to the concourse leading to the airline boarding area. He was approached by two detectives, who previously had observed him and believed that his characteristics fit a "drug-courier profile." Upon request, but without oral consent, Royer produced his airline ticket and driver's license, which carried his correct name. When the detectives asked about the discrepancy in names, Royer explained that a friend had made the ticket reservation in the assumed name. The detectives then informed Royer that they were narcotics investigators and that they had reason to suspect him of transporting narcotics, and, without returning his airline ticket or driver's license, asked him to accompany them to a small room adjacent to the concourse. Without Royer's consent, one of the detectives retrieved his luggage from the airline and brought it to the room. While he did not respond orally to the detectives' request that he consent to a search of the luggage, Royer produced a key and unlocked one of the suitcases, in which marijuana was found. When Royer said he did not know the combination to the lock on the second suitcase but did not object to its being opened, the officers pried it open and found more marijuana. Royer was then arrested. Following the Florida trial court's denial of his pretrial motion

FLORIDA v. ROYER *(cont.)*

to suppress the evidence obtained in the search of the suitcases, Royer was convicted of felony possession of marijuana. The Florida Court of Appeals reversed, holding that Royer had been involuntarily confined without probable cause, that at the time his consent to search was obtained, the involuntary detention had exceeded the limited restraint permitted by *Terry v. Ohio,* and that such consent was therefore invalid because tainted by the unlawful confinement. The U.S. Supreme Court granted certiorari.

ISSUE

Is consent to search valid if it is obtained by the police during a seizure that was not based on probable cause?

HOLDING

No. Royer's consent was not valid because it was tainted by the illegal seizure.

RATIONALE

"Detective Johnson testified at the suppression hearing and the Florida District Court of Appeal held that there was no probable cause to arrest until Royer's bags were opened. Clearly, then, probable cause to arrest Royer did not exist at the time he consented to the search of his luggage. The facts are that a nervous young man with two American Tourister bags paid cash for an airline ticket to a 'target city.' These facts led to inquiry, which in turn revealed that the ticket had been bought under an assumed name. The proffered explanation did not satisfy the officers. We cannot agree with the state that every nervous young man paying cash for a ticket to New York City under an assumed name and carrying two heavy American Tourister bags may be arrested and held to answer for a serious felony charge. Because we affirm the Florida District Court of Appeals' conclusion that Royer was being illegally detained when he consented to the search of his luggage, we agree that the consent was tainted by the illegality and was ineffective to justify the search. The judgment of the Florida District Court of Appeal is accordingly affirmed."

CASE EXCERPT

"Probable cause to arrest Royer did not exist at the time he consented to the search of his luggage. The facts are that a nervous young man with two American Tourister bags paid cash for an airline ticket to a 'target city.'

These facts led to inquiry, which in turn revealed that the ticket had been bought under an assumed name. The proffered explanation did not satisfy the officers. We cannot agree with the State, if this is its position, that every nervous young man paying cash for a ticket to New York City under an assumed name and carrying two heavy American Tourister bags may be arrested and held to answer for a serious felony charge."

CASE SIGNIFICANCE

This case stands for the proposition that consent obtained by the police during an illegal seizure is not valid. This means the police must make sure that they do not exceed their authority to detain a suspect before seeking consent. Once a seizure is deemed to have occurred, the full protections of the Fourth Amendment apply.

ILLINOIS v. RODRIGUEZ
497 U.S. 177 (1990)

FACTS

Rodriguez was arrested in his apartment and charged with possession of illegal drugs, which the police had observed in plain view and seized. The officers did not have an arrest or search warrant, but gained entry to the apartment with the assistance of Gail Fischer, who represented that the apartment was "ours" and that she had clothes and furniture there, unlocked the door with her key, and gave the officers permission to enter. The trial court granted Rodriguez's motion to suppress the seized evidence, holding that at the time Fischer consented to the entry she did not have common authority because she had moved out of the apartment. The Appellate Court of Illinois affirmed, and the U.S. Supreme Court granted certiorari.

ISSUE

May the police enter without a warrant based upon the consent of a third party whom the police, at the time of entry, believe to possess common authority over the premises, but who in fact does not?

HOLDING

Yes. A warrantless entry is valid when based upon the consent of a third party whom the police, at the time of the entry, reasonably believe to possess common authority over the premises, but who in fact does not.

RATIONALE

"What Rodriguez is assured by the Fourth Amendment is not that no government search of his house will occur unless he consents; but that no such search will occur that is unreasonable. As with the many other factual determinations that must regularly be made by government agents in the Fourth Amendment context, the reasonableness of a police determination of consent to enter must be judged not by whether the police were correct in their assessment, but by the objective standard of whether the facts available at the moment would warrant a person of reasonable caution in the belief that the consenting party had authority over the premises. If not, then warrantless entry without further inquiry is unlawful unless authority actually exists. But if so, the search is valid."

CASE EXCERPT

"As *Stoner* demonstrates, what we hold today does not suggest that law enforcement officers may always accept a person's invitation to enter premises. Even when the invitation is accompanied by an explicit assertion that the person lives there, the surrounding circumstances could conceivably be such that a reasonable person would doubt its truth and not act upon it without further inquiry. As with other factual determinations bearing upon search and seizure, determination of consent to enter must 'be judged against an objective standard: would the facts available to the officer at the moment . . . "warrant a man of reasonable caution in the belief" ' that the consenting party had authority over the premises? If not, then warrantless entry without further inquiry is unlawful unless authority actually exists. But if so, the search is valid."

CASE SIGNIFICANCE

This case stands for the proposition that police may enter a building based on the consent of a person who lives there or has the authority to exclude others. The police need not ask if the person in fact has such authority; rather, they may make that assumption based on their observation of the situation. So long as the conclusion is reasonable, the consent will be upheld by the courts. This is known as the "apparent authority" rule. It means that at times police may be better off not asking if the person giving consent to a search has the authority to give such consent.

FLORIDA v. JIMENO

500 U.S. 248 (1991)

FACTS

Having stopped Jimeno's car for a traffic infraction, Officer Trujillo, who had been following the car after overhearing Jimeno arranging what appeared to be a drug transaction, declared that he had reason to believe that Jimeno was carrying narcotics in the car, and asked permission to search it. Jimeno consented, and Trujillo found cocaine inside a folded paper bag on the car's floorboard. Jimeno was charged with possession with intent to distribute cocaine in violation of Florida law, but the state trial court granted his motion to suppress the cocaine on the ground that his consent to search the car did not carry with it specific consent to open the bag and examine its contents. The Florida District Court of Appeals and Florida Supreme Court affirmed, and the U.S. Supreme Court granted certiorari.

ISSUE

Does consent to search a car include consent to search closed containers located within a car?

HOLDING

Yes. A criminal suspect's Fourth Amendment right to be free from unreasonable searches is not violated when, after he gives police permission to search his car, they open a closed container found within the car that might reasonably hold the object of the search.

RATIONALE

"The Amendment is satisfied when, under the circumstances, it is objectively reasonable for the police to believe that the scope of the suspect's consent permitted them to open the particular container. Here, the authorization to search extended beyond the car's interior surfaces to the bag, since Jimeno did not place any explicit limitation on the scope of the search, and was aware that Trujillo would be looking for narcotics in the car, and since a reasonable person may be expected to know that narcotics are generally carried in some form of container. There is no basis for adding to the Fourth Amendment's basic test of objective reasonableness a requirement that, if police wish to search closed containers within a car, they must separately request permission to search each container."

FLORIDA v. JIMENO *(cont.)*

CASE EXCERPT

"The scope of a search is generally defined by its expressed object. In this case, the terms of the search's authorization were simple. Respondent granted Officer Trujillo permission to search his car, and did not place any explicit limitation on the scope of the search. Trujillo had informed respondent that he believed respondent was carrying narcotics, and that he would be looking for narcotics in the car. We think that it was objectively reasonable for the police to conclude that the general consent to search respondent's car included consent to search containers within that car which might bear drugs. A reasonable person may be expected to know that narcotics are generally carried in some form of a container."

CASE SIGNIFICANCE

This case clarified the scope of consent to search an automobile. Prior Supreme Court cases were in conflict whether such consent extended to containers within the car. One case held that it did, while another case held that the police could seize, but not search, containers within the car. This case made it clear that consent to search a car extends to all containers within the car.

UNITED STATES v. DRAYTON ET AL.

536 U.S. 194 (2002)

FACTS

Drayton and a friend traveling together on a bus in Florida were approached during a bus sweep and asked for consent to search their luggage for drugs or weapons. Finding nothing in their carry-on baggage, the officer then asked the men for consent to search their persons. A pat down of the first subject (Brown) revealed packages of drugs taped to both thighs underneath his clothing. A consensual pat down of the second subject (Drayton) revealed the same. Both men were arrested and charged with conspiracy to distribute cocaine. At trial in federal district court, Drayton moved to suppress the evidence on grounds of coercive police conduct. Finding none, the district court denied the motion, whereupon Drayton was convicted. The Eleventh Circuit Court of Appeals reversed and remanded with instructions to grant the motion to suppress, and the U.S. Supreme Court granted certiorari.

ISSUE

May the police randomly approach individuals and ask for consent to search their luggage (or personal belongings, person, etc.) absent any indication that criminal activity is afoot?

HOLDING

Yes. The police are authorized to approach individuals, even when they have no basis for suspecting that criminal activity is afoot, and ask for consent to search their luggage (or personal belongings, person, etc.) so long as compliance is not induced by coercive means.

RATIONALE

The Court has long held that the police do not violate the Fourth Amendment by simply approaching an individual and asking questions even when there is no evidence that criminal activity is afoot. If, however, an individual refuses to speak with the police he or she must be allowed to go on his or her way unfettered. Furthermore, refusal to engage the police in conversation or consent to a search cannot be used as a basis for detention. Finally, officers are prohibited from using coercive or intimidating tactics in order to gain consent for a search. These principles, traceable to the Court's earlier ruling in the similar case of *Florida v. Bostick* (1991), are again reinforced by this decision. Where the individual is free to leave and go about his or her business, no seizure has occurred under the Fourth Amendment. Having determined that respondents in the present case were not coerced but, instead, consented freely to the search at issue, no Fourth Amendment violation was deemed to have occurred.

CASE EXCERPT

"In a society based on law, the concept of agreement and consent should be given a weight and dignity of its own. Police officers act in full accord with the law when they ask citizens for consent. It reinforces the rule of law for the citizen to advise the police of his or her wishes and for the police to act in reliance on that understanding. When this exchange takes place, it dispels inferences of coercion."

CASE SIGNIFICANCE

The decision in this case reaffirmed the Court's earlier ruling in *Florida v. Bostick*. Both cases authorized the police to approach individuals in public and not only ask questions, but also ask them for consent to search even in situations where there is no evidence that criminal activity is under way. If the individual refuses to talk and the officer lacks reasonable suspicion to believe that something is amiss, he or she must be allowed to leave unfettered. The fact that an individual refuses to answer an officer's otherwise groundless questions or refuses to give consent for a search cannot be used as a basis for detention. In other words, just because someone refuses to talk to the police does not automatically justify a detention of that individual. In reality, it is not at all difficult for an officer to develop reasonable suspicion that an individual who refuses to answer questions or consent to a search may actually be trying to conceal involvement in some form of unlawful activity. Once the officer has developed reasonable suspicion to believe that criminal activity is afoot, he or she has a legally justifiable basis to detain the individual.

GEORGIA v. RANDOLPH
547 U.S. 103 (2006)

FACTS
Randolph and his wife separated in 2001 and the wife moved out of the home, taking her son to live with her parents in Canada. A few months after the separation, the wife returned to the home and a domestic disturbance took place. Randolph took the child to a neighbor's house. The police arrived and were given conflicting versions of the events leading up to the disturbance, with each spouse accusing the other of illegal drug use. Mrs. Randolph advised police that evidence of drug use was inside the home. When the officers asked Randolph if they could search the house, he refused. Mrs. Randolph, however, consented and led the officer to Randolph's bedroom, where a drinking straw with a white powdery substance (likely cocaine) was found. The officer left the house and called the District Attorney, who advised the officer to stop the search and call in for a warrant. Upon the officer's return to the home, Mrs. Randolph withdrew her consent. The officers took the straw and the Randolphs to the police station, obtained a search warrant, and returned to the home, where they found additional evidence of drug use. Scott Randolph was charged with possession of cocaine. He moved to suppress the evidence, challenging his wife's consent to the search of the bedroom.

ISSUE
As co-occupants of the residence, was the consent of Mrs. Randolph valid after Mr. Randolph refused?

HOLDING
No. When a physically present inhabitant gives express refusal to a police search of his home, the consent of another occupant is invalid unless there are exigent circumstances.

RATIONALE
In previous cases, the court found valid consent in circumstances where an individual is present at a dwelling and any reasonable person would believe he or she lived at the residence—for example, a woman answers the door with a baby on her hip. However, in this case the court addresses the issue of an officer entering a home on consent of one occupant that is immediately challenged by another occupant at the scene.

The Court held that when there are people living in the same residence who disagree over "common quarters," then it is better to resolve the conflict with a "voluntary accommodation" but not one party appealing to the authorities. "Unless the people living together fall within some recognized hierarchy, like a household of parent and child or barracks housing military personnel of different grades, there is no societal understanding of superior and inferior." When an officer searches the home based on one co-tenant's consent, this cannot be considered "reasonable," which is a requirement under the Fourth Amendment.

CASE EXCERPT
"Disputed permission is thus no match for this central value of the Fourth Amendment, and the State's other countervailing claims do not add up to outweigh it. Yes, we recognize the consenting tenant's interest as a citizen in bringing criminal activity to light. And we understand a co-tenant's legitimate self-interest in siding with the police to deflect suspicion raised by sharing quarters with a criminal."

CASE SIGNIFICANCE
This case is significant because it is the first time the Supreme Court addressed the issue of a disagreement between co-tenants over the consent to search a home. By focusing on the reasonableness aspect of the inquiry, the Court determined that both individuals must give valid consent.

DISCUSSION QUESTIONS

1. What is your opinion of consent searches? Who do they favor, suspects or law enforcement officials?

2. The police are not required to advise people of their right to refuse consent. Do you agree with this? Why or why not?

3. Should parents be allowed to give consent to have police search the rooms of their children? What if the children are over eighteen and pay rent?

4. Should a person who consents to a search be able to define the scope of the consent given? If so, what possible problems could this pose?

5. If the police confront a person in an airport and ask consent to search the person's bag, and the person refuses, what is the likely consequence of this action?

6. How does the State establish that a consent to search was given voluntarily?

7. Should third parties be able to consent to the search of the property of another? Why or why not?

8. Discuss the concept of apparent authority.

9. Should probable cause be required even when consent is obtained?

10. Should one co-occupant's refusal to consent be a barrier to obtaining consent from the other co-occupant?

CHAPTER ELEVEN

PLAIN VIEW SEARCHES

TEXAS v. BROWN, *460 U.S. 730 (1983)*

ARIZONA v. HICKS, *480 U.S. 321 (1987)*

HORTON v. CALIFORNIA, *496 U.S. 128 (1990)*

INTRODUCTION

Untrained observers frequently suggest that "plain view" applies in situations where evidence can be seen without having to "search" for it. While this may be a *literal* interpretation of what it means for something to be in plain view, it is not the interpretation the courts use. Plain view has a very specific meaning in criminal procedure, and the doctrine applies in only certain situations.

The plain view doctrine first emerged in the Supreme Court's decision in *Coolidge v. New Hampshire,* 403 U.S. 443 (1971). The issue in *Coolidge* was whether evidence seized during a search of cars belonging to Coolidge was admissible. The police had a warrant to search the cars, but it was later deemed invalid, so the state argued that the evidence should still be admissible because the cars were in "plain view" from a public street and from the house in which Coolidge was arrested. The Court did not buy this argument, pointing out that just because the police could *see* the cars from where they were was not enough to permit seizure of the evidence in question. However, the Court did point out that had the police been *in* an area such as a car and house, evidence that is "immediately apparent as such" and is discovered "inadvertently" would be admissible. In other words, part of the reason the evidence was not admissible in *Coolidge* was that the police officers were not lawfully "in" the cars when the evidence was seized.

To summarize, the Court decided in *Coolidge* that a plain view *seizure* is authorized when (1) the police are lawfully *in* the area where the evidence is located;

(2) the items are "immediately apparent" as subject to seizure; and (3) the discovery of the evidence is "inadvertent." The first prong of the *Coolidge* ruling—the lawful access prong—has remained relatively stable over time. The second and third prongs, however, have undergone significant interpretation in recent years. We now consider each prong separately.

First, for the plain view doctrine to apply, the police must have lawful access to the object to be seized. Consider what the Supreme Court had to say in *Coolidge*: "[P]lain view *alone* is never enough to justify the warrantless seizure of evidence. This is simply a corollary of the familiar principle...that no amount of probable cause can justify a warrantless search or seizure absent 'exigent circumstances.' Incontrovertible testimony of the senses that an incriminating object is on premises belonging to a criminal suspect may establish the fullest possible measure of probable cause. But even where the object is contraband, this Court has repeatedly stated and enforced the basic rule that the police may not enter and make a warrantless seizure."

This excerpt from the Court's opinion in *Coolidge* reinforces the requirement that just because the police may *see* contraband does not necessarily mean they can seize it. If, for example, evidence is seen laying in a vacant lot or other public place, it may be seized. In such a situation, a search has not occurred. However, evidence that may be viewed from a public place but is in fact on private property cannot be seized unless a warrant is obtained or exigent circumstances are present. So, if a police officer on foot patrol observes a marijuana plant in the window of a private citizen, he or she may not enter the premises and seize the plant, even though such observation establishes "the fullest possible measure of probable cause."

What is meant by *lawful vantage point*? There are four specific situations where police officers can be found in a lawful vantage point for purposes of the plain view doctrine. The first is during a warranted search. For example, if an officer comes upon an article during the execution of a valid search warrant, the plain view doctrine may apply, subject to further restrictions described below. Second, officers are in a lawful vantage point during a valid arrest. This includes warrantless arrests in public, warrantless arrests based on exigent circumstances, and arrests with warrants. Third, when a warrantless search is conducted, the police officer is in a lawful vantage point, assuming of course that the warrantless search is based on probable cause. Finally, as illustrated in the previous paragraph, officers are always in a lawful vantage point during "nonsearches."

In addition to the requirement that the police have lawful access to an object for the plain view doctrine to apply, it must also be "immediately apparent" that the object is subject to seizure. "Immediately apparent" means that the officer has probable cause to seize the object. This was the decision reached in *Arizona v. Hicks*. In that case, the police entered the defendant's apartment without a warrant because a bullet had been fired through his floor into an apartment below, injuring a person. The warrantless entry was based on the exigency of looking for the shooter, for other potential victims, and for the weapon used in the incident. Once inside the apartment, the officer observed new stereo equipment that seemed out of place given the surroundings. The officer suspected the stereo equipment was stolen but did not have probable cause to believe as such, so he picked up a turntable so that he could obtain its serial number. He then called in the information and confirmed that it was stolen. The Court held that this warrantless action did not satisfy the plain view doctrine: it was not immediately apparent to the officer that the stereo equipment was stolen.

Keep in mind that probable cause to seize and "immediately apparent" are one and the same. Officers do not need to be absolutely certain that the object is subject to seizure for the plain view doctrine to apply. This was the decision reached in *Texas v. Brown*. In that case, Brown was stopped late at night at a routine driver's license checkpoint. Brown opened the glove box to look for his license, at which point an opaque balloon, knotted at the opening, fell from his hand onto the floor of the passenger side of the vehicle. The officer observed what he perceived to be drug paraphernalia in the glove compartment and ultimately seized the balloon and its contents. The balloon was later proved to contain heroin, and Brown was convicted of narcotics offenses. The Texas Court of Criminal Appeals reversed Brown's conviction, pointing that the plain view doctrine did not apply because the officer did not *know* incriminatory evidence was before him when he seized the balloon. A unanimous Supreme Court reversed, stating: "The fact that [the officer] could not see through the opaque fabric of the balloon is all but irrelevant; the distinctive character of the balloon itself spoke volumes as to its contents—particularly to the trained eye of the officer."

The role of inadvertency in the plain view determination has received considerable attention. The original position of the Supreme Court in *Coolidge v. New Hampshire* 403 U.S. 443 (1971) was that objects seized under the plain view doctrine must not have been "anticipated" by the police. For example, assume that a police officer obtains a warrant to search a suspect's home for the proceeds from a robbery. Assume further that the officer *expects* to find guns in the house, but does not state in the warrant that guns will be sought. If, during the search, the officer finds guns, under the Supreme Court's old ruling, the guns would not be admissible because the officers expected to find them. This restriction on the plain view doctrine came to be known as the *inadvertency requirement*. The rationale for this restriction was that an officer who anticipates discovering evidence of a crime should seek prior judicial authorization (i.e., a warrant). Further, the Fourth Amendment's particularity requirement would be compromised if "general" searches were permitted.

In *Horton v. California*, the Court declared that inadvertency, although a "characteristic of most legitimate 'plain view' seizures, . . . is not a necessary condition" of the doctrine. The Court offered two reasons for abandoning the inadvertency requirement imposed in *Coolidge*. First, according to *Horton*, as long as a warrant particularly describes the places to be searched and the objects to be seized, the officer cannot expand the area of the search once the evidence is found. In other words, it is unlikely that once officers find the evidence listed in the warrant they will go on "fishing expeditions," looking for evidence not listed in the warrant. According to the Court, the particularity requirement itself ensures that people's privacy is protected.

Second, the Court noted that "[E]venhanded law enforcement is best achieved by the application of objective standards of conduct, rather than standards that depend upon the subjective state of mind of the officer." An inadvertency requirement would force the courts to dwell on police officers' subjective motivations, which would be both time consuming and distracting. The Court went on to note that "[t]he fact that an officer is interested in an item of evidence and fully expects to find it in the course of a search should not invalidate its seizure if the search is confined in area and duration by the terms of the warrant or a valid exception to the warrant requirement."

TEXAS v. BROWN
460 U.S. 730 (1983)

FACTS
A Fort Worth, Texas, police officer stopped Brown's automobile at night at a routine driver's license checkpoint. While asking Brown for his license, the police officer shined his flashlight into the car and saw an opaque, green balloon, knotted near the tip, fall from Brown's hand to the seat beside him. Based on his experience, the officer was aware that narcotics were frequently packaged in such balloons, and while Brown was looking in the glove compartment for his license, the officer shifted his position to obtain a better view of the interior of the automobile. He then noticed small plastic vials, loose white powder, and an open bag of balloons in the glove compartment. After Brown said that he had no driver's license in his possession and complied with the officer's request to get out of the car, the officer picked up the green balloon, which contained a powdery substance within its tied-off portion. Brown was then advised that he was under arrest, an on-the-scene inventory search of the car was conducted, and other items were seized. At a suppression hearing, a police department chemist testified that heroin was contained in the balloon seized by the officer and that narcotics frequently were so packaged. Brown was subsequently convicted. The Texas Court of Criminal Appeals reversed, holding that the evidence should have been suppressed. Rejecting the state's contention that the so-called "plain view" doctrine justified the seizure, the court concluded that

for that doctrine to apply, not only must the officer be legitimately in a position to view the object, but also it must be "immediately apparent" to the police that they have evidence before them. The U.S. Supreme Court then granted certiorari.

ISSUE
For the plain view exception to apply, must it be "immediately apparent" that the items seen by the officer are contraband?

HOLDING
No. there is no such requirement for the plain view exception.

RATIONALE
The plain view doctrine provides grounds for a warrantless seizure of a suspicious item when the officer's access to the item has some prior justification under the Fourth Amendment. This rule merely reflects an application of the Fourth Amendment's central requirement of reasonableness to the law governing seizures of property. Here, the officer's initial stop of Brown's vehicle was valid, and his actions in shining his flashlight into the car and changing his position to see what was inside did not violate any Fourth Amendment rights. The "immediately apparent" language in *Coolidge* does not establish a requirement that a police officer "know" that certain items are contraband or evidence of a crime. "The seizure of property in plain view involves no invasion of privacy and is presumptively reasonable, assuming that there is probable cause to associate the property with criminal activity." Probable cause is a flexible, commonsense standard, merely requiring that the facts available to the officer would warrant a man of reasonable caution to believe that certain items may be contraband or stolen property or useful as evidence of a crime; it does not demand any showing that such a belief be correct or more likely true than false. In view of the police officer's testimony here, corroborated by that of the police department chemist, as to the common use of balloons in packaging narcotics, the officer had probable cause to believe that the balloon contained an illicit substance. Moreover, the requirement of the plain view doctrine under *Coolidge* that the officer must discover incriminating evidence "inadvertently," without knowing in advance the location of the particular evidence and intending to seize it by use of the doctrine as a pretext, was no bar to the seizure here.

TEXAS v. BROWN *(cont.)*
CASE EXCERPT
"The fact that Maples changed [his] position and bent down at an angle so [he] could see what was inside Brown's car is irrelevant to Fourth Amendment analysis. The general public could peer into the interior of Brown's automobile from any number of angles; there is no reason Maples should be precluded from observing as an officer what would be entirely visible to him as a private citizen. There is no legitimate expectation of privacy shielding that portion of the interior of an automobile which may be viewed from outside the vehicle by either inquisitive passersby or diligent police officers. In short, the conduct that enabled Maples to observe the interior of Brown's car and of his open glove compartment was not a search within the meaning of the Fourth Amendment."

CASE SIGNIFICANCE
This case clarifies the holding in *Coolidge v. New Hampshire,* in which the Supreme Court created the "plain view" exception to the search warrant requirement. There is no requirement that a police officer know with absolute certainty that an item he or she sees in plain view is contraband. In addition, officers may adjust their position and use items such as flashlights to improve their vision; so long as they are lawfully present, the plain view exception still applies.

ARIZONA v. HICKS
480 U.S. 321 (1987)

FACTS
A bullet fired through the floor of Hicks' apartment injured a man on the floor below. Police entered Hicks' apartment to search for the shooter, for other victims, and for weapons, and there seized three weapons and discovered a stocking-cap mask. While there, one of the policemen noticed two sets of expensive stereo components and, suspecting that they were stolen, read and recorded their serial numbers—moving some of them, including a turntable, to do so—and phoned in the numbers to headquarters. Upon learning that the turntable had been taken in an armed robbery, the officer seized it immediately. Hicks was subsequently indicted for the robbery, but the state trial court granted his motion to suppress the evidence that had been seized, and the Arizona Court of Appeals affirmed. Relying upon a statement in *Mincey v. Arizona* that a

warrantless search must be "strictly circumscribed by the exigencies which justify its initiation," the court of appeals held that the policeman's obtaining the serial numbers violated the Fourth Amendment because it was unrelated to the shooting, the exigent circumstance that justified the initial entry and search. Both state courts rejected the contention that the policeman's actions were justified under the "plain view" doctrine. The U.S. Supreme Court then granted certiorari.

ISSUE
Is a "plain view" search exempt from the requirement for probable cause?

HOLDING
No. The policeman's actions come within the purview of the Fourth Amendment. The mere recording of the serial numbers did not constitute a "seizure" since it did not meaningfully interfere with Hicks' possessory interest in either the numbers or the stereo equipment. However, the moving of the equipment was a "search" separate and apart from the search that was the lawful objective of entering the apartment.

RATIONALE
"The fact that the search uncovered nothing of great personal value to Hicks is irrelevant. The plain view doctrine does not render the search "reasonable" under the Fourth Amendment. The policeman's action directed to the stereo equipment was not *ipso facto* unreasonable simply because it was unrelated to the justification for entering the apartment. That lack of relationship always exists when the "plain view" doctrine applies. However, the search was invalid because the policeman had only a "reasonable suspicion" (i.e., less than probable cause to believe) that the stereo equipment was stolen. Probable cause is required to invoke the "plain view" doctrine as it applies to seizures...The policeman's action cannot be upheld on the ground that it was not a "full-blown search" but was only a "cursory inspection" that could be justified by reasonable suspicion instead of probable cause. A truly cursory inspection—one that involves merely looking at what is already exposed to view, without disturbing it—is not a "search" for Fourth Amendment purposes, and therefore does not even require reasonable suspicion. Merely inspecting those parts of the turntable that came into view during the latter search would not have constituted an independent search, because it would have produced no additional invasion of Hicks' privacy interest.

CASE EXCERPT

"Officer Nelson's moving of the equipment, however, did constitute a 'search' separate and apart from the search for the shooter, victims, and weapons that was the lawful objective of his entry into the apartment. Merely inspecting those parts of the turntable that came into view during the latter search would not have constituted an independent search, because it would have produced no additional invasion of respondent's privacy interest. But taking action, unrelated to the objectives of the authorized intrusion, which exposed to view concealed portions of the apartment or its contents, did produce a new invasion of respondent's privacy unjustified by the exigent circumstance that validated the entry."

CASE SIGNIFICANCE

This case made clear that the plain view doctrine does not allow police officers to seize, on less than probable cause, any item they happen to see that is in "plain view." In addition, the officers must have reason to believe the item is seizable—that it is contraband.

HORTON v. CALIFORNIA
496 U.S. 128 (1990)

FACTS

A California policeman determined that there was probable cause to search Horton's home for the proceeds of a robbery and the robbers' weapons. His search warrant affidavit referred to police reports that described both the weapons and the proceeds, but the warrant issued by the magistrate authorized only a search for the proceeds. Upon executing the warrant, the officer did not find the stolen property but did find the weapons in plain view and seized them. The trial court refused to suppress the seized evidence, and Horton was convicted of armed robbery. The California Court of Appeals affirmed. Since the officer had testified that while he was searching Horton's home for the stolen property he was also interested in finding other evidence connecting Horton to the robbery, the seized evidence was not discovered "inadvertently." However, in rejecting Horton's argument that *Coolidge v. New Hampshire* required suppression of that evidence, the court of appeals relied on a state supreme court decision holding that *Coolidge*'s discussion of the inadvertence limitation on the "plain view" doctrine was not binding because it was contained in a four-justice plurality opinion. The U.S. Supreme Court then granted certiorari.

ISSUE

Is inadvertence a requirement of the "plain view" doctrine?

HOLDING

No. The Fourth Amendment does not prohibit the warrantless seizure of evidence in plain view even though the discovery of the evidence was not inadvertent. Although inadvertence is a characteristic of most legitimate plain view seizures, it is not a necessary condition.

RATIONALE

"For a warrantless seizure of an object in plain view to be valid, two conditions must be satisfied in addition to the essential predicate that the officer did not violate the Fourth Amendment in arriving at the place from which the object could be plainly viewed. First, the object's incriminating character must be immediately apparent. Although the cars in *Coolidge* were obviously in plain view, their probative value remained uncertain until after their interiors were swept and examined microscopically. Second, the officer must have a lawful right of access to the object itself...evenhanded law enforcement is best achieved by applying objective standards of conduct, rather than standards that depend upon the officer's subjective state of mind. The fact that an officer is interested in an item and fully expects to find it should not invalidate its seizure if the search is confined in area and duration by a warrant's terms or by a valid exception to the warrant requirement. Second, the suggestion that the inadvertence requirement is necessary to prevent the police from conducting general searches, or from converting specific warrants into general warrants, is not persuasive because that interest is already served by the requirements that an unparticularized warrant not be issued and that a warrantless search be circumscribed by the exigencies which justify its initiation. Here, the search's scope was not enlarged by the warrant's omission of reference to the weapons; indeed, no search for the weapons could have taken place if the named items had been found or surrendered at the outset. The prohibition against general searches and warrants is based on privacy concerns, which are not implicated when an officer with a lawful right of access to an item in plain view seizes it without a warrant."

HORTON v. CALIFORNIA *(cont.)*

CASE EXCERPT

"The suggestion that the inadvertence requirement is necessary to prevent the police from conducting general searches, or from converting specific warrants into general warrants, is not persuasive because that interest is already served by the requirements that no warrant issue unless it particularly describes the place to be searched and the persons or things to be seized, by the exigencies which justify its initiation. Scrupulous adherence to these requirements serves the interests in limiting the area and duration of the search that the inadvertence requirement inadequately protects. Once those commands have been satisfied and the officer has a lawful right of access, however, no additional Fourth Amendment interest is furthered by requiring that the discovery of evidence be inadvertent."

CASE SIGNIFICANCE

This case made clear that there is no requirement that the discovery of evidence be inadvertent, or accidental, for the plain view doctrine to apply. Consequently, so long as a police officer is lawfully present, if he or she observes something that he or she knows is contraband, he or she may seize it.

DISCUSSION QUESTIONS

1. How is "plain view" used differently in the legal sense compared to everyday use?
2. The Supreme Court has dispensed with the inadvertency requirement with respect to plain view seizures. Do you agree with this decision?
3. Pursuant to the plain view doctrine, it must be immediately apparent to the police that an item is subject to seizure. Do you agree with this requirement? Why or why not?
4. Describe how the plain view doctrine might be used to the advantage of law enforcement officials.
5. Does the plain view doctrine favor suspects or the police? List several reasons for your answer.

CHAPTER TWELVE

OPEN FIELDS SEARCHES

OLIVER v. UNITED STATES, *466 U.S. 170 (1984)*

CALIFORNIA v. CIRAOLO, *476 U.S. 207 (1986)*

UNITED STATES v. DUNN, *480 U.S. 294 (1987)*

INTRODUCTION

The physical setting in which police activity takes place is also important in determining whether the Fourth Amendment applies. Clearly, the inside of a residence is protected by the Fourth Amendment, but what about the outside? If the outside is protected, how far beyond the residence can the strictures of the Fourth Amendment be expected to apply? In answer to these questions, courts refer to the term "curtilage." Curtilage has been defined by the Supreme Court as the "area to which extends the intimate activity associated with the sanctity of a man's home and the privacies of life." This definition should be contrasted with the definition of an "open field." An open field is any unoccupied or undeveloped real property falling outside the curtilage of a home (*Oliver v. United States*).

Open fields do not enjoy Fourth Amendment protection, but homes and curtilage do. Note, however, that open fields need not be "open" or "fields" to fall beyond the reach of the Fourth Amendment. If a barn located 50 yards from a house is not used for "intimate activities," it *can* be considered an open field, even though it is located on private property (see *United States v. Dunn*). This is because "Open fields do not provide the setting for those intimate activities that the [Fourth] Amendment is intended to shelter from government interference or surveillance" (*Oliver v. United States*).

In *Oliver,* the Court went on to observe that "there is no societal interest in protecting the privacy of those activities, such as the cultivation of crops, that occur in open fields. Moreover, as a practical matter, these lands usually are accessible to the public and the police in ways that a home, office or commercial structure would not be. It is not generally true that fences or ["No Trespassing"] signs effectively bar the public from viewing open fields in rural areas."

The courts consider four different factors when distinguishing between open fields and curtilage: (1) the proximity of the area to the house; (2) whether the area is included within fences or other enclosures surrounding the house; (3) the nature of the use to which the land/property is being put; and (4) the steps taken by the resident to protect the area from observation (*United States v. Dunn*). These four issues were considered by the Court in *United States v. Dunn.* In that case police entered the defendant's property without a warrant, climbed over several fences, and peered inside his barn. They eventually obtained a warrant to search the barn, but the Court ruled that their earlier activity was a search within the meaning of the Fourth Amendment.

A twist on the aforementioned scenarios occurs when the police perform so-called "flyovers"— that is, when they perform aerial surveillance from fixed-wing aircraft and/or helicopters. In *California v. Ciraolo,* the Supreme Court ruled that naked-eye observation of a fenced-in backyard from a height of 1,000 feet did not constitute a search. The logic offered by the Court was that in "an age where private and commercial flight in the public airways is routine, it is unreasonable for respondent to expect that his marijuana plants were constitutionally protected" from such observation.

Similarly, in *Florida v. Riley,* 488 U.S. 445 (1989), the Court held that the Fourth Amendment was not implicated when the police flew a helicopter at an altitude of 400 feet over the defendant's partially covered greenhouse, which was found to contain marijuana. "Riley no doubt intended and expected that his greenhouse would not be open to public inspection, and the precautions he took [including placing a wire fence around the greenhouse and a "Do Not Enter" sign] protected against ground-level observation," but the fact that any person could position himself or herself over the greenhouse in a helicopter was not enough to amount to a Fourth Amendment violation. The Court supported its position in this matter by noting that the helicopter's altitude was within legal parameters and Federal Aviation Administration guidelines.

OLIVER v. UNITED STATES
466 U.S. 170 (1984)

FACTS
Acting on reports that marijuana was being raised on Oliver's farm, narcotics agents of the Kentucky State Police went to the farm to investigate. Arriving at the farm, they drove past Oliver's house to a locked gate with a "No Trespassing" sign, but with a footpath around one side. The agents then walked around the gate and along the road and found a field of marijuana over a mile from Oliver's house. Oliver was arrested and indicted for manufacturing a controlled substance in violation of a federal statute. After a pretrial hearing, the district court suppressed evidence of the discovery of the marijuana field, applying *Katz v. United States,* 389 U.S. 347 (1967) and holding that petitioner had a reasonable expectation that the field would remain private and that it was not an "open" field that invited casual intrusion. The court of appeals reversed, holding that *Katz* had not impaired the vitality of the open fields doctrine of *Hester v. United States,* 265 U.S. 57 (1924) which permits police officers to enter and search a field without a warrant. The U.S. Supreme Court then granted certiorari.

ISSUE
Does the "open fields doctrine" apply when a property owner attempts to create a "reasonable expectation of privacy" by excluding others from the property?

HOLDING
Yes. The open fields doctrine should be applied in both cases to determine whether the discovery or seizure of the marijuana in question was valid. There is no expectation of privacy, despite the property owner's attempts to exclude the public.

RATIONALE
The open fields doctrine was founded upon the explicit language of the Fourth Amendment, whose special protection accorded to persons, houses, papers, and effects does not extend to the open fields. Open fields are not "effects" within the meaning of the Amendment, the term "effects" being less inclusive than "property" and not encompassing open fields. The government's intrusion upon open fields is not one of those "unreasonable searches" proscribed by the Amendment. Because open fields are accessible to the public and the police in ways that a home, office, or commercial structure would not be, and because fences or "No Trespassing" signs do not effectively bar the public from viewing open fields, the asserted expectation of privacy in open fields is not one that society recognizes as reasonable. Moreover, the common law, by implying that only the land immediately surrounding and associated with the home warrants the Fourth Amendment protections that attach to the home, conversely implies that no expectation of privacy legitimately attaches to open fields. Steps taken to protect privacy, such as planting the marijuana on secluded land and erecting fences and "No Trespassing" signs around the property, do not establish that expectations of privacy in an open field are legitimate in the sense required by the Fourth Amendment.

CASE EXCERPT
"Nor is the government's intrusion upon an open field a search in the constitutional sense because that intrusion is a trespass at common law. The existence of a property right is but one element in determining whether expectations of privacy are legitimate . . . Even a property interest in premises may not be sufficient to establish a legitimate expectation of privacy with respect to particular items located on the premises or activity conducted thereon. The common law may guide consideration of what areas are protected by the Fourth Amendment by defining areas whose invasion by others is wrongful. The law of trespass, however, forbids intrusions upon land that the Fourth Amendment would not proscribe. For trespass law extends to instances where the exercise of the right to exclude vindicates no legitimate privacy

interest. Thus, in the case of open fields, the general rights of property protected by the common law of trespass have little or no relevance to the applicability of the Fourth Amendment."

CASE SIGNIFICANCE

This case is important because it made clear that "open fields" are not protected by the Fourth Amendment, even under a "reasonable expectation of privacy" analysis. This gives police the authority to ignore fences and "No Trespassing" signs and seize evidence that may be used against a criminal suspect, even though the police violated criminal law in obtaining it.

CALIFORNIA v. CIRAOLO
476 U.S. 207 (1986)

FACTS

Santa Clara, California, police received an anonymous telephone tip that marijuana was growing in Ciraolo's backyard, which was enclosed by two fences and shielded from view at ground level. Officers who were trained in marijuana identification secured a private airplane, flew over Ciraolo's house at an altitude of 1,000 feet, and readily identified marijuana plants growing in the backyard. A search warrant was later obtained on the basis of one of the officer's naked-eye observations and an aerial photograph of the backyard. The search warrant was executed, and numerous marijuana plants were seized. After the trial court denied Ciraolo's motion to suppress the evidence of the search, he pled guilty to a charge of cultivation of marijuana. The California Supreme Court reversed on the ground that the warrantless aerial observation of Ciraolo's yard violated the Fourth Amendment, and the U.S. Supreme Court granted certiorari.

ISSUE

Does a warrantless aerial observation of the curtilage violate the Fourth Amendment?

HOLDING

No. The Fourth Amendment is not violated by the naked-eye aerial observation of areas within the curtilage.

RATIONALE

"The touchstone of Fourth Amendment analysis is whether a person has a constitutionally protected reasonable expectation of privacy, which involves the two inquiries of whether the individual manifested a subjective expectation of privacy in the object of the challenged search, and whether society is willing to recognize that expectation as reasonable. In pursuing the second inquiry, the test of legitimacy is not whether the individual chooses to conceal assertedly 'private activity,' but whether the government's intrusion infringes upon the personal and societal values protected by the Fourth Amendment. On the record here, Ciraolo's expectation of privacy from all observations of his backyard was unreasonable. That the backyard and its crop were within the 'curtilage' of Ciraolo's home did not itself bar all police observation. The mere fact that an individual has taken measures to restrict some views of his activities does not preclude an officer's observation from a public vantage point where he has a right to be and which renders the activities clearly visible. The police observations here took place within public navigable airspace, in a physically nonintrusive manner. The police were able to observe the plants readily discernible to the naked eye as marijuana, and it was irrelevant that the observation from the airplane was directed at identifying the plants and that the officers were trained to recognize marijuana. Any member of the public flying in this airspace who cared to glance down could have seen everything that the officers observed. The Fourth Amendment simply does not require police traveling in the public airways at 1,000 feet to obtain a warrant in order to observe what is visible to the naked eye."

CASE EXCERPT

"The mere fact that an individual has taken measures to restrict some views of his activities does not preclude an officer's observation from a public vantage point where he has a right to be and which renders the activities clearly visible."

CASE SIGNIFICANCE

This case limited the protection afforded by the curtilage. At common law, the curtilage was considered the grounds and buildings closely surrounding a dwelling. Other Supreme Court decisions have extended the protections afforded the home to the curtilage. If something is in the open fields, the Fourth Amendment simply does not apply. If an area is within the curtilage, the Fourth Amendment does apply. This case, however, limits such protection. So long as police make their observation of the curtilage from the air, and have a legal right to be in the airspace, no search warrant is required.

UNITED STATES v. DUNN

480 U.S. 294 (1987)

FACTS

Drug Enforcement Administration agents, having discovered that Carpenter had bought large quantities of chemicals and equipment used to make controlled substances, placed tracking "beepers" in some of the equipment and one of the chemical containers, which, when transported in Carpenter's truck, led the agents to Dunn's ranch. Aerial photographs of the ranch showed the truck backed up to a barn behind the ranch house. The ranch was completely encircled by a perimeter fence and contained several interior barbed wire fences, including one around the house approximately 50 yards from the barn, and a wooden fence enclosing the front of the barn, which had an open overhang and locked, waist-high gates. Without a search warrant, agents crossed the perimeter fence, several of the barbed wire fences, and the wooden fence in front of the barn. They were led there by the smell of chemicals. They did not enter the barn but stopped at the locked gate and shined a flashlight inside, observing what they took to be a drug laboratory. They then left the ranch but entered it twice the next day to confirm the laboratory's presence. They then obtained a search warrant and executed it, arresting Dunn and seizing chemicals and equipment, as well as bags of amphetamines they discovered in the house. After the district court denied Dunn's motion to suppress all evidence seized pursuant to the warrant, Dunn was convicted of conspiracy to manufacture controlled substances and related offenses. However, the court of appeals reversed, holding that the barn was within the residence's curtilage and therefore within the Fourth Amendment's protective ambit. The U.S. Supreme Court then granted certiorari.

ISSUE

Was the barn located 50 yards from the house and surrounded by a fence within the curtilage of the residence, and therefore protected by the Fourth Amendment?

HOLDING

No. The area near the barn was not within the curtilage of the house for Fourth Amendment purposes.

RATIONALE

Extent-of-curtilage questions should be resolved with particular reference to the following four factors, at least to the extent that they bear upon whether the area claimed to be curtilage is so intimately tied to the home itself that it should be placed under the home's "umbrella" of protection: (1) the proximity of the area to the home; (2) whether the area is within an enclosure surrounding the home; (3) the nature and uses to which the area is put; and (4) the steps taken by the resident to protect the area from observation by passersby. Applying the first factor to the instant case, the barn's substantial distance from the fence surrounding the house (50 yards) and from the house itself (60 yards) supports no inference that it should be treated as an adjunct of the house. Second, the barn did not lie within the fence surrounding the house, which plainly demarks the area that is part and parcel of the house, but stands out as a distinct and separate portion of the ranch. Third, it is especially significant that the officers possessed objective data indicating that the barn was not being used as part of Dunn's home, in that the aerial photographs showed that Carpenter's truck was backed up to the barn, apparently to unload its contents, which included the chemical container, and the officers detected strong chemical odors coming from, and heard a motor running in, the barn. Fourth, Dunn did little to protect the barn area from observation by those standing outside, the ranch's fences being of the type used to corral livestock, not to ensure privacy. Dunn's contention that, because the barn is essential to his business, he possessed an expectation of privacy in it and its contents independent from his home's curtilage, is without merit. Even assuming that the barn could not be entered lawfully without a warrant, Dunn's argument ignores the fact that, prior to obtaining the warrant, the officers never entered the barn but conducted their observations from the surrounding open fields after crossing over Dunn's ranch-style fences. The Court's prior decisions have established that the government's intrusion upon open fields is not an unreasonable search; that the erection of fences on an open field—at least of the type involved here—does not create a constitutionally protected privacy interest; that warrantless naked-eye observation of an area protected by the Fourth Amendment is not unconstitutional; and that shining a flashlight into a protected area, without probable cause to search the area, is permissible.

CASE EXCERPT

"Drawing upon the Court's own cases and the cumulative experience of the lower courts that have grappled with the task of defining the extent of a home's curtilage, we believe that curtilage questions should be resolved with particular reference to four factors: the proximity of the area claimed to be curtilage to the home, whether the area is included within an enclosure surrounding the home, the nature of the uses to which the area is put, and the steps taken by the resident to protect the area from observation by people passing by."

CASE SIGNIFICANCE

This case sets out the Court's definition of curtilage. This is important because if an item is within the curtilage, the Fourth Amendment applies and police officers are limited in their ability to conduct warrantless searches. If an item is determined to be outside the curtilage, then it is by definition considered within the "open fields," which are not covered by the protections of the Fourth Amendment. Police are not barred by the Constitution from conducting warrantless searches in the open fields.

DISCUSSION QUESTIONS

1. According to the Supreme Court, it is possible for someone to have an "open field" on his or her private property. Do you agree with this decision? Why or why not?
2. What steps must a property owner take to ensure that some part of his or her land falls within the curtilage of a home?
3. Clearly, there are no bright-line Supreme Court decisions concerning the definition of curtilage. Should there be?
4. The Supreme Court has permitted aerial surveillance of people's private property. Do you agree with this decision?
5. Do the Supreme Court's open fields decisions favor law enforcement or criminal suspects? Offer several reasons for your answer.

CHAPTER THIRTEEN

VEHICLE SEARCHES

INTRODUCTION

Although the Fourth Amendment generally requires the issuance of a warrant based upon probable cause before a search can be undertaken, there exist a number and variety of judicially created exceptions to this rule. One such exception is that pertaining to vehicle searches. This chapter outlines the principal Supreme Court cases that guide the authority of law enforcement officers to conduct warrantless vehicle searches where there exists probable cause to believe that a crime has been or is being committed. Because this line of cases forms a basis for many of today's drug trafficking arrests made on the nation's roadways, it is imperative that officers understand the constitutional limits of their authority in this continuously evolving area of the law.

The authority of law enforcement officers to undertake a warrantless roadside search of a motor vehicle dates back to the 1920s (*Carroll v. United States*), when Prohibition agents stopped two brothers and seized the alcohol they were bootlegging. On appeal, the Supreme Court ruled that the warrantless search was permissible based upon the agents' articulable belief that criminal activity was afoot. Furthermore, the Court recognized that if the agents had taken time to secure a warrant, the vehicle would have likely fled the scene before they could return. Thus was born the vehicle search exception to the Fourth Amendment's warrant requirement.

In the decades since this initial decision, the Supreme Court has greatly expanded the authority of officers to undertake warrantless vehicle searches so that they may now inspect an entire vehicle as well as any closed containers (purses, luggage, etc.) found therein so long as there exists articulable probable cause to believe that evidence of criminal activity will be discovered (e.g., *Wyoming v. Houghton*). However, this is not to suggest that police behavior has gone totally unchecked or unrestrained in this area of the law. Although it is true that the Supreme Court condoned the practice of pretextual traffic stops in the case of *Whren v. United States,* it has in other instances condemned police behavior such as the detention of motorists without probable cause. Combine these seemingly contradictory holdings with the dozen or so other landmark decisions in this area, and it becomes quickly apparent why this body of law is of such relevance to the daily activities of all law enforcement personnel.

In sum, the cases that follow outline the general authority of officers to conduct warrantless vehicle searches where there exists probable cause to believe that evidence of criminal activity will be discovered therein. While many cases serve to strengthen the crime-fighting ability of police, others stand as examples of officer behavior that border or fall beyond the boundaries of reasonableness and thereby violate the Fourth Amendment.

CARROLL v. UNITED STATES
267 U.S. 132 (1925)

FACTS
Prohibition agents engaged in routine patrol along the highways leading into and out of Detroit observed the "Carroll boys" en route to Grand Rapids. Based upon knowledge that the boys were bootleggers in Grand Rapids and, having been previously unable to catch them in the act of transporting then-illegal alcoholic beverages, the federal agents stopped the pair and conducted a search of the vehicle, resulting in discovery of the expected incriminating evidence. The evidence was admitted at trial and the pair was convicted of violating the National Prohibition Act. The U.S. Supreme Court granted certiorari to determine whether the roadside search of the vehicle violated the Fourth Amendment's warrant requirement.

ISSUE
Does the Fourth Amendment prohibit officers from conducting the warrantless roadside search of a vehicle where there exists probable cause to believe that evidence of criminal activity will be found therein?

HOLDING
No. Police are authorized to undertake the warrantless roadside search of a vehicle if there exists probable cause to believe that evidence of criminal activity contained therein will be lost or destroyed if time is taken to secure a warrant.

RATIONALE
To determine whether the roadside search of petitioner's vehicle violated the Fourth Amendment, the Court first traced the legislative history of the National Prohibition Act passed by Congress for purposes of enforcing the Eighteenth Amendment. Specific attention was given to the scope of search and seizure powers granted to officials responsible for enforcing the Act's statutory provisions. In a portion of the Act known as the Stanley Amendment, Congress provided for the punishment of officers who searched a private dwelling or building without a warrant or in a manner that was malicious and lacked probable cause. A strict reading of this section led the Justices to observe that Congress had not specifically prohibited agents from searching automobiles or vehicles of transportation without a warrant. Noting that the language of the Fourth Amendment did not prohibit all searches and seizures but only those of an "unreasonable" nature, the Court concluded that the Act was not inconsistent with these constitutional principles. Finally, and most importantly, the Court acknowledged the fact that if the agents had taken time to secure a warrant before undertaking their roadside search, there was a high likelihood that both the suspect vehicle and the evidence contained therein would have been lost or destroyed. Given the situation where there exists probable cause to believe that a car contains evidence of criminal activity, accentuated by the risk that evidence will be lost or destroyed if time is taken to secure judicial authorization, the Court excepted roadside vehicle searches from the Fourth Amendment's warrant requirement.

CASE EXCERPT
"The Fourth Amendment does not denounce all searches or seizures, but only such as are unreasonable...if the search and seizure without a warrant are made upon probable cause, that is, upon a belief, reasonably arising out of circumstances known to the seizing officer, that an automobile or other vehicle contains that which by law is subject to seizure and destruction, the search and seizure are valid. The Fourth Amendment is to be construed in the light of what was deemed an unreasonable search and seizure when it was adopted, and in a manner which will conserve public interests as well as the interests and rights of individual citizens."

CASE SIGNIFICANCE
This landmark case established the principle of law that officers are constitutionally authorized to undertake the warrantless roadside search of a vehicle where

CARROLL v. UNITED STATES (cont.)

there exists probable cause to believe that it contains evidence of criminal activity. This authority is premised upon the knowledge that if time is taken to secure judicial authorization before undertaking a search, the vehicle and its occupants as well as the evidence concealed therein will likely be "long gone" when the officers return. This case not only established what is known as the "automobile exception" to the Fourth Amendment's warrant requirement but, in doing so, serves as a fundamental basis for many of the ancillary roadside authorities exercised by law enforcement personnel today.

CHAMBERS v. MARONEY
399 U.S. 42 (1970)

FACTS

Chambers was arrested along with three other men when the vehicle they were traveling in was stopped by police following the reported armed robbery of a gas station. The vehicle was driven to a nearby police station, where a warrantless search revealed two revolvers, several "dumdum" bullets, money taken from the gas station attendant, and cards bearing the name of another station attendant who reported being robbed a week earlier. In a warrant authorizing the search of Chambers' home the following morning, officers seized additional "dumdum" bullets similar to those recovered from the vehicle. This evidence was introduced, but Chambers' first trial ended in a mistrial. Chambers was represented by a different court-appointed attorney and convicted of committing both robberies upon retrial. Chambers filed unsuccessful habeas corpus appeals in both the Pennsylvania Supreme Court and federal district court. The Court of Appeals for the Third Circuit affirmed, and the U.S. Supreme Court granted certiorari.

ISSUE

Does the Fourth Amendment prohibit the warrantless search of a vehicle that has been moved from the original location where it was stopped to a police station?

HOLDING

No. The warrantless search of a vehicle that has been transported to a police station does not violate the Fourth Amendment so long as officers have probable cause to believe that it contains evidence of criminal activity.

RATIONALE

In deciding this case, the Supreme Court noted that although the search in question was not justifiable under the "incident to a lawful arrest" exception, it was permissible on grounds of exigency. More specifically, the Court referred to its prior ruling in *Carroll v. United States,* which established the principle of law that a warrantless vehicle search may be undertaken where the police have probable cause to believe that evidence of criminal activity will be found therein but there exists no time to secure a warrant. With regard to the facts of the present case, the Court saw no constitutional difference between seizing the suspect vehicle and then awaiting judicial authorization as compared to immediately undertaking a warrantless search; in either instance, the outcome would have been the same. Thus, so long as there exists probable cause to believe that a vehicle contains evidence of criminal activity, the police are constitutionally authorized to undertake an immediate search of that vehicle even in situations where time permits them to obtain a warrant before doing so.

CASE EXCERPT

"On the facts before us, the blue station wagon could have been searched on the spot when it was stopped since there was probable cause to search and it was a fleeting target for a search. The probable-cause factor still obtained at the station house and so did the mobility of the car unless the Fourth Amendment permits a warrantless seizure of the car and the denial of its use to anyone until a warrant is secured."

CASE SIGNIFICANCE

This case is important insofar as it eliminated the requirement that officers delay a vehicle search where there exists time for them to first obtain a warrant. This decision clearly expanded the standard definition of an exigent circumstance previously relied upon by lower courts hearing similar cases. Prior to this decision, officers were required to first obtain a warrant unless there existed a risk that the vehicle might flee the scene or that evidence of a crime might somehow be destroyed. Today, this requirement no longer applies. Thus, if the police make an arrest and for some reason are unable to immediately undertake a search of the vehicle at the scene, they may indefinitely delay doing so where there exists probable cause to believe that evidence of criminal activity will be found therein. Of course, the safest method to ensure that any evidence seized during a vehicle search will be admitted at trial is to secure a properly authorized warrant where time permits.

DELAWARE v. PROUSE
440 U.S. 648 (1979)

FACTS
A Delaware patrol officer stopped a vehicle and, upon making his approach, observed within plain view a quantity of marijuana of the floorboard. Prouse, a passenger in the vehicle, was arrested and subsequently indicted for possession of a controlled substance. Prior to trial, Prouse entered a motion to suppress the evidence as the result of an unlawful traffic stop. The patrol officer testified at the hearing that he had not observed any violations or suspicious activity. Rather, he admitted to having made the stop solely for purposes of checking the driver's license and registration. The officer was not acting pursuant to any established standards, guidelines, or procedures promulgated by his agency or the state for purposes of conducting such spot checks. The trial court granted Prouse's motion to suppress on grounds that the stop and detention were capricious and thus violative of the Fourth Amendment. The Delaware Supreme Court affirmed, noting that a random stop of a motorist in the absence of specific articulable facts that justify the stop by indicating a reasonable suspicion that a violation of the law has occurred is constitutionally impermissible and violative of the Fourth and Fourteenth Amendments to the U.S. Constitution. The Supreme Court granted certiorari to resolve an apparent conflict between this decision, which had been embraced by five other jurisdictions, and a contrary determination adopted by six others that the Fourth Amendment does not prohibit such groundless stops.

ISSUE
Does the Fourth Amendment prohibit officers from stopping a vehicle being operated on a public roadway for purposes of checking the driver's license and vehicle registration in the absence of probable cause or some violation of law?

HOLDING
Yes. Except in situations where there is at least articulable and reasonable suspicion that a motorist is unlicensed or that a vehicle is unregistered, or that either the vehicle or occupants are subject to seizure for some violation of law, stopping a car solely for purposes of checking the driver's license and registration is unreasonable under the Fourth Amendment. In other words, the police may not make random traffic stops for purposes of checking a driver's license or vehicle registration in the absence of some violation of law.

RATIONALE
Both the Fourth and Fourteenth Amendments were triggered in this case due to the fact that stopping a vehicle and detaining its occupants, even if only for a brief period of time, constitute a seizure. During a traffic stop, motorists are required to pull to the side of the road generally as the result of an officer's unsettling show of authority. Not only does the ensuing detention interfere with the motorist's freedom of physical movement, but it is also inconvenient and can cause a substantial amount of psychological anxiety. Given these eventualities, the question becomes one of balancing the interests of the state against those of the individual. In its defense, the State of Delaware argued that it had a vested interest in keeping unsafe drivers and vehicles off the public roadways and, although the officer was not acting pursuant to any established standards or procedures, such spot checks were an essential element in its comprehensive traffic safety program. The Court rejected this assertion, however, on the grounds that the state presented no empirical evidence to demonstrate that the spot checks were an effective deterrent. With regard to individual interests, the Court noted that just as an individual does not lose all protections of the Fourth Amendment when stepping from his home onto the sidewalk, neither should these protections be lost when an individual steps from the sidewalk into a car. In the end, the Court remained unconvinced that the incremental contribution to highway safety of the random spot checks justifies the practice under the Fourth Amendment. The decision of the Delaware Supreme Court that the traffic stop had been illegal was thus affirmed.

CASE EXCERPT
"The Fourth and Fourteenth Amendments are implicated in this case because stopping an automobile and detaining its occupants constitute a 'seizure' within the meaning of those Amendments, even though the purpose of the stop is limited and the resulting detention quite brief... The marginal contribution to roadway safety possibly resulting from a system of spot checks cannot justify subjecting every occupant of

DELAWARE v. PROUSE *(cont.)*

every vehicle on the roads to a seizure—limited in magnitude compared to other intrusions but nonetheless constitutionally cognizable—at the unbridled discretion of law enforcement officials."

CASE SIGNIFICANCE

This case is significant in several regards. First, it is interesting to note that it was not until this decision was rendered in 1979 that traffic stops lacking the element of probable cause or at least reasonable, articulable suspicion were held unconstitutional under the Fourth Amendment as a general rule of law. Second, the case clearly required that officers develop, at a minimum, reasonable, articulable suspicion that a violation of law has occurred before making a traffic stop. In simple terms, this case stands for the principle of law that officers must develop some violation of the law, moving or otherwise, before making a traffic stop. In the absence of some lawful basis, the traffic stop will be deemed unconstitutional and any derived evidence will most likely be ruled inadmissible. Third, the Court noted that the Fourth Amendment prohibited random spot checks, but not necessarily full-scale roadblocks where every passing motorist is stopped. This caveat, along with the Court's fixation on the absence of any policy or standards for guiding officer behavior, has implications for the manner in which state legislatures frame their roadway safety programs. Thus, the Court seems to suggest that if states develop detailed standards for conducting blanket roadside checks of driver's licenses, such procedures may pass constitutional muster.

NEW YORK v. BELTON
453 U.S. 454 (1981)

FACTS

Belton was the passenger of a vehicle stopped for speeding by a New York state police officer. Upon making contact the officer not only sensed an odor of burnt marijuana but also spotted an envelope believed to contain an additional quantity of the substance. Everyone was told to exit the vehicle, whereupon each was arrested for possession. While searching the vehicle's interior incident to arrest, the officer found within a coat belonging to Belton a quantity of cocaine. At trial, Belton entered a motion to suppress on grounds that the evidence had been improperly seized. When

this motion was denied, Belton pled guilty to a lesser-included offense while still preserving his claim that the seizure had been unwarranted. The Appellate Division of the New York Supreme Court upheld the search and seizure based upon the rationale that once a suspect has been lawfully arrested, an officer has authority to search the immediate area for additional contraband. However, this ruling was overturned by the New York Court of Appeals on the grounds that "[a] warrantless search of the zippered pockets of an inaccessible jacket may not be upheld as a search incident to a lawful arrest where there is no longer any danger that the arrestee or a confederate might gain access to the article." The U.S. Supreme Court then granted certiorari.

ISSUE

Do officers have authority to search the passenger compartment of a vehicle and its contents incident to a lawful arrest?

HOLDING

Yes. Officers may search the passenger compartment of a vehicle and its contents incident to a lawful arrest. Not only may they may look inside the glove compartment and other storage receptacles, but they may also examine any other closed containers, even if there is a low probability that incriminating evidence will be discovered.

RATIONALE

Chimel v. California, 395 U.S. 752 (1969), established the general rule of law that officers are authorized to search an individual and his or her immediate surroundings incident to a lawful arrest in order to prevent escape or the destruction of evidence. While this principle seemed straightforward enough at the time, there continued to exist considerable ambiguity among lower courts in defining the scope of an arrestee's immediate surroundings. In the interest of establishing more specific parameters for the meaning of this phrase, the Court concluded that the relatively limited space of a vehicle's passenger compartment constituted an area "into which an arrestee might reach in order to grab a weapon or evidentiary item." With little additional elaboration it was thus established that "when a policeman has made a lawful custodial arrest of the occupant of an automobile, he may, as a contemporaneous incident of that arrest, search the passenger compartment of that automobile." Furthermore, it was determined that officers are free to examine the contents of any containers—open or closed—given the relative ease with which one can reach almost anywhere inside a passenger compartment. Lastly, the Court noted that containers within the passenger compartment are subject to search even if there is a low probability that they will yield evidence related to the original offense for which the individual has been arrested.

CASE EXCERPT

"We hold that when a policeman has made a lawful custodial arrest of the occupant of an automobile, he may, as a contemporaneous incident of that arrest, search the passenger compartment of that automobile…It follows from this conclusion that the police may also examine the contents of any containers found within the passenger compartment, for if the passenger compartment is within reach of the arrestee, so also will containers in it be within his reach."

CASE SIGNIFICANCE

Prior to this decision, officers were restricted to searching the "wingspan" within an arrestee's immediate control. This case, however, expanded the permissible scope of a vehicle search incident to lawful arrest. In particular, it allowed officers to search not only the entire passenger compartment, but also any open or closed containers found therein. Perhaps not surprisingly, members of the criminal element will attempt to conceal evidence of their illegal activity inside the otherwise "innocent-looking" containers one might naturally expect to find inside a car—cigarette packages, purses, glove boxes, cassette cases, ashtrays, cosmetic bags, etc. An officer is now authorized to search these articles for evidence and weapons, even after an arrestee has been physically removed from the vehicle and no longer has access to them. Furthermore, officers are empowered to look inside such containers even when there is a low probability of discovering evidence related to the initial offense for which the subject was arrested. For example, an officer who arrests a motorist on traffic warrants may search the entire passenger compartment and all containers therein even in the absence of any belief that evidence or weapons will be found. In other words, officers who have made a lawful arrest are not required to articulate any belief or suspicion in order to search the interior of a vehicle. In turn, it is no longer valid for an individual to claim that arresting officers lacked an articulable reason for searching the interior of a vehicle in which he or she was traveling. Finally, it is important to point

out that the Supreme Court did not address within the context of this case whether the same rules applied to the search of a vehicle's trunk; this issue would later be addressed in a separate case (*United States v. Ross*).

UNITED STATES v. ROSS
456 U.S. 798 (1982)

FACTS

Washington, D.C. police, acting upon information that an individual was selling drugs kept in the trunk of a vehicle, proceeded to the location, stopped the car, and arrested the driver. One of the officers opened the vehicle's trunk and looked inside a closed brown paper bag to discover several glassine bags containing a white powdery substance that later tested positive as heroin. The officer drove the vehicle to a police station, where another warrantless search was undertaken. This time, a zippered leather pouch containing cash was recovered. The evidence was admitted at trial over objection, and Ross was convicted of possession with intent to distribute. A federal court of appeals reversed on grounds that although the officers had a legal basis for stopping and searching the entire car, including its trunk, they did not have a justifiable basis to open the paper bag or leather pouch without a warrant. The U.S. Supreme Court then granted certiorari.

ISSUE

Does the Fourth Amendment prohibit officers from opening closed containers during the course of conducting a warrantless vehicle search?

HOLDING

No. Officers may open closed containers found during the course of a warrantless vehicle search so long as they have probable cause to believe that contraband may be found therein.

RATIONALE

In reaching this decision, the Supreme Court first noted that warrantless vehicle searches are authorized in situations where an officer has probable cause to believe that contraband may be found therein. Moreover, the scope of this search is not limited by the nature of a container that may be used to conceal the object of the search. Instead, the scope of a search is more appropriately defined by the object being sought and the types of places in which it may be concealed. Thus, the

UNITED STATES v. ROSS *(cont.)*

smaller an object, the broader the permissible scope of a search becomes.

CASE EXCERPT

"The rationale justifying a warrantless search of an automobile that is believed to be transporting contraband arguably applies with equal force to any movable container that is believed to be carrying an illicit substance…In the same manner, an individual's expectation of privacy in a vehicle and its contents may not survive if probable cause is given to believe that the vehicle is transporting contraband. Certainly the privacy interests in a car's trunk or glove compartment may be no less than those in a movable container. An individual undoubtedly has a significant interest that the upholstery of his automobile will not be ripped or a hidden compartment within it opened. These interests must yield to the authority of a search, however, which—in light of *Carroll*—does not itself require the prior approval of a magistrate."

CASE SIGNIFICANCE

This case is important insofar at it broadens the authority of officers to conduct warrantless vehicle searches. As long as an officer has probable cause to believe that a vehicle contains contraband or evidence of illegal activity, he or she may undertake a warrantless search for such evidence. If the object of that search is large in size, then the permissible scope of a search for that object must be limited to places where it might reasonably be secreted. Thus, one cannot look for a long-barreled rifle in a book bag or purse. If, on the other hand, one is looking for narcotic evidence, which can be hidden almost anywhere, then the permissible scope of a search becomes much broader and could very well extend to a book bag or an even smaller receptacle. Accordingly, officers must tailor the scope of a search to only those places where the object of interest might reasonably be concealed.

MICHIGAN v. LONG
463 U.S. 1032 (1983)

FACTS

Two officers observed Long drive his vehicle into a ditch. Stopping to investigate, they also observed Long exit the vehicle in a manner suggesting that he was intoxicated. When the officers asked Long to produce his license and registration he turned and began walking back to his vehicle. The officers followed and observed a hunting knife on the driver's-side floorboard of the vehicle. The officers conducted a pat-down search of Long's person but did not find any weapons. One of the officers then observed something protruding from under a front seat armrest and, upon lifting its cover, discovered a baggie of marijuana. Long was placed under arrest for possession of marijuana. An inventory search of the vehicle revealed an additional quantity of marijuana in the trunk. Long's objection to introduction of the evidence at trial was denied and he was convicted. An appeals court affirmed, ruling that the protective search of the vehicle's passenger compartment was valid under *Terry v. Ohio* and that the inventory search of the trunk was also valid under *South Dakota v. Opperman*. The Michigan Supreme Court reversed on grounds that *Terry* did not justify the passenger compartment search and that the marijuana found in the trunk was therefore the fruit of an illegal search. The U.S. Supreme Court then granted certiorari.

ISSUE

Are the police authorized under the principles of *Terry v. Ohio* to conduct a limited protective search of a vehicle's passenger compartment for weapons?

HOLDING

Yes. A protective search of a vehicle's passenger compartment for weapons is reasonable under the principles articulated in *Terry v. Ohio*.

RATIONALE

In *Terry v. Ohio,* the Court ruled that police are authorized to conduct limited protective pat-down searches for weapons that may endanger their safety or that of others. The language of that decision did not restrict protective searches to the person. In the interest of officer and public safety, the scope of a protective search may be expanded beyond the immediate person to include the passenger compartment of a vehicle in instances where the officer has reasonable and articulable suspicion that the suspect is armed and dangerous.

CASE EXCERPT

"Our past cases indicate then that protection of police and others can justify protective searches when police have a reasonable belief that the suspect poses a danger, that roadside encounters between police and suspects are especially hazardous, and that danger may arise from the possible presence of weapons in the area surrounding a suspect. These principles compel our conclusion that the search of the passenger compartment of an automobile, limited to those areas in which a weapon may be placed or hidden, is permissible if the police officer possesses a reasonable belief based on 'specific and articulable facts which, taken together with the rational inferences from those facts, reasonably warrant' the officer in believing that the suspect is dangerous and the suspect may gain immediate control of weapons."

CASE SIGNIFICANCE

This case is important because it extended the *Terry* "stop and frisk" doctrine beyond the person to also include vehicles. This means that a limited protective search of a vehicle's passenger compartment is authorized in situations where an officer possesses reasonable belief that the suspect is dangerous and might gain control of a weapon. The decision does not allow officers to conduct an exhaustive search of the vehicle; rather, it authorizes them to undertake a cursory overview of the passenger compartment to see if any weapons are readily accessible. Officers may only take a "quick peek" in open areas such as between or underneath the seats and on the floorboards. The decision does not allow officers to look inside the glove box, trunk, or closed containers—only those areas where a suspect might gain immediate control of a weapon. Finally, it is important to note that even though a suspect may be under a state of control—such as being in handcuffs—officers are still authorized to undertake a limited search of the vehicle's passenger compartment for weapons that might be used to harm them.

CALIFORNIA v. CARNEY
471 U.S. 386 (1985)

FACTS

A federal drug enforcement agent developed information that Carney was using his motor home located in a downtown San Diego parking lot as a location to exchange marijuana for sex. After observing individuals enter and leave the motor home, the agent stopped a youth who confirmed that he had in fact been given a quantity of marijuana in return for sex. The agent convinced the young man to return to the motor home and lure Carney outside. As Carney answered the door and stepped out, an accompanying agent entered the motor home and confirmed the presence of marijuana. The motor home was impounded and taken to a nearby police station, where closer inspection revealed additional marijuana. Carney was charged with possession of marijuana for sale, his motion to suppress was denied, and he was convicted. A state court of appeals affirmed, but the California Supreme Court later reversed on grounds that the motor vehicle exception to the Fourth Amendment did not apply insofar as Carney's expectation of privacy was equivalent to that which applies to dwellings. The U.S. Supreme Court then granted certiorari.

ISSUE

Does the motor vehicle exception to the Fourth Amendment's warrant requirement apply to motor homes?

HOLDING

Yes. A motor home that is being used on the public roadways in a manner other than as a residence or dwelling qualifies as an automobile for purposes of conducting a warrantless search under established Fourth Amendment standards.

RATIONALE

A six-justice majority reversed the California Supreme Court's ruling that Carney's motor home constituted a residence/dwelling for purposes of Fourth Amendment analysis. More specifically, the Court reasoned that two well-established exceptions to the Fourth Amendment's warrant requirement apply where motor homes are being used on public roadways—first, the vehicle is readily mobile and, second, pervasive governmental regulation of vehicles creates a diminished expectation of privacy for the occupants. In making this finding, the Court avoided creating confusion on such matters by eliminating the need for lower courts to consider factors such as a given motor home's size and "quality of its appointments" in order to determine whether it should be regarded as more of a vehicle or dwelling. Finally, the Court also noted that excluding motor homes from the already well-established automobile exception to the Fourth Amendment would obviously ignore the fact that they could easily be used for purposes of trafficking drugs and/or concealing other forms of illegal activity.

CALIFORNIA v. CARNEY (cont.)

CASE EXCERPT

"The public is fully aware that it is accorded less privacy in its automobiles because of this compelling governmental need for regulation. Historically, individuals always [have] been on notice that movable vessels may be stopped and searched on facts giving rise to probable cause that the vehicle contains contraband, without the protection afforded by a magistrate's prior evaluation of those facts…While it is true that respondent's vehicle possessed some, if not many of the attributes of a home, it is equally clear that the vehicle falls clearly within the scope of the exception laid down in *Carroll* and applied in succeeding cases. Like the automobile in *Carroll*, respondent's motor home was readily mobile. Absent the prompt search and seizure, it could readily have been moved beyond the reach of the police."

CASE SIGNIFICANCE

This case is important for law enforcement purposes insofar as it settled the question of whether or not a motor home constitutes a "residence" within the meaning of the Fourth Amendment. More specifically, the Court ruled that a motor home that is used on the public roadways in a manner other than as a residence or dwelling qualifies as an "automobile" for purposes of conducting warrantless searches. This decision authorizes officers to search motor homes traveling on the open roadways or situated in locations not regularly used for residential purposes (i.e., a parking lot) on the basis of exigency so long as there exists probable cause to believe that evidence of criminal activity will be found therein. It is important to note, however, that the decision failed to address the question of whether or not officers are authorized to search motor homes located in an area that is commonly used for residential purposes (i.e., a camping facility). In these types of situations officers are advised to treat the motor home as a "residence," requiring the issuance of a warrant before undertaking a search of its contents.

FLORIDA v. WELLS

495 U.S. 1 (1990)

FACTS

Wells, who had been arrested for driving under the influence, gave a Florida state trooper permission to open the trunk of his vehicle for purposes of conducting an inventory search. Two marijuana cigarette butts were found in the ashtray, along with a locked suitcase inside the trunk. The trooper directed two employees of the impound lot to forcibly open the suitcase, revealing a large quantity of marijuana. At trial, Wells' motion to suppress the marijuana found in the suitcase was denied. He pleaded no contest to possession of a controlled substance but retained his right to appeal the motion to suppress. An intermediate appeals court held that the trial court erred in denying the motion to suppress. The Florida Supreme Court affirmed this ruling. Specifically, the Florida Supreme Court relied upon language in *Colorado v. Bertine*, 479 U.S. 367 (1987) requiring departments to adopt policies carefully circumscribing officer discretion during inventory searches. The U.S. Supreme Court granted certiorari to determine whether its opinion in *Bertine* had been correctly applied to the facts in Wells' case.

ISSUE

Should trial courts exclude evidence discovered within a closed container during a vehicle search in which the officer's discretion to look therein was not narrowly guided by policy?

HOLDING

Yes. Evidence that is found within a closed container should be excluded in cases where the officer's discretion to look therein was not narrowly guided by agency policy.

RATIONALE

In *Colorado v. Bertine,* the U.S. Supreme Court held that law enforcement agencies must adopt policies narrowly limiting officer discretion during vehicle inventory searches. In seeking to resolve the evidentiary question presented by Wells' case, the Florida appellate judiciary strictly interpreted this as an "either-or" proposition—either officers are to be given complete liberty in opening closed containers found during vehicle searches, or they are to be absolutely prohibited from doing so. In other words, a decision that had traditionally been left to officer discretion (whether or not to open a closed container and look therein) was now to be replaced by a generalized *a priori* policy stating how such situations were to be routinely handled. In revisiting this issue as it applied to the present case, the U.S. Supreme Court expressed concern with the Florida judiciary's "all-or-nothing" approach. On one hand the majority noted that giving officers too much discretion could easily turn an inventory search into "a ruse for a general rummaging in order to discover incriminating evidence." On the other hand, it admitted seeing no reason for reducing inventory searches into purely mechanical operations. In the end, the Court struck a balance between the two extremes by stating: "A police officer must be allowed sufficient latitude to determine whether a particular container should or should not be opened in light of the nature of the search and characteristics of the container itself." Thus, where the contents of a particular container are not readily discernible from exterior examination, officers should retain the discretion to probe further in the interest of protecting the owner's property. This finding did not, however, dispense with the existing requirement under *Bertine* that officer behavior during inventory searches be at least generally guided by agency policy. Because the Florida Highway Patrol did not have any policy whatsoever, the evidence against Wells should have been excluded at trial.

CASE EXCERPT

"Our view that standardized criteria or established routine must regulate the opening of containers found during inventory searches is based on the principle that an inventory search must not be a ruse for a general rummaging in order to discover incriminating evidence. The policy or practice governing inventory searches should be designed to produce an inventory. The individual police officer must not be allowed so much latitude that inventory searches are turned into 'a purposeful and general means of discovering evidence of crime.'"

CASE SIGNIFICANCE

The primary significance of this case is to be found in the fact that it clarified the Court's position on the previous matter of *Colorado v. Bertine*. In particular, it steered lower courts away from the same type of "all-or-nothing" approach applied by the Florida appellate judiciary. Had this early trend not been corrected, law enforcement might eventually have found itself in a situation where officer discretion was altogether eliminated, or at least severely restrained, during vehicle inventory searches. Some observers might argue that the element of officer discretion should never enter into such matters and that behavior in these situations should be closely controlled by standardized policies in order to avoid potential abuse. Others observers might assert that even in the most routine inventory searches there frequently arise unique circumstances

or considerations that defy generalized rules and procedures. Apparently, the majority tried to pacify both positions by stating that, consistent with its earlier holding in *Bertine,* agencies must adopt policies that "rein in" officer behavior during inventory searches while at the same time allowing for limited latitude in situations that defy generalized treatment.

CALIFORNIA v. ACEVEDO

500 U.S. 565 (1991)

FACTS

California police officers received information from a federal DEA agent regarding a shipment of drugs being sent via Federal Express to one Jamie Daza within their jurisdiction. Officers observed Daza claim the package and proceed with it to his residence. Shortly thereafter they observed an individual enter and then leave the apartment with a half-full knapsack. Officers stopped the vehicle in which this individual was traveling, searched the knapsack, and seized 1.5 pounds of marijuana that was contained therein. Later still, the officers observed Acevedo enter the residence and leave carrying a brown paper bag they knew to be consistent with the packaging of the initial shipment. Acevedo placed the bag in the trunk of his vehicle and drove off, whereupon officers in an unmarked vehicle who feared imminent destruction of the evidence stopped him. The officers opened the trunk of his vehicle, looked inside the bag, and discovered a quantity of marijuana. Acevedo was arrested and charged with violation of state drug laws. At trial, Acevedo pled guilty after his motion to suppress was denied. A reconsideration of the motion prevailed when an appellate court concluded that although the officers had probable cause to believe that the bag contained marijuana, they were not authorized to open it without a search warrant. The California Supreme Court denied the prosecution's petition for review, and the U.S. Supreme Court granted certiorari.

ISSUE

Does the Fourth Amendment prohibit officers from opening a container suspected of holding contraband while conducting a warrantless vehicle search?

HOLDING

No. Police officers are authorized to search any container found within a vehicle without having to first secure a warrant so long as they have probable cause

CALIFORNIA v. ACEVEDO *(cont.)*
to believe that it holds contraband or other evidence of criminal activity.

RATIONALE
In this case the Court was asked to clarify whether or not the police may lawfully search a container believed to hold contraband while conducting a warrantless vehicle search. Following an examination of the relevant case law, a six-justice majority decided that the doctrine established in 1925 by *Carroll v. United States* controls all automobile searches. This means that the police may search a vehicle as well as any containers so long as there exists probable cause to believe that contraband or evidence of illegal behavior will be found therein.

CASE EXCERPT
"The line between probable cause to search a vehicle and probable cause to search a package in that vehicle is not always clear, and separate rules that govern the two objects to be searched may enable the police to broaden their power to make warrantless searches and disserve privacy interests. We noted this in *Ross* in the context of a search of an entire vehicle. Recognizing that, under *Carroll*, the 'entire vehicle itself…could be searched without a warrant,' we concluded that prohibiting police from opening immediately a container in which the object of the search is most likely to be found, and instead forcing them first to comb the entire vehicle, would actually exacerbate the intrusion on privacy interests."

CASE SIGNIFICANCE
The decision in this case not only served to reinforce the authority of officers to conduct warrantless vehicle searches but, in fact, greatly extended it. In the past, officers had been prohibited from opening any closed containers (i.e., luggage, purses, etc.) found inside a vehicle on grounds that the owner possessed a heightened expectation of privacy. This restriction was lifted, however, by the Court's decision in *United States v. Ross,* which held that the warrantless search of a vehicle included any closed containers found therein so long as there exists probable cause to search the vehicle. The immediate decision expanded upon this ruling to authorize police to search closed containers found within a vehicle so long as there exists probable cause to believe that the container—as opposed to the vehicle itself—will reveal evidence of criminal activity. In simple terms, there is no requirement that the police

have probable cause to search the vehicle; all that is needed is probable cause to search the container itself.

OHIO v. ROBINETTE
519 U.S. 33 (1996)

FACTS
Robinette, who had been stopped for speeding and given a verbal warning, was asked before being released from the scene if his vehicle contained any contraband. Answering in the negative, he gave permission for the car to be searched. Discovered therein was a small amount of marijuana and a pill that later tested positive for methamphetamine. Robinette was arrested and charged with possession of a controlled substance. The trial court rejected a motion to suppress, whereupon Robinette pleaded no contest and was convicted. The Ohio Court of Appeals reversed the conviction and the Ohio Supreme Court affirmed on grounds that the continued detention constituted an illegal seizure. Specifically, it stated that officers must inform motorists that they are free to leave before asking for consent to search. The U.S. Supreme Court then granted certiorari.

ISSUE
Does an officer have to specifically inform a motorist that he or she is free to leave the scene before requesting consent to search the vehicle?

HOLDING
No. Police officers are not required under the Fourth Amendment to inform a motorist that he or she is free to leave before requesting consent to search a vehicle.

RATIONALE
An eight-justice majority reversed the Ohio Supreme Court's ruling that officers must inform a motorist that he or she is "free to go" prior to asking for consent to search his or her vehicle. In particular, it was reasoned that in assessing the validity of a given consent search, the element of voluntariness is the most important factor to be considered. However, it is not necessary for the state to establish that an individual possesses the specific knowledge that he or she has the right to refuse a consent search in order for one to be valid. Finally, the Court concluded that it would be unrealistic to require that police officers always inform motorists that they are free to go in order for a given consent search to be considered both voluntary and valid.

CASE EXCERPT

"In *Schneckloth* v. *Bustamonte*, it was argued that such a consent could not be valid unless the defendant knew that he had a right to refuse the request. We rejected this argument. While knowledge of the right to refuse consent is one factor to be taken into account, the government need not establish such knowledge as the sine qua non of an effective consent. And just as it would be thoroughly impractical to impose on the normal consent search the detailed requirements of an effective warning, so too would it be unrealistic to require police officers to always inform detainees that they are free to go before a consent to search may be deemed voluntary."

CASE SIGNIFICANCE

The decision in this case was one that clearly favored and facilitated the law enforcement endeavor. By refusing to require that police officers specifically inform motorists that they are free to leave before requesting permission to search a vehicle, the Court emphasized that the determination of whether or not a particular consent to search is voluntary should not turn on a single statement. Rather, this determination should be based on a totality of the circumstances. While the Court has decreed that officers do not have to inform a motorist that he or she is free to leave, this does not absolve officers of the responsibility to ensure that the totality of the circumstances surrounding the stop remain as noncoercive as is reasonably possible. In sum, a court that is asked to determine whether or not a particular consent to search was voluntarily given or coerced is going to put greater emphasis on evaluating the full range of circumstances under which consent was given than it will on some brief disclaimer made by the officer. Finally, states may choose to provide citizens with increased protection beyond the minimal standards required by the Constitution. Thus, some jurisdictions may require officers to provide such a warning before seeking consent, but this will vary from state to state.

PENNSYLVANIA v. LABRON
518 U.S. 938 (1996)

FACTS

Police officers observed Labron participate in a number of street-corner drug transactions that subsequently led to his arrest. A search of the vehicle involved in these transactions yielded a quantity of cocaine that was submitted for consideration as evidence at trial. The trial court, however, suppressed this evidence and the state supreme court affirmed. In essence, the Pennsylvania Supreme Court concluded from its reading of previous U.S. Supreme Court opinions on warrantless vehicle searches that the exception applied only in instances where there existed both probable cause and some exigent circumstance. Because the circumstances surrounding Labron's arrest did not present any apparent form of exigency, the state supreme court ultimately held that the evidence had been improperly seized and had thus been properly excluded at trial. The U.S. Supreme Court granted certiorari to determine whether the language in its prior decisions had been properly interpreted and applied.

ISSUE

Where time clearly permits, does the Fourth Amendment require that officers first obtain a warrant before searching a vehicle that has been lawfully stopped?

HOLDING

No. The very fact that a vehicle is mobile creates an exigent circumstance precluding the need for officers to first obtain a warrant before searching a vehicle that has been lawfully stopped. In other words, officers are not required to secure a warrant before searching a vehicle so long as they have solid probable cause to believe that incriminating evidence may be found therein.

RATIONALE

In a *per curiam* opinion, the U.S. Supreme Court reversed the lower court's conclusion that the evidence against Labron had been improperly introduced at trial. More specifically, a seven-justice majority held that the search in question fell squarely within the automobile exception to the Fourth Amendment. Thus, it was reasoned that although the officers may have had time to secure a warrant, the search of Labron's vehicle was nonetheless justified on two grounds. Primary among these justifications was the vehicle's mobility. Secondly, the officers had probable cause to believe that the vehicle contained evidence of criminal activity. The fact that these two justifications were present thereby precludes the need for officers to obtain a warrant prior to undertaking searches of this type. However, had these two justifications (mobility and probable cause) been lacking, the search would have violated the Fourth Amendment.

PENNSYLVANIA v. LABRON *(cont.)*

CASE EXCERPT

"If a car is readily mobile and probable cause exists to believe it contains contraband, the Fourth Amendment thus permits police to search the vehicle without more. As the state courts found, there was probable cause in both of these cases: Police had seen respondent Labron put drugs in the trunk of the car they searched, and had seen respondent Kilgore act in ways that suggested he had drugs in his truck. We conclude the searches of the automobiles in these cases did not violate the Fourth Amendment."

CASE SIGNIFICANCE

The Court's decision in this case clearly weighed in favor of law enforcement. Specifically, the case expanded the authority of police to conduct warrantless vehicle searches even where there is time to obtain a warrant. Recall that the Court first sanctioned warrantless vehicle searches due to exigency in the case of *Carroll v. United States*. In that case, it was decided that Prohibition agents were authorized to search the Carroll vehicle because they did not have time to obtain a warrant—had they taken the time to do so, either the vehicle would have left the scene or the occupants would have destroyed the evidence in question. In the years that have elapsed since the *Carroll* decision, lower courts have not allowed the police to conduct warrantless vehicle searches where there was adequate time to obtain a judicial order. The decision in the present case altogether dispensed with the requirement that officers obtain a warrant where there exists time or opportunity to do so. Thus, even if an officer has time to get a warrant before searching a car, he or she is no longer required to do so.

WHREN v. UNITED STATES
517 U.S. 806 (1996)

FACTS

Plainclothes officers working an area known for its high prevalence of drug transactions observed a truck waiting at a stop sign for an uncharacteristically long period of time. Abruptly, the truck turned the corner and departed at a high rate of speed. The officers gave chase, eventually stopping the truck for the observed traffic violations. Upon approaching the vehicle, officers saw several baggies of crack cocaine in Whren's hands, resulting in his and the driver's arrest. Prior

to trial on federal drug charges, Whren moved to suppress the evidence on grounds that not only did the officers lack probable cause to believe that drug-related activity had occurred, but that the stop itself was purely pretextual in nature. The motion to suppress was denied, Whren was convicted, and the court of appeals affirmed. The U.S. Supreme Court then granted certiorari.

ISSUE

Do pretextual traffic stops—those made for no other reason than to identify vehicle occupants—violate the Fourth Amendment?

HOLDING

No. Pretextual traffic stops are constitutional so long as an officer has probable cause to believe that a traffic violation or some other offense has occurred.

RATIONALE

A unanimous Supreme Court affirmed Whren's conviction, holding that officers need only possess probable cause to believe that a crime has been committed in order to make a traffic stop. In reaching this conclusion, the Court denied Whren's request to replace this standard with one limiting officers to only those stops that are reasonable. Acknowledging that the prevailing standard lends itself to potential abuse by officers who might make stops based upon impermissible factors such as a motorist's race, the Court nonetheless remained unpersuaded that a change in standards was necessary. More specifically, the Court reasoned that the standard proposed by *Whren* would make the Fourth Amendment's protection turn on trivialities concerning police enforcement practices that would no doubt vary considerably from place to place and time to time.

CASE EXCERPT

"We think these [prior Supreme Court] cases foreclose any argument that the constitutional reasonableness of traffic stops depends on the actual motivations of the individual officers involved. We of course agree with petitioners that the Constitution prohibits selective enforcement of the law based on considerations such as race. But the constitutional basis for objecting to intentionally discriminatory application of laws is the Equal Protection Clause, not the Fourth Amendment. Subjective intentions play no role in ordinary, probable-cause Fourth Amendment analysis."

CASE SIGNIFICANCE

This case is important for day-to-day law enforcement purposes insofar as it affirmed the authority of officers to make traffic stops so long as there exists probable cause to believe that an offense has been committed. In particular, the decision endorses a practice known as "pretextual stops" in which an officer detains a motorist on one or more traffic violations although the true motivation for making the stop may lie in identifying the vehicle's occupants and probing for further evidence of criminal activity. Clearly, as the Court duly acknowledged, the inherent danger in affirming this authority is to be found in its potential for abuse. To be sure, pretextual stops are at the core of today's heated debate concerning racial profiling.

MARYLAND v. WILSON

519 U.S. 408 (1997)

FACTS

A Maryland state trooper observed a speeding vehicle with registration violations. While attempting to stop the car the trooper noticed that two of the three passengers repeatedly ducked out of view as if trying to hide something. When the vehicle finally yielded and the trooper made contact with the driver, he also noticed that the front-seat passenger, Wilson, appeared to be extremely nervous. While the driver searched for the vehicle's rental paperwork, the trooper directed Wilson to step out and speak with him. Upon doing so, a small quantity of crack cocaine fell to the ground, resulting in his arrest for possession with intent to distribute. Prior to trial Wilson entered a motion to suppress on grounds that the trooper's order to exit the vehicle constituted an unreasonable seizure under the Fourth Amendment. The Circuit Court for Baltimore County granted Wilson's motion, which was in turn unsuccessfully challenged by prosecutors before a court of special appeals. The U.S. Supreme Court then granted certiorari.

ISSUE

Does the Fourth Amendment prohibit police officers from requiring passengers to exit the vehicle during a lawful traffic stop?

HOLDING

No. Police officers may direct any and all passengers to exit and remain outside of a vehicle that has been lawfully stopped.

RATIONALE

In reaching the determination that officers can require any and all passengers to exit a vehicle that has been lawfully stopped, a seven-justice majority balanced the public interests at stake against those of the individual. On the public interest side, it was noted that the risk to officer safety during a traffic stop remains high regardless of whether an individual is the driver or a passenger. It was further noted that the danger to officer safety during a traffic stop is likely to be greater when a vehicle contains multiple occupants in addition to the driver. In examining the personal liberty interests at stake, the Court first noted that by ordering a passenger to exit the vehicle, all that has changed in terms of the inconvenience imposed is the individual's physical location. In other words, he or she has already been detained as a result of the initial traffic stop, so requiring him or her to also exit the vehicle does not require any further inconvenience than that which has already been imposed. Additionally, the Court noted that by requiring a passenger to exit the vehicle, he or she would be denied access to any possible weapon that might be concealed therein. Given the minimal inconvenience imposed upon the passengers, the Court ruled in favor of the officer safety interests at stake, thereby reversing the lower court's judgment.

CASE EXCERPT

"In summary, danger to an officer from a traffic stop is likely to be greater when there are passengers in addition to the driver in the stopped car. While there is not the same basis for ordering the passengers out of the car as there is for ordering the driver out, the additional intrusion on the passenger is minimal. We therefore hold that an officer making a traffic stop may order passengers to get out of the car pending completion of the stop."

CASE SIGNIFICANCE

This case clarified an officer's authority to lawfully order any and all passengers out of the vehicle during a traffic stop. The authority to lawfully order the driver out of a vehicle was previously established by the *Mimms* decision in 1977. However, the opinion in that case failed to specify whether or not this authority extended to all occupants of the vehicle. The decision in the immediate case put this issue to rest. Here again, the Court ruled in favor of the state out of concern for officer safety over the slight inconvenience imposed upon a passenger who is required to briefly exit the vehicle. In terms

MARYLAND v. WILSON *(cont.)*

of day-to-day law enforcement practice, an officer's directive that all passengers exit the vehicle during a traffic stop can sometimes lead to roadside disagreements, especially where passengers take issue with whether or not the officer can lawfully require them to do so. Thus, the decision in this case can be a dual-edged sword, to the extent that although it is intended to ensure officer safety, it also has the potential to jeopardize officer safety by inadvertently escalating the tempers of traffic violators and their passengers.

KNOWLES v. IOWA
525 U.S. 113 (1998)

FACTS
Iowa law authorized police officers to either cite or arrest traffic violators. Knowles, who had been stopped for speeding, was issued a citation by the attending officer, who then proceeded to conduct a full search of the vehicle before releasing him. During this search the officer found a quantity of marijuana and narcotic paraphernalia, resulting in Knowles' arrest. Prior to trial Knowles entered a motion to suppress the evidence on grounds that since he had received a citation but was not arrested, the search did not qualify under the "incident to arrest" exception created in *United States v. Robinson.* The trial court rejected this claim, finding Knowles guilty. The Iowa Supreme Court affirmed by creating a "search incident to citation" exception to the Fourth Amendment. In essence, the court reasoned that so long as an officer has probable cause, an actual arrest is not necessary in order for the search to be constitutionally permissible. The U.S. Supreme Court then granted certiorari.

ISSUE
Does the Fourth Amendment prohibit officers from undertaking a full vehicle search in situations where the traffic violator is issued a citation instead of being placed under arrest?

HOLDING
Yes. The full search of a vehicle incident to a traffic stop in which the officer issues a citation rather than arresting the motorist violates the Fourth Amendment.

RATIONALE
In a unanimous opinion, the U.S. Supreme Court reversed the Iowa Supreme Court's decision creating

a "search incident to citation" exception to the Fourth Amendment. This ruling was based on the fact that neither of the two historical rationales for allowing officers to conduct such searches (i.e., mobility and/or the need to disarm a dangerous suspect) was present to justify the search of Knowles' vehicle. The Court further reasoned that the risk to officer safety while issuing a traffic citation is "a good deal less" than when making a custodial arrest. Lastly, it was noted that officers have other bases for conducting a vehicle search without having to create a new "incident to citation" exception.

CASE EXCERPT
"Iowa nevertheless argues that a `search incident to citation' is justified because a suspect who is subject to a routine traffic stop may attempt to hide or destroy evidence related to his identity (*e.g.,* a driver's license or vehicle registration), or destroy evidence of another, as yet undetected crime. As for the destruction of evidence relating to identity, if a police officer is not satisfied with the identification furnished by the driver, this may be a basis for arresting him rather than merely issuing a citation. As for destroying evidence of other crimes, the possibility that an officer would stumble onto evidence wholly unrelated to the speeding offense seems remote."

CASE SIGNIFICANCE
Many states allow officers the discretion to issue a citation in lieu of making a full custodial arrest for certain types of traffic violations. This option does not, however, give the officer authority to conduct a search incident to a citation. In situations where an officer decides to let a violator leave the scene after issuing a summons, the only acceptable basis for conducting a search of the vehicle is by developing probable cause or obtaining informed consent. In the absence of one of these two grounds, officers are prohibited under the *Knowles* decision from searching a vehicle based solely on the issuance of a citation.

WYOMING v. HOUGHTON
526 U.S. 295 (1999)

FACTS
A Wyoming state trooper stopped a vehicle in which Houghton and two others were traveling. The trooper inquired about the trio's use of illegal drugs after

noticing a syringe in the driver's shirt pocket. The driver confirmed that he in fact used drugs, whereupon the trooper initiated a search of the vehicle's passenger compartment. Lying in the back seat was a purse that Houghton, who had lied to the trooper about her true identity, admitted to owning. Looking inside the purse, presumably for some form of identification, the trooper found a quantity of methamphetamine and related narcotic paraphernalia. Houghton was arrested and convicted for possession of a controlled substance despite arguing at trial that the evidence should have been suppressed under the Fourth Amendment. The Wyoming Supreme Court reversed the conviction on grounds that the officer had no justifiable basis for searching the purse. The U.S. Supreme Court then granted certiorari.

ISSUE
Does the Fourth Amendment prohibit officers from searching a passenger's personal belongings (i.e., purse, bag, or other such receptacle) during a warrantless vehicle search?

HOLDING
No. Where officers have probable cause to conduct a warrantless vehicle search, they are also authorized to search a passenger's personal belongings where there exists the possibility that contraband may be contained therein.

RATIONALE
The U.S. Supreme Court reversed the ruling of the Wyoming Supreme Court. More specifically, the search of Houghton's purse was found not to have violated the Fourth Amendment on the grounds that neither the Court's earlier decision in *United States v. Ross* nor the historical evidence relied upon in that case raised a distinction among packages or containers based upon ownership. In simple terms, the Court clarified that under the *Ross* decision, all receptacles—regardless of whom they belong to—were subject to search where officers have probable cause to believe that the vehicle may contain contraband. Thus, it does not matter whom the purse, bag, or container belongs to: if it is found within a vehicle that is being searched by the police, it may be opened for purposes of determining whether or not it contains contraband. Finally, the Court noted two additional reasons for allowing officers to search any and all containers found within a vehicle despite ownership. Among these was the fact that not only is a

passenger's expectation of privacy considerably diminished while traveling in a vehicle, but that the governmental interests in preventing the loss or intentional destruction of evidence are substantial.

CASE EXCERPT
"Whereas the passenger's privacy expectations are, as we have described, considerably diminished, the governmental interests at stake are substantial. Effective law enforcement would be appreciably impaired without the ability to search a passenger's personal belongings when there is reason to believe contraband or evidence of criminal wrongdoing is hidden in the car. As in all car-search cases, the ready mobility of an automobile creates a risk that the evidence or contraband will be permanently lost while a warrant is obtained."

CASE SIGNIFICANCE
The practical significance of this case for law enforcement lies in the fact that it allows officers to search the personal belongings of all passengers in a vehicle so long as the vehicle has been lawfully stopped and there is probable cause to believe that the search will reveal evidence of criminal activity. Thus, where an officer makes a traffic stop and then develops probable cause to believe that the vehicle contains contraband or other evidence of criminal activity, he or she may undertake a search not only of the vehicle, but of any personal belongings of the passengers as well. This means that officers no longer have to obtain the consent of the passenger whose belongings are to be searched.

MARYLAND v. PRINGLE
540 U.S. 366 (2003)

FACTS
A police officer stopped a car for speeding at 3:16 a.m.; searched the car, seizing $763 from the glove compartment and cocaine from behind the back-seat armrest; and arrested the car's three occupants after they denied ownership of the drugs and money. Respondent Pringle, the front-seat passenger, was convicted of possession with intent to distribute cocaine and possession of cocaine and was sentenced to 10 years' incarceration without the possibility of parole. The Maryland Court of Special Appeals affirmed, but the State Court of Appeals reversed, holding that, absent specific facts tending to show Pringle's knowledge and dominion or control over the drugs, the mere finding of cocaine in

MARYLAND v. PRINGLE (cont.)

the back armrest when Pringle was a front-seat passenger in a car being driven by its owner was insufficient to establish probable cause for an arrest for possession.

ISSUE

Can the passenger of a vehicle be charged with possession of a controlled substance (or other illegal object) without specific proof that the contraband belonged to him or her?

HOLDING

Yes. The passenger of a car can be charged with possession of contraband absent a specific showing that the object(s) belonged to him or her.

RATIONALE

Maryland law authorizes police officers to execute warrantless arrests where the officer has probable cause to believe that a felony has been committed or is being committed in the officer's presence. Here, it is uncontested that the officer, upon recovering the suspected cocaine, had probable cause to believe a felony had been committed; the question is whether he had probable cause to believe Pringle committed that crime. The "substance of all the definitions of probable cause is a reasonable ground for belief of guilt," and that belief must be particularized with respect to the person to be searched or seized. To determine whether an officer had probable cause to make an arrest, a court must examine the events leading up to the arrest and then decide "whether these historical facts, viewed from the standpoint of an objectively reasonable police officer, amount to" probable cause. As it is an entirely reasonable inference from the facts here that any or all of the car's occupants had knowledge of, and exercised dominion and control over, the cocaine, a reasonable officer could conclude that there was probable cause to believe Pringle committed the crime of possession of cocaine, either solely or jointly.

CASE EXCERPT

"This case is quite different from *Ybarra*. Pringle and his two companions were in a relatively small automobile, not a public tavern. In *Wyoming* v. *Houghton*, we noted that 'a car passenger—unlike the unwitting tavern patron in *Ybarra*—will often be engaged in a common enterprise with the driver, and have the same interest in concealing the fruits or the evidence of their wrongdoing.' Here we think it was reasonable for the officer to infer a common enterprise among the three men. The quantity of drugs and cash in the car indicated the likelihood of drug dealing, an enterprise to which a dealer would be unlikely to admit an innocent person with the potential to furnish evidence against him."

CASE SIGNIFICANCE

This case is important insofar as it opens the door to prosecutions in instances where the police stop a car full of people and no one claims ownership of contraband found therein. Previously, the police would have to prove that a specific person had domain and control over the contraband. That is now no longer the case. Thus, when the police stop a vehicle, both the driver and passenger(s) are deemed to be individually responsible for any contraband found therein.

ILLINOIS v. LIDSTER
540 U.S. 419 (2004)

FACTS

On Saturday, August 23, 1997, just after midnight, an unknown motorist traveling eastbound on a highway in Lombard, Illinois, struck and killed a 70-year-old bicyclist. The motorist drove off without identifying himself. About one week later at about the same time of night and at about the same place, local police set up a highway checkpoint designed to obtain more information about the accident from the motoring public.

Police cars with flashing lights partially blocked the eastbound lanes of the highway. The blockage forced traffic to slow down, leading to lines of up to 15 cars in each lane. As each vehicle drew up to the checkpoint, an officer would stop it for 10 to 15 seconds, ask the occupants whether they had seen anything happen there the previous weekend, and hand each driver a flyer. The flyer said "ALERT … FATAL HIT & RUN ACCIDENT" and requested "assistance in identifying the vehicle and driver in this accident which killed a 70 year old bicyclist." Robert Lidster, the respondent, drove a minivan toward the checkpoint. As he approached the checkpoint, his van swerved, nearly hitting one of the officers. The officer smelled alcohol on Lidster's breath. He directed Lidster to a side street, where another officer administered a sobriety test and then arrested Lidster. Lidster was tried and convicted in Illinois state court of driving under the influence of alcohol. Lidster challenged the lawfulness of his arrest and conviction on the ground that the government had obtained much of the relevant evidence through use of a checkpoint stop that violated the Fourth Amendment. The trial court rejected that challenge, but an Illinois appellate court reached the opposite conclusion. The Illinois Supreme Court agreed with the appellate court. It held (by a vote of 4 to 3) that its decision in *Indianapolis v. Edmond* required it to find the stop unconstitutional. Because lower courts have reached different conclusions about this matter, the Supreme Court granted certiorari.

ISSUE
Did the manner in which the police conducted this checkpoint in order to solicit information regarding a prior deadly accident in the area violate the Fourth Amendment?

HOLDING
No. The manner in which the police conducted the checkpoint stop did not violate the Fourth Amendment.

RATIONALE
The stops "interfered only minimally with liberty of the sort the Fourth Amendment seeks to protect. Viewed objectively, each stop required only a brief wait in line—a very few minutes at most. Contact with the police lasted only a few seconds. Police contact consisted simply of a request for information and the distribution of a flyer. Viewed subjectively, the contact provided little reason for anxiety or alarm. The police stopped all vehicles systematically, and there is no allegation here that the police acted in a discriminatory or otherwise unlawful manner while questioning motorists during stops."

CASE EXCERPT
"The relevant public concern was grave. Police were investigating a crime that had resulted in a human death. No one denies the police's need to obtain more information at that time. And the stop's objective was to help find the perpetrator of a specific and known crime, not of unknown crimes of a general sort. The

stop advanced this grave public concern to a significant degree. The police appropriately tailored their checkpoint stops to fit important criminal investigatory needs. The stops took place about one week after the hit-and-run accident, on the same highway near the location of the accident, and at about the same time of night. And police used the stops to obtain information from drivers, some of whom might well have been in the vicinity of the crime at the time it occurred."

CASE SIGNIFICANCE
This case validated the efforts of police who were conducting a checkpoint in order to solicit information from motorists regarding a hit-and-run death that had previously occurred within the area. Here the Court reasoned that the manner in which the checkpoint was conducted did not violate the Fourth Amendment because the intrusion caused by the stop was minimal and the public concern was "grave." This decision opens the door for police to conduct limited traffic checkpoints to generate information regarding serious crimes (not minor offenses) and, in effect, widens the figurative net that sometimes catches other types of violations that have occurred or, more likely, are in progress.

DISCUSSION QUESTIONS

1. Why does the Supreme Court allow police officers to search motor vehicles without a warrant?
2. If police officers have information that criminal activity is taking place inside a motor home that is parked at a campground, must they first obtain a warrant in order to conduct a search?
3. Are police officers at liberty to completely disassemble a motor vehicle on the side of the road? Why or why not?
4. Why is it important for police departments to develop specific policies guiding officer behavior during inventory searches?
5. What should police officers do if they encounter a locked briefcase in the trunk of a vehicle that has already been seized in conjunction with a drug trafficking offense?

CHAPTER FOURTEEN

REGULATORY SEARCHES & EXIGENT CIRCUMSTANCES

SOUTH DAKOTA v. OPPERMAN, *428 U.S. 364 (1976)*

ILLINOIS v. LAFAYETTE, *462 U.S. 640 (1983)*

CAMARA v. MUNICIPAL COURT, *387 U.S. 523 (1967)*

NEW YORK v. BURGER, *482 U.S. 691 (1987)*

UNITED STATES v. MARTINEZ-FUERTE, *428 U.S. 543 (1976)*

MICHIGAN DEPARTMENT OF STATE POLICE v. SITZ, *496 U.S. 444 (1990)*

CITY OF INDIANAPOLIS v. EDMOND, *531 U.S. 32 (2000)*

NEW JERSEY v. T.L.O., *469 U.S. 325 (1985)*

O'CONNOR v. ORTEGA, *480 U.S. 709 (1987)*

VERNONIA SCHOOL DISTRICT 47J v. ACTON, *515 U.S. 646 (1995)*

FERGUSON v. CHARLESTON, *523 U.S. 67 (2001)*

BOARD OF EDUCATION OF INDEPENDENT SCHOOL DISTRICT v. EARLS, *536 U.S. 822 (2002)*

GRIFFIN v. WISCONSIN, *483 U.S. 868 (1987)*

UNITED STATES v. KNIGHTS, *534 U.S. 112 (2001)*

BRIGHAM CITY v. STUART, *547 U.S. 398 (2006)*

ONTARIO v. QUON, *560 U.S.—(2010)*

KENTUCKY v. KING,—U.S.—*(2011)*

INTRODUCTION

The Supreme Court has authorized numerous varieties of searches under the administrative justification exception to the Fourth Amendment's probable cause and warrant requirements. Sometimes they are described as "special needs beyond law enforcement" searches; other times they are called "regulatory" searches. To avoid confusion, this book calls them "regulatory searches." The types of searches considered in this chapter are (1) inventory searches, (2) inspections, (3) checkpoints, (4) school disciplinary searches, (5) government employee searches, (6) drug and alcohol testing, and (7) probation supervision searches.

Inventories can be of vehicles and/or of a person's personal items. Usually, a search occurs under the automobile exception (in the case of an automobile) or a search incident to arrest (when a person is involved), and an inventory is taken after the fact for the purpose of developing a record of items in custody.

Vehicle inventories occur under a number of situations, usually after a car has been impounded

for traffic or parking violations. In *South Dakota v. Opperman,* the Supreme Court held that warrantless inventories are permissible on administrative/regulatory grounds; however, they must (1) follow a *lawful* impoundment, (2) be of a routine nature, following standard operating procedures, and (3) not be a "pretext concealing an investigatory police motive." Thus, even though an inventory search can be perceived as a fallback measure that permits a search when probable cause is lacking, it cannot be used in lieu of a "regular" search requiring probable cause.

The inventory search exception to the Fourth Amendment's warrant requirement applies in the case of person inventories as well. Such searches are often called "arrest inventories." The general rule is that the police may search an arrestee and his or her personal items, including containers found in his or her possession, as part of a routine inventory incident to the booking and jailing procedure. Neither a search warrant nor probable cause is required (*Illinois v. Lafayette*).

Concerning home inspections, in *Camara v. Municipal Court* the Court noted that nonconsensual administrative searches of private residences amount to a significant intrusion upon the interests protected by the Fourth Amendment. Nowadays, then, warrants are required for authorities to engage in home inspections. However, the meaning of "probable cause" in such warrants differs from that discussed earlier. The Court has stated that if an area "as a whole" needs inspection, based on factors such as the time, age, and condition of the building, then the probable cause requirement will be satisfied. The key is that probable cause in the inspection context is not "individualized" as in the typical warrant. That is to say, inspections of this sort are geared toward buildings, not persons.

In a later case, *Donovan v. Dewey,* 452 U.S. 494 (1981), the Court modified the "closely regulated business" exception. The Court decided that it is not enough that an industry is "pervasively regulated" for the business inspection exception to apply. Three additional criteria must be met: (1) the government must have a "substantial" interest in the activity at stake, (2) warrantless searches must be necessary to the effective enforcement of the law, and (3) the inspection protocol must provide "a constitutionally adequate substitute for a warrant."

The Court clarified the *Dewey* criteria in *New York v. Burger.* In that case, the Court upheld the warrantless inspection of a vehicle junkyard for the purpose of identifying "vehicle dismantlers." Justice Blackman noted that *Dewey*'s first criterion was satisfied because vehicle theft was a serious problem in New York. The second criterion was satisfied because "surprise" inspections were necessary if stolen vehicles and parts were to be identified, and the third criterion—adequate substitute—was satisfied because junkyard operators were notified that inspections would be unannounced and conducted during normal business hours.

Now we turn our attention to checkpoints. In *United States v. Martinez-Fuerte* the Court upheld the Immigration and Naturalization Service's (INS) decision to establish roadblocks near the Mexican border designed to discover illegal aliens. The Court offered a number of reasons for its decision. First, "[t]he degree of intrusion upon privacy that may be occasioned by a search of a house hardly can be compared with the minor interference with privacy resulting from the mere stop for questioning as to residence." Second, motorists could avoid the checkpoint if they so desired. Third, the Court noted that the traffic flow

near the border was heavy, so individualized suspicion was not possible. Fourth, the location of the roadblock was not decided by the officers in the field "but by officials responsible for making overall decisions." Finally, a requirement that such stops be based on probable cause "would largely eliminate any deterrent to the conduct of well-disguised smuggling operations, even though smugglers are known to use these highways regularly."

In *Michigan Department of State Police v. Sitz* the Court upheld warrantless, suspicionless checkpoints designed to detect evidence of drunk driving. In that case, police checkpoints were set up at which all drivers were stopped and briefly (approximately 25 seconds) observed for signs of intoxication. If such signs were found, the driver would be detained for sobriety testing and, if the indication was that the driver was intoxicated, an arrest would be made. The Court weighed the magnitude of the governmental interest in eradicating the drunk driving problem against the slight intrusion to motorists stopped briefly at such checkpoints. Key to the constitutionality of Michigan's checkpoint were two additional factors: (1) evenhandedness was ensured because the locations of the checkpoints were chosen pursuant to written guidelines and every driver was stopped and (2) the officers themselves were not given discretion to decide whom to stop. Significantly, the checkpoint was deemed constitutional even though motorists were *not* notified of the upcoming checkpoint *or* given an opportunity to turn around and go the other way.

The regulatory search rationale is *not* acceptable, by comparison, to detect evidence of criminal activity. This was the decision reached in the recent Supreme Court case *City of Indianapolis v. Edmond.* There the Court decided whether a city's suspicionless checkpoints for detecting illegal drugs were constitutional.

With respect to disciplinary searches, public school administrators and teachers may search students without a warrant if they possess reasonable suspicion that the search will yield evidence that the student has violated the law or is violating the law or rules of the school. However, such school disciplinary searches must not be "excessively intrusive in light of the age and sex of the students and the nature of the infraction." This was the decision reached in *New Jersey v. T.L.O.* In *T.L.O.,* a high-school student was caught smoking in a school bathroom (in violation of school policy) and was sent to the assistant vice-principal. The assistant vice-principal searched the student's purse for cigarettes and found evidence implicating the student in the sale of marijuana. The Court held that the evidence was admissible because the administrator had sufficient justification to search the purse for evidence concerning the school's anti-smoking policy.

In a case very similar to *T.L.O.,* although not involving a public-school student, the Court held that neither a warrant nor probable cause was needed to search a government employee's office, but the search must be "a noninvestigatory work-related intrusion or an investigatory search for evidence of suspected work-related employee misfeasance" (*O'Connor v. Ortega*). Justice O'Connor summarized the Court's reasoning: "[T]he delay in correcting the employee misconduct caused by the need for probable cause rather than reasonable suspicion will be translated into tangible and often irreparable damage to the agency's work, and ultimately to the public interest."

It is important to note, however, that the Court was limiting its decision strictly to work-related matters: "[W]e do not address the appropriate standard when an employee is being investigated for criminal misconduct or breaches of other nonwork-related statutory or regulatory standards."

Concerning drug testing, in a recent case, *Ferguson v. Charleston,* the Supreme Court addressed the constitutionality of drug testing of hospital patients. The question before the Supreme Court was: Is the Fourth Amendment violated when hospital personnel, working with the police, test pregnant mothers for drug use without their consent? Not surprisingly, the Court answered yes.

The Supreme Court has recently extended its drug-testing decisions to include public-school students. Specifically, in *Vernonia School District 47J v. Acton* the Court upheld a random drug-testing program for school athletes. The program had been instituted because the district had been experiencing significant student drug use. Under the program, all students who wished to play sports were required to be tested at the beginning of the season and then to be retested randomly later in the season. The Court noted that athletes enjoy a lesser expectation of privacy given the semipublic nature of locker rooms where the testing took place. Also, athletes are often subject to other intrusions, including physical exams, so drug testing involved "negligible" privacy intrusions according to the Court.

Even more recently, the Supreme Court affirmed *Vernonia School District* in *Board of Education of Independent School District v. Earls.* However, the Supreme Court held that random, suspicionless drug testing of students who participate in extracurricular activities "is a reasonable means of furthering the School District's important interest in preventing and deterring drug use among its schoolchildren and does not violate the Fourth Amendment."

Finally, it has been established that people on probation enjoy a lesser expectation of privacy than the typical citizen. In *Griffin v. Wisconsin* the Court held that a state law or agency rule permitting probation officers to search probationers' homes without a warrant and based on reasonable grounds is not unconstitutional. The majority (of only five justices) concluded that probation supervision "is a 'special need' of the State permitting a degree of impingement upon privacy that would not be constitutional if applied to the public at large." The same almost certainly applies to parolees, but the Supreme Court has not addressed this issue.

In *United States v. Knights,* the Supreme Court held that warrantless searches of probationers are permissible not only for probation-related purposes (e.g., to ensure that probation conditions are being conformed with), but for investigative purposes. In that case, a probationer was suspected of vandalizing utility company facilities. A police detective searched the probationer's residence and found incriminating evidence. The Supreme Court held that "[t]he warrantless search of Knights, supported by reasonable suspicion and authorized by a probation condition, satisfied the Fourth Amendment."

SOUTH DAKOTA v. OPPERMAN
428 U.S. 364 (1976)

FACTS

Opperman's car had been previously impounded on several occasions for parking violations. Police finally impounded Opperman's car and, following standard department procedures, they inventoried the contents of the car. In doing so they discovered marijuana in the glove compartment. Opperman was arrested and charged with narcotics offenses. He sought suppression of the evidence and the U.S. Supreme Court granted certiorari.

ISSUE

Do police inventory searches of impounded vehicles violate the Fourth Amendment?

HOLDING

No. A warrantless, suspicionless inventory search of an impounded vehicle does not violate the Fourth Amendment. However, the impoundment must be lawful, the search should follow "standard operating procedures," and the search should not be used as a pretext concealing a motive to obtain incriminating evidence.

RATIONALE

"The police procedures followed in this case did not involve an 'unreasonable' search in violation of the Fourth Amendment. The expectation of privacy in one's automobile is significantly less than that relating to one's home or office.... When vehicles are impounded, police routinely follow caretaking procedures by securing and inventorying the cars' contents. These procedures have been widely sustained as reasonable under the Fourth Amendment. This standard practice was followed here, and there is no suggestion of any investigatory motive on the part of the police."

CASE EXCERPT

"In applying the reasonableness standard adopted by the Framers, this Court has consistently sustained police intrusions into automobiles impounded or otherwise in lawful police custody where the process is aimed at securing or protecting the car and its contents...we conclude that in following standard police procedures, prevailing throughout the country and approved by the overwhelming majority of courts, the conduct of the police was not unreasonable under the Fourth Amendment."

CASE SIGNIFICANCE

This case is important because it was the first to constitutionally sanction police inventory searches. The Court permitted regulatory searches of this nature on less than probable cause for several reasons, such as the needs to protect the owner's property while an impounded vehicle is in possession of the police, protect against claims of lost or stolen property, and protect the public from dangerous items (such as weapons) that might be concealed in the car. Even though the Court stated that inventory searches should not be relied upon to obtain incriminating evidence, it is clear that, if the police do not have probable cause to engage in a conventional search, inventories can act as something of a fallback measure. In a recent decision, *Whren v. United States,* 517 U.S. 806 (1996)

(see Chapter Thirteen), the Supreme Court basically sanctioned pretextual searches, so the Court's admonition in *Opperman* against using inventory searches for more than just inventorying can probably be taken with a grain of salt.

ILLINOIS v. LAFAYETTE

462 U.S. 640 (1983)

FACTS

Lafayette was arrested for disturbing the peace and was taken to the police station. Lafayette's shoulder bag was subjected to a warrantless search as part of the process of booking him. The search was done for the purpose of inventorying his possessions but also turned up amphetamine pills. Lafayette was charged with drug possession but prior to trial sought suppression of the drugs on the grounds that they were obtained via an unconstitutional search. The trial court suppressed the drugs and the U.S. Supreme Court granted certiorari.

ISSUE

May the police search an arrestee, including his or her personal items, as part of a routine inventory incident to booking and jailing?

HOLDING

Yes. The police may search a person, including his or her personal effects, as part of a routine inventory incident to the booking and jailing procedure. However, the arrest leading to booking and jailing must be lawful.

RATIONALE

"Consistent with the Fourth Amendment, it is reasonable for police to search the personal effects of a person under lawful arrest as part of the routine administrative procedure at a police station incident to booking and jailing the suspect. The justification for such searches does not rest on probable cause, and hence the absence of a warrant is immaterial to the reasonableness of the search. Here, every consideration of orderly police administration—protection of a suspect's property, deterrence of false claims of theft against the police, security, and identification of the suspect—benefiting both the police and the public points toward the appropriateness of the examination of Lafayette's shoulder bag."

ILLINOIS v. LAFAYETTE *(cont.)*

CASE EXCERPT

"The question here is whether, consistent with the Fourth Amendment, it is reasonable for police to search the personal effects of a person under lawful arrest as part of the routine administrative procedure at a police station house incident to booking and jailing the suspect. The justification for such searches does not rest on probable cause, and hence the absence of a warrant is immaterial to the reasonableness of the search. Indeed, we have previously established that the inventory search constitutes a well-defined exception to the warrant requirement…A so-called inventory search is not an independent legal concept but rather an incidental administrative step following arrest and preceding incarceration. To determine whether the search of respondent's shoulder bag was unreasonable we must 'balanc[e] its intrusion on the individual's Fourth Amendment interests against its promotion of legitimate governmental interests.'"

CASE SIGNIFICANCE

This case permitted an inventory of an arrestee's personal items as part of the booking procedure. This is an important and logical part of the booking process. Allowing such searches preserves police and suspect safety, according to the Supreme Court.

CAMARA v. MUNICIPAL COURT
387 U.S. 523 (1967)

FACTS

Camara was charged with violating the San Francisco Housing Code for refusing to allow housing inspectors to engage in a warrantless inspection of the apartment where he resided. While awaiting trial, Camara claimed that the inspection ordinance was unconstitutional because it permitted searches without warrants or any suspicion, in violation of the Fourth Amendment. The U.S. Supreme Court granted certiorari.

ISSUE

Does the Fourth Amendment bar prosecution of persons who refuse to permit warrantless code inspections of their personal residences?

HOLDING

Yes. Nonconsensual administrative searches of private residences violate the Fourth Amendment. Under the Fourth Amendment, people have a constitutional right to insist that code inspectors obtain a warrant to search their private residences.

RATIONALE

"Under the present system, when the inspector demands entry, the occupant has no way of knowing whether enforcement of the municipal code involved requires inspection of his premises, no way of knowing the lawful limits of the inspector's power to search, and no way of knowing whether the inspector himself is acting under proper authorization. These are questions which may be reviewed by a neutral magistrate without any reassessment of the basic agency decision to canvass an area. Yet, only by refusing entry and risking a criminal conviction can the occupant at present challenge the inspector's decision to search. And even if the occupant possesses sufficient fortitude to take this risk, as appellant did here, he may never learn any more about the reason for the inspection than that the law generally allows housing inspectors to gain entry. The practical effect of this system is to leave the occupant subject to the discretion of the official in the field. This is precisely the discretion to invade private property which we have consistently circumscribed by a requirement that a disinterested party warrant the need to search…. We simply cannot say that the protections provided by the warrant procedure are not needed in this context; broad statutory safeguards are no substitute for individualized review, particularly when those safeguards may only be invoked at the risk of a criminal penalty."

CASE EXCERPT

"The final justification suggested for warrantless administrative searches is that the public interest demands such a rule: it is vigorously argued that the health and safety of entire urban populations is dependent upon enforcement of minimum fire, housing, and sanitation standards, and that the only effective means of enforcing such codes is by routine systematized inspection of all physical structures. Of course, in applying any reasonableness standard, including one of constitutional dimension, an argument that the public interest demands a particular rule must receive careful consideration. But we think this argument misses the mark. The question is not, at this stage at least, whether these inspections may be made, but whether they may be made without a warrant…administrative searches of the kind at issue here are significant intrusions upon the interests protected by the Fourth Amendment, that such searches when authorized and conducted without a warrant procedure lack the traditional safeguards which the Fourth Amendment guarantees to the individual, and that the reasons put forth for upholding these warrantless searches are insufficient to justify so substantial a weakening of the Fourth Amendment's protections."

CASE SIGNIFICANCE

This case is important because it prohibited warrantless, nonconsensual "inspections" of private residences. The decision reinforced the Supreme Court's interest in preserving the privacy of people in their homes. Code inspections of the nature discussed in *Camara* are still permissible, but authorities are now required to obtain a warrant to "inspect" beforehand. The only time government officials are permitted to enter a residence without a warrant is either with valid consent or exigent circumstances. Neither was present in this case.

NEW YORK v. BURGER

482 U.S. 691 (1987)

FACTS

Burger owned a junkyard at which automobiles were dismantled and their parts sold. Pursuant to a New York statute authorizing warrantless inspections of automobile junkyards, police officers entered Burger's junkyard and asked to see his license as well as records describing the automobiles and parts on the premises. Burger stated that he did not have such documents, which are required by law. The officers announced their intentions to "inspect" the junkyard. They found stolen vehicles and parts. Burger was charged with possession of stolen property and another offense. He sought suppression of the evidence, arguing that the statute permitting the inspections was unconstitutional, and the U.S. Supreme Court granted certiorari.

ISSUE

Do inspections of vehicle junkyards fall within the "closely regulated business" exception to the Fourth Amendment's warrant requirement?

HOLDING

Yes. Warrantless inspections of vehicle junkyards for the purpose of identifying vehicle dismantlers do not violate the Fourth Amendment.

RATIONALE

"The New York regulatory scheme satisfies the three criteria necessary to make reasonable warrantless inspections pursuant to [the statute in question]. First, the State has a substantial interest in regulating the vehicle-dismantling and automobile-junkyard industry because motor vehicle theft has increased in the State and because the problem of theft is associated with this industry.... Second, regulation of the vehicle-dismantling industry reasonably serves the State's substantial interest in eradicating automobile theft... [and third, the statute] provides a 'constitutionally adequate substitute for a warrant.... The statute informs the operator of a vehicle dismantling business that inspections will be made on a regular basis.... Thus, the vehicle dismantler knows that the inspections to which he is subject do not constitute discretionary acts by a government official but are conducted pursuant to the statute.'"

CASE EXCERPT

"Because the owner or operator of commercial premises in a 'closely regulated' industry has a reduced expectation of privacy, the warrant and probable-cause requirements, which fulfill the traditional Fourth Amendment standard of reasonableness for a government search, have lessened application in this context. Rather, we conclude that, as in other situations of 'special need,' where the privacy interests of the owner are weakened and the government interests in regulating particular business are concomitantly heightened, a warrantless inspection of commercial premises may well be reasonable within the meaning of the Fourth Amendment."

CASE SIGNIFICANCE

This case is important for two reasons. First, the Court recognized that automobile junkyards are closely regulated businesses, and this permits warrantless inspections. This case is also important because in it the Court clearly announced the three requirements for an inspection of the type considered here to be constitutionally valid. First, there must be a "substantial" government interest in improving the health and safety of the public. Second, the inspections must be necessary to further the regulatory scheme. Finally, the statute authorizing the inspection must serve as a constitutionally adequate substitute for a warrant, providing the owner with notice that search is being made pursuant to the law and has a limited scope and

NEW YORK v. BURGER *(cont.)*

limiting the discretion of the officers who engage in the search. The Court felt all three conditions were satisfied in this case.

UNITED STATES v. MARTINEZ-FUERTE
428 U.S. 543 (1976)

FACTS
Martinez-Fuerte and others, traveling by vehicle from Mexico to the United States, were arrested at the permanent immigration checkpoint operated by the U.S. Border Patrol away from the international border with Mexico. Each sought suppression of certain evidence based on the ground that the immigration checkpoint violated the Fourth Amendment's proscription against unreasonable searches and seizures, and the U.S. Supreme Court granted certiorari.

ISSUE
Do roadblocks near the Mexican border designed to discover illegal aliens violate the Fourth Amendment?

HOLDING
No. Roadblocks near international borders for the purpose of detecting illegal aliens do not need to be authorized in advance by a judicial warrant.

RATIONALE
"To require that such stops always be based on reasonable suspicion would be impractical because the flow of traffic tends to be too heavy to allow the particularized study of a given car necessary to identify it as a possible carrier of illegal aliens. Such a requirement also would largely eliminate any deterrent to the conduct of well-disguised smuggling operations, even though smugglers are known to use these highways regularly.... [Further, w]hile the need to make routine checkpoint stops is great, the consequent intrusion on Fourth Amendment interests is quite limited, the interference with legitimate traffic being minimal and checkpoint operations involving less discretionary enforcement activity than roving-patrol stops.... Under the circumstances of these checkpoint stops, which do not involve searches, the Government or public interest in making such stops outweighs the constitutionally protected interest of the private citizen."

CASE EXCERPT
"Our previous cases have recognized that maintenance of a traffic-checking program in the interior is necessary because the flow of illegal aliens cannot be controlled effectively at the border. We note here only the substantiality of the public interest in the practice of routine stops for inquiry at permanent checkpoints, a practice which the Government identifies as the most important of the traffic-checking operations. These checkpoints are located on important highways; in their absence such highways would offer illegal aliens a quick and safe route into the interior. Routine checkpoint inquiries apprehend many smugglers and illegal aliens who succumb to the lure of such highways. And the prospect of such inquiries forces others onto less efficient roads that are less heavily traveled, slowing their movement and making them more vulnerable to detection by roving patrols."

CASE SIGNIFICANCE
The checkpoint considered in this case was one operated by the Border Patrol several miles inside the U.S. border, near the convergence of two main roads and in an area that restricts vehicle passage around the checkpoint. The Court sanctioned the stops because they were brief and done with the sole purpose of detecting illegal aliens. Most drivers are simply waved on by, and only a handful of motorists are ordered to pull over into a holding area where citizenship is determined. In the Court's words, "Neither the vehicle nor its occupants are searched, and visual inspection of the vehicle is limited to what can be seen without a search." Had the agents been given vast discretion to search the whole of people's cars, the checkpoint probably would not have been lawful.

MICHIGAN DEPARTMENT OF STATE POLICE v. SITZ
496 U.S. 444 (1990)

FACTS
The Michigan Department of State Police instituted a sobriety checkpoint program under guidelines set forth by an advisory committee. The guidelines described how the checkpoints were to be operated, where they were to be set up, and how public notice was to be provided. The guidelines further provided that checkpoints would be set up along certain state roads and that all vehicles passing through would be stopped and their drivers briefly examined for signs of intoxication.

If signs of intoxication were detected, the driver would be directed out of the flow of traffic and subjected to a field sobriety test. The checkpoint at issue in this case was one that was in operation for about 75 minutes, during which time 126 vehicles passed through. The average delay per car was 25 seconds. Two drivers were detained for sobriety testing; one was arrested. Another person drove through the checkpoint without stopping but was followed and stopped a short time thereafter. One day before the checkpoint went into operation, a group of drivers filed a complaint in the Circuit Court of Wayne County, Michigan, claiming that the checkpoints were unconstitutional, and the U.S. Supreme Court granted certiorari.

ISSUE
Do warrantless, suspicionless highway sobriety checkpoints violate the Fourth Amendment?

HOLDING
No. Warrantless, suspicionless highway sobriety checkpoints are consistent with the Fourth Amendment.

RATIONALE
"No one can seriously dispute the magnitude of the drunken driving problem or the States' interest in eradicating it. Media reports of alcohol-related death and mutilation on the Nation's roads are legion. The anecdotal is confirmed by the statistical.... For decades, this Court has 'repeatedly lamented the tragedy.'... Conversely, the weight bearing on the other scale—the measure of the intrusion on motorists stopped briefly at sobriety checkpoints—is slight."

CASE EXCERPT
"Here, checkpoints are selected pursuant to the guidelines, and uniformed police officers stop every approaching vehicle. The intrusion resulting from the brief stop at the sobriety checkpoint is for constitutional purposes indistinguishable from the checkpoint stops we upheld in *Martinez-Fuerte*...the balance of the State's interest in preventing drunken driving, the extent to which this system can reasonably be said to advance that interest, and the degree of intrusion upon individual motorists who are briefly stopped, weighs in favor of the state program."

CASE SIGNIFICANCE
This case is important because it upheld warrantless, suspicionless sobriety checkpoints. The Court

held that such checkpoints do not violate the Fourth Amendment, but it suggested that part of the reason for this was that the checkpoints were operated pursuant to clearly defined policies, every vehicle was stopped, and there was little discretion (in terms of who would be stopped) accorded to each individual officer. Also, the detentions were, on average, very brief, so the Court looked favorably on the checkpoints, even though they technically amounted to "seizures" within the meaning of the Fourth Amendment.

CITY OF INDIANAPOLIS v. EDMOND
531 U.S. 32 (2000)

FACTS
The city of Indianapolis operated a checkpoint program under which officers, without any suspicion, would stop certain vehicles at roadblocks throughout the city for the purpose of discovering unlawful narcotics. Once a vehicle was stopped, at least one officer would approach the car, advise the driver that he or she was stopped at a narcotics checkpoint, ask the driver for his or her license and registration, look for signs of impairment, conduct an open-view examination of the vehicle from the outside, and allow a trained drug dog to walk around the outside of the car. Two people stopped at the checkpoints filed suit in the U.S. District Court for the Southern District of Indiana, asserting that the checkpoints violated the Fourth Amendment. The U.S. Supreme Court granted certiorari.

ISSUE
Do suspicionless vehicle checkpoints for detecting illegal drugs violate the Fourth Amendment?

HOLDING
Yes. Because suspicionless vehicle checkpoints for detecting illegal drugs are "indistinguishable from the general interest in crime control," the checkpoints violate the Fourth Amendment.

RATIONALE
"We have never approved a checkpoint program whose primary purpose was to detect evidence of ordinary criminal wrongdoing. Rather, our checkpoint cases have recognized only limited exceptions to the general rule that a seizure must be accompanied by some measure of individualized suspicion.

CITY OF INDIANAPOLIS v. EDMOND *(cont.)*

We suggested in *Prouse* that we would not credit the 'general interest in crime control' as justification for a regime of suspicionless stops....Consistent with this suggestion, each of the checkpoint programs that we have approved was designed primarily to serve purposes closely related to the problems of policing the border or the necessity of ensuring roadway safety. Because the primary purpose of the Indianapolis narcotics checkpoint program is to uncover evidence of ordinary criminal wrongdoing, the program contravenes the Fourth Amendment."

CASE EXCERPT

"Nor can the narcotics-interdiction purpose of the checkpoints be rationalized in terms of a highway safety concern similar to that present in *Sitz*. The detection and punishment of almost any criminal offense serves broadly the safety of the community, and our streets would no doubt be safer but for the scourge of illegal drugs. Only with respect to a smaller class of offenses, however, is society confronted with the type of immediate, vehicle-bound threat to life and limb that the sobriety checkpoint in *Sitz* was designed to eliminate...The primary purpose of the Indianapolis narcotics checkpoints is in the end to advance the general interest in crime control. We decline to suspend the usual requirement of individualized suspicion where the police seek to employ a checkpoint primarily for the ordinary enterprise of investigating crimes. We cannot sanction stops justified only by the generalized and ever-present possibility that interrogation and inspection may reveal that any given motorist has committed some crime."

CASE SIGNIFICANCE

This case is important because it addressed checkpoints that were markedly different from those discussed in the previous cases. The checkpoints operated in Indianapolis were different because their sole purpose was to detect evidence of criminal activity. In the other checkpoint cases already discussed, the focus was on patrolling the borders and/or ensuring roadway safety. The Court held that because Indianapolis's checkpoint program served little more than a general crime-control function—instead of being concerned with broader issues of safety—it violated the Fourth Amendment's proscription against unreasonable searches and seizures.

NEW JERSEY v. T.L.O.

469 U.S. 325 (1985)

FACTS

A high-school teacher caught a 14-year-old freshman smoking in the restroom, in violation of a school rule. The student was brought to the principal's office and was questioned by the assistant vice-principal. The student denied that she had been smoking. The assistant vice-principal then demanded to see her purse, opened the purse, and found a pack of cigarettes. The assistant vice-principal also noticed a pack of rolling papers, which are often used to roll marijuana. A more thorough search of the student's purse revealed a small amount of marijuana, a pipe, several empty plastic bags, cash, and other incriminating information. The evidence was admitted against the student in a New Jersey juvenile court proceeding. The New Jersey court held that school officials can search a student if the official has reasonable suspicion or reasonable cause to believe a search is necessary to enforce a school policy. The U.S. Supreme Court then granted certiorari.

ISSUE

Is probable cause necessary for a school disciplinary search?

HOLDING

No. School officials do not need a warrant or probable cause for a school disciplinary search. Instead, the search should be judged on its reasonableness and premised on "reasonable grounds" that it will turn up the evidence sought.

RATIONALE

"Schoolchildren have legitimate expectations of privacy. They may find it necessary to carry with them a variety of legitimate, non-contraband items, and there is no reason to conclude that they have necessarily waived all rights to privacy in such items by bringing them onto school grounds. But striking a balance between schoolchildren's legitimate expectations of privacy and the school's equally legitimate need to maintain an environment in which learning can take place requires some easing of the restrictions to which searches by public authorities are ordinarily subject. Thus, school officials need not obtain a warrant before searching a student who is under their authority. Moreover, school officials need not be held subject to the requirement that searches be based on probable cause to believe that the subject of the search has violated or is violating the law. Rather, the legality of a search of a student should depend simply on the reasonableness, under all the circumstances, of the search. Determining the reasonableness of any search involves a determination of whether the search was justified at its inception and whether, as conducted, it was reasonably related in scope to the circumstances that justified the interference in the first place. Under ordinary circumstances the search of a student by a school official will be justified at its inception where there are reasonable grounds for suspecting that the search will turn up evidence that the student has violated or is violating either the law or the rules of the school."

CASE EXCERPT

"The school setting also requires some modification of the level of suspicion of illicit activity needed to justify a search. Ordinarily, a search—even one that may permissibly be carried out without a warrant—must be based upon 'probable cause' to believe that a violation of the law has occurred. However, probable cause is not an irreducible requirement of a valid search. The fundamental command of the Fourth Amendment is that searches and seizures be reasonable, and although 'both the concept of probable cause and the requirement of a warrant bear on the reasonableness of a search,…in certain limited circumstances neither is required.'"

CASE SIGNIFICANCE

The case serves as a prime example of the Court's balancing approach used in judging the constitutionality of so-called regulatory searches. The Court felt that even though a search of T.L.O. took place, the school's interest in maintaining an environment conducive to learning was more important. Even so, the Court did require that "reasonable grounds" be in place before disciplinary searches can commence. This way, public-school students cannot be searched on a whim. Note that this case dealt with grades K–12; the story is markedly different for college students. The courts have generally held that college students enjoy Fourth Amendment protection and cannot be searched and/or seized on less than probable cause.

O'CONNOR v. ORTEGA

480 U.S. 709 (1987)

FACTS

Dr. Ortega was Chief of Professional Education at Napa State Hospital for 17 years. His primary duty was to train young physicians in psychiatric residency programs. In July 1981, hospital officials began to suspect Ortega of possible job-related malfeasance. Allegations surfaced that Ortega coerced subordinates to contribute funds for the purchase of a computer and that he had sexually harassed and inappropriately disciplined several residents. While he was on administrative leave, hospital officials searched his office. State property and several personal items were seized, which were then used against Ortega in a dismissal hearing. He brought a Section 1983 suit (see Chapter 20), alleging that his Fourth Amendment rights were violated. The U.S. Supreme Court granted certiorari.

ISSUE

Do government employees enjoy Fourth Amendment protection in their offices?

HOLDING

Yes. Neither a warrant nor probable cause is necessary to search a government employee's office, but the search must be noninvestigative and intended to discover evidence of work-related malfeasance. Searches and seizures by government employers of their employees are subject to the restrictions of the Fourth Amendment. However, probable cause is not necessary for searches and seizures that are noninvestigative and work-related. The search and seizure must be judged in terms of its "reasonableness."

RATIONALE

"Searches and seizures by government employers or supervisors of the private property of their employees…are subject to the restraints of the Fourth Amendment.…The workplace includes those areas and items that are related to work and are generally within the employer's control. At a hospital, for example, the hallways, cafeteria, offices, desks, and file cabinets, among other areas, are all part of the workplace. These areas remain part of the workplace context even if the employee has placed personal items in them, such as a photograph placed in a desk or a letter posted on an employee bulletin board.…We hold, therefore,

O'CONNOR v. ORTEGA *(cont.)*

that public employer intrusions on the constitutionally protected privacy interests of government employees for non-investigatory, work-related purposes, as well as for investigations of work-related misconduct, should be judged by the standard of reasonableness under all the circumstances. Under this reasonableness standard, both the inception and the scope of the intrusion must be reasonable."

CASE EXCERPT

"The employee's expectation of privacy must be assessed in the context of the employment relation. An office is seldom a private enclave free from entry by supervisors, other employees, and business and personal invitees. Instead, in many cases offices are continually entered by fellow employees and other visitors during the workday for conferences, consultations, and other work-related visits... Requiring an employer to obtain a warrant whenever the employer wished to enter an employee's office, desk, or file cabinets for a work-related purpose would seriously disrupt the routine conduct of business and would be unduly burdensome... In contrast to other circumstances in which we have required warrants, supervisors in offices such as at the Hospital are hardly in the business of investigating the violation of criminal laws. Rather, work-related searches are merely incident to the primary business of the agency."

CASE SIGNIFICANCE

This case is important because it provided that government employees enjoy Fourth Amendment protection in the workplace. However, even though the Court said government employees enjoy this protection, it did not require that probable cause, or even reasonable suspicion, be in place to search and seize property. Instead, as in *T.L.O.*, the search and seizure should be judged in terms of their reasonableness. Note that this decision does not apply to searches of private employees' offices by private employers; private employers are not bound by the strictures of the Fourth Amendment.

VERNONIA SCHOOL DISTRICT 47J v. ACTON

515 U.S. 646 (1995)

FACTS

Officials in an Oregon public school district noticed an increase in student drug use and became particularly concerned that it could also increase the risk of sports-related injuries. A parent "input night" was held during which the parents in attendance gave unanimous support for a policy of drug testing, through urinalysis, of student athletes. The policy that was adopted provided that all students who wished to participate in athletics had to sign a form consenting to drug testing, that all athletes were tested near the beginning of the season, and that 10 percent of the athletes would be randomly tested at weekly intervals after that. A seventh-grade student was not allowed to participate in sports because he and his parents refused to sign the consent form. The student and his parents filed a lawsuit, claiming that the drug testing procedure violated the Fourth Amendment, and the U.S. Supreme Court granted certiorari.

ISSUE

Do random, suspicionless drug tests of school athletes violate the Fourth Amendment?

HOLDING

No. Random, suspicionless drug tests of school athletes do not violate the Fourth Amendment. The decreased expectation of privacy of students who participate in school sports, the relative unobtrusiveness of the search, and the need to promote student safety all combine to mean that the Oregon public school district's policy did not violate the Fourth Amendment.

RATIONALE

"State-compelled collection and testing of urine constitutes a 'search' under the Fourth Amendment.... [T]he 'reasonableness' of [such] a search is judged by balancing the intrusion on the individual's Fourth Amendment interests against the promotion of legitimate governmental interests.... The first factor to be considered in determining reasonableness is the nature of the privacy interests on which the search intrudes. Here, the subject of the policy are children who have been committed to the temporary custody of the State as schoolmaster; in that capacity, the State may exercise a degree of supervision and control greater than it could exercise over free adults. The requirements that public school children submit to physical examinations and be vaccinated indicated that they have a lesser privacy expectation with regard to medical examinations and procedure than the general population. Student athletes have even less of a legitimate privacy expectation, for an element of communal undress is inherent in athletic participation, and athletes are subject to preseason physical exams and rules regulating their conduct. Finally, the privacy interests compromised by the process of obtaining urine samples under the Policy are negligible, since the conditions of collection are nearly identical to those typically encountered in public restrooms. In addition, the tests look only for standard drugs, not medical conditions, and the results are released to a limited group."

CASE EXCERPT

"Fourth Amendment rights, no less than First and Fourteenth Amendment rights, are different in public schools than elsewhere; the `reasonableness' inquiry cannot disregard the schools' custodial and tutelary responsibility for children...Legitimate privacy expectations are even less with regard to student athletes...There is an additional respect in which school athletes have a reduced expectation of privacy. By choosing to `go out for the team,' they voluntarily subject themselves to a degree of regulation even higher than that imposed on students generally...Somewhat like adults who choose to participate in a `closely regulated industry,' students who voluntarily participate in school athletics have reason to expect intrusions upon normal rights and privileges, including privacy."

CASE SIGNIFICANCE

This case was the first to uphold random, suspicionless drug tests of students seeking to participate in school athletics. The Court adopted a balancing approach, weighing the privacy interests of each individual student with the school district's interest of promoting safety during sports-related activities. The Court felt that the district's interest was more important than each individual student's privacy rights, so, even though the drug tests are considered "searches," the Court held that no justification is necessary for officials to conduct them.

FERGUSON v. CHARLESTON

523 U.S. 67 (2001)

FACTS

In the fall of 1988, staff at the Charleston, South Carolina, public hospital became concerned over the apparent increase in the use of cocaine by patients who received prenatal treatment. Staff at the hospital approached the city and agreed to cooperate in

prosecuting pregnant mothers who tested positive for drugs. A task force was set up consisting of hospital personnel, police, and other local officials. The task force formulated a policy for how to conduct the tests, preserve the evidence, and use it to prosecute those who tested positive. Ferguson and several other women tested positive for cocaine, and the case came before the U.S. Supreme Court.

ISSUE

Is the Fourth Amendment violated when hospital personnel, working with the police, test pregnant mothers for drug use without their consent?

HOLDING

Yes. When hospital personnel test patients without their consent for drug use and then turn the evidence over to the police, this violates the Fourth Amendment.

RATIONALE

"Because the hospital seeks to justify its authority to conduct drug tests and to turn the results over to police without the patients' knowledge or consent, this case differs from the four previous cases in which the Court considered whether comparable drug tests fit within the closely guarded category of constitutionally permissible suspicionless searches....Those cases employed a balancing test weighing the intrusion on the individual's privacy interest against the 'special needs' that supported the program. The invasion of privacy here is far more substantial than in those cases. In previous cases, there was no misunderstanding about the purpose of the test or the potential use of the test results, and there were protections against the dissemination of the results to third parties. Moreover, those cases involved disqualification from eligibility for particular benefits, not the unauthorized dissemination of test results. The critical difference, however, lies in the nature of the 'special needs' asserted. In each of the prior cases, the 'special need' was divorced from the State's general law enforcement interest. Here, the policy's central and indispensable feature from its inception was the use of law enforcement to coerce patients into substance abuse treatment."

CASE EXCERPT

"As respondents have repeatedly insisted, their motive was benign rather than punitive. Such a motive, however, cannot justify a departure from Fourth Amendment protections, given the pervasive

FERGUSON v. CHARLESTON (cont.)

involvement of law enforcement with the development and application of the MUSC policy. The stark and unique fact that characterizes this case is that Policy M-7 was designed to obtain evidence of criminal conduct by the tested patients that would be turned over to the police and that could be admissible in subsequent criminal prosecutions. While respondents are correct that drug abuse both was and is a serious problem, the gravity of the threat alone cannot be dispositive of questions concerning what means law enforcement officers may employ to pursue a given purpose. The Fourth Amendment's general prohibition against nonconsensual, warrantless, and suspicionless searches necessarily applies to such a policy."

CASE SIGNIFICANCE

This case is important because it placed restrictions on the so-called regulatory or suspicionless search doctrine. The Court reaffirmed the requirement that regulatory searches be conducted without special law enforcement interests in mind. Instead, the benefit to public safety must outweigh individual privacy interests for suspicionless searches to be constitutionally valid. The Court felt that the public interest in capturing pregnant women who abused drugs was not as significant as the women's privacy interests.

BOARD OF EDUCATION OF INDEPENDENT SCHOOL DISTRICT v. EARLS

536 U.S. 822 (2002)

FACTS

The Student Activities Drug Testing Policy implemented by the Board of Education of Independent School District No. 92 of Pottawatomie County required students participating in extracurricular activities to submit to random, suspicionless urine tests intended to detect the use of illegal drugs. Together with their parents, two students, Lindsay Earls and Daniel James, brought a Section 1983 lawsuit against the school district, alleging that the drug testing policy violated the Fourth Amendment as incorporated to the states through the due process clause of the Fourteenth Amendment. The district court found in favor of the school district, but the Tenth Circuit reversed, holding that the policy violated the Fourth Amendment. It concluded that random, suspicionless drug tests would be permissible only were there some identifiable drug abuse problem. The U.S. Supreme Court then granted certiorari.

ISSUE

Do random, suspicionless drug tests of students who participate in extracurricular activities violate the Fourth Amendment?

HOLDING

No. Suspicionless drug tests of students participating in extracurricular activities do not violate the Fourth Amendment.

RATIONALE

"[T]he Court concludes that the invasion of students' privacy is not significant, given the minimally intrusive nature of the sample collection and the limited uses to which the test results are put. The degree of intrusion caused by collecting a urine sample depends upon the manner in which production of the sample is monitored. Under the Policy, a faculty monitor waits outside the closed restroom stall for the student to produce a sample and must listen for the normal sounds of urination to guard against tampered specimens and ensure an accurate chain of custody. This procedure is virtually identical to the 'negligible' intrusion approved in *Vernonia School District 47J v. Acton.* ... The Policy clearly requires that test results be kept in confidential files separate from a student's other records and released to school personnel only on a 'need to know' basis. Moreover, the test results are not turned over to any law enforcement authority. Nor do the test results lead to the imposition of discipline or have any academic consequences. Rather, the only consequences of a failed drug test is to limit the student's privilege of participating in extracurricular activities."

CASE EXCERPT

"Students who participate in competitive extracurricular activities voluntarily subject themselves to many of the same intrusions on their privacy as do athletes. Some of these clubs and activities require occasional off-campus travel and communal undress. All of them have their own rules and requirements for participating students that do not apply to the student body as a whole."

CASE SIGNIFICANCE
This case is easily reconciled with *Ferguson*. There, the urine tests were handed over to law enforcement personnel. Here, the tests were used only to determine whether a student should be allowed to participate in extracurricular activities. The Court concluded that the policy in question here served the school district's interest in protecting the health and safety of its students, so the minimal intrusions did not violate the Fourth Amendment. This case is therefore important because it carefully outlines the requirements of a constitutional regulatory drug testing program.

GRIFFIN v. WISCONSIN
483 U.S. 868 (1987)

FACTS
In September 1980, Griffin was convicted on charges of resisting arrest, disorderly conduct, and obstructing an officer. He was placed on probation. One of the conditions of his probation was that he allow any probation officer to search his home without a warrant as long as the probation officer's supervisor approved and that there were "reasonable grounds" to believe contraband would be found. On April 5, 1983, a detective of the Beloit Police Department informed Lew, Griffin's probation officer's supervisor, that there might be guns at Griffin's apartment. Lew, who was accompanied by another probation officer and three plainclothes police officers, went to Griffin's apartment. Griffin answered the door and Lew told him that they were there to search his apartment. A handgun was found during the search. Griffin was convicted of possession of a firearm by a felon. The U.S. Supreme Court then granted certiorari.

ISSUE
Can probationers be forced to submit to warrantless searches of their residences?

HOLDING
Yes. Probationers can be forced to submit to warrantless searches of their residences. However, "reasonable grounds" that contraband will be found is the necessary level of justification.

RATIONALE
"A State's operation of a probation system, like its operation of a school, government office or prison, or its supervision of a regulated industry, likewise presents

'special needs' beyond normal law enforcement that may justify departures from the usual warrant and probable cause requirements.... To a greater or lesser degree, it is always true of probationers (as we have said it to be true of parolees) that they do not enjoy 'the absolute liberty to which every citizen is entitled, but only... conditional liberty properly dependent on observance of special [probation] restrictions.'"

CASE EXCERPT
"A warrant requirement would interfere to an appreciable degree with the probation system, setting up a magistrate rather than the probation officer as the judge of how close a supervision the probationer requires. Moreover, the delay inherent in obtaining a warrant would make it more difficult for probation officials to respond quickly to evidence of misconduct... We think that the probation regime would also be unduly disrupted by a requirement of probable cause... In some cases—especially those involving drugs or illegal weapons—the probation agency must be able to act based upon a lesser degree of certainty than the Fourth Amendment would otherwise require in order to intervene before a probationer does damage to himself or society. The agency, moreover, must be able to proceed on the basis of its entire experience with the probationer, and to assess probabilities in the light of its knowledge of his life, character, and circumstances."

CASE SIGNIFICANCE
This case is important because it treats probationers differently from ordinary citizens. The Court sanctioned warrantless searches of probationers' residences because, it argued, they enjoy a lesser expectation of privacy as part of being placed on probation. The Court has sanctioned similar searches of parolees' homes as well; the same logic applies. In this case the Court focused more on the "special needs" of law enforcement than a balancing approach, weighing the individual's privacy interests with the state's interest in promoting public safety.

UNITED STATES v. KNIGHTS
534 U.S. 112 (2001)

FACTS
As a condition of his probation on drug charges, Knights was required to submit to searches conducted

UNITED STATES v. KNIGHTS *(cont.)*

by any probation or law enforcement officer even in the absence of a warrant or probable cause. Knights was convicted on drug charges and given probation. Three days into probation, Knights became the primary suspect in an arson case. A sheriff's deputy investigating the case drove by Knights' residence and noticed in the bed of a pickup truck several potentially incriminating items, not the least of which was a Molotov cocktail and various explosive materials. Knowing the terms of Knights' probation, the deputy undertook a search of the apartment, resulting in the discovery of additional incriminating evidence. Knights was arrested and indicted by a federal grand jury. A motion to suppress the evidence found in his apartment was accepted on grounds that the purpose of the search was more investigatory than probationary in nature. The Ninth Circuit Court of Appeals affirmed on grounds that the terms of Knights' probation were limited to probationary searches and not investigatory searches. The U.S. Supreme Court then granted certiorari.

ISSUE

Is evidence seized from a warrantless search of a probationer's apartment admissible under the Fourth Amendment when the search is legally authorized by the terms of probation?

HOLDING

Yes. The warrantless search of Knights' apartment resulting in the discovery of incriminating criminal evidence did not violate the Fourth Amendment because Knights' probation conditions required that he submit to warrantless searches.

RATIONALE

"The Fourth Amendment's touchstone is reasonableness, and a search's reasonableness is determined by assessing, on the one hand, the degree to which it intrudes upon an individual's privacy and, on the other, the degree to which it is needed to promote legitimate government interests. . . . Knights' status as a probationer subject to a search condition informs both sides of that balance. In assessing the governmental interest, it must be remembered that the very assumption of probation is that the probationer is more likely than others to violate the law. . . . The State's interest in apprehending criminal law violators, thereby protecting potential victims, may justifiably focus on probationers in a way that it does not on the ordinary citizen.

On balance, no more than reasonable suspicion was required to search this probationer's house. The degree of individualized suspicion required is a determination that a sufficiently high probability of criminal conduct makes the intrusion on the individual's privacy interest reasonable. Although the Fourth Amendment ordinarily requires probable cause, a lesser degree satisfies the Constitution when the balance of governmental and private interests makes such a standard reasonable."

CASE EXCERPT

"The judge who sentenced Knights to probation determined that it was necessary to condition the probation on Knights's acceptance of the search provision. It was reasonable to conclude that the search condition would further the two primary goals of probation—rehabilitation and protecting society from future criminal violations. The probation order clearly expressed the search condition and Knights was unambiguously informed of it. The probation condition thus significantly diminished Knights's reasonable expectation of privacy."

CASE SIGNIFICANCE

This case gave the police authority to conduct investigatory searches where required by the terms of an individual's probation. In other words, if the terms of an individual's probation require submission to a warrantless search, any incriminating evidence discovered as a result should be ruled admissible under the Fourth Amendment. Caution must be exercised, however, to ensure that searches of an investigatory nature are not excluded from the terms of the probationary contract. To the extent that investigatory searches are excluded, officers will be limited in their authority to initiate such warrantless intrusions. Where such searches are not specifically excluded from the terms of probation, this ruling serves to greatly expand the authority of officers conducting investigations focusing upon previously adjudicated and therefore known offenders.

BRIGHAM CITY v. STUART
547 U.S. 398 (2006)

FACTS

This case arises out of a melee that occurred in a Brigham City, Utah, home in the early-morning hours of July 23, 2000. At about 3 a.m., four police officers responded to a call regarding a loud party at a residence.

Upon arriving at the house, they heard shouting from inside and proceeded down the driveway to investigate. There, they observed two juveniles drinking beer in the backyard. They entered the backyard, and saw—through a screen door and windows—an altercation taking place in the kitchen of the home. According to the testimony of one of the officers, four adults were attempting, with some difficulty, to restrain a juvenile. The juvenile eventually "broke free, swung a fist and struck one of the adults in the face." The officer testified that he observed the victim of the blow spitting blood into a nearby sink. The other adults continued to try to restrain the juvenile, pressing him up against a refrigerator with such force that the refrigerator began moving across the floor. At this point, an officer opened the screen door and announced the officers' presence. Amid the tumult, nobody noticed. The officer entered the kitchen and again cried out, and as the occupants slowly became aware that the police were on the scene, the altercation ceased. The officers subsequently arrested respondents and charged them with contributing to the delinquency of a minor, disorderly conduct, and intoxication. In the trial court, respondents filed a motion to suppress all evidence obtained after the officers entered the home, arguing that the warrantless entry violated the Fourth Amendment. The court granted the motion, and the Utah Court of Appeals affirmed. Before the Supreme Court of Utah, Brigham City argued that although the officers lacked a warrant, their entry was nevertheless reasonable on either of two grounds. The court rejected both contentions and, over two dissenters, affirmed. First, the court held that the injury caused by the juvenile's punch was insufficient to trigger the so-called "emergency aid doctrine" because it did not give rise to an "objectively reasonable belief that an unconscious, semi-conscious, or missing person feared injured or dead [was] in the home." Furthermore, the court suggested that the doctrine was inapplicable because the officers had not sought to assist the injured adult but instead had acted "exclusively in their law enforcement capacity." The court also held that the entry did not fall within the exigent circumstances exception to the warrant requirement. This exception applies, the court explained, where police have probable cause and where "a reasonable person [would] believe that the entry was necessary to prevent physical harm to the officers or other persons." Under this standard, the court stated, the potential harm need not be as serious as that required to invoke the emergency aid exception.

Although it found the case "a close and difficult call," the court nevertheless concluded that the officers' entry was not justified by exigent circumstances.

ISSUE

Were the officers authorized under the exigent circumstances exception to the Fourth Amendment in entering the house to render aid to the assaulted individual?

HOLDING

Yes. Under the exigent circumstance exception to the Fourth Amendment, police officers are authorized to enter a residence in the interest of protecting the welfare of a person when there exists an objectively reasonable basis for believing that person may be in peril.

RATIONALE

Because the Fourth Amendment's ultimate touchstone is "reasonableness," the warrant requirement is subject to certain exceptions. For example, one exigency obviating the requirement is the need to render emergency assistance to occupants of private property who are seriously injured or threatened with such injury. This Court has repeatedly rejected respondents' contention that, in assessing the reasonableness of an entry, consideration should be given to the subjective motivations of individual officers. Because the officers' subjective motivation is irrelevant, it does not matter here whether they entered the kitchen to arrest respondents and gather evidence or to assist the injured and prevent further violence. Relying on the Court's holding in *Welsh v. Wisconsin* that "an important factor to be considered when determining whether any exigency exists is the gravity of the underlying offense for which the arrest is being made," respondents further contend that their conduct was not serious enough to justify the officers' intrusion into the home. This contention is misplaced. In *Welsh*, the "only potential emergency" confronting the officers was the need to preserve evidence of the suspect's blood-alcohol level, an exigency the Court held insufficient under the circumstances to justify a warrantless entry into the suspect's home. Here, the officers were confronted with *ongoing* violence occurring *within* the home, a situation *Welsh* did not address.

CASE EXCERPT

"The officers' entry here was plainly reasonable under the circumstances. Given the tumult at the house when

BRIGHAM CITY v. STUART *(cont.)*

they arrived, it was obvious that knocking on the front door would have been futile. Moreover, in light of the fracas they observed in the kitchen, the officers had an objectively reasonable basis for believing both that the injured adult might need help and that the violence was just beginning. Nothing in the Fourth Amendment required them to wait until another blow rendered someone unconscious, semiconscious, or worse before entering."

CASE SIGNIFICANCE

This case stands for the principle of law that police are authorized to enter a private residence when they have an objectively reasonable basis for believing that someone inside may be in peril. Thus, they do not have to first secure a warrant to lawfully enter if they hear, for example, a struggle ensuing or someone calling for help.

ONTARIO v. QUON
560 U.S.—(2010)

FACTS

Jeff Quon was member of the Ontario, California, Police Department (OPD) SWAT team. To improve communications for SWAT team members, OPD purchased pagers for members of the SWAT team to use for work. The OPD had an electronic privacy policy, which stated employees should not have an expectation of privacy and were subject to monitoring without notice on computer, Internet, and email usage. While the policy did not explicitly deal with text messages, Quon and other employees were told that the city would treat text messages the same way they treated emails. Quon repeatedly exceeded his text limit and reimbursed the city for the overages each time. His supervisor, wanting to determine whether the department needed to increase the texting limit on the pagers, requested transcripts for two months of texts where there were overages in order to determine whether the overages were work-related or personal use. The supervisor determined that the majority of texts were for personal use and that some texts were sexually explicit. The matter was referred to Internal Affairs, which investigated and determined that Quon violated OPD rules, and Quon was disciplined. Quon appealed to the federal district court, arguing his Fourth Amendment rights were violated. The district court determined that the OPD did not violate the Fourth Amendment but the Ninth Circuit reversed,

holding that Quon did have a reasonable expectation of privacy and that OPD violated his privacy right because the search was not reasonable in scope.

ISSUE

Did the administrative review of Quon's text-messaging records violate his Fourth Amendment privacy rights?

HOLDING

No. Because the search of Quon's text messages was reasonable, petitioners did not violate respondent's Fourth Amendment rights.

RATIONALE

The Court must proceed with care when considering the whole concept of privacy expectations in communications made on electronic equipment owned by a government employer. The judiciary risks error by elaborating too fully on the Fourth Amendment implications of emerging technology before its role in society has become clear. In *Katz* (389 U.S. 347, 1967), the Court relied on its own knowledge and experience to conclude that there is a reasonable expectation of privacy in a telephone booth. It is not so clear that courts at present are on so sure a ground. Prudence counsel's caution before the facts in the instant case are used to establish far-reaching premises that define the existence, and extent, of privacy expectations enjoyed by employees when using employer-provided communication devices.

CASE EXCERPT

"A broad holding concerning employees' privacy expectations vis-à-vis employer-provided technological equipment might have implications for future cases that cannot be predicted. It is preferable to dispose of this case on narrower grounds. For present purposes we assume several propositions arguendo: First, Quon had a reasonable expectation of privacy in the text messages sent on the pager provided to him by the City; second, petitioners' review of the transcript constituted a search within the meaning of the Fourth Amendment; and third, the principles applicable to a government employer's search of an employee's physical office apply with at least the same force when the employer intrudes on the employee's privacy in the electronic sphere."

CASE SIGNIFICANCE

This case is significant for employees of all types insofar as it allows employers to monitor their electronic communiqué in and related to the workplace. The significant aspect here seems to be that of notice: where the employer gives the employee fair notice that electronic communications, especially those involving work-related devices, are subject to monitoring, then any such action will likely be construed by a reviewing court as reasonable and, therefore, permissible under the Fourth Amendment.

KENTUCKY V. KING
—U.S.—(2011)

FACTS
This case concerns the search of an apartment in Lexington, Kentucky. Police officers set up a controlled buy of crack cocaine outside an apartment complex. Undercover Officer Gibbons watched the deal take place from an unmarked car in a nearby parking lot. After the deal occurred, Gibbons radioed uniformed officers to move in on the suspect. He told the officers that the suspect was moving quickly toward the breezeway of an apartment building, and he urged them to "hurry up and get there" before the suspect entered an apartment. In response to the radio alert, the uniformed officers drove into the nearby parking lot, left their vehicles, and ran to the breezeway. Just as they entered the breezeway, they heard a door shut and detected a very strong odor of burnt marijuana. At the end of the breezeway, the officers saw two apartments, one on the left and one on the right, and they did not know which apartment the suspect had entered. Gibbons had radioed that the suspect was running into the apartment on the right, but the officers did not hear this statement because they had already left their vehicles. Because they smelled marijuana smoke emanating from the apartment on the left, they approached the door of that apartment. Officer Steven Cobb, one of the uniformed officers who approached the door, testified that the officers banged on the left apartment door "as loud as [they] could" and announced, "This is the police" or "Police, police, police." Cobb said that "[a]s soon as [the officers] started banging on the door," they "could hear people inside moving," and "[i]t sounded as [though] things were being moved inside the apartment." These noises, Cobb testified, led the officers to believe that drug-related evidence was about to be destroyed. At that point, the officers announced that they "were going to make entry inside the apartment." Cobb then

kicked in the door, the officers entered the apartment, and they found three people in the front room: respondent Hollis King, respondent's girlfriend, and a guest who was smoking marijuana. The officers performed a protective sweep of the apartment, during which they saw marijuana and powder cocaine in plain view. In a subsequent search, they also discovered crack cocaine, cash, and drug paraphernalia. Police eventually entered the apartment. Inside, they found the suspected drug dealer who was the initial target of their investigation.

ISSUE
Did police-created "exigency" justify a warrantless entry and search of the home under the Fourth Amendment?

HOLDING
No. An exigent circumstance that is created by police officers does not justify entry and search under existing exceptions to the Fourth Amendment.

RATIONALE
The proper test follows from the principle that permits warrantless searches: warrantless searches are allowed when the circumstances make it reasonable, within the meaning of the Fourth Amendment, to dispense with the warrant requirement. Thus, a warrantless entry based on exigent circumstances is reasonable when the police did not create the exigency by engaging or threatening to engage in conduct violating the Fourth Amendment.

CASE EXCERPT
"In applying this exception for the 'creation' or 'manufacturing' of an exigency by the police, courts require something more than mere proof that fear of detection by the police caused the destruction of evidence."

CASE SIGNIFICANCE
This case limits the authority of the police to conduct exigent-based searches, especially where the police themselves created the exigency. The facts of this case are a textbook example of what is meant by use of the term "police-created exigency." In essence, the police cannot allow a situation to escalate into an "emergency" type of situation and then use the exigent circumstance exception to the Fourth Amendment as a basis for undertaking a subsequent search or seizure.

DISCUSSION QUESTIONS

1. Regulatory searches require no justification, yet they are still searches. What is your assessment of regulatory searches?

2. Which types of regulatory searches are more invasive than others? Why?

3. As of this writing, the Supreme Court is hearing a case on whether the police should be able to institute checkpoints to ask people whether they have information about a crime, and then arrest drunk drivers and people with contraband in plain view. How should the Court rule?

4. A controversial practice with respect to probation searches is the emerging practice of police–probation partnerships. This practice teams police officers with probationers to conduct spot checks of certain probationers once they come on probation. What is your opinion of this practice?

5. Identify examples of closely regulated businesses that would fall under the regulatory searches exception to the Fourth Amendment.

CHAPTER FIFTEEN

ELECTRONIC SURVEILLANCE

OLMSTEAD v. UNITED STATES, *277 U.S. 438 (1928)*

BERGER v. NEW YORK, *388 U.S. 41 (1967)*

KATZ v. UNITED STATES, *389 U.S. 347 (1967)*

UNITED STATES v. KARO, *468 U.S. 705 (1984)*

UNITED STATES v. JONES, *—U.S.—(2012)*

INTRODUCTION

Law enforcement has historically been constrained in the collection of evidence by electronic means on at least two grounds. Primary among these has been the Supreme Court ruling that electronic eavesdropping constitutes a search under the Fourth Amendment (*Katz v. United States*). Secondly, there has long existed a general lack of technological resources and competence within law enforcement circles. While it is difficult to accurately predict what the future holds, it seems relatively safe to assert that both of these constraints are rapidly evaporating as the result of recent terrorist attacks against U.S. interests. In other words, the events of September 11, 2001, have placed an unprecedented emphasis on the use of various technologies to detect, prevent, and prosecute criminal activities both before and after the fact. Changes in this area of the law are likely to be very dramatic as the "War on Terror" escalates and continues into the indefinite future.

Although the cases included here stem from less dramatic events, each contributes to a comprehensive understanding of the constitutional principles guiding the collection of evidence by electronic means. Upon close review of these cases, a few important points bear mention. First, there are only a limited number of cases in this particular area of the law, and there are even fewer cases dealing with the countless new forms of technology and the varieties of crime that they often breed (generally through the use of computers, etc.). Also, the cases within this area are rather dated

insofar as they do not remain abreast of the current public-safety interests that are at stake (again, referring to the risk of terrorist attacks). When these three facts are taken together, it becomes readily apparent how and why this area of the law is so fertile for future growth.

Be that as it may, the cases briefed within this chapter deal not only with wiretapping (e.g., *Olmstead* and *Katz*) but with other forms of electronic eavesdropping as well. These include the use of homing devices to track the movement of people, packages, or objects (*United States v. Karo*). While these cases are indeed narrowly focused, numerically few, and historically dated, they nonetheless continue to guide the manner in which law enforcement utilizes such investigative resources.

OLMSTEAD v. UNITED STATES
277 U.S. 438 (1928)

FACTS

Olmstead was convicted in federal court for violation of the National Prohibition Act. In essence, he was the principal actor in a large-scale alcohol smuggling operation. The evidence used to convict Olmstead was obtained by Prohibition agents who electronically eavesdropped on a number of telephone conversations. More specifically, the bugging devices were placed on phone lines outside the location from where the calls were both made and received. The Ninth Circuit Court

OLMSTEAD v. UNITED STATES *(cont.)*

of Appeals affirmed Olmstead's conviction, and the U.S. Supreme Court granted certiorari.

ISSUE

Does electronic eavesdropping (i.e., wiretapping) constitute a search within the meaning of the Fourth Amendment where there occurs no physical trespass or intrusion into a protected area?

HOLDING

No. Electronic eavesdropping does not constitute a search within the meaning of the Fourth Amendment unless there occurs a physical intrusion or trespass into a protected area.

RATIONALE

In reaching the conclusion that electronic eavesdropping does not constitute a search unless there occurs a physical intrusion or trespass into a protected area, the Supreme Court gave a very strict interpretation of the Fourth Amendment's language. Specifically, the Court observed: "The Amendment does not forbid what was done here. There was no searching. There was no seizure. The evidence was secured by the use of the sense of hearing and that only. There was no entry of the houses or the offices of the defendants." The majority further reasoned that: "[O]ne who installs in his house a telephone instrument with connecting wires intends to project his voice to those quite outside, and that the wires beyond his house, and message while passing over them, are not within the protection of the Fourth Amendment."

CASE EXCERPT

"A standard which would forbid the reception of evidence, if obtained by other than nice ethical conduct by government officials, would make society suffer and give criminals greater immunity than has been known heretofore. In the absence of controlling legislation by Congress, those who realize the difficulties in bringing offenders to justice may well deem it wise that the exclusion of evidence should be confined to cases where rights under the Constitution would be violated by admitting it."

CASE SIGNIFICANCE

Although the *Olmstead* decision no longer serves as controlling precedent, it was the prevailing rule of law guiding the use of electronic eavesdropping devices until the Court revisited the issue some four decades later in *Katz v. United States.* Initially, the decision as to whether or not electronic eavesdropping constituted a search turned upon a strict interpretation of the language contained in the Fourth Amendment. Under such an approach, officers were allowed to gather oral/conversational evidence against suspects that could later be admitted at trial so long as there was no physical intrusion into a protected area. Today, however, such tactics are no longer permissible, and any form of electronic eavesdropping—even in the absence of a physical trespass—constitutes a search protected by Fourth Amendment standards.

BERGER v. NEW YORK

388 U.S. 41 (1967)

FACTS

Berger was convicted for attempting to bribe a public official. The chief evidence used against him was gathered using an electronic eavesdropping device or "bug." The device was planted pursuant to a state law authorizing prosecutors or police officials at the rank of sergeant or above to issue a bugging order that would be valid for up to two months. The statute did not, however, require the state officials to detail specific information regarding the content of the conversations, nor did it provide guidelines for a "return" of the gathered information. The New York appellate courts upheld the constitutionality of the statute and affirmed Berger's conviction, and the U.S. Supreme Court granted certiorari.

ISSUE

Did the statute authorizing state officials to eavesdrop on private conversations using a bugging device violate the Fourth Amendment protection against unreasonable searches and seizures?

HOLDING

Yes. Electronic eavesdropping constitutes a search, which, in the absence of clearly limited guidelines regarding the information sought and how it is to be "returned," violates the Fourth Amendment prohibition against unreasonable searches and seizures.

RATIONALE

In concluding that the evidence used to convict Berger was illegally obtained, it was first noted that the use of electronic devices to monitor private conversations constitutes a search within the meaning of the Fourth Amendment. Thus, any such law or action by the state must comply with the standards set forth therein. For example, the Fourth Amendment requires officers to particularly describe the person or things to be seized. Because the New York law did not comply with this prerequisite, it was constitutionally defective. In the absence of this requirement, officers would possess "roving" authority to seize any and all private conversations. Yet another defective element of the law was that which authorized officers to listen in on conversations for up to two months. The Court equated this characteristic to a series of conventional searches conducted pursuant to a single showing of probable cause. Still other defective elements included (1) the power of extension up to two additional months without any further showing of probable cause, (2) the absence of a specific termination date, (3) no requirement for a showing of exigency, and (4) no provision for "return" of the warrant and disclosure of how the obtained evidence would be used. In light of the breadth and gravity associated with these defective characteristics, the law in question was deemed unconstitutional under both the Fourth and Fourteenth Amendments.

CASE EXCERPTS

"The Fourth Amendment commands that a warrant issue not only upon probable cause supported by oath or affirmation, but also `particularly describing the place to be searched, and the persons or things to be seized.' New York's statute lacks this particularization. It merely says that a warrant may issue on reasonable ground to believe that evidence of crime may be obtained by the eavesdrop. It lays down no requirement for particularity in the warrant as to what specific crime has been or is being committed, nor `the place to be searched,' or `the persons or things to be seized' as specifically required by the Fourth Amendment. The need for particularity and evidence of reliability in the showing required when judicial authorization of a search is sought is especially great in the case of eavesdropping. By its very nature eavesdropping involves an intrusion on privacy that is broad in scope."

CASE SIGNIFICANCE

This case is important on several grounds, not the least of which is that it is one of two electronic eavesdropping decisions rendered by the Court in 1967 (see *Katz*

v. United States). It also clarified the requisite elements for an eavesdropping statute to pass constitutional scrutiny. First, the law must particularly describe the conversations to be surveilled. Second, probable cause to believe that criminal activity is afoot must be established. Third, the duration of the eavesdropping must be limited—extensions may be made, however, where an adequate showing can be made. Fourth, the individual(s) whose conversations are to be monitored must be named in the judicial order. Fifth, a return showing what conversations were monitored and the intended use of any evidence must be made available to the issuing court. Last, the eavesdropping must cease once the desired information has been obtained. While these requirements for electronic eavesdropping may seem commonplace today, they were revolutionary when they were announced. In fact, it was only one year later that Congress enacted the Omnibus Crime Control and Safe Streets Act, which more specifically addressed such matters. Although not widely cited or relied upon as precedent, the *Berger* decision may very well find renewed significance in today's era of rapid technological expansion characterized by dramatic increases in Internet and computer-based crime.

KATZ v. UNITED STATES
389 U.S. 347 (1967)

FACTS

Katz was indicted and convicted on federal charges for transmitting wagering (betting) information across state lines by way of telephone. The evidence used to convict was obtained by FBI agents who had attached an electronic eavesdropping and recording device to a public pay phone used by Katz. Naturally, Katz objected to the introduction of this evidence at trial, but his motion to suppress was denied. A federal appellate court affirmed the conviction on grounds that there was no physical intrusion into an occupied area. The U.S. Supreme Court then granted certiorari.

ISSUE

Is a public telephone booth constitutionally protected from electronic eavesdropping by the Fourth Amendment even where there is no physical intrusion?

HOLDING

Yes. Despite the fact that a telephone booth exists in public, individuals who make use of it possess a

KATZ v. UNITED STATES (*cont.*)

reasonable expectation of privacy. Thus, any electronic monitoring of the phone constitutes a search. No physical intrusion needs to occur in order for the Fourth Amendment to be triggered.

RATIONALE

In resolving this particular case, the Court was asked to first determine whether or not a public telephone booth is a constitutionally protected area under the Fourth Amendment. The second issue to be resolved was whether or not there must be an actual physical intrusion into the booth itself or, instead, whether a nonphysical intrusion such as that which occurs with electronic eavesdropping can also trigger the Fourth Amendment. As to the first of these issues—whether or not a public telephone booth is constitutionally protected under the Fourth Amendment—the Court rejected the government's position that individuals have a diminished expectation of privacy when using public pay phones because the typical booth is at least partially walled by glass. Thus, the Court showed reluctance to accept the government's argument that just because an individual can be observed through the glass walls of a pay phone, the affairs he or she conducts therein automatically become public rather than remaining private in nature. The fact that an individual closes the door of the booth clearly indicates a desire to keep the details of his or her conversation confidential. On these and similarly related grounds it was ultimately concluded that an individual who uses a pay phone possesses a reasonable expectation that his or her conversation will remain private and not be broadcast to or listened in upon by others. Having resolved this issue, the Court turned its attention to the second issue—that of determining whether there must be an actual physical intrusion into the protected space or, instead, whether a nonphysical intrusion such as that which occurs with electronic eavesdropping can also trigger the Fourth Amendment. With regard to this question, the Court changed its position established by two earlier cases—*Olmstead v. United States* (wiretapping does not violate the Fourth Amendment unless there is a physical trespass into a constitutionally protected area) and *Goldman v. United States,* 316 U.S. 129 (1942) (the Fourth Amendment is limited only to searches and seizures of tangible property). In opposition to these prior rulings, the Court now asserted that once it has been acknowledged that the Fourth Amendment governs not only the seizure of tangible items but also extends to the recording of private conversations, its application cannot depend solely upon the relative presence or absence of a physical intrusion into a given enclosed space. Combined, these two lines of reasoning allowed the Court to conclude that public telephone booths are constitutionally protected from electronic eavesdropping by the Fourth Amendment even where no physical intrusion occurs.

CASE EXCERPT

"We conclude that the underpinnings of *Olmstead* and *Goldman* have been so eroded by our subsequent decisions that the 'trespass' doctrine there enunciated can no longer be regarded as controlling. The Government's activities in electronically listening to and recording the petitioner's words violated the privacy upon which he justifiably relied while using the telephone booth and thus constituted a 'search and seizure' within the meaning of the Fourth Amendment. The fact that the electronic device employed to achieve that end did not happen to penetrate the wall of the booth can have no constitutional significance."

CASE SIGNIFICANCE

The *Katz* decision is important in several regards. First, it served to overturn the decision previously rendered in *Olmstead v. United States* establishing the rule of law that wiretapping does not constitute a search unless there occurs some trespass into a constitutionally protected area. Thus, the Court's decision in this case broadens the Fourth Amendment's protective scope so that even in the absence of physical intrusion into a protected space, electronic eavesdropping constitutes a search. Beyond establishing a new rule of law, the decision also sets forth the notion that just because an individual conducts his or her business in public view (i.e., a partially glassed-in phone booth), this does not mean that he or she has a diminished expectation of privacy. As the Court pointed out, despite the fact that a phone booth has glass walls that allow others to see inside, the conversation or communication that occurs within the confines of the booth remains private. Given these distinguishing characteristics, the *Katz* decision remains the rule of law controlling police behavior in the area of electronic eavesdropping.

UNITED STATES v. KARO

468 U.S. 705 (1984)

FACTS
DEA agents learned from an informant that Karo and two other individuals had arranged to purchase two cans of ether to be used for purposes of extracting cocaine from clothing that had been imported into the United States. With the informant's consent and court approval, a homing device was affixed to one of the ether containers so that agents could track its movement. After being transported between several locations, the agents secured a search warrant for the residence where the container finally came to rest. Upon executing the warrant a quantity of cocaine was found and Karo, along with others, was charged with various drug-related offenses. During federal pretrial proceedings, Karo moved to suppress the evidence on grounds that the original warrant authorizing placement of the homing device was defective, thereby rendering all subsequent evidence inadmissible. The government unsuccessfully appealed the motion to suppress, and the U.S. Supreme Court granted certiorari.

ISSUE
Did the warrantless monitoring of the homing device inside a private residence violate the Fourth Amendment?

HOLDING
Yes. The warrantless monitoring of a homing device inside a private residence violates the Fourth Amendment.

RATIONALE
Although planting a homing device does not in and of itself violate the Constitution, monitoring its presence and movement inside a private residence does offend the Fourth Amendment. The Court reasoned that because a residence is not open to visual surveillance, the government's surreptitious use of the homing device to obtain information was akin to conducting a warrantless search. At the same time, however, the justices concluded that monitoring the movements of the container over the open roads provided ample probable cause to sustain the issuance of the second search warrant for the residence. In the end, the suppression order was reversed, allowing the evidence to be admitted upon retrial.

CASE EXCERPT
"In this case, had a DEA agent thought it useful to enter the Taos residence to verify that the ether was actually in the house and had he done so surreptitiously and without a warrant, there is little doubt that he would have engaged in an unreasonable search within the meaning of the Fourth Amendment. For purposes of the Amendment, the result is the same where, without a warrant, the Government surreptitiously employs an electronic device to obtain information that it could not have obtained by observation from outside the curtilage of the house…We cannot accept the Government's contention that it should be completely free from the constraints of the Fourth Amendment to determine by means of an electronic device, without a warrant and without probable cause or reasonable suspicion, whether a particular article—or a person, for that matter—is in an individual's home at a particular time. Indiscriminate monitoring of property that has been withdrawn from public view would present far too serious a threat to privacy interests in the home to escape entirely some sort of Fourth Amendment oversight."

CASE SIGNIFICANCE
This decision is somewhat confusing insofar as it ruled the monitoring of the homing device to be in violation of the Fourth Amendment while at the same time reversing the suppression order on other grounds. Specifically, the justices objected to the monitoring of the device while it was inside a private residence. On the other hand, the Court held that tracking the movement of the container over the open road created enough probable cause by itself to render issuance of the residential search warrant valid. For day-to-day police operations, this decision means that the police are authorized to use homing devices in open areas (roadways, etc.) but not in private areas (residences, etc.). They cannot, however, rely on its mere presence inside a private dwelling as probable cause for a search warrant because such places afford property owners a reasonable expectation of privacy under the Fourth Amendment. Once a container is inside such a location, a warrant authorizing its seizure must be predicated upon other known facts or elements of probable cause.

UNITED STATES v. JONES
—U.S.—(2012)

FACTS

The Government obtained a search warrant permitting it to install a Global Positioning System (GPS) tracking device on a vehicle registered to respondent Jones's wife. The warrant authorized installation in the District of Columbia and within 10 days, but agents installed the device on the 11th day and in Maryland. The Government then tracked the vehicle's movements for 28 days. It subsequently secured an indictment of Jones and others on drug trafficking conspiracy charges. The District Court suppressed the GPS data obtained while the vehicle was parked at Jones's residence but held the remaining data admissible because Jones had no reasonable expectation of privacy when the vehicle was on public streets. Jones was convicted. The D.C. Circuit reversed, concluding that admission of the evidence obtained by warrantless use of the GPS device violated the Fourth Amendment.

ISSUE

Does the use of a GPS device mounted to a vehicle for purposes of monitoring a person's movements constitute a search under the Fourth Amendment?

HOLDING

Yes. The Government's attachment of the GPS device to the vehicle, and its use of that device to monitor the vehicle's movements, constitutes a search under the Fourth Amendment.

RATIONALE

The Fourth Amendment protects the "right of the people to be secure in their persons, houses, papers, and effects, against unreasonable searches and seizures." Here, the Government's physical intrusion on an "effect" for the purpose of obtaining information constitutes a "search." This type of encroachment on an area enumerated in the Amendment would have been considered a search within the meaning of the Amendment at the time it was adopted.

CASE EXCERPT

"In cases involving even short-term monitoring, some unique attributes of GPS surveillance relevant to the *Katz* analysis will require particular attention. GPS monitoring generates a precise, comprehensive record of a person's public movements that reflects a wealth of detail about her familial, political, professional, religious, and sexual associations. The Government can store such records and efficiently mine them for information years into the future. And because GPS monitoring is cheap in comparison to conventional surveillance techniques and, by design, proceeds surreptitiously, it evades the ordinary checks that constrain abusive law enforcement practices: limited police resources and community hostility."

CASE SIGNIFICANCE

This case represents an important victory for privacy-right advocates who are concerned with governmental intrusion into individual affairs via electronic technology. In essence, the Court reaffirmed the principle established in *Katz* that electronic eavesdropping constitutes a search. The right of the people to be secure in their papers, houses, papers, and effects has now been interpreted to mean that the government cannot electronically track individuals even with a search warrant.

DISCUSSION QUESTIONS

1. Discuss how changes in technology are likely to influence future Supreme Court decisions in the area of electronic surveillance/eavesdropping.
2. Do individuals still have a reasonable expectation of privacy even though communications via cellular phone can be easily intercepted by a radio scanner? Why or why not?
3. Do individuals have a reasonable expectation of privacy in communications via the Internet (e.g., email, one-on-one chatting, chat rooms, etc.)? Why or why not?
4. What does the decision in *Jones* mean for police who want to use GPS technology?
5. Should the meaning of the Fourth Amendment stay the same as when it was written in 1791? Can it, in light of technological developments?

CHAPTER SIXTEEN

PRETRIAL IDENTIFICATION PROCEDURES

UNITED STATES v. WADE, *388 U.S. 218 (1967)*

KIRBY v. ILLINOIS, *406 U.S. 682 (1972)*

MANSON v. BRATHWAITE, *432 U.S. 98 (1977)*

UNITED STATES v. CREWS, *445 U.S. 463 (1980)*

PERRY v. NEW HAMPSHIRE, *—U.S.—(2012)*

INTRODUCTION

During the course of day-to-day police operations, officers frequently need to obtain eyewitness identification without the luxury of being able to organize and conduct a formal lineup at the stationhouse. In such instances, it would not be uncommon for the police to accomplish this pressing objective by one of two means: (1) transport a suspect back to the scene of a crime so that a victim or witness can make a positive identification or (2) present the witness or victim with a collection of photographs, hoping that he or she will be able to positively identify the suspect of interest. In both cases, officers must proceed with extreme caution to avoid prejudicially influencing the victim/witness identification. At the same time, officers must be intimately familiar with other due process requirements related to pretrial identification procedures: specifically, they must know when a suspect is or is not entitled to the assistance of counsel during such instances. To this important end, the cases briefed within this chapter outline the basic constitutional concerns that arise during pretrial identification procedures.

Contrary to popular belief, suspects who have not been formally charged with a criminal offense are not entitled to the assistance of counsel during pretrial identification procedures. This principle of law may be directly traced to the Supreme Court's ruling in *Kirby v. Illinois.* While this decision clearly benefits law enforcement interests, there exist other cases that

ardently protect the due process rights of criminal suspects. For example, *United States v. Wade* established the principle of law that once an individual has been formally charged with a crime, he or she is entitled to have an attorney present during any subsequent police-orchestrated lineups.

UNITED STATES v. WADE
388 U.S. 218 (1967)

FACTS

Having been indicted on federal bank robbery and conspiracy charges, Wade was placed in a lineup without the benefit of counsel and, along with other participants, made to wear a disguise and repeat words like those reportedly used by the robber. Two bank employees identified him as having been involved in the robbery. This identification testimony was subsequently introduced at trial, prompting Wade to enter a motion for acquittal on the grounds that the lineup procedures had violated his Fifth Amendment right to avoid self-incrimination as well as his Sixth Amendment right to counsel. The motion was denied and Wade was convicted. On appeal, the conviction was reversed on the grounds that although there had been no Fifth Amendment violation, his right to counsel under the Sixth Amendment had been abridged during the lineup. A new trial was ordered with instructions that

UNITED STATES v. WADE (cont.)

the identification testimony be excluded, and the U.S. Supreme Court granted certiorari.

ISSUE

Does the Fifth Amendment prohibit the state from requiring a criminal defendant to appear in a postindictment lineup for identification purposes? Does the Sixth Amendment require the presence of a criminal defendant's attorney during postindictment lineups conducted for identification purposes? Are courtroom identifications of a criminal defendant that are the product of a postindictment lineup conducted without the benefit of counsel admissible at trial?

HOLDING

No, yes, and no. The Fifth Amendment does not prohibit the state from requiring a defendant to participate in a postindictment lineup conducted for identification purposes. However, the Sixth Amendment requires the presence of counsel during such procedures, given their critical nature. Any identification testimony derived from a postindictment lineup procedure in which a defendant was denied the right to counsel is violative of the Sixth Amendment and is thus inadmissible at trial.

RATIONALE

The Court has long held that the Fifth Amendment was intended to protect a defendant from being forced to testify against himself or herself or otherwise provide incriminating evidence of a "communicative" nature. For example, the Fifth Amendment does not protect a suspect from the state's demand that he or she submit to "fingerprinting, photography, or measurement, to write or speak for identification, to appear in court, to stand, to assume a stance, to walk, or to make a particular gesture." Thus, requiring Wade to repeat language allegedly used by the robber during the lineup procedure in no way violated his Fifth Amendment right to avoid self-incrimination. The question of whether or not the Sixth Amendment required the presence of counsel during a postindictment lineup was, however, an altogether different matter. Most importantly, the Court noted that "[a]s early as *Powell v. Alabama* (1932), we recognized that the period from arraignment to trial was perhaps the most critical period of the proceedings ... during which the accused requires the guiding hand of counsel." This guiding principle, combined with the potential for unfairness inherent

in most identification procedures, led to a conclusion that the best way to protect defendants from any risk of irreparable prejudice was to extend the right to counsel to postindictment lineups. Thus, any identification testimony derived from a postindictment lineup procedure in which a defendant was denied the right to counsel must be excluded from evidence at trial.

CASE EXCERPT

"Counsel can hardly impede legitimate law enforcement; on the contrary, for the reasons expressed, law enforcement may be assisted by preventing the infiltration of taint in the prosecution's identification evidence. That result cannot help the guilty avoid conviction but can only help assure that the right man has been brought to justice. Legislative or other regulations, such as those of local police departments, which eliminate the risks of abuse and unintentional suggestion at lineup proceedings and the impediments to meaningful confrontation at trial may also remove the basis for regarding the stage as 'critical.' But neither Congress nor the federal authorities have seen fit to provide a solution. What we hold today in no way creates a constitutional strait-jacket which will handicap sound efforts at reform, nor is it intended to have this effect."

CASE SIGNIFICANCE

This case is important insofar as it established the general rule of law that criminal defendants have a right to counsel during any postindictment lineup/ identification procedures. Under *Wade*, the filing of formal charges against a defendant was regarded by the Court as a "critical stage" of the adversarial process, thereby triggering this particular aspect of the Sixth Amendment. As a consequence of this determination, it is imperative that authorities know the "status" of a given case before requiring a suspect to participate in a lineup. Where formal charges have been filed, the state must not only give a defendant and his or her attorney advance notice of intent to conduct a lineup, but the attorney must also be allowed to attend in order to ensure that no unfair or prejudicial actions take place. It is worth noting that the opinion in *Wade* failed to specify whether suspects who have not yet been charged with a crime enjoy the same level of constitutional protection. Instead, this question became the subject of a later case—*Kirby v. Illinois.*

KIRBY v. ILLINOIS

406 U.S. 682 (1972)

FACTS

Petitioner, Kirby, and a companion, Bean, were stopped by Chicago police and asked for identification. Officers became suspicious when the two men produced documents (social security card and traveler's checks) belonging to another individual not in their immediate company. Unable to convincingly explain how these items came into their possession, the two were arrested and taken to the stationhouse. Upon arrival, the arresting officers learned of a street robbery that had been reported just the day before. The victim, Willie Shard, reported that two men had stolen his wallet containing, among other items, his social security card and some traveler's checks. A police unit was dispatched to Shard's place of employment for purposes of bringing him in to make an identification of the two suspects. As soon as Shard entered the stationhouse, he confirmed to an officer that Kirby and Bean were in fact the two men who had robbed him. At the time of this identification, neither suspect had been informed of his right to counsel, neither had asked for assistance of counsel, nor was an attorney present in the stationhouse. Kirby and Bean were subsequently indicted for the robbery, received appointed counsel, and pled not guilty. A pretrial motion to suppress Shard's stationhouse identification of the two men was denied and both were found guilty. Kirby's conviction was affirmed by a state appellate court, which found no error in the admission of Shard's testimony regarding how he had identified the two men to police. Specifically, the state appellate court held that the *Wade-Gilbert per se* exclusionary rule did not apply to preindictment lineups. The Supreme Court granted certiorari limited to this question.

ISSUE

Does the *Wade-Gilbert per se* exclusionary rule, which prohibits police from conducting postindictment lineups in the absence of legal counsel, also apply to preindictment lineups? In other words, does the Sixth Amendment require the presence of a suspect's attorney at preindictment lineups?

HOLDING

No. The Sixth Amendment does not require that a suspect's attorney be present for any preindictment lineups conducted by the police for identification purposes.

RATIONALE

The *Wade-Gilbert per se* exclusionary rule stems from the guarantee of the right to counsel contained in the Sixth Amendment as it is applied to the states through the Fourteenth Amendment. Specifically, the *Wade-Gilbert* rule established the principle that criminal defendants are "entitled to the assistance of counsel at any critical stage of the prosecution, and that a postindictment lineup is such a critical stage." With very little elaboration on the matter, the Court flatly stated that it declined "to import into a routine police investigation an absolute constitutional guarantee historically and rationally applied only after the onset of formal prosecutorial proceedings." The Court noted, however, that its reluctance to apply a *per se* exclusionary rule to preindictment lineups should not be interpreted as a decision that condones unnecessarily suggestive or prejudicial lineup procedures. Instead, it issued a strong cautionary reminder that such actions were still strictly prohibited by the Fifth Amendment's due process clause.

CASE EXCERPT

"In this case we are asked to import into a routine police investigation an absolute constitutional guarantee historically and rationally applicable only after the onset of formal prosecutorial proceedings. We decline to do so. Less than a year after *Wade* and *Gilbert* were decided, the Court explained the rule of those decisions as follows: 'The rationale of those cases was that an accused is entitled to counsel at any "critical stage of the prosecution," and that a post-indictment lineup is such a "critical stage."' We decline to depart from that rationale today by imposing a per se exclusionary rule upon testimony concerning an identification that took place long before the commencement of any prosecution whatever."

CASE SIGNIFICANCE

The Court's refusal to extend the right to counsel to preindictment lineups conducted for identification purposes not only signaled a shift in its philosophy regarding suspects' rights but, more importantly, established a bright line standard for the point at which the right to counsel in criminal matters takes effect. Although the Court did not specifically mention the burden that would otherwise be imposed upon law

KIRBY v. ILLINOIS (cont.)

enforcement had it decided to extend the *Wade-Gilbert per se* exclusionary rule to preindictment lineups, it nonetheless seems important to point out that many of the roadside identifications that no doubt occur on a day-to-day basis owe their permissibility to the decision in this case. Thus, it seems reasonable to speculate that had the Court extended the *Wade-Gilbert per se* exclusionary rule to preindictment identifications, the ability of law enforcement personnel to effectively combat crime would have been significantly hampered. Although suspects do not enjoy a right to counsel during preindictment identifications, law enforcement personnel must nonetheless remain cognizant of suggestive behaviors, influential factors, or inappropriate comments that may prejudice the outcome of a lineup. Otherwise, they run a considerable risk of losing the case not on Sixth Amendment grounds but, instead, on violations of the Fifth Amendment's due process clause.

MANSON v. BRATHWAITE

432 U.S. 98 (1977)

FACTS

An undercover Connecticut state trooper assigned to the narcotics division was taken by an informant to an apartment building for purposes of buying drugs. The pair knocked on a third-floor apartment door and was met by an unidentified black male who exchanged drugs for money. During the transaction, the door was opened some 12 to 18 inches and the black male stood no more than two feet away from the trooper for a period of five to seven minutes. Upon leaving the building, the trooper radioed a physical description of the dealer to backup officers. Upon returning to work two days later, the trooper found on his desk a photo of the dealer that had been retrieved from local archives by one of his backup officers. The photo was used for purposes of identifying Brathwaite as the dealer, a statement accepted into evidence without objection at his trial for possession and sale of heroin. Brathwaite was convicted and the state's supreme court affirmed his sentence. Brathwaite subsequently filed a petition for habeas corpus in district court claiming that admission of the identification testimony at trial violated his Fourteenth Amendment due process rights. The district court dismissed the petition. However, the U.S. Court of Appeals for the Second Circuit reversed

this holding and ordered that a writ be issued unless the state expressed intent to retry Brathwaite within a reasonable period of time and absent the identification testimony. The U.S. Supreme Court then granted certiorari.

ISSUE

Does the Fourteenth Amendment's due process clause require the *per se* exclusion of a police officer's testimony where identification of the defendant was based upon a procedure that may have been unnecessarily suggestive?

HOLDING

No. The Fourteenth Amendment does not require the automatic exclusion of testimony based upon a police officer's identification of the defendant even if it was obtained as the result of a procedure that may have been unnecessarily suggestive.

RATIONALE

In the context of this particular case, the Supreme Court noted that there are two possible standards for determining the admissibility of identification testimony resulting from procedures that may have been biased or unnecessarily suggestive. A strict standard would require the automatic (*per se*) exclusion of any testimony obtained as the result of a biased or suggestive identification procedure. A second standard would determine admissibility of the testimony following consideration of the totality of circumstances surrounding the identification procedure in question. It was the latter of these two standards—one that considers the totality of circumstances—that the Court deemed most appropriate for cases of this nature. Under the totality of circumstances standard, the reliability of the identification is a critical factor. In other words, identification of a defendant arising from a biased or suggestive procedure does not have to be automatically excluded from evidence if it can be shown that the identification possesses certain qualities of reliability. Although these may be greater or fewer in number depending upon the facts of a given case, the Court enunciated five criteria that may be used to establish the reliability of an otherwise questionable identification. These include but are not limited to (1) the opportunity to view, (2) the degree of attention, (3) the accuracy of the description, (4) the witness's level of certainty, and (5) the time between the crime and the confrontation. Applying these five criteria to the facts in the present case, the Court concluded that (1) the undercover trooper had ample opportunity to view the suspect (an elapsed time of several minutes) under adequate lighting, (2) the trooper was a trained observer cognizant of the fact that he would later be called upon to identify the suspect, thus prompting him to take especially close note of Brathwaite's distinguishing features, (3) the trooper's oral description of Brathwaite to backup officers was so detailed that one was able to find a photo of him without even having seen him, (4) the trooper was absolutely certain in his identification of Brathwaite both in court and by photograph, and (5) the amount of time that elapsed between the trooper's exchange with Brathwaite and his viewing of the photograph was minimal as compared to days, weeks, or even months. In sum, the Court concluded that these factors created enough reliability to offset any unfairness or risk of error that may have occurred as the result of a suggestive identification procedure. Thus, the Supreme Court reversed the decision of the court of appeals, which ultimately had the effect of letting Brathwaite's conviction stand.

CASE EXCERPT

"Although identifications arising from single-photograph displays may be viewed in general with suspicion, we find in the instant case little pressure on the witness to acquiesce in the suggestion that such a display entails. D'Onofrio had left the photograph at Glover's office and was not present when Glover first viewed it two days after the event. There thus was little urgency and Glover could view the photograph at his leisure. And since Glover examined the photograph alone, there was no coercive pressure to make an identification arising from the presence of another. The identification was made in circumstances allowing care and reflection."

CASE SIGNIFICANCE

This case represented an effort on behalf of the Supreme Court to resolve an apparent conflict among lower courts regarding the appropriate standard for determining the admissibility of questionable identification testimony. At the same time, it had important implications for law enforcement. Specifically, the case acknowledged that there will no doubt arise circumstances in which police—for one reason or another—are unable to conduct a lineup that is free from suggestive influence. For example, consider a situation in which the police have apprehended a suspect

believed to be responsible for assaulting a victim who is hospitalized and perhaps not expected to live. The police do not have the time to wait for the victim to get better before asking him or her to make an identification. Similarly, they may not be able to bring the victim to the jail or other facility to make an identification because of his or her critical condition. Thus, the only reasonable alternative is to bring the suspect into the hospital room and ask the victim to try and make an identification. Clearly, such an approach is wrought with suggestive elements. However, the Court recognized through its opinion in the present case that an identification from such a procedure need not always be subject to automatic exclusion at trial. Instead, a more tempered approach—one the Court embraced—allows these types of questionable identifications to be considered under a totality of circumstances to determine whether or not they possess qualities of reliability that offset any risk of misidentification. This is but one of several implications this case posed for law enforcement. The case also reaffirmed the notion that, where possible, investigators should incorporate procedures into the identification process that will negate the claim that a particular lineup was unfairly suggestive. Simple measures, such as ensuring that photo lineups consist of more than one picture (a montage) depicting subjects with physical characteristics roughly similar to those of the primary suspect, will help ensure the admissibility of critical identification testimony at trial. Identification procedures such as those at issue in the present case may be marginally acceptable, but they are not ideal.

UNITED STATES v. CREWS
445 U.S. 463 (1980)

FACTS

Immediately after being assaulted and robbed at gunpoint, the victim notified the police and gave them a full description of her assailant. Several days later, Crews, who matched the suspect's description, was seen by the police around the scene of the crime. After an attempt to photograph him proved unsuccessful, Crews was taken into custody, ostensibly as a suspected truant from school, and was detained at police headquarters, where he was briefly questioned, photographed, and then released. Thereafter, the victim identified Crews' photograph as that of her assailant. Crews was again taken into custody and at a court-ordered lineup was

UNITED STATES v. CREW *(cont.)*

identified by the victim. Crews was then indicted for armed robbery and other offenses. On Crews' pretrial motion to suppress all identification testimony, the trial court found that the initial detention at the police station constituted an arrest without probable cause and accordingly ruled that the products of that arrest—the photographic and lineup identifications—could not be introduced at trial, but further held that the victim's ability to identify Crews in court was based upon independent recollection untainted by the intervening identifications and that therefore such testimony was admissible. At trial, the victim once more identified Crews as her assailant, and he was convicted of armed robbery. The District of Columbia Court of Appeals reversed, holding that the in-court identification testimony should have been excluded as a product of the violation of Crews' Fourth Amendment rights. The U.S. Supreme Court then granted certiorari.

ISSUE

Should the in-court identification testimony have been excluded, since it may have been tainted by earlier illegal photographic and lineup identifications?

HOLDING

No. The in-court identification need not be suppressed as the fruit of Crews' concededly unlawful arrest but is admissible because the police's knowledge of Crews' identity and the victim's independent recollections of him both antedated the unlawful arrest and were thus untainted by the constitutional violation.

RATIONALE

The victim's presence in the courtroom at Crews' trial was not the product of any police misconduct. Her identity was known long before there was any official misconduct, and her presence in court was thus not traceable to any Fourth Amendment violation. Nor did the illegal arrest infect the victim's ability to give accurate identification testimony. At trial, she merely retrieved her mnemonic representation of the assailant formed at the time of the crime, compared it to the figure of Crews in the courtroom, and positively identified him as the robber. Insofar as Crews challenges his own presence at trial, he cannot claim immunity from prosecution simply because his appearance in court was precipitated by an unlawful arrest. Crews is not himself a suppressible "fruit," and the illegality of his detention cannot deprive the government of the opportunity to prove his guilt through the introduction of evidence wholly untainted by the police misconduct.

CASE EXCERPT

"In this case the record plainly discloses that prior to his illegal arrest, the police both knew respondent's identity and had some basis to suspect his involvement in the very crimes with which he was charged. Moreover, before they approached respondent, the police had already obtained access to the 'evidence' that implicated him in the robberies, i. e., the mnemonic representations of the criminal retained by the victims and related to the police in the form of their agreement upon his description. In short, the Fourth Amendment violation in this case yielded nothing of evidentiary value that the police did not already have in their grasp. Rather, respondent's unlawful arrest served merely to link together two extant ingredients in his identification. The exclusionary rule enjoins the Government from benefiting from evidence it has unlawfully obtained; it does not reach backward to taint information that was in official hands prior to any illegality."

CASE SIGNIFICANCE

This case is important because it introduced the "independent source" exception to the exclusionary rule. Under this exception, an initial police illegality may not prevent the introduction of seized evidence, if the prosecution can establish that the police could have learned of the evidence through lawful means. Thus police misconduct may not necessarily bar the introduction of important evidence.

PERRY v. NEW HAMPSHIRE
—U.S.—(2012)

FACTS

Around 3 a.m. on August 15, 2008, the Nashua, New Hampshire, Police Department received a call reporting that an African-American male was trying to break into cars parked in the lot of the caller's apartment building. When an officer responding to the call asked eyewitness Nubia Blandon to describe the man, Blandon pointed to her kitchen window and said the man she saw breaking into the car was standing in the parking lot, next to a police officer. Petitioner Barion Perry's arrest followed this identification.

Before trial, Perry moved to suppress Blandon's identification on the ground that admitting it at trial would violate due process. The New Hampshire trial court denied the motion. To determine whether due process prohibits the introduction of an out-of-court identification at trial, the Superior Court said, this Court's decisions instruct a two-step inquiry: The trial court must first decide whether the police used an unnecessarily suggestive identification procedure; if they did, the court must next consider whether that procedure so tainted the resulting identification as to render it unreliable and thus inadmissible. Perry's challenge, the court found, failed at step one, for Blandon's identification did not result from an unnecessarily suggestive procedure employed by the police. A jury subsequently convicted Perry of theft by unauthorized taking.

On appeal, Perry argued that the trial court erred in requiring an initial showing that police arranged a suggestive identification procedure. Suggestive circumstances alone, Perry contended, suffice to require court evaluation of the reliability of an eyewitness identification before allowing it to be presented to the jury. The New Hampshire Supreme Court rejected Perry's argument and affirmed his conviction. The U.S. Supreme Court then granted certiorari.

ISSUE

Does the due process clause require a preliminary judicial inquiry into the reliability of an eyewitness identification?

HOLDING

No. The due process clause does not require a preliminary judicial inquiry into the reliability of an eyewitness identification when the identification was not procured under unnecessarily suggestive circumstances arranged by law enforcement.

RATIONALE

The Supreme Court reasoned that there were sufficient safeguards in place—such as the burden of proof beyond a reasonable doubt—to minimize eyewitness identifications that may be subject to problems of reliability. Furthermore, the justices were concerned that allowing lower courts to entertain preliminary judicial inquiry into all cases involving eyewitness identifications would inappropriately widen the door of due process.

CASE EXCERPT

"Given the safeguards generally applicable in criminal trials, protections availed of by the defense in Perry's case, we hold that the introduction of Blandon's eyewitness testimony, without a preliminary judicial assessment of its reliability, did not render Perry's trial fundamentally unfair."

CASE SIGNIFICANCE

In this case it was argued that a pretrial identification that was first deemed accurate but then contradicted when the witness could not later identify the suspect should be subject to judicial scrutiny as unreliable. The Court, however, rejected this argument and held firm with its line of cases ruling that eyewitness identifications are in some instances exempt from such review. To do otherwise, the Court reasoned, would unnecessarily invite such review into every case involving eyewitness identification, causing an unnecessary due process burden on lower courts when sufficient safeguards against faulty identification are already in place.

DISCUSSION QUESTIONS

1. Why do suspects not enjoy the right to have an attorney present during pretrial identification procedures?
2. Why are suspects entitled to have an attorney present during identification procedures once they have been charged with a crime?
3. What measures can the police take to make sure that pretrial identification procedures are not unduly prejudicial?
4. What practical measures can be taken during a pretrial lineup to minimize claims of prejudicial influence when the suspect of primary interest has a unique identifying characteristic that clearly sets him or her apart from others (e.g., physical handicap, especially tall/short, hair color or style, etc.)?
5. How does the Supreme Court's decision in Perry affect the use of eyewitness testimony at trial?

CHAPTER SEVENTEEN

RIGHT TO COUNSEL

POWELL ET AL. v. ALABAMA, *287 U.S. 45 (1932)*

GIDEON v. WAINWRIGHT, *372 U.S. 335 (1963)*

ESCOBEDO v. ILLINOIS, *378 U.S. 478 (1964)*

MASSIAH v. UNITED STATES, *377 U.S. 201 (1964)*

UNITED STATES v. HENRY, *447 U.S. 264 (1980)*

ROTHGERY v. GILLESPIE COUNTY, *554 U.S. 191 (2008)*

KANSAS v. VENTRIS, *556 U.S.—(2009)*

MONTEJO v. LOUISIANA, *556 U.S. 778 (2009)*

INTRODUCTION

The right to counsel is specifically enumerated by the Sixth Amendment to the Constitution, which states in relevant part, "In all criminal prosecutions, the accused shall enjoy the right to . . . the assistance of counsel for his defense." Initially, this provision applied only to criminal trials; however, it has since been extended to other "critical stages" of the justice process. This chapter traces the evolution of this right from its initial application in *Powell et al. v. Alabama* to *United States v. Henry*.

In *Powell et al. v. Alabama,* also known as the "Scottsboro Boys" case, the Supreme Court held that the denial of legal counsel in a capital case violated the standards of due process. The issue was revisited three decades later in *Gideon v. Wainwright,* a case involving an indigent defendant who had been denied assistance of counsel during trial for felony burglary in Florida. In that matter, the Supreme Court reversed Gideon's conviction, concluding that the right to counsel applies not only to capital cases but to felony prosecutions as well. *Escobedo v. Illinois* and *Massiah v. United States* were both decided the very next term. In *Escobedo,* the justices ruled that a suspect has the right to request and confer with an attorney during custodial interrogations. In *Massiah,* the Court held that the Sixth Amendment prohibits the government from surreptitiously eliciting incriminating statements once an individual has secured the assistance of counsel. More recently, the Court in *United States v. Henry* prohibited the government from enlisting the assistance of jailhouse informants for purposes of obtaining incriminating statements from a defendant.

Although limited in number compared to decisions in other areas of criminal procedure, the cases included in this chapter established the parameters of a very important area of the law. In particular, they defined the boundaries within which police and prosecutors must operate when seeking to obtain confessions lest their actions come into conflict with Sixth Amendment jurisprudence. Where such established rules are disregarded, even with the best or most naive of intentions, there exists likelihood that the obtained information will be later ruled as inadmissible. Accordingly, representatives of the government must remain keenly aware of these cases at the Supreme Court level, as well as those guiding state-level procedure.

POWELL ET AL. v. ALABAMA
287 U.S. 45 (1932)

FACTS

Powell was one of nine black youths charged with the rape of two white girls. The judge presiding over the arraignment appointed all members of the local bar to serve as legal counsel for the boys, although no specific attorney was named until the day of trial. All nine defendants were convicted and sentenced to death. The Alabama Supreme Court affirmed the convictions, and the U.S. Supreme Court granted certiorari.

ISSUE

Does the denial of legal counsel in a capital case constitute a violation of due process under the Fourteenth Amendment?

HOLDING

Yes. The denial of legal counsel in a capital case constitutes a violation of due process under the Fourteenth Amendment.

RATIONALE

In deciding this case, the Supreme Court first noted that criminal defendants should, at a minimum, be afforded the opportunity to secure their own legal counsel. Because Powell and his codefendants were financially unable to secure their own attorneys, combined with the fact that the trial court specifically appointed none, the men were effectively rendered incapable of protecting their liberty interest in what was certainly a serious criminal matter. Furthermore, an Alabama state law required that capital defendants who are unable to secure their own attorney be appointed legal counsel by the trial court. Given these circumstances, the U.S. Supreme Court reversed the nine convictions on Fourteenth Amendment grounds.

CASE EXCERPT

"In a capital case, where the defendant is unable to employ counsel, and is incapable adequately of making his own defense because of ignorance, feeble-mindedness, illiteracy, or the like, it is the duty of the court, whether requested or not, to assign counsel for him as a necessary requisite of due process of law; and that duty is not discharged by an assignment at such a time or under such circumstances as to preclude the giving of effective aid in the preparation and trial of the case. To hold otherwise would be to ignore the fundamental postulate, already adverted to, `that there are certain immutable principles of justice which inhere in the very idea of free government which no member of the Union may disregard.'"

CASE SIGNIFICANCE

This early decision, which has since come to be known as the infamous "Scottsboro Boys" case, affirmed the constitutional principle that criminal defendants, especially those facing capital charges, are entitled to the assistance of legal counsel. Where a defendant is unable to secure an attorney it becomes the affirmative duty of the trial court to appoint one. An interesting aspect about this case is that it was decided not on Sixth Amendment grounds, as one might initially expect, but instead on Fourteenth Amendment grounds; at the time the *Powell* case was heard, the Sixth Amendment and its attending rights did not apply to state criminal proceedings. Thus, the Fourteenth Amendment was the only mechanism available at the time to intervene in state judicial matters. Over the years and decades since this case was decided, the Supreme Court has selectively incorporated specific portions of the Bill of Rights to the states so that today such claims are more appropriately litigated on Sixth rather than Fourteenth Amendment grounds.

GIDEON v. WAINWRIGHT
372 U.S. 335 (1963)

FACTS

Gideon was arrested and charged with felony burglary. At trial, he requested that the court appoint legal counsel based upon his indigent status. The request was denied on grounds that Florida law required appointment of counsel only for indigent defendants charged with a capital crime. The trial proceeded with Gideon representing himself as adequately as possible. Pronounced guilty and sentenced to prison, Gideon filed an unsuccessful writ of habeas corpus with the state supreme court alleging violation of his Sixth Amendment right to counsel. The U.S. Supreme Court then granted certiorari.

ISSUE

Does the Sixth Amendment require that legal counsel be appointed to represent an indigent defendant in state felony prosecutions?

HOLDING

Yes. The Sixth Amendment requires the appointment of legal counsel to represent an indigent defendant facing prosecution on state felony charges.

GIDEON v. WAINWRIGHT *(cont.)*
RATIONALE
In deciding that indigent defendants are entitled to court-appointed counsel in state felony prosecutions, the Supreme Court overturned its previous ruling in the case of *Betts v. Brady,* 316 U.S. 455 (1942). In *Betts,* the Court held that a refusal to appoint counsel for an indigent defendant charged with a felony did not violate the due process clause of the Fourteenth Amendment. In making this shift, it was specifically asserted that "in our adversary system of criminal justice, any person haled [*sic*] into court, who is too poor to hire a lawyer, cannot be assured a fair trial unless counsel is provided for him." Consequently, the Sixth Amendment right to counsel in felony cases was deemed so fundamental to the American system of justice that it should also be applied to state prosecutions.

CASE EXCERPT
"Not only these precedents but also reason and reflection require us to recognize that in our adversary system of criminal justice, any person haled into court, who is too poor to hire a lawyer, cannot be assured a fair trial unless counsel is provided for him. This seems to us to be an obvious truth. Governments, both state and federal, quite properly spend vast sums of money to establish machinery to try defendants accused of crime. Lawyers to prosecute are everywhere deemed essential to protect the public's interest in an orderly society. Similarly, there are few defendants charged with crime, few indeed, who fail to hire the best lawyers they can get to prepare and present their defenses. That government hires lawyers to prosecute and defendants who have the money hire lawyers to defend are the strongest indications of the widespread belief that lawyers in criminal courts are necessities, not luxuries. The right of one charged with crime to counsel may not be deemed fundamental and essential to fair trials in some countries, but it is in ours. From the very beginning, our state and national constitutions and laws have laid great emphasis on procedural and substantive safeguards designed to assure fair trials before impartial tribunals in which every defendant stands equal before the law. This noble ideal cannot be realized if the poor man charged with crime has to face his accusers without a lawyer to assist him."

CASE SIGNIFICANCE
This landmark decision applied the Sixth Amendment right to counsel to state felony prosecutions. This means not only that defendants are entitled to legal representation in such cases, but that an attorney must be provided free of charge for those who cannot afford one on their own means. This protection was afforded on a limited basis to defendants in capital cases as a result of the Court's previous decision in *Powell et al. v. Alabama. Powell,* however, was decided on Fourteenth Amendment grounds, whereas *Gideon* is based squarely on the Sixth Amendment. Thus, the *Gideon* case serves as an example of how the protections contained in the Bill of Rights have been selectively incorporated to the states by a judicially active and liberal Supreme Court. Finally, it is important to note that the Court did not specifically define what level of income (or lack thereof) constitutes "indigence" for purposes of determining whether or not an individual qualifies for court-appointed representation.

ESCOBEDO v. ILLINOIS
378 U.S. 478 (1964)

FACTS
Escobedo was arrested by police in connection with the shooting death of his brother-in-law. Escobedo was never informed of his right to remain silent and, although his attorney was present in the building at the time of questioning, his repeated requests for assistance of counsel were refused. An incriminating statement made to a government attorney was admitted at trial and Escobedo was convicted of murder. The state supreme court initially reversed the conviction but later accepted the state's motion for a rehearing, whereupon it allowed the conviction to stand. The U.S. Supreme Court then granted certiorari.

ISSUE
Does the Sixth Amendment require that police allow a suspect to confer with an attorney if one has been requested during a custodial interrogation?

HOLDING
Yes. The police must allow a suspect to speak with an attorney if one is requested during a custodial interrogation.

RATIONALE
In determining that suspects are constitutionally entitled to request and speak with an attorney during custodial interrogation, the Supreme Court considered

several important factors. For example, it was noted that the investigation centered squarely on Escobedo as a primary suspect. Secondly, he was subjected to questioning in an environment intended to elicit incriminating statements. Finally, Escobedo was not informed of his absolute right to remain silent. These findings, taken into consideration with one another, amounted to a violation of his Sixth Amendment right to counsel requiring reversal of the conviction.

CASE EXCERPT

"Where, as here, the investigation is no longer a general inquiry into an unsolved crime but has begun to focus on a particular suspect, the suspect has been taken into police custody, the police carry out a process of interrogations that lends itself to eliciting incriminating statements, the suspect has requested and been denied an opportunity to consult with his lawyer, and the police have not effectively warned him of his absolute constitutional right to remain silent, the accused has been denied 'the Assistance of Counsel' in violation of the Sixth Amendment to the Constitution as made obligatory upon the States by the Fourteenth Amendment, and that no statement elicited by the police during the interrogation may be used against him at a criminal trial."

CASE SIGNIFICANCE

This landmark decision is credited with forming the nexus between the Fifth Amendment right to remain silent and the Sixth Amendment right to counsel during custodial interrogation that would later culminate in *Miranda v. Arizona,* 384 U.S. 436 (1966). Although some regarded the *Escobedo* decision as an important step forward in protecting the rights of suspects during custodial interrogation, others criticized the ruling on the grounds that it unduly complicated law enforcement efforts. Part of the reason that *Escobedo* is today overshadowed by *Miranda* is that it left several important issues unresolved, primary among them being the question of exactly when and under what types of circumstances the right to counsel becomes applicable. Does it apply only to serious crimes such as rape, robbery, and murder, or does it also apply to petty offenses such as vandalism, shoplifting, and the like? What exactly constitutes a custodial interrogation and, similarly, at what point does one become the "focus" of an investigation? Because of these and other lingering questions, the decision is not as routinely relied upon today as it was initially. Instead, as noted earlier,

it is credited with laying a foundation for the Court's decision in *Miranda* and its progeny.

MASSIAH v. UNITED STATES
377 U.S. 201 (1964)

FACTS
While employed as a merchant marine, Massiah conspired with others to smuggle drugs into the country aboard a U.S. vessel. Acting upon this information, federal customs officers boarded and searched the ship when it arrived in port. The expected cache of drugs was discovered, leading to Massiah's indictment. He was arraigned, retained a lawyer, pled not guilty, and was released on bail. Several days later one of Massiah's coconspirators began cooperating with the government by allowing agents to electronically eavesdrop on a postindictment conversation between the two men. During the conversation, Massiah made incriminating statements that were introduced over objection at trial. Massiah was convicted in federal district court, and a federal court of appeals affirmed. The U.S. Supreme Court then granted certiorari.

ISSUE
Do incriminating statements surreptitiously elicited by the police from a suspect who has already been charged with a crime and retained an attorney violate the Sixth Amendment right to counsel?

HOLDING
Yes. The Sixth Amendment prohibits the police from surreptitiously obtaining incriminating statements from a suspect who has previously been charged with a crime and retained an attorney.

RATIONALE
In holding that the surreptitiously obtained incriminating statements violated Massiah's constitutional rights, the Court referred to its prior decision in *Spano v. New York,* 360 U.S. 315 (1959) overturning the petitioner's conviction on grounds that he had confessed to murder after being indicted and without the benefit of legal counsel. Also cited was the case of *Powell et al. v. Alabama,* in which the Court reversed the capital conviction of nine defendants on grounds that they had been denied legal counsel during trial. Although these two cases were decided on Fourteenth Amendment grounds, it was reasoned that the need for assistance of

MASSIAH v. UNITED STATES *(cont.)*

counsel during postindictment activities such as those in the immediate matter was so great that it could not reasonably be ignored. Accordingly, the Court ruled that the Sixth Amendment right to counsel was directly applicable to the facts present in Massiah's case, resulting in reversal of the federal conviction.

CASE EXCERPT

"We do not question that in this case, as in many cases, it was entirely proper to continue an investigation of the suspected criminal activities of the defendant and his alleged confederates, even though the defendant had already been indicted. All that we hold is that the defendant's own incriminating statements, obtained by federal agents under the circumstances here disclosed, could not constitutionally be used by the prosecution as evidence against him at his trial."

CASE SIGNIFICANCE

This case prohibited the police from surreptitiously gathering incriminating evidence from a suspect who has already been indicted for a crime. Once charged, the police cannot elicit incriminating statements from a suspect without his or her attorney being present. If, however, the suspect has not been charged, the government behavior prohibited by this ruling would have otherwise been deemed constitutionally acceptable. One last point to note is that this case involved the use of an electronic eavesdropping device, thereby also raising a Fourth Amendment issue. However, the Court did not address this particular issue because of the manner in which it resolved the case. Instead, this issue has been addressed by an altogether different line of cases beginning with *Katz v. United States,* 389 U.S. 347 (1967) (see Chapter Fifteen).

UNITED STATES v. HENRY

447 U.S. 264 (1980)

FACTS

Henry was indicted on federal bank robbery charges and was being held in jail awaiting trial when he made incriminating statements to a jailhouse informant operating under the guidance of government agents. The informant testified against Henry, who was convicted. Henry moved to have the sentence vacated on grounds that his Sixth Amendment right to counsel

had been violated as a result of the informant's actions. A federal district court denied the motion but the court of appeals reversed, citing *Massiah v. United States* as controlling precedent. The U.S. Supreme Court then granted certiorari.

ISSUE

Does the use of a jailhouse informant operating under guidance of government for purposes of gathering incriminating information from a criminal defendant violate the Sixth Amendment right to counsel?

HOLDING

Yes. The government cannot enlist the assistance of a jailhouse informant for purposes of gathering incriminating information from a criminal defendant.

RATIONALE

The Supreme Court's decision that the government cannot enlist the assistance of a jailhouse informant for purposes of gathering incriminating information was predicated on two factors. First, it was concluded that the informant acted as an agent of the government. Secondly, Henry was under indictment when the informant gathered the incriminating information, thereby rendering his statements inadmissible under *Massiah v. United States.*

CASE EXCERPT

"The question here is whether under the facts of this case a Government agent `deliberately elicited' incriminating statements from Henry within the meaning of *Massiah.* Three factors are important. First, Nichols was acting under instructions as a paid informant for the Government; second, Nichols was ostensibly no more than a fellow inmate of Henry; and third, Henry was in custody and under indictment at the time he was engaged in conversation by Nichols."

CASE SIGNIFICANCE

This case limited the use of jailhouse informants by police. More specifically, it prohibited the police from actively enlisting the assistance of jailhouse informants for purposes of gathering incriminating information from other prisoners. However, the decision did not appear to prohibit the use of such information so long as the government does not actively solicit individuals to work on its behalf. Equally important, if not more so, is the fact that once an individual is charged, he or she may not be "questioned"—even by another prisoner—without having an attorney present.

ROTHGERY v. GILLESPIE COUNTY

554 U.S. 191 (2008)

FACTS

Texas police relied on erroneous information that petitioner Rothgery had a previous felony conviction to arrest him as a felon in possession of a firearm. The officers brought Rothgery before a magistrate judge, as required by state law, for a so-called "article 15.17 hearing," at which the Fourth Amendment probable-cause determination was made, bail was set, and Rothgery was formally apprised of the accusation against him. After the hearing, the magistrate judge committed Rothgery to jail, and he was released after posting a surety bond. Rothgery had no money for a lawyer and made several unheeded oral and written requests for appointed counsel. He was subsequently indicted and rearrested, his bail was increased, and he was jailed when he could not post the bail. Subsequently, Rothgery was assigned a lawyer, who assembled the paperwork that prompted the indictment's dismissal.

Rothgery then brought this 42 U.S.C. §1983 action against respondent County, claiming that if it had provided him a lawyer within a reasonable time after the article 15.17 hearing, he would not have been indicted, rearrested, or rejailed. He asserted that the County's unwritten policy of denying appointed counsel to indigent defendants out on bond until an indictment is entered violated his Sixth Amendment right to counsel. The District Court granted the County summary judgment, and the Fifth Circuit affirmed, considering itself bound by Circuit precedent to the effect that the right to counsel did not attach at the article 15.17 hearing because the relevant prosecutors were not aware of, or involved in, Rothgery's arrest or appearance at the hearing, and there was no indication that the officer at Rothgery's appearance had any power to commit the State to prosecute without a prosecutor's knowledge or involvement.

ISSUE

Does an article 15.17 hearing, which involves, among other things, a determination of charges against a defendant, constitute a significant event in the adversarial judicial process such that appointment of counsel under the Sixth Amendment is constitutionally required?

HOLDING

Yes. A criminal defendant's initial appearance before a magistrate judge, where he learns the charge against him and his liberty is subject to restriction, marks the initiation of adversary judicial proceedings that trigger attachment of the Sixth Amendment right to counsel.

RATIONALE

The County tried to downplay the significance of the initial appearance by saying that an attachment rule unqualified by prosecutorial involvement would lead to the conclusion "that the State has statutorily committed to prosecute *every* suspect arrested by the police," given that "state law requires an article 15.17 hearing for every arrestee." The answer, though, is that the State has done just that, subject to the option to change its official mind later. The State may rethink its commitment at any point: it may choose not to seek indictment in a felony case, say, or the prosecutor may enter *nolle prosequi* after the case gets to the jury room. But without a change of position, a defendant subject to accusation after his or her initial appearance is headed for trial and needs to get a lawyer working, whether to attempt to avoid that trial or to be ready with a defense when the trial date arrives.

CASE EXCERPT

"We do not decide whether the 6-month delay in appointment of counsel resulted in prejudice to Rothgery's Sixth Amendment rights, and have no occasion to consider what standards should apply in deciding this. We merely reaffirm what we have held before and what an overwhelming majority of American jurisdictions understand in practice: a criminal defendant's initial appearance before a judicial officer, where he learns the charge against him and his liberty is subject to restriction, marks the start of adversary judicial proceedings that trigger attachment of the Sixth Amendment right to counsel."

CASE SIGNIFICANCE

This case reaffirms and further clarifies previous decisions in which the Court has ruled that the Sixth Amendment right to counsel attaches at critical stages of the adversarial judicial process like that which occurred in the article 15.17 hearing. Simply stated,

ROTHGERY v. GILLESPIE COUNTY *(cont.)*
once a suspect or arrestee has been informed of the charges against him or her and has been informed of his or her rights under *Miranda*, the Sixth Amendment right to counsel has been triggered. Consequently, all subsequent police action must be undertaken in light of this situation.

KANSAS v. VENTRIS

556 U.S.—(2009)

FACTS

Ventris was in jail awaiting trial on murder and robbery charges. Police placed a jailhouse informant in his cell in an effort to obtain incriminating statements, a practice condemned by the Supreme Court in *Massiah v. United States* (1964). The informant was instructed to ask Ventris about the crimes, and Ventris made incriminating statements to the informant. The prosecution did not use introduce these statements in its case in chief but did call the informant to rebut Ventris' testimony that someone else was the killer. Ventris was convicted. On appeal his conviction was reversed by the Kansas supreme court, which held that the eliciting of incriminating statements by an informant acting as a state agent without counsel violated the Sixth Amendment. The U.S. Supreme Court then granted certiorari.

ISSUE

Did use of the jailhouse informant for purposes of rebutting Ventris' testimony violate the Sixth Amendment under the Court's previous decision in *Massiah*?

HOLDING

No. Incriminating statements obtained in violation of the Sixth Amendment right to counsel may be used to impeach the testimony of the defendant. Such statements cannot be used to prove guilt, however.

RATIONALE

It is illogical to say that the right is not violated until trial counsel's task of opposing conviction has been undermined by the statement's admission into evidence. A defendant is not denied counsel merely because the prosecution has been permitted to introduce evidence of guilt, even evidence so overwhelming that the attorney's job of gaining an acquittal is rendered impossible. In such circumstances the accused continues to enjoy the assistance of counsel; the assistance is simply not worth much. The assistance of counsel has been denied, however, at the prior critical stage that produced the inculpatory evidence.

CASE EXCERPT

"This case does not involve, therefore, the prevention of a constitutional violation, but rather the scope of the remedy for a violation that has already occurred. Our precedents make clear that the game of excluding tainted evidence for impeachment purposes is not worth the candle. The interests safeguarded by such exclusion are outweighed by the need to prevent perjury and to assure the integrity of the trial process. It is one thing to say that the Government cannot make an affirmative use of evidence unlawfully obtained. It is quite another to say that the defendant can... 'provide himself with a shield against contradiction of his untruths.' Once the defendant testifies in a way that contradicts prior statements, denying the prosecution use of the traditional truth-testing devices of the adversary process is a high price to pay for vindication of the right to counsel at the prior stage."

CASE SIGNIFICANCE

In the earlier case of *Massiah*, the Supreme Court ruled that the use of jailhouse informants for purposes of eliciting incriminating statements was unconstitutional under the Sixth Amendment. Here, a caveat is created: while prosecutors cannot use inculpatory statements elicited by jailhouse informants as evidence in chief against a defendant, the information can be used to impeach the testimony of the defendant. Thus, while the use of jailhouse informants was previously rendered unconstitutional in *Massiah*, the practice is partly resurrected by this decision insofar as it allows prosecutors to make some salvageable use of such information, but only for impeachment purposes.

MONTEJO v. LOUISIANA

556 U.S. 778 (2009)

FACTS

Montejo was arrested and charged with first-degree murder in Louisiana. He was appointed counsel at his first court appearance, a fact that he did not acknowledge. Police officers subsequently re-Mirandized him and asked him if he would accompany them on a search for the murder weapon; in the course of doing so he provided them with a letter of apology he had written to the victim's wife. When the incriminating letter was admitted at trial, Montejo objected, arguing that it had been obtained in violation of his Sixth Amendment right to counsel since the police had obtained it without his counsel being present. In *Michigan v. Jackson* (1986), the Supreme Court held that statements obtained by police during an interview without counsel after the suspect had invoked his right to counsel at an arraignment were not admissible. The trial court and state supreme court upheld the admission of the letter, on the ground that *Jackson* did not apply since Montejo had not affirmatively acknowledged his acceptance of appointed counsel during his first court appearance.

ISSUE

Was the incriminating letter properly admitted into evidence even though it was obtained by investigators in the absence of the suspect's attorney?

HOLDING

Yes. The Supreme Court held that the letter was properly admitted and, in doing so, explicitly overruled *Michigan v. Jackson*, stating that it had proved unworkable and that there were sufficient safeguards of the right to counsel in place without the additional complexity that the rule added.

RATIONALE

In practice, *Montejo*'s rule would prevent police-initiated interrogation entirely once the Sixth Amendment right attaches, at least in those States that appoint counsel promptly without request from the defendant. As the dissent in *Jackson* pointed out, with no expressed disagreement from the majority, the opinion "most assuredly [did] *not* hold that the *Edwards per se* rule prohibiting all police-initiated interrogations applies from the moment the defendant's Sixth Amendment right to counsel attaches, with or without a request for counsel by the defendant." That would have constituted a "shockingly dramatic restructuring of the balance this Court has traditionally struck between the rights of the defendant and those of the larger society."

CASE EXCERPT

"Although our holding means that the Louisiana Supreme Court correctly rejected Montejo's claim under *Jackson*, we think that Montejo should be given an opportunity to contend that his letter of apology should still have been suppressed under the rule of *Edwards*. If Montejo made a clear assertion of the right to counsel when the officers approached him about accompanying them on the excursion for the murder weapon, then no interrogation should have taken place unless Montejo initiated it. Even if Montejo subsequently agreed to waive his rights, that waiver would have been invalid had it followed an unequivocal election of the right."

CASE SIGNIFICANCE

This case once again reaffirms the principle that acknowledgment or rejection of Constitutional rights must be made in a clear and unequivocal manner. More simply and directly stated, had Montejo requested an attorney, one would have been provided and no interview would have occurred. Because, however, he failed to acknowledge his right to counsel, it seemed at the time reasonably safe to assume that he did not want to speak with an attorney before investigators took him on a search for the murder weapon.

DISCUSSION QUESTIONS

1. Why is the right to assistance of counsel of such vital importance in capital cases as compared to misdemeanor cases? Where should the line be drawn? That is, to what types of cases should the right apply and, conversely, to what types of cases (if any) should it not?

2. In Constitutional terms, what is the major difference between the police prompting a jailhouse informant to obtain incriminating evidence or statements from a defendant, as compared to a situation in which the informant gathers the incriminating evidence on his or her own without having been asked to do so by agents of the state?

3. Describe and discuss the Supreme Court's rationale in extending the Sixth Amendment right to include felony prosecutions when in the past this right had applied only to capital cases.

4. Discuss how the Supreme Court's decision in *Escobedo* relates to the decision in *Miranda v. Arizona* (see next chapter). How are the two cases related to one another in chronological, constitutional, and practical terms?

5. What do the Supreme Court's most recent decisions regarding the right to counsel suggest about the Court's perception of the extent of that right?

THE DEVELOPMENT AND SCOPE OF THE *MIRANDA* WARNINGS

BROWN v. MISSISSIPPI, *297 U.S. 278 (1936)*

MIRANDA v. ARIZONA, *384 U.S. 436 (1966)*

EDWARDS v. ARIZONA, *451 U.S. 477 (1981)*

SOUTH DAKOTA v. NEVILLE, *459 U.S. 553 (1983)*

BERKEMER v. MCCARTY, *468 U.S. 420 (1984)*

NEW YORK v. QUARLES, *467 U.S. 649 (1984)*

OREGON v. ELSTAD, *470 U.S. 298 (1985)*

COLORADO v. CONNELLY, *479 U.S. 157 (1986)*

COLORADO v. SPRING, *479 U.S. 564 (1987)*

PATTERSON v. ILLINOIS, *487 U.S. 285 (1988)*

ARIZONA v. ROBERSON, *486 U.S. 675 (1988)*

DUCKWORTH v. EAGAN, *492 U.S. 195 (1989)*

MINNICK v. MISSISSIPPI, *498 U.S. 146 (1990)*

PENNSYLVANIA v. MUNIZ, *496 U.S. 582 (1990)*

ARIZONA v. FULMINANTE, *499 U.S. 279 (1991)*

MCNEIL v. WISCONSIN, *501 U.S. 171 (1991)*

DAVIS v. UNITED STATES, *512 U.S. 452 (1994)*

MISSOURI v. SEIBERT, *542 U.S. 600 (2004)*

UNITED STATES v. PATANE, *542 U.S. 360 (2004)*

FLORIDA v. POWELL, *559 U.S.—(2010)*

MARYLAND v. SHATZER, *559 U.S.—(2010)*

BERGHUIS v. THOMPKINS, *560 U.S.—(2010)*

J.D.B. v. NORTH CAROLINA, *564 U.S.—(2011)*

INTRODUCTION

*M*iranda v. Arizona is one of the most influential criminal procedure cases ever decided by the Supreme Court. The practical effects of this 5–4 decision on day-to-day police operations have been so profound that it has taken almost 50 years to decipher exactly how far and in what contexts the decreed protections actually apply. Contrast this enduring need for clarification against the fact that average members of the public can generally recite key phrases of the decision with amazing accuracy, and it is not surprising to find that many police officers widely bemoan its perceived restraining effect on their ability to fight crime.

The cases in this chapter are of two broad types— those affirming the *Miranda* decision and those weakening it. A history of the warnings' development is traced through cases such as *Brown v. Mississippi* (confessions obtained by torture are not admissible), *Edwards v. Arizona* (officers may not reinitiate contact with a suspect who has previously invoked the right to remain silent), and *Michigan v. Jackson* (the police may not interrogate a suspect who has asked for assistance of counsel until he or she has had an opportunity to meet with an attorney). By comparison, a number of decisions eroding the warnings' protective intent are briefed as well. These include cases such as *New York v. Quarles* (concern for public safety outweighs strict adherence to the *Miranda* decision), *Duckworth v. Eagan* (it is not necessary for the warnings to be recited exactly as they appeared in the original case), and *Pennsylvania v. Muniz* (the police ask routine questions of DWI suspects and videotape the responses without having to inform arrestees of their *Miranda* rights).

In summarizing these and the dozen or so other decisions highlighted within this chapter, three important points bear mention. First, the clearly diverse array of cases that follow have contributed to the development of an extremely confusing area of the law—one that requires constant updating and review by law enforcement personnel in all types of investigative and enforcement assignments. Second, unlike the exclusionary rule, whose application is at least somewhat tempered by the "good faith" exception, the judiciary rarely gives latitude to officers who are blasé or haphazard in their respect for a suspect's right to remain silent. Last, whether or not one agrees with the *Miranda* decision and its progeny of related cases, the established principles it stands for now serve as immutable facts of life in police work.

BROWN v. MISSISSIPPI
297 U.S. 278 (1936)

FACTS
Brown was confronted at his home by a deputy sheriff who asked that he accompany him to another residence where a murder had taken place. Once at the scene, Brown was accused of the crime and twice hanged from a tree until he was ready to talk. Once lowered to the ground, Brown was tied to the tree and whipped before being set free. Several days later the deputy returned to Brown's residence and placed him under arrest. The deputy beat Brown again while en route to the jail until he finally confessed to the murder. Unbeknownst to Brown, two other men were also arrested and beaten until they confessed. Despite testifying that the confessions had been beaten out of them, the three men were convicted and sentenced to death. The Mississippi Supreme Court affirmed the conviction and the U.S. Supreme Court granted certiorari.

ISSUE
Were the confessions, obtained by way of physical torture, properly admitted into evidence?

HOLDING
No. Confessions that are obtained by way of physical torture, coercion, or brutality on the part of law enforcement officials are not admissible at trial under the Fourteenth Amendment's due process clause.

RATIONALE
In deciding that physical brutality automatically renders a confession inadmissible at trial, the Supreme Court noted that although states are generally free to run their courts as they see fit, they are nonetheless required to observe certain fundamental constitutional principles. Chief among these is the right of a defendant to be free from physical torture aimed at obtaining a confession. Similarly, the state may not deny a defendant the assistance of legal counsel. The absence of such fundamental protections in Brown's case, the Court reasoned, amounted to a clear denial of due process, requiring reversal of the conviction.

CASE EXCERPT
"In the instant case, the trial court was fully advised by the undisputed evidence of the way in which the confessions had been procured. The trial court knew that there was no other evidence upon which conviction and sentence could be based. Yet it proceeded to permit conviction and to pronounce sentence. The conviction and sentence were void for want of the essential elements of due process, and the proceeding thus vitiated could be challenged in any appropriate manner."

CASE SIGNIFICANCE
This case, decided in 1936, established the principle of law that confessions obtained by way of physical torture, coercion, or brutality on the part of law enforcement officials are inadmissible at trial under the Fourteenth Amendment's due process clause. Although representing a clear step toward eliminating coerced confessions, it was not until the Supreme Court rendered its decision in *Miranda v. Arizona* some 30 years later that the full weight of the Constitution would be brought to bear. However, the Court prohibited only those confessions obtained by physically coercive means as compared to those more subtly obtained by psychologically coercive means. Despite this limitation, the *Brown* decision stands as a landmark case upholding the rights of criminal defendants to be free from the injustice suffered as a result of being physically coerced into making a false confession.

MIRANDA v. ARIZONA
384 U.S. 436 (1966)

FACTS
Miranda was taken into police custody in connection with a kidnapping and sexual assault. Interrogated at length by detectives, he eventually provided a full written confession that was admitted at trial, resulting in

MIRANDA v. ARIZONA *(cont.)*
conviction on both charges. Miranda appealed, but the state court upheld his conviction. The U.S. Supreme Court then granted certiorari.

ISSUE
Must the police inform a suspect of his or her dual constitutional rights to legal representation and protection from self-incrimination during custodial interrogation?

HOLDING
Yes. The police must inform a suspect of his or her constitutional right to legal representation and protection from self-incrimination during custodial interrogation. Any incriminating statements obtained in violation of these rights are inadmissible at trial.

RATIONALE
In ruling that prosecutors are constitutionally prohibited from introducing incriminating admissions obtained during custodial interrogation from an individual who has not been advised of his or her right to avoid self-incrimination under the Fifth Amendment and to legal representation under the Sixth Amendment, the Supreme Court scrutinized the coercive conditions under which such statements are generally obtained. Specifically, the Court reviewed a litany of questionable tactics employed by investigators to "persuade" a suspect to talk about and/or confess to involvement in a given crime. Given the long history with which the Fifth Amendment's privilege against self-incrimination had been applied to trial proceedings, it seemed only reasonable to extend its protection to settings such as custodial interrogation where it was also needed. In conjunction with extending the Fifth Amendment privilege against self-incrimination, the Court spelled out the language of the warning that must be given to suspects prior to custodial interrogation. Specifically, a suspect must be informed that he or she has the right to remain silent; anything he or she says will be used against him or her in court; he or she has the right to consult with a lawyer and to have the lawyer present during interrogation; and if he or she cannot afford an attorney one will be appointed.

In addition to this language, the Court admonished officers that if a suspect invokes the right to remain silent prior to or during the interrogation, all questioning must immediately cease. If a suspect chooses not to invoke these rights and allows the interrogation to proceed without requesting an attorney, the government bears the burden of proving that these rights were both knowingly and intelligently waived. Finally, the option to rescind a waiver of these rights rests with the suspect so that, at any time, he or she may invoke the privilege to avoid self-incrimination and request the presence of an attorney. Where any of these rights are violated, the obtained statements will be inadmissible at trial.

CASE EXCERPT
"There can be no doubt that the Fifth Amendment privilege is available outside of criminal court proceedings and serves to protect persons in all settings in which their freedom of action is curtailed in any significant way from being compelled to incriminate themselves. We have concluded that without proper safeguards the process of in-custody interrogation of persons suspected or accused of crime contains inherently compelling pressures which work to undermine the individual's will to resist and to compel him to speak where he would not otherwise do so freely. In order to combat these pressures and to permit a full opportunity to exercise the privilege against self-incrimination, the accused must be adequately and effectively apprised of his rights and the exercise of those rights must be fully honored... At the outset, if a person in custody is to be subjected to interrogation, he must first be informed in clear and unequivocal terms that he has the right to remain silent. For those unaware of the privilege, the warning is needed simply to make them aware of it—the threshold requirement for an intelligent decision as to its exercise. More important, such a warning is an absolute prerequisite in overcoming the inherent pressures of the interrogation atmosphere. It is not just the subnormal or woefully ignorant who succumb to an interrogator's imprecations, whether implied or expressly stated, that the interrogation will continue until a confession is obtained or that silence in the face of accusation is itself damning and will bode ill when presented to a jury. Further, the warning will show the individual that his interrogators are prepared to recognize his privilege should he choose to exercise it... The warning of the right to remain silent must be accompanied by the explanation that anything said can and will be used against the individual in court. This warning is needed in order to make him aware not only of the privilege, but also of the consequences of forgoing it... Once warnings have been given, the subsequent procedure is clear. If the individual indicates in any

CHAPTER EIGHTEEN *MIRANDA* WARNINGS 159
manner, at any time prior to or during questioning, that he wishes to remain silent, the interrogation must cease. At this point he has shown that he intends to exercise his Fifth Amendment privilege; any statement taken after the person invokes his privilege cannot be other than the product of compulsion, subtle or otherwise."

CASE SIGNIFICANCE

Arguably one of the most significant rulings of the due process revolution, *Miranda* is so widely recognized by the general public that many can recite portions of its language from memory. Unfortunately, however, a considerable degree of misconception surrounds its provisions despite the uncommon specificity with which the opinion was written. For example, many believe that *Miranda* applies in its entirety any time they are approached by the police. It is thought that officers must always warn an individual before asking even the most innocuous of questions. This is, of course, not true. Instead (and as other cases in this chapter illustrate), the police are required to warn individuals only during custodial interrogation—*Miranda* does not apply to roadside questioning during a traffic stop, nor when asking routine questions as part of the booking procedure. This misinformation, attributable in large part to the popular media and fictionalized television portrayals, leads to much controversy between the police and those with whom they come into contact. Finally, although the decision is widely looked upon by crime-control advocates as unnecessarily hindering the law enforcement mission, it has nonetheless served to curtail otherwise questionable tactics previously used to extract confessions, thereby enhancing ethical standards within the profession.

EDWARDS v. ARIZONA
451 U.S. 477 (1981)

FACTS

Edwards was arrested by police on a warrant for the offenses of robbery, burglary, and first-degree murder. Having been informed of his *Miranda* rights upon arrival at the stationhouse, Edwards willingly submitted to questioning regarding his involvement in the alleged offenses. The officer conducting the interrogation told Edwards he had been implicated by another suspect also in custody. Edwards gave a taped statement denying his involvement but nonetheless offered

to "make a deal." Lacking the authority to enter into such an agreement, the officer allowed Edwards to call a county attorney. The record does not provide any details regarding the nature of this call other than to indicate that after a few brief moments Edwards hung up and stated, "I want an attorney before making a deal." The investigating officer dutifully ceased the interrogation and returned Edwards to his cell. The following morning, two altogether different detectives arrived at the jail requesting to see Edwards, who stated that he did not want to talk to anyone. The jailer conveying the message told Edwards that "he had" to talk to the detectives. The pair of officers informed Edwards of his *Miranda* rights a second time, followed by a request that he talk with them about the alleged offenses. Edwards asked that he be allowed to hear the taped statement of his accomplice. The officers played the tape for several minutes, whereupon Edwards agreed to make an oral statement on the condition that it not be recorded. The detectives informed him that it was irrelevant whether or not the statement was recorded since they could still testify in court as to anything he said. Edwards stated that he would tell the detectives whatever they wanted to know but reaffirmed his demand that the statement not be recorded. Detectives accommodated this condition and Edwards offered information implicating his involvement in the crimes. Prior to trial, Edwards moved to suppress the statement on the basis that officers had violated his *Miranda* rights by returning to question him a second time without allowing him access to counsel. The trial court granted the motion to suppress but later reversed the ruling when presented with a controlling decision by a superior Arizona court. The statement was admitted at trial and Edwards was convicted. The state's supreme court, considering the matter on appeal, determined that Edwards had indeed invoked his right to remain silent and have counsel present during the initial interrogation. Because the altogether different pair of detectives who visited Edwards the next morning correctly informed him of his rights, which he then voluntarily waived, the Arizona Supreme Court upheld the decision of the trial court to allow his confession into evidence and the convictions were affirmed. The U.S. Supreme Court then granted certiorari.

ISSUE

Are officers prohibited from reinitiating contact with a suspect once he or she has invoked the right to remain

EDWARDS v. ARIZONA *(cont.)*

silent and have the assistance of counsel during custodial interrogation?

HOLDING

Yes. Officers may not reinitiate contact with a suspect who has previously invoked the right to remain silent and have the assistance of counsel during custodial interrogation. In other words, once a suspect states that he or she desires legal representation during custodial interrogation, the questioning must stop immediately and may not resume until the request has been satisfied, even if only to inquire whether or not the individual has had a change of mind and wants to confess. The conviction was overturned.

RATIONALE

The Court's decision in *Miranda* established the principle of law that criminal suspects have the right not only to remain silent but also to have legal counsel present while undergoing custodial interrogation by state agents. Once these rights are invoked, all questioning must immediately cease until an attorney is present. If a suspect chooses to waive these rights, the burden of demonstrating that this decision was both informed and voluntary is placed upon the state. In the immediate case, neither the trial court nor the state supreme court undertook an inquiry to determine whether Edwards had made the waiver in an informed and voluntary manner. Instead, both courts erroneously assumed that the waiver met these criteria based solely upon the fact that Edwards was responsive to a police-initiated follow-up interrogation. Consequently, the decision of the Arizona Supreme Court that Edwards had knowingly and freely waived his right to the presence of counsel during the second interrogation was overturned.

CASE EXCERPT

"*Miranda* itself indicated that the assertion of the right to counsel was a significant event and that once exercised by the accused, 'the interrogation must cease until an attorney is present.' Our later cases have not abandoned that view... We reconfirm these views and, to lend them substance, emphasize that it is inconsistent with *Miranda* and its progeny for the authorities, at their instance, to reinterrogate an accused in custody if he has clearly asserted his right to counsel."

CASE SIGNIFICANCE

The Court's decision in the *Edwards* case had several notable implications. First, it clearly reaffirmed the *Miranda* decision and its progeny to the extent that once a suspect invokes the right to remain silent and requests the presence of legal counsel, all questioning must immediately cease until an attorney is physically present. Second, it established "bright line" procedures for how state agents are to act in these types of situations. More specifically, the case established the clear and unequivocal standard that once these joint rights are invoked, officers are prohibited from reinitiating contact and inquiry with the suspect even if they again inform him or her anew of his or her *Miranda* rights. For courts and the judges who preside over them, the decision helps clarify previously established guidelines for determining whether or not a suspect's waiver of these rights was both voluntary and informed. Third, the decision serves as a prophylactic that protects suspects from the pressures inherent in the custodial environment. In the absence of such protection, the Court feared that suspects will eventually waive their rights and confess to police in the absence of counsel during follow-up interrogation sessions simply because they have been worn down. Thus, one might imagine a situation in which a suspect invokes the right to remain silent and have counsel present during questioning. The interview might then stop only to be resumed at a later time by other officers who again read the *Miranda* warning and proceed with questioning until such time as the rights are again invoked. Still later, other officers might again do the same until such time as the suspect waives his rights because he senses that he will never be presented with an attorney during the interrogations. A fourth implication specifically noted in the Court's opinion centers upon the issue of initiation—that is, who undertakes the subsequent contact in which the rights are waived and a confession is proffered. Writing for the Court, Justice White noted that the protections established by *Edwards* would not apply in situations where the suspect initiates subsequent contact, conversation, or communication with the police. In the final analysis, this decision prevents police and state agents from repeatedly interrogating a suspect who has invoked the right to remain silent and have counsel present during such questioning, even if they inform him or her of his or her rights anew each and every time. It also has the effect of prohibiting the police from even checking in on a suspect who is in custody to see if he or she has had a "change of heart" about wanting to talk.

SOUTH DAKOTA v. NEVILLE

459 U.S. 553 (1983)

FACTS

Neville was stopped by officers for running a stop sign. Unable to satisfactorily perform a series of field sobriety tests, he was arrested, informed of his *Miranda* rights, and asked to submit to a blood-alcohol test. Neville refused, stating that he was too drunk to pass the test. Under South Dakota law, the fact that a DWI arrestee refuses to submit to a blood-alcohol test may be introduced into evidence at trial. In Neville's case, however, the trial court judge suppressed such evidence on the grounds that officers had failed to inform him of the consequences for refusing to take the test. The state supreme court affirmed the suppression order on grounds that the introduction of such evidence would violate the Fifth Amendment protection to avoid self-incrimination. The U.S. Supreme Court then granted certiorari.

ISSUE

Does the Fifth Amendment privilege against self-incrimination prohibit the state from introducing evidence that a DWI defendant refused to take a blood-alcohol test? Does an officer's failure to inform a DWI suspect that refusal to take a blood-alcohol test may later be introduced as evidence at trial constitute a violation of due process?

HOLDING

No. Admission into evidence of a DWI defendant's refusal to take a blood-alcohol test does not violate the Fifth Amendment right to avoid self-incrimination. The failure of an officer to inform a DWI suspect that refusal to take a blood-alcohol test may be introduced at trial does not constitute a violation of due process.

RATIONALE

The U.S. Supreme Court overturned the South Dakota Supreme Court's decision prohibiting prosecutors from introducing into evidence the fact that a DWI defendant refused to take a blood-alcohol test. Specifically, the Court reasoned that such evidence does not violate the Fifth Amendment right to avoid self-incrimination

due to the fact that an officer's request to take the blood-alcohol test is not of a coercive nature. Because the Fifth Amendment is limited to prohibiting the use of physical or moral compulsion exerted on the person asserting the privilege, its protection does not apply to the facts in Neville's case. In other words, an officer's request that a DWI suspect take a blood-alcohol test is no different than asking someone to submit to fingerprinting. A suspect who refuses to be fingerprinted may have this evidence introduced against him or her at trial without violating the Fifth Amendment. The same rules apply to the present case. Finally, the Court also ruled that it is not fundamentally unfair for the prosecution to use a suspect's refusal to take the blood-alcohol test as evidence at trial even though he or she was not specifically warned of its potential use. This finding stems from the fact that the defendant's right to refuse the test is a matter of grace bestowed by the state legislature, and an officer's failure to warn the suspect of its potential use does not constitute a promise that the refusal will not be used as evidence at trial.

CASE EXCERPT

"We do not think it fundamentally unfair for South Dakota to use the refusal to take the test as evidence of guilt, even though respondent was not specifically warned that his refusal could be used against him at trial. First, the right to silence underlying the *Miranda* warnings is one of constitutional dimension, and thus cannot be unduly burdened. Respondent's right to refuse the blood-alcohol test, by contrast, is simply a matter of grace bestowed by the South Dakota Legislature."

CASE SIGNIFICANCE

The decision in this case not only endorsed the growing practice among states to require that DWI suspects provide a sample of their blood, breath, or urine for purposes of determining blood-alcohol content, but it also permitted the introduction of one's refusal to submit a sample as evidence suggesting guilt at trial. Consistent with the trend to more harshly deter and punish DWI, offenders are now left with no choice in the matter—either submit a sample and run the risk of disclosing one's guilt, or refuse the request and run the risk of refusal being used as suggestive evidence of guilt when the case comes to trial. A second implication raised by this decision involves day-to-day police procedure in the processing of DWI cases and

SOUTH DAKOTA v. NEVILLE (cont.)

evidence. Specifically, it clarified the fact that officers are not required to inform DWI suspects of all potential consequences of the decisions they make during the documentation stage.

BERKEMER v. MCCARTY
468 U.S. 420 (1984)

FACTS

An Ohio state trooper observed McCarty's vehicle being operated in an erratic manner consistent with drunk driving. Once stopped, the trooper asked McCarty to exit the vehicle—a request that was fulfilled despite considerable difficulty maintaining balance on the operator's part. The trooper decided that McCarty would be taken into custody and was not free to leave the scene but did not announce his intention until McCarty had clearly failed several standardized field sobriety tests. When asked if he was under the influence of drugs or alcohol during this roadside detention, McCarty admitted that he had recently consumed two beers and smoked some marijuana. McCarty was placed under arrest and transported to jail, where a subsequent test failed to detect any alcohol in his bloodstream. The trooper continued asking questions of McCarty, who made incriminating statements about his condition in the absence of being given the *Miranda* warnings. McCarty was charged with a misdemeanor offense for operating a vehicle under the influence of drugs and/or alcohol. At trial, McCarty entered a motion to have the incriminating statements excluded from consideration on the basis that he had not been informed of his rights under *Miranda*. The trial court rejected this claim, McCarty pled no contest to the charges, and he was convicted. The conviction was affirmed on appeal by the county court and the Ohio Supreme Court denied review. Seeking habeas corpus relief in federal district court, the petition for review was denied but then reversed by the Sixth Circuit Court of Appeals, which held that the *Miranda* warning must be given to all individuals prior to custodial interrogation regardless of whether or not the offense alleged is a felony or misdemeanor. The court of appeals vacated the conviction but failed to specify which statements, if any, made by McCarty could be admitted at retrial. The U.S. Supreme Court then granted certiorari.

ISSUE

(1) Must the *Miranda* warning be given to a suspect prior to custodial interrogation regarding involvement in a misdemeanor offense? In simple terms, do the police have to read misdemeanor suspects their rights before asking them questions about their involvement in the offense? (2) Does the roadside questioning of a motorist who has been lawfully detained for a traffic violation trigger the *Miranda* doctrine? In simple terms, do police officers have to read motorists the *Miranda* warning every time they make a traffic stop?

HOLDING

Yes, and no. As to the first issue, the Court held that suspects are entitled to the procedural safeguards established under *Miranda* any time they are exposed to custodial interrogation regardless of whether the offense alleged is classified as a felony or misdemeanor. As to the second issue, the Court held that the roadside questioning of a motorist who is detained pursuant to a lawful traffic stop does not constitute a custodial interrogation; consequently, officers are not required to inform traffic violators of their *Miranda* rights.

RATIONALE

In *Miranda v. Arizona,* the Supreme Court announced a principle of law designed to protect criminal suspects from the coercive pressures inherent in custodial interrogations that might otherwise give rise to self-incrimination—a protection specifically guaranteed by the Fifth Amendment. This principle has been affirmed over the years by a number of associated cases. In this particular matter, the Court was asked to create an exception to the general rule that suspects must be informed of their constitutional rights under *Miranda* when exposed to custodial interrogation related to involvement in a misdemeanor offense. The Court flatly rejected making such an exception on the basis that doing so would "substantially undermine" the simplicity of the *Miranda* rule. Furthermore, the Court reasoned, there often arise situations in which officers at the time of arrest or interrogation may be uncertain as to which charge (e.g., a felony or misdemeanor) is most appropriate. The example provided by the Court to illustrate this point is one in which an intoxicated driver is involved in a motor vehicle accident. Depending upon the facts surrounding the accident and its outcome, the driver might be charged with a misdemeanor if the behavior in question is determined to be only negligent in intent. Alternatively, if someone dies as a result of the accident or the behavior in question is determined to be reckless in its intent, then a felony charge is in order. In such ambiguous situations, officers might have to ask probative questions that, if answered by a suspect in the absence of being read the *Miranda* warning, could be self-incriminating. Another scenario envisioned by the justices was one in which a seemingly minor offense gradually escalated into one of a more serious nature. The question would then become one of determining the point at which the *Miranda* rule should be applied. Last, the Court also expressed reluctance to create the proposed exception on the basis that doing so would create a situation in which affected cases would have to be so closely scrutinized that they would be disruptive of the law enforcement function. Thus, the Court did not see fit to alter the existing rule's simplistic nature. Accordingly, the court held that officers must inform criminal suspects of their *Miranda* rights when conducting a custodial interrogation regardless of the severity of the alleged offense.

In seeking to resolve the second issue—that of determining whether or not traffic stops constitute a form of custodial interrogation, thereby triggering the requirement that officers inform motorists of their *Miranda* rights—the Court concluded that such encounters do not create the type of situation in which individuals will be forced to divulge information they might not otherwise disclose. In simple terms, the Court decided that a traffic stop does not constitute a custodial interrogation. In reaching this conclusion, the Court cited two factors that serve to mitigate the danger that a person might be forced to make self-incriminating statements. First, a vast majority of traffic stops are brief in duration. Motorists likely know that eventually they will be sent on their way after answering a few questions. The type of questioning that occurs during a routine traffic stop, the Court asserted, is considerably different than that which occurs at the stationhouse when a person is brought in for detailed and more considerably prolonged questioning. And, although an armed uniformed officer projects an undeniable air of authority that may be intimidating to some, this concern is offset by the fact that traffic stops, unlike stationhouse interrogations, generally occur in public so that officers are deterred from employing less-than-legitimate means for extracting information from the detained motorist. Given these mitigating considerations, the Court ruled that motorists who are temporarily detained during a lawful traffic stop are not the subjects of a custodial

interrogation requiring recitation of the *Miranda* warning.

CASE EXCERPT

"A person subjected to custodial interrogation is entitled to the benefit of the procedural safeguards enunciated in *Miranda*, regardless of the nature or severity of the offense of which he is suspected or for which he was arrested... Two features of an ordinary traffic stop mitigate the danger that a person questioned will be induced to speak where he would not otherwise do so freely, First, detention of a motorist pursuant to a traffic stop is presumptively temporary and brief. The vast majority of roadside detentions last only a few minutes... Questioning incident to an ordinary traffic stop is quite different from stationhouse interrogation, which frequently is prolonged, and in which the detainee often is aware that questioning will continue until he provides his interrogators the answers they seek... Second, circumstances associated with the typical traffic stop are not such that the motorist feels completely at the mercy of the police. To be sure, the aura of authority surrounding an armed, uniformed officer and the knowledge that the officer has some discretion in deciding whether to issue a citation, in combination, exert some pressure on the detainee to respond to questions. But other aspects of the situation substantially offset these forces."

CASE SIGNIFICANCE

The implications of this case for day-to-day law enforcement were multifold. First, in the event that there was ever any doubt, the decision expanded the *Miranda* rule to all custodial interrogations whether they involve a felony or misdemeanor offense. Thus, individuals who are subjected to custodial interrogation for misdemeanor offenses are covered by the protections afforded under *Miranda*. While this ruling may appear to some observers as an impediment to effective law enforcement, it is counterbalanced by the finding that officers do not have to read the *Miranda* warning each and every time they make a lawful traffic stop and request information of a driver. Still in question, however, is the issue of determining exactly when one is deemed to be "in custody" for purposes of triggering the *Miranda* rule. The Court openly acknowledged that lower courts would still be forced to answer this question almost on a case-by-case basis. In the present instance, the state trooper decided in the early stages of the traffic stop to take McCarty into custody

BERKEMER v. MCCARTY (cont.)

but did not verbally articulate this intention. Thus, in the trooper's mind McCarty was under arrest almost from the outset. McCarty, on the other hand, may very well have been under the impression that he would soon be free to leave, and the notion of being in custody may have never entered his mind. Situations like this, which likely characterize countless traffic stops on a daily basis, remain ambiguous and will continue to elude precise definition. Fortunately, however, the Court has provided some guidance to lower courts in resolving such dilemmas. Specifically, the Court stated that "a policeman's unarticulated plan has no bearing on the question of whether a suspect was 'in custody' at a particular time." Rather, what is most important in making such a determination "is how a reasonable man in the suspect's position would have understood his situation." One additional implication of the present decision is the contention that exempting traffic stops from the *Miranda* rule will induce officers to conduct their interrogations on the roadside rather than in the stationhouse. That is, some fear that this decision will result in officers exploiting the fact that traffic stops do not constitute an "in-custody" interrogation and delaying the arrest of an individual with an eye toward obtaining self-incriminating information they might not otherwise discover if the suspect is placed into immediate custody. Unfortunately, there appears to be no easy solution to this possibility other than to say that the facts surrounding such eventualities will be given consideration in hindsight and, where necessary, remedied through exclusion of the statements in question.

NEW YORK v. QUARLES
467 U.S. 649 (1984)

FACTS
Two officers were approached by a female who informed them that she had just been raped by an armed man who was last seen entering a nearby supermarket. Spotting an individual who matched the description given, one of the officers gave chase. Once cornered, the suspect was frisked and found to be wearing an empty shoulder holster. Asked where the gun was, he nodded toward some empty cartons and said, "The gun is over there." Quarles was placed under arrest and, having been properly informed of his *Miranda* rights, admitted to owning the weapon. At trial, both the weapon and Quarles'

initial statement as to the gun's location were excluded on the basis that he had not yet been informed of his *Miranda* rights. Consequently, the statements that followed were also excluded on grounds that they were tainted by the *Miranda* violation. Both the Appellate Division of the New York Supreme Court and the New York Court of Appeals affirmed. The U.S. Supreme Court granted certiorari.

ISSUE
Should the trial court have accepted into evidence Quarles' admission regarding the gun's location and ownership? Does the concern for public safety outweigh strict adherence to the *Miranda* warning?

HOLDING
Yes. The lower courts erred in excluding Quarles' statement regarding the weapon's location and ownership, as well as his subsequent admission, as illegal fruits of the *Miranda* violation. The concern for public safety in this type of case clearly outweighs strict adherence to the principles of *Miranda*.

RATIONALE
The Supreme Court reversed the decision of the lower court, finding that the statement made by Quarles as to the gun's location should have been admitted at trial despite the fact that he had not been informed of his *Miranda* rights. In making this determination, the Court conducted a balancing test in which it weighed the public-safety interest against the suspect's right to avoid self-incrimination. In doing so, the Court noted that the doctrinal underpinnings of the *Miranda* decision do not require that the warnings be applied with total rigor to situations in which the police ask questions reasonably prompted by a concern for public safety. In other words, the Court acknowledged that had the officer taken time to inform Quarles of his *Miranda* rights, the cost associated with failing to immediately locate the gun would have been greater than the exclusion of evidence at trial. Thus, in the overwhelming interest of public safety, the Court concluded that officers are authorized to ask certain limited questions of criminal suspects without having to first read the *Miranda* warnings.

CASE EXCERPT
"There is a 'public safety' exception to the requirement that *Miranda* warnings be given before a suspect's answers may be admitted into evidence, and that the

availability of that exception does not depend upon the motivation of the individual officers involved. In a kaleidoscopic situation such as the one confronting these officers, where spontaneity rather than adherence to a police manual is necessarily the order of the day, the application of the exception which we recognize today should not be made to depend on post hoc findings at a suppression hearing concerning the subjective motivation of the arresting officer. Undoubtedly most police officers, if placed in Officer Kraft's position, would act out of a host of different, instinctive, and largely unverifiable motives—their own safety, the safety of others, and perhaps as well the desire to obtain incriminating evidence from the suspect."

CASE SIGNIFICANCE

Narrowly applied, the *Miranda* decision prohibited authorities from asking any questions whatsoever of a suspect who is in custody until he or she has been informed of and waives certain rights extended under the Fifth Amendment. The facts of the present case, however, were substantially different from the day-to-day situations in which officers interrogate suspects about crimes that do not pose an immediate threat to others. Instead, this case clearly involved an encounter between the police and a suspect who was believed to have been both armed and dangerous. The fact that Quarles was found to be wearing an empty shoulder holster created an apparent and immediate concern not only for the safety of the officer, but for the safety of others as well. Thus, the primary significance of this case lies in the fact that it created a public-safety exception to the *Miranda* rule. Interestingly, the Court did not identify other specific situations to which the exception might apply but left the determination to the individual officer on the scene. Despite the fact that this decision weighed in favor of law enforcement and the public interest, due caution must be exercised so that the exception does not become the subject of abuse. Where this occurs with widespread pattern or frequency, the Court may retract the public-safety exception in favor of protecting the rights of suspects from arbitrary abuse.

OREGON v. ELSTAD
470 U.S. 298 (1985)

FACTS

Two officers went to the residence of Elstad's mother to arrest him on a burglary warrant. While explaining

that he had been implicated in the alleged offense, Elstad openly commented to one of the officers, "Yes, I was there." Elstad was transported to the police station and, upon arrival, properly informed of his *Miranda* rights. He subsequently made a voluntary waiver of these rights, providing investigating officers with a written statement detailing his involvement in the crime. At trial, the state sought to introduce both Elstad's written statement and his initial unwarned comment to the arresting officer. The trial court ruled the unwarned oral statement inadmissible but allowed the written confession. The Oregon Court of Appeals reversed and the U.S. Supreme Court granted certiorari.

ISSUE

Does a suspect's unwarned and unsolicited statement automatically render a properly obtained subsequent confession inadmissible?

HOLDING

No. A confession that is properly obtained subsequent to an unsolicited and unwarned statement is not automatically rendered inadmissible under the Fifth Amendment.

RATIONALE

In reaching the conclusion that a prior unwarned and unsolicited statement does not automatically render a subsequent properly obtained confession inadmissible, the Court rejected an assertion that the exclusionary rule's "fruit of the poisonous tree" doctrine should be broadly applied to such Fifth Amendment issues. Instead, a six-justice majority reasoned that while a failure to administer the *Miranda* warnings creates a presumption of involuntariness, there is no accompanying presumption that the information derived from otherwise voluntary statements be regarded as inherently tainted. In simple terms, the justices did not think it prudent to broadly apply the "fruit of the poisonous tree" doctrine to fact situations such as those in the present case. Absent any evidence to suggest that the police deliberately coerced or tricked Elstad into making the initial unwarned statement, the fact that they later took care to properly warn him of his *Miranda* rights remedied the condition that otherwise made it inadmissible. Lastly, the Court noted that not only was Elstad's fully warned confession knowingly and voluntarily given, but so too was his first, within the meaning of the Fifth Amendment.

OREGON v. ELSTAD (*cont.*)

CASE EXCERPT

"After an accused has once let the cat out of the bag by confessing, no matter what the inducement, he is never thereafter free of the psychological and practical disadvantages of having confessed. He can never get the cat back in the bag. The secret is out for good. In such a sense, a later confession may always be looked upon as fruit of the first. But this Court has never gone so far as to hold that making a confession under circumstances which preclude its use, perpetually disables the confessor from making a usable one after those conditions have been removed."

CASE SIGNIFICANCE

The decision in this case partially eroded the rigors of *Miranda* insofar as it allowed a suspect who has previously responded to unwarned questioning to subsequently confess after being properly informed of his or her rights. In practical terms, this means that trial courts are not required to automatically exclude confessions that are obtained after a suspect has "let the cat out of the bag," as occurred in this case. Prior to this decision, lower courts would frequently suppress such evidence as fruit of the poisonous tree. Thus, a suspect who makes an incriminating statement without having first been read his or her *Miranda* rights can still be questioned later by the police so long as he or she is properly warned at that time. While the initial unwarned statement might not necessarily be admissible at trial, under this ruling the second warned statement certainly should be.

COLORADO v. CONNELLY

479 U.S. 157 (1986)

FACTS

Connelly approached a Denver police officer and confessed to a murder. The officer promptly advised Connelly of his *Miranda* rights, but he nonetheless insisted on talking about the crime in order to clear his conscience. Upon arrival at police headquarters, Connelly related his story in full detail and eventually accompanied officers to the crime scene. The following morning, Connelly became visibly disoriented and claimed that he was hearing voices, whereupon he was taken to a state hospital for psychiatric evaluation. In a pretrial hearing on the murder charge, the defense moved to suppress Connelly's statements on grounds that his psychotic condition had prompted him to confess. The trial court accepted this argument and ordered the initial statements suppressed although the police had done nothing coercive to obtain them. The Colorado Supreme Court affirmed and the U.S. Supreme Court granted certiorari.

ISSUE

Can a suspect who is lacking a fully rational state of mind validly waive his or her *Miranda* rights?

HOLDING

Yes. A suspect who is lacking a fully rational state of mind may validly waive his or her *Miranda* rights, and, in the absence of any coercive police behavior, any incriminating statements are admissible under state rules of evidence.

RATIONALE

A majority of the Court, led by Chief Justice Rehnquist, asserted that incriminating statements made by an individual who is lacking a fully rational state of mind but who has been properly informed of his or her *Miranda* rights should not be subject to automatic exclusion. In reaching this decision, the majority reasoned that in order for a violation of due process to occur, there must be evidence of coercive police activity. In the present case, there was none—Connelly freely confessed without any pressure from police. Consequently, neither the taking of his statement nor its admission into evidence constituted a violation of his due process rights.

CASE EXCERPT

"Coercive police activity is a necessary predicate to the finding that a confession is not 'voluntary' within the meaning of the Due Process Clause of the Fourteenth Amendment…*Miranda* protects defendants against government coercion leading them to surrender rights protected by the Fifth Amendment; it goes no further than that. Respondent's perception of coercion flowing from the 'voice of God,' however important or significant such a perception may be in other disciplines, is a matter to which the United States Constitution does not speak."

CASE SIGNIFICANCE

This case stands as yet another example of a ruling weakening the *Miranda* decision. The basis for this assertion is found in the Court's conclusion that the

Fifth Amendment privilege against self-incrimination applies only to evidence that is obtained by coercive means. Because the police did not coerce Connelly into making the statement, there was no Fifth Amendment violation. Finally, the fact that Connelly apparently lacked a fully rational state of mind was determined to have no bearing on the case—he was properly warned, gave a valid waiver, and freely confessed without any pressure from police. In the absence of any coercive activity by police, the admissibility of such statements is left to state rules of evidence. Although the frequency with which the police encounter such situations is unknown, officers are allowed to take an individual's statement so long as he or she is properly Mirandized and a valid waiver of the attending rights is obtained.

COLORADO v. SPRING

479 U.S. 564 (1987)

FACTS
Federal agents arrested Spring on charges of selling stolen firearms. Spring was given the *Miranda* warning but provided a written waiver of his right to remain silent. During this initial interrogation, agents gradually refocused their questioning upon Spring's involvement in an unsolved Colorado homicide case. Colorado authorities, having again advised Spring of his *Miranda* rights, later questioned him about the murder, at which time he confessed to having aided the actual killer. At trial, Spring moved to have his confession to involvement in the murder suppressed on grounds that his waiver extended only to the agents' questions regarding the federal weapons charge. Because the agents had not given Spring advance notice that they would question him about the homicide, the defense argued that he had not waived his *Miranda* rights for that particular offense. Rejecting this assertion, the trial court found Spring guilty of first-degree murder. The Colorado Court of Appeals reversed and remanded the case for retrial, accepting Spring's argument in favor of suppression. The Colorado Supreme Court affirmed the reversal and the U.S. Supreme Court granted certiorari.

ISSUE
Must a suspect be given advance notice of all possible topics of interrogation in order for his or her waiver of *Miranda* rights to be valid?

HOLDING
No. The police are not required to provide suspects with advance notice of all possible topics of interrogation in order for a waiver of *Miranda* rights to be valid. In other words, the police do not have to tell a suspect which specific crime(s) they intend to ask questions about.

RATIONALE
In reaching the decision that Spring's initial waiver of his *Miranda* rights was valid, the Court first noted that there was no evidence to suggest that he had been unduly influenced or pressured by the police. To the contrary, the written waiver of these rights further demonstrated that Spring clearly understood that he retained the right to remain silent and that anything he revealed could be used as evidence against him at trial. The Court then went on to assert that no provision of the Constitution requires the state to inform a suspect of every possible consequence that might arise from a waiver of the Fifth Amendment right to remain silent. That the police did not specifically spell out in advance every topic of interrogation has no bearing on determining whether or not the waiver is valid—more important for making such a determination is whether the suspect did so voluntarily, knowingly, and intelligently. Absent any evidence to the contrary, the initial written waiver must be held valid and, therefore, admissible.

CASE EXCERPT
"There is no doubt that Spring's decision to waive his Fifth Amendment privilege was voluntary. He alleges no 'coercion of a confession by physical violence or other deliberate means calculated to break [his] will,' and the trial court found none. His allegation that the police failed to supply him with certain information does not relate to any of the traditional indicia of coercion: 'the duration and conditions of detention…the manifest attitude of the police toward him, his physical and mental state, the diverse pressures which sap or sustain his powers of resistance and self-control.'"

CASE SIGNIFICANCE
This case is important insofar as it established the general principle of law that police are not required to inform a suspect of all possible offenses about which he or she might be asked during an interrogation. Once the police have informed a suspect of his or her *Miranda* rights and these protections have been validly

COLORADO v. SPRING *(cont.)*

waived, the police may probe any area they choose. In the immediate case, government agents began the interrogation by asking Spring about his involvement in a minor offense, then shifted the focus of their inquiry to more serious matters (i.e., murder). On appeal, it was argued that the police should be required to provide a suspect with advance notice of all crimes about which he or she will be asked during the interrogation. This argument was rejected, and it was instead concluded that the police do not have to tell a suspect what areas they intend to explore.

PATTERSON v. ILLINOIS
487 U.S. 285 (1988)

FACTS
Patterson, who had been indicted for participation in a gang-related murder, began to make a statement about the homicide to an attending officer. The officer promptly interrupted Patterson and presented him with a waiver form clearly spelling out five provisions of the *Miranda* warning. Patterson read and signed the form and then gave the officer, and later a state attorney, an incriminating statement regarding his involvement in the murder. These statements were introduced over objection at trial and Patterson was convicted. On appeal, it was argued that the statements should have been excluded on grounds that the Sixth Amendment requires a higher standard for showing waiver of the right to counsel than that which is required for *Miranda* waivers. The Appellate Court of Illinois affirmed the conviction and the U.S. Supreme Court granted certiorari.

ISSUE
Does a suspect's waiver of the Fifth Amendment right to remain silent under *Miranda* simultaneously waive his or her Sixth Amendment right to counsel?

HOLDING
Yes. A suspect who has been properly advised of his or her *Miranda* rights during postindictment questioning is deemed to have also been sufficiently informed of the accompanying Sixth Amendment right to counsel. A valid waiver of the *Miranda* rights simultaneously implicates both the Fifth Amendment right to remain silent and the Sixth Amendment right to counsel.

RATIONALE
On appeal to the Supreme Court, it was asserted that Patterson should have received an altogether separate warning regarding his Sixth Amendment right to counsel. By a 5–4 vote, the Court rejected this argument on grounds that it was inappropriate to designate one right (the Sixth Amendment right to counsel) as "superior" or "more difficult" to waive than another (the Fifth Amendment right to remain silent). Instead, the Court concluded that the appropriate method for resolving such Sixth Amendment issues is one that examines the utility of counsel at the particular stage of proceedings in question. In the end, it was reasoned that the *Miranda* warnings were sufficient for protecting Patterson's Sixth Amendment right due to the fairly limited role played by counsel at that particular stage of the adversarial proceedings.

CASE EXCERPT
"An accused who is admonished with the warnings prescribed by this Court in *Miranda* has been sufficiently apprised of the nature of his Sixth Amendment rights, and of the consequences of abandoning those rights, so that his waiver on this basis will be considered a knowing and intelligent one…Once it is determined that a suspect's decision not to rely on his rights was uncoerced, that he at all times knew he could stand mute and request a lawyer, and that he was aware of the State's intention to use his statements to secure a conviction, the analysis is complete and the waiver is valid as a matter of law."

CASE SIGNIFICANCE
This case rejected the notion that suspects must be given two distinct sets of warnings and waive each prior to custodial interrogation. Specifically, Patterson argued that he should have received a separate warning regarding the Sixth Amendment right to counsel in addition to the standard *Miranda* warning dealing solely with the Fifth Amendment right to avoid self-incrimination. This argument was rejected on the basis that while suspects possess a right to counsel during custodial interrogation, the intent of this right is limited to protecting the individual from self-incrimination. For purposes of day-to-day law enforcement, officers are still required to read the *Miranda* warning to a suspect prior to custodial interrogation. They are not required to inform the suspect of any additional rights beyond those specifically contained in the language of the warning.

ARIZONA v. ROBERSON
486 U.S. 675 (1988)

FACTS
Roberson was apprehended at the scene of a burglary and, upon being informed of his *Miranda* rights by the arresting officer, stated that he "wanted a lawyer before answering any questions"—a fact noted by the officer in his report. Three days later, Roberson was approached by a different officer who was unaware that he had previously invoked the right to assistance of counsel. The officer advised Roberson of his *Miranda* rights and then proceeded to interrogate him about his involvement in a separate burglary offense. During the interrogation, Roberson disclosed information that incriminated him in the second, unrelated offense that was of interest to this particular officer. At trial for the second burglary offense, Roberson's statement was suppressed under the *Edwards* rule establishing that once a suspect expresses a desire to deal with the police only through counsel, he or she may not be subjected to further interrogation until such time as the request is fulfilled or the accused initiates further communication with the authorities. Recall, however, that in *Edwards v, Arizona* the suspect was repeatedly questioned about his involvement in a single offense without the benefit of counsel being present, whereas in the immediate matter Roberson was subjected to questioning about his involvement in two separate, unrelated offenses. The U.S. Supreme Court granted certiorari.

ISSUE
Does the *Edwards* rule prohibit officers from initiating an interrogation with a suspect regarding an unrelated offense if he or she has invoked the Fifth Amendment right to assistance of counsel in a previous interrogation conducted by other officers?

HOLDING
Yes. The Supreme Court held that the previously established *Edwards* rule prohibits officers from initiating repeated interrogations of a suspect once he or she has invoked the Fifth Amendment right to counsel even if the subsequent interrogation focuses on an altogether separate offense.

RATIONALE
The state of Arizona asserted that the rule previously established under *Edwards* prohibiting police from conducting repeated custodial interrogations

of a suspect who has invoked the Fifth Amendment right to counsel should not be applied to the facts in the immediate matter on two grounds. First, the state pointed to the Court's earlier decision in *Michigan v. Mosley,* 423 U.S. 96 (1975), holding that the police may question a suspect about an unrelated offense even if he or she has previously cut off communications where two conditions are met: (1) a significant amount of time passes and (2) the suspect is again informed of his or her *Miranda* rights. This argument, however, was rejected by the Court on the basis that "a suspect's decision to cut off questioning, unlike his request for counsel, does not raise the presumption that he is unable to proceed without a lawyer's advice." In effect, the Court drew a distinction between suspects who simply refuse to talk with police and those who refuse to talk without the benefit of counsel. A second argument raised by the state was premised upon the Court's earlier decision in *Connecticut v. Barrett,* 479 U.S. 523 (1987), involving a suspect who refused to give the police a written statement without assistance of counsel but did, however, agree to continue "talking" with them about the incident in question. In this particular case, the Court determined that Barrett himself had drawn a distinction between oral and written statements, thereby voluntarily allowing officers to continue their questioning of him. The state asserted that Roberson's request for counsel was similarly limited so that it applied only to questions regarding his involvement in the burglary for which he was initially arrested. The Court, however, viewed this argument to be flawed on both legal and factual grounds. On legal grounds, a suspect's request for counsel creates the presumption that one is unable to deal with the pressures of custodial interrogation alone. This presumption, the Court continued, "does not disappear simply because the police have approached the suspect, still in custody, still without counsel, about a separate investigation." On factual grounds, it may be recalled, Roberson told the arresting officer that he "wanted a lawyer before answering any questions." In a literal sense, then, the police were prohibited from asking further questions given Roberson's specific use of the term "any."

CASE EXCERPT
"Whether a contemplated reinterrogation concerns the same or a different offense, or whether the same or different law enforcement authorities are involved in the second investigation, the same need to determine

ARIZONA v. ROBERSON *(cont.)*

whether the suspect has requested counsel exists. The police department's failure to honor that request cannot be justified by the lack of diligence of a particular officer."

CASE SIGNIFICANCE

The Court's decision in this case is significant to the extent that it not only affirmed the *Miranda* decision but also expanded the prophylactic measures created under *Edwards*. Naturally, the majority's decision drew sharp criticism from dissenting justices, who acknowledged the realities of day-to-day law enforcement where suspects are frequently wanted in connection with multiple offenses. The *Roberson* decision, the dissenters astutely noted, effectively "bar[s] law enforcement officials, even those from some other city or other jurisdiction, from questioning a suspect about an unrelated matter if he is in custody and has requested counsel to assist in answering questions put to him about the crime for which he was arrested." Thus, crime-control advocates often criticize the Court's "broad brush" expansion of the *Edwards* rule on the basis that it unnecessarily impedes effective law enforcement. Furthermore, the decision requires arresting officers to pay very close attention to detail. Specifically, officers must carefully note whether a suspect states that he or she does not want to answer questions about the specific offense for which he or she has been arrested or, as did Roberson, states that he or she does not want to answer "any" questions whatsoever. Perhaps most importantly, this information must be conveyed to any and all investigators who wish to interrogate the suspect. If this information is not specifically conveyed, such a breakdown in communication may very well lead to a situation in which any or all incriminating statements are ruled inadmissible at trial.

DUCKWORTH v. EAGAN

492 U.S. 195 (1989)

FACTS

Prior to questioning Eagan in connection with a stabbing, Indiana police read him a *Miranda* waiver form, including the provision that a lawyer would be appointed "if and when you go to court." Eagan signed the form and provided investigators with an incriminating statement that was later admitted into evidence at his trial for attempted murder. Eagan was convicted and, upon exhausting available state-level appeals, filed a writ of habeas corpus in federal court. The writ was denied in district court but granted on appeal by the Seventh Circuit on grounds that the language contained in the warning was constitutionally defective. The U.S. Supreme Court then granted certiorari.

ISSUE

Did the waiver form, which included the phrase "if and when you go to court," violate the requirements of *Miranda v. Arizona*?

HOLDING

No. It is not necessary for the *Miranda* warnings to be presented or recited exactly as they appeared in the original case.

RATIONALE

The Supreme Court reversed the judgment of the Seventh Circuit Court of Appeals, ruling that the warning given to Eagan was adequate for purposes of satisfying the intent of the *Miranda* decision. In reaching this decision, a five-justice majority first noted that the Court had never insisted on the warnings being given in a specific or exact form. Rather, the underlying objective had been to ensure that officers "reasonably convey" to a suspect his or her constitutional rights during custodial interrogation or its functional equivalent. To the extent that this objective is reasonably satisfied, no violation has occurred. The fact that the warning in question included language not found in the original *Miranda* opinion simply serves to clarify for the suspect other stages of the process when he or she can expect to have the assistance of counsel. Finally, the Court further clarified that the police are not required to provide a suspect with counsel upon demand, as might be inferred from a literal reading of the *Miranda* decision. Instead, all that is required is that the police cease questioning until such time as an attorney has been made available to the suspect by whatever procedural mechanism has been put in place.

CASE EXCERPT

"We think the initial warnings given to respondent touched all of the bases required by *Miranda*. The police told respondent that he had the right to remain silent, that anything he said could be used against him in court, that he had the right to speak to an attorney before and during questioning, that he had 'this right to the advice and presence of a lawyer even if [he could] not afford to hire one,' and that he had the 'right to stop answering at any time until [he] talked to a lawyer.' As noted, the police also added that they could not provide respondent with a lawyer, but that one would be appointed 'if and when you go to court.' "

CASE SIGNIFICANCE

This case is important for law enforcement purposes on two grounds. First, it resolved the question of whether the police must inform a suspect of the *Miranda* warning verbatim or, instead, if minor variations are acceptable. In clarifying this issue, the Court ruled that police officers do not have to inform suspects of their *Miranda* rights verbatim. This means that minor variations of the warning are acceptable so long as its substantive meaning remains the same. A second question resolved by this decision was whether or not the police must immediately produce an attorney for a suspect once one is requested. This issue was resolved by the Court's ruling that police are not required to immediately produce an attorney once a suspect has requested one. In simple terms, then, this case stands for two principles of law: (1) The police are not required to inform a suspect of the *Miranda* warning verbatim so long as its substantive meaning remains intact and (2) The police are not required to immediately produce an attorney once a suspect has requested one.

MINNICK v. MISSISSIPPI

498 U.S. 146 (1990)

FACTS

Minnick, wanted on capital murder charges in Mississippi, was arrested in California and held for extradition. While awaiting arrival of Mississippi officials, Minnick was questioned by federal agents, who terminated their interrogation upon his request to speak with an attorney, which he was allowed to do two or three times. Upon arrival, the deputy sheriff from Mississippi resumed interrogation and told Minnick that he could not refuse to talk. While being questioned by the deputy, Minnick confessed to involvement in the murder. At trial, a motion to suppress the confession was denied, whereupon Minnick was convicted and sentenced to death. The Mississippi Supreme Court rejected Minnick's appeal alleging that the confession had been obtained in violation of

his Fifth Amendment right to counsel. Specifically, the state's high court reasoned that the *Edwards* rule, which prohibits the police from reinitiating interrogation of a suspect until counsel is made available, was not applicable in Minnick's case because his request for representation had been granted before the deputy resumed questioning. The U.S. Supreme Court then granted certiorari.

ISSUE

Does protection established under the *Edwards* rule cease to exist once a suspect has consulted with an attorney? In other words, if a suspect asks for counsel during interrogation and this request is granted, may the police later resume the interrogation?

HOLDING

No. When, during custodial interrogation, a suspect asks for counsel, all questioning must immediately cease and may not resume until such time as counsel is present in the room.

RATIONALE

In this case the Supreme Court clarified its earlier ruling in *Edwards* and, in doing so, expanded the scope of Fifth Amendment protection afforded suspects during custodial interrogation. In particular, the Court's majority interpreted the requirement in *Edwards* that counsel be made available to the accused upon request to mean that before questioning by police may resume, an attorney must be physically present in the room. Thus, "the requirement that counsel be made available to the accused refers to more than an opportunity to consult with an attorney outside the interrogation room." The Court felt this expansion was necessary given that "[a] single consultation with an attorney does not remove the suspect from persistent attempts by officials to persuade him to waive his rights, or from the coercive pressures that accompany custody and that may increase as custody is prolonged." At one point, the State contended that a suspect could simply reinstate his or her desire for assistance of counsel during subsequent interrogations. The Court noted, however, that such a formulation would likely create unnecessary confusion by allowing the rule to pass in and out of existence multiple times. Thus, in the interest of protecting suspects' Fifth Amendment rights while at the same time maintaining *Edwards*' "bright line" standards, Minnick's conviction was reversed and remanded.

MINNICK v. MISSISSIPPI (cont.)

CASE EXCERPT

"The need for counsel to protect the Fifth Amendment privilege comprehends not merely a right to consult with counsel prior to questioning, but also to have counsel present during any questioning if the defendant so desires."

CASE SIGNIFICANCE

This case poses significant implications for law enforcement on several grounds. First, it clearly establishes the standard that once a suspect under custodial interrogation requests assistance of counsel, all questioning must immediately cease and be held in abeyance until an attorney is physically present in the room. It is not adequate to simply allow the suspect to communicate with an attorney by phone before resuming the interrogation; officers must refrain from asking any questions whatsoever until the suspect's attorney arrives at the location where the interrogation is being conducted. Any effort whatsoever by officers from any jurisdiction to reestablish communications with the suspect without his or her attorney being present is also strictly forbidden. As might be expected, this expansion of the Fifth Amendment by the Court's majority drew sharp criticism from the dissenting justices, who noted that even if a suspect genuinely and freely desired to do so, he or she could never consent to an interview with police unless an attorney is present. Thus, a criminal who is truly repentant cannot confess to a crime without waiting for an attorney to arrive on the scene. As the dissenting justices stated: "The value of any prophylactic rule must be assessed not only on the basis of what is gained, but also on the basis of what is lost." In effect, the dissenting justices suggested that although increased protection for criminal suspects has indeed been gained as a result of this decision, that which has been lost—a certain measure of power on the part of police to find those who have violated the law—may be of greater cost in the end.

PENNSYLVANIA v. MUNIZ

496 U.S. 582 (1990)

FACTS

Muniz was arrested for drunk driving and transported to a booking center where officers, as a matter of practice with such suspects, videotaped the intake procedure. During this procedure, Muniz responded to routine questions about his name, address, date of birth, etc. One particular question asked of Muniz was the date of his sixth birthday, which he was unable to correctly answer. While attempting to perform a variety of standardized sobriety tests, Muniz openly commented on his state of inebriation. He also refused a request to submit a sample of his breath for analysis. Muniz was then informed of his *Miranda* rights for the first time, signed a waiver of those rights, and admitted on video to driving while intoxicated. The booking video was admitted into evidence at Muniz's bench trial and he was convicted. An appeal for retrial was granted by a superior court on grounds that the audio portion of the tape violated Muniz's Fifth Amendment protection against self-incrimination insofar as he had been asked questions without having first been properly warned. The Supreme Court of Pennsylvania denied the prosecution's request for review, and the U.S. Supreme Court granted certiorari.

ISSUE

Did the police violate Muniz's Fifth Amendment protection against self-incrimination by videotaping the booking procedure without first advising him of his right to remain silent?

HOLDING

No. Not only may the police ask routine questions of DWI suspects during booking procedures, but they are also allowed to videotape the responses without having to first inform the arrestee of his or her *Miranda* rights.

RATIONALE

In resolving the claim that police violated Muniz's Fifth Amendment protection against self-incrimination by videotaping his responses to routine booking questions without having first properly Mirandized him, the Supreme Court reversed and remanded the case for further proceedings. More specifically, a majority of the justices agreed that Muniz's Fifth Amendment rights were violated by admitting into evidence that portion of the tape in which he was unable to correctly provide the date of his sixth birthday. Aside from this limited portion, however, the remainder of the tape was properly admitted. Those portions of the video depicting the sobriety test as well as Muniz's refusal to provide a sample of his breath had been properly admitted into evidence. The Fifth Amendment protects suspects from being compelled to provide the government with incriminating evidence of a testimonial or communicative nature. The fact that Muniz's speech was slurred and he apparently lacked muscular coordination constituted "non-testimonial" components of the recorded responses that fall beyond the protective scope of the Fifth Amendment. Furthermore, Muniz's statements during the sobriety tests as well as the refusal to provide a sample of his breath were all voluntary insofar as they were not elicited as the result of a custodial interrogation.

CASE EXCERPT

"Officer Hosterman's dialogue with Muniz concerning the physical sobriety tests consisted primarily of carefully scripted instructions as to how the tests were to be performed. These instructions were not likely to be perceived as calling for any verbal response and therefore were not 'words or actions' constituting custodial interrogation, with two narrow exceptions not relevant here. The dialogue also contained limited and carefully worded inquiries as to whether Muniz understood those instructions, but these focused inquiries were necessarily 'attendant to' the police procedure held by the court to be legitimate. Hence, Muniz's incriminating utterances during this phase of the videotaped proceedings were 'voluntary' in the sense that they were not elicited in response to custodial interrogation."

CASE SIGNIFICANCE

This case is important for law enforcement purposes insofar as it authorizes officers to interview DWI suspects and videotape their responses without first having to inform them of their *Miranda* rights. However, the questions must be a "routine" part of the booking procedure (i.e., questions such as name, age, height, weight, place of residence, etc.). Thus, questions that are not part of the regular booking protocol may not be admitted unless the suspect has been properly warned (i.e., questions regarding how much alcohol he or she has consumed, where the individual had been drinking, etc.). From a due process perspective, the decision in this case reinforces the notion that the Fifth Amendment protects suspects from being compelled to provide self-incriminating evidence of a testimonial or communicative nature. Because Muniz lacked muscular coordination and manifested slurred speech—evidence of a physical rather than communicative nature—the Fifth Amendment was deemed inapplicable to the videotaped evidence.

ARIZONA v. FULMINANTE
499 U.S. 279 (1991)

FACTS

While incarcerated in a New York federal prison, Fulminante befriended a fellow inmate, Sarivola, who was acting as a paid informant for the FBI. Sarivola, having heard rumors that Fulminante had killed his 11-year-old stepdaughter while residing in Arizona, approached him and offered protection from the other inmates on the condition that he confess. Fulminante confided that he had indeed killed the girl and disclosed several details about the crime. After his release from prison, Fulminante was traveling by car to Pennsylvania with Sarivola and Sarivola's wife. The latter of the two asked why he was going to Pennsylvania instead of returning to Arizona. In response, Fulminante freely cited the murder of his stepdaughter as the reason that he could not return and proceeded to provide even greater detail about the crime than he had to her husband while in prison. Fulminante was subsequently indicted for the young girl's murder, presumably as the result of Sarivola's relationship with the FBI, and held for trial. Prior to trial, Fulminante moved to suppress both confessions on the basis that the first was coerced while the second was a "fruit" of the first. The trial court denied the motion and both confessions were admitted, whereupon Fulminante was convicted and sentenced to death. On appeal to the Arizona Supreme Court, Fulminante claimed that the admission of both confessions violated his due process rights under the Fifth and Fourteenth Amendments. The Arizona high court initially held that Fulminante's prison confession was coerced given the totality of the circumstances (i.e., fear that if he did not confess in exchange for protection he would be the target of attack by other inmates). At the same time, however, the court determined that the confession's admission at trial amounted to a "harmless error" because, even in its absence, there existed enough evidence to convict. Thus, Fulminante's conviction was initially allowed to stand. Upon motion for reconsideration, the state supreme court later changed its position, reversed the conviction, and ordered that Fulminante be retried without the use of the confession. The U.S. Supreme Court then granted certiorari.

ISSUE

Was Fulminante's prison confession "coerced" for purposes of Fifth Amendment analysis? Does the

ARIZONA v. FULMINANTE *(cont.)*

"harmless error" doctrine apply to cases involving involuntary confessions later admitted at trial? Was the admission of Fulminante's prison confession a "harmless error" that had no bearing upon his conviction?

HOLDING

Yes, yes, and no. As to the first issue, the Court held that Fulminante's prison confession to Sarivola was coerced under traditional Fifth Amendment analysis. As to the second issue, the Court held that the "harmless error" doctrine is applicable to cases involving the improper admission of an involuntary confession at trial. As to the third issue, the Court held that the introduction of Fulminante's prison confession at trial was more than a "harmless error" and thus required reversal of the conviction.

RATIONALE

The first order of business addressed by the Court was a determination of whether or not the Arizona Supreme Court had applied the appropriate test in reaching its conclusion that Fulminante's prison confession to Sarivola was coerced under traditional Fifth Amendment analysis. On this point, the justices held that the applicable standard was one that considered the totality of the circumstances. Because this was the standard the lower court had applied, its finding that the confession had not been freely given was deemed to be without error. In particular, the justices seemed receptive to the Arizona Supreme Court's acknowledgment that "[T]he confession was obtained as a direct result of extreme coercion, and was tendered in the belief that the defendant's life was in jeopardy if he did not confess. This is a true coerced confession in every sense of the word." Next, the Court considered the question of whether or not the "harmless error" rule established under *Chapman v. California*, 386 U.S. 18 (1967), was applicable in situations where an involuntary confession was improperly admitted at trial, as had occurred in Fulminante's case. Under considerable criticism by four dissenting justices, a majority of the Court nonetheless determined that the rule should be extended to such situations on the basis that it had previously been applied to numerous other types of trial errors. This extension of the rule is counterbalanced, the majority argued, by placing a burden upon the state to prove that the error in question was harmless beyond a reasonable doubt. Last, the Court sought to determine whether the admission of Fulminante's coerced confession at trial constituted a harmless error or, instead, so adversely affected the proceedings as to render the outcome unfair. Referring again to its previous decision in *Chapman,* the justices concluded that the state did not, as required, adequately carry its burden of demonstrating beyond a reasonable doubt that the error was of harmless consequence. In so deciding, the majority recognized that "[a] confession is like no other evidence" in that it comes straight from the defendant himself or herself and can have such a dramatic impact on the minds of the jurors that they would likely not be able to disregard it even if told to do so. Because Fulminante's prison confession was coerced and because its introduction was deemed harmful to the trial's outcome, a majority of the justices affirmed the state supreme court's decision to grant him a retrial in which the tainted statement was not to be admitted.

CASE EXCERPT

"Our cases have made clear that a finding of coercion need not depend upon actual violence by a government agent; a credible threat is sufficient."

CASE SIGNIFICANCE

This case presented multiple issues and raised at least as many implications for criminal procedure. First, the decision affected the manner in which police use prisoners for purposes of gaining confessions from other prisoners. Specifically, when police use jailhouse informants for purposes of obtaining incriminating statements from other prisoners, they must be certain that the informants do not elicit confessions under coercive conditions. Where jailhouse informants create in the minds of other prisoners the belief that unless they confess to the act in question, something bad will happen to them, statements become inadmissible under the Fifth Amendment. Thus, state agents must be absolutely certain that jailhouse informants understand that they cannot engage in language or behavior that amounts to coercion. A second implication of this case is to be found in its application of what is known as the "harmless error" doctrine. In particular, the *Fulminante* decision established the procedural rule that the improper admission of an involuntary confession into evidence does not require an automatic reversal upon appeal. A third implication arising from this centers upon whether or not Fulminante's confession amounted to a "harmless error" or was so grave as to constitute a violation of procedural due process.

Because the Court found that Fulminante's confession was both improperly admitted and amounted to more than harmless error, the conviction required reversal on procedural due process grounds.

MCNEIL v. WISCONSIN
501 U.S. 171 (1991)

FACTS
McNeil was arrested for armed robbery. He requested and received representation by a public defender at a bail hearing on the charge. While still in detention, McNeil was approached by an officer seeking information regarding his involvement in a murder and other related offenses that occurred in a nearby town. McNeil was properly Mirandized, waived the attending rights, and made incriminating statements. At trial for these offenses, McNeil moved to suppress the statements on grounds that his request for a lawyer during the bail hearing on the armed robbery charges constituted an invocation of his *Miranda* rights and thereby prohibited further police interrogations. The motion to suppress was denied and McNeil was convicted. An appeal to the Wisconsin Supreme Court was equally unsuccessful. The U.S. Supreme Court then granted certiorari.

ISSUE
Does a request for assistance of counsel at a bail hearing constitute an invocation of the Fifth Amendment right to counsel under *Miranda* for other uncharged offenses?

HOLDING
No. A request for assistance of counsel at a bail hearing does not constitute an invocation of the Fifth Amendment right to counsel under *Miranda* for other uncharged offenses.

RATIONALE
In *Edwards v. Arizona,* the Court held that once a suspect asserts the right to counsel during custodial interrogation, not only must all questioning stop until an attorney has been made available, but the police are also barred from approaching the suspect regarding any other offense unless an attorney is present. In other words, the right to counsel afforded under *Miranda* is not "offense-specific." The same does not hold true, however, for the Sixth Amendment right to counsel,

which *is* offense-specific. Thus, the Sixth Amendment right to counsel cannot be broadly invoked as a protective shield from future questioning about other offenses that have not yet been charged. To do otherwise, the Court reasoned, would unnecessarily frustrate public interest and impede law enforcement investigations.

CASE EXCERPT
"Petitioner urges upon us the desirability of providing a clear and unequivocal guideline for the police: no police-initiated questioning of any person in custody who has requested counsel to assist him in defense or in interrogation. But the police do not need our assistance to establish such a guideline; they are free, if they wish, to adopt it on their own. Of course, it is our task to establish guidelines for judicial review. We like them to be clear and unequivocal, but only when they guide sensibly, and in a direction we are authorized to go. Petitioner's proposal would, in our view, do much more harm than good, and is not contained within, or even in furtherance of, the Sixth Amendment's right to counsel or the Fifth Amendment's right against compelled self-incrimination."

CASE SIGNIFICANCE
In this case, McNeil claimed that his request for counsel at a bail hearing simultaneously triggered his Fifth Amendment *Miranda* rights, thereby precluding officers from questioning him about other offenses for which charges had not yet been filed. The Court rejected this assertion, instead concluding that the Sixth Amendment right to counsel is "offense-specific." This decision thus authorized officers to question a suspect about other crimes that have not yet been charged even where he or she has requested assistance of counsel during pretrial proceedings. Naturally, the police are prohibited from asking the suspect additional questions about the offense charged unless his or her attorney is present. Equally clear is the requirement that before asking questions about other offenses not yet charged, the suspect must be properly Mirandized and validly waive all attending rights.

DAVIS v. UNITED STATES
512 U.S. 452 (1994)

FACTS
While serving as a member of the U.S. Navy, Davis was identified by the Naval Intelligence Service (NIS)

DAVIS v. UNITED STATES *(cont.)*

as a murder suspect. Brought in for questioning, Davis was properly informed of but nonetheless waived his *Miranda* rights. Approximately an hour and a half into the interrogation Davis remarked, "Maybe I should talk to a lawyer." The NIS agent tried to clarify what Davis meant by this comment and concluded that he had not specifically asked for a lawyer. The agent then reminded Davis of his rights and the questioning resumed for another hour until Davis made the comment again, whereupon the interview immediately ceased. During court-martial, Davis's motion to have the statement suppressed was denied on grounds that not only had the agents properly sought to determine what he had meant by the comment, but his statement had not taken the form more closely associated with such a request. Davis was convicted and both a court of military review as well as the U.S. Court of Military Appeals affirmed. The U.S. Supreme Court then granted certiorari.

ISSUE

If a suspect has knowingly and voluntarily waived his or her *Miranda* rights and then, during questioning, makes a comment that does not qualify as an unambiguous invocation of the right to counsel, must the interrogation immediately cease?

HOLDING

No. Authorities may continue to question a suspect who has knowingly and voluntarily waived his or her *Miranda* rights until he or she clearly asks for assistance of counsel.

RATIONALE

The U.S. Supreme Court affirmed Davis's conviction by a 5–4 vote. The Court first noted the critical assumption that military tribunals are governed by the same rules of evidence as civilian criminal courts. Where this assumption is met, the Court continued by stating that the general rule of law created under *Edwards v. Arizona* requiring the police to respect a suspect's request for counsel during custodial interrogation would become distorted beyond utility by requiring officers to cease questioning every time a suspect made an ambiguous statement along such lines. Thus, not only did the Court conclude that an interrogation may continue until a suspect clearly requests assistance of counsel, but it also added that officers are not required to stop and clarify what is meant by otherwise ambiguous comments such as those in the present case.

CASE EXCERPT

"The suspect must unambiguously request counsel. As we have observed, 'a statement either is such an assertion of the right to counsel or it is not.' Although a suspect need not speak with the discrimination of an Oxford don, he must articulate his desire to have counsel present sufficiently clearly that a reasonable police officer, in the circumstances, would understand the statement to be a request for an attorney. If the statement fails to meet the requisite level of clarity, *Edwards* does not require that the officers stop questioning the suspect."

CASE SIGNIFICANCE

In this case, the Supreme Court slightly relaxed the rule established by *Edwards v. Arizona* requiring that all questioning immediately cease once a suspect invokes the right to counsel. The basis for this retraction is to be found in the specific language a suspect uses. In *Edwards,* the suspect's unequivocal request for an attorney required immediate cessation of the interrogation. By comparison, Davis did not specifically ask for an attorney but, instead, only vaguely remarked that he should probably talk to one. While Davis's comment may strike some as a valid request for counsel, the Court apparently regarded it as a slippery slope with the potential to distort the *Edwards* rule beyond utility. Thus, instead of requiring an interview to cease each time such an ambiguous statement is made, the appropriate standard for determining whether or not the right has been invoked is from the perspective of a reasonable interrogator. Where a reasonable interrogator would interpret a suspect's request for counsel as unambiguous, all questioning must immediately cease under the *Edwards* rule. Where, however, the request is vague, questioning may continue until such time as the suspect clearly invokes the right to counsel. The practical implication of this decision lies in the need to adequately document a suspect's exact language during interrogation in the event that questions are raised at trial regarding the clarity of any such requests.

MISSOURI v. SEIBERT

542 U.S. 600 (2004)

FACTS

Respondent Seibert feared charges of neglect when her son, afflicted with cerebral palsy, died in his sleep.

She was present when two of her sons and their friends discussed burning her family's mobile home to conceal the circumstances of her son's death. Donald, an unrelated mentally ill 18-year-old living with the family, was left to die in the fire, in order to avoid the appearance that Seibert's son had been unattended. Five days later, the police arrested Seibert but did not inform her of her rights under *Miranda v. Arizona*. At the police station, Officer Hanrahan questioned her for 30 to 40 minutes, obtaining a confession that the plan was for Donald to die in the fire. He then gave her a 20-minute break, returned to give her *Miranda* warnings, and obtained a signed waiver. He resumed questioning, confronting Seibert with her prewarning statements and getting her to repeat the information. Seibert moved to suppress both her prewarning and postwarning statements. Hanrahan testified that he made a conscious decision to withhold *Miranda* warnings, question first, then give the warnings, and then repeat the question until he got the answer previously given. The District Court suppressed the prewarning statement but admitted the postwarning one, and Seibert was convicted of second-degree murder. The Missouri Court of Appeals affirmed, finding the case indistinguishable from *Oregon v. Elstad,* in which this Court held that a suspect's unwarned inculpatory statement made during a brief exchange at his house did not make a later, fully warned inculpatory statement inadmissible. In reversing, the State Supreme Court held that, because the interrogation was nearly continuous, the second statement, which was clearly the product of the invalid first statement, should be suppressed, and distinguished *Elstad* on the ground that the warnings had not intentionally been withheld there.

ISSUE

Did the "two-step" technique of interrogation used here violate Seibert's Fifth Amendment rights?

HOLDING

Yes. The two-step technique of questioning a suspect first, then warning him or her, then questioning again, violates the Fifth Amendment.

RATIONALE

That the interrogating officer relied on respondent's prewarning statement to obtain the postwarning one used at trial shows the temptations for abuse inherent in the two-step technique. Reference to the prewarning statement was an implicit, and false, suggestion that the mere repetition of the earlier statement was not independently incriminating. The *Miranda* rule would be frustrated were the police permitted to undermine its meaning and effect. However, the plurality's test—that whenever a two-stage interview occurs, the postwarning statement's admissibility depends on whether the midstream warnings could have been effective enough to accomplish their object given the case's specific facts—cuts too broadly. The admissibility of postwarning statements should continue to be governed by *Elstad*'s principles unless the deliberate two-step strategy is employed. Then, the postwarning statements must be excluded unless curative measures are taken before they were made. Such measures should be designed to ensure that a reasonable person in the suspect's situation would understand the import and effect of the *Miranda* warning and waiver. For example, a substantial break in time and circumstances between the prewarning statement and the warning may suffice in most instances, as may an additional warning explaining the likely inadmissibility of the prewarning statement. Because no curative steps were taken in this case, the postwarning statements are inadmissible and the conviction cannot stand.

CASE EXCERPT

"The contrast between *Elstad* and this case reveals a series of relevant facts that bear on whether *Miranda* warnings delivered midstream could be effective enough to accomplish their object: the completeness and detail of the questions and answers in the first round of interrogation, the overlapping content of the two statements, the timing and setting of the first and the second, the continuity of police personnel, and the degree to which the interrogator's questions treated the second round as continuous with the first. In *Elstad*, it was not unreasonable to see the occasion for questioning at the station house as presenting a markedly different experience from the short conversation at home; since a reasonable person in the suspect's shoes could have seen the station house questioning as a new and distinct experience, the *Miranda* warnings could have made sense as presenting a genuine choice whether to follow up on the earlier admission."

CASE SIGNIFICANCE

The police use a number and variety of established practices to elicit information from suspects. One such

MISSOURI v. SEIBERT *(cont.)*

technique, known as the "two-step" method of interrogation, came under scrutiny in this particular case. In the two-step technique, police first elicit an unwarned inculpatory statement and then later advise the suspect of his or her *Miranda* rights, followed by another round of questioning meant to reaffirm the prior incriminating statements. This strategy is no longer a viable option for law enforcement. Thus, officers are now prohibited from using the technique, thereby narrowing the variety of interrogation strategies commonly used to elicit confessions.

UNITED STATES v. PATANE

542 U.S. 360 (2004)

FACTS

After Officer Fox began to investigate respondent's apparent violation of a temporary restraining order, a federal agent told Fox's colleague, Detective Benner, that respondent, a convicted felon, illegally possessed a pistol. Officer Fox and Detective Benner proceeded to respondent's home, where Fox arrested him for violating the restraining order. Benner attempted to advise respondent of his rights under *Miranda v. Arizona,* but respondent interrupted, asserting that he knew his rights. Benner then asked about the pistol and retrieved and seized it. Respondent was indicted for possession of a firearm by a convicted felon. The District Court granted his motion to suppress the pistol, reasoning that the officers lacked probable cause to arrest him and declining to rule on his alternative argument that the gun should be suppressed as the fruit of an unwarned statement. The Tenth Circuit reversed the probable-cause ruling but affirmed the suppression order on respondent's alternative theory. Rejecting the Government's argument that *Oregon v. Elstad* and *Michigan v. Tucker* foreclosed application of the fruit of the poisonous tree doctrine of *Wong Sun v. United States* to the present context, the appeals court reasoned that *Oregon* and *Tucker*, which were based on the view that *Miranda* announced a prophylactic rule, were incompatible with *Dickerson v. United States,* in which this Court held that *Miranda* announced a constitutional rule. The appeals court thus equated *Dickerson*'s ruling with the proposition that a failure to warn pursuant to *Miranda* is itself a violation of the suspect's Fifth Amendment rights.

ISSUE

Does a failure to give a suspect the warnings prescribed by *Miranda v. Arizona* require suppression of the physical fruits of the suspect's unwarned but voluntary statements?

HOLDING

No. A failure to provide a suspect with the *Miranda* warning does not automatically require the suppression of physical evidence that is the product of an otherwise voluntary statement.

RATIONALE

The *Miranda* rule is a prophylactic employed to protect against violations of the self-incrimination clause. That clause's core protection is a prohibition on compelling a criminal defendant to testify against himself at trial. It cannot be violated by the introduction of nontestimonial evidence obtained as a result of voluntary statements. The Court has recognized and applied several prophylactic rules designed to protect the core privilege against self-incrimination. For example, the *Miranda* rule creates a presumption of coercion in custodial interrogations, in the absence of specific warnings, that is generally irrebuttable for purposes of the prosecution's case in chief. But because such prophylactic rules necessarily sweep beyond the self-incrimination clause's actual protections, any further extension of one of them must be justified by its necessity for the protection of the actual right against compelled self-incrimination. Thus, uncompelled statements taken without *Miranda* warnings can be used to impeach a defendant's testimony at trial, although the fruits of actually compelled testimony cannot. A blanket rule requiring suppression of statements noncompliant with the *Miranda* rule could not be justified by reference to the "Fifth Amendment goal of assuring trustworthy evidence" or by any deterrence rationale and would therefore fail the Court's requirement that the closest possible fit be maintained between the self-incrimination clause and any rule designed to protect it. Furthermore, the clause contains its own exclusionary rule that automatically protects those subjected to coercive police interrogations from the use of their involuntary statements (or evidence derived from their statements) in any subsequent criminal trial. This explicit textual protection supports a strong presumption against expanding the *Miranda* rule any further. Finally, nothing in *Dickerson* calls into question the Court's continued insistence on its close-fit requirement.

CASE EXCERPT

"The fact that the books contain some exceptions to the *Miranda* exclusionary rule carries no weight here. In *Harris v. New York*, it was respect for the integrity of the judicial process that justified the admission of unwarned statements as impeachment evidence. But Patane's suppression motion can hardly be described as seeking to 'pervert' *Miranda* 'into a license to use perjury' or otherwise handicap the 'traditional truth-testing devices of the adversary process.' Nor is there any suggestion that the officers' failure to warn Patane was justified or mitigated by a public emergency or other exigent circumstance, as in *New York v. Quarles*. And of course the premise of *Oregon v. Elstad* is not on point; although a failure to give *Miranda* warnings before one individual statement does not necessarily bar the admission of a subsequent statement given after adequate warnings, that rule obviously does not apply to physical evidence seized once and for all."

CASE SIGNIFICANCE

This case allows the introduction of physical evidence that was obtained by way of an unwarned but otherwise voluntary statement. In the present instance the police did not interrogate the suspect for purposes of eliciting incriminating oral statements. The firearm was recovered in a manner not inconsistent with prior Supreme Court decisions. In *Oregon v. Elstad* the court held that a failure to give the *Miranda* warnings prior to a single inculpatory statement does not necessarily bar the admission of a subsequent properly warned statement. Here, the Court applied the logic of *Elstad* to its decision but further reasoned that the Fifth Amendment protection applies narrowly to evidence of a testimonial nature and not to physical evidence such as the firearm recovered from Patane's residence.

FLORIDA v. POWELL
559 U.S.—(2010)

FACTS

Tampa police officers were called to an apartment rented by Powell's girlfriend. After seeing Powell exiting a bedroom in the apartment the officers searched the room and found a loaded handgun under the bed. Powell was arrested and transported to the police department. He was read the standard *Miranda* warnings and release form used in that department. The form specifically stated that Powell had the right to talk to a lawyer before

answering any questions and that he had the right to any of the rights listed on the form at any time during the interview. Powell acknowledged that he understood his rights, signed the form, and admitted to the officers that the handgun was his and that he knew he was not allowed to possess it. He was then charged with being a felon in possession of a firearm. Powell made a motion to suppress his incriminating statements, arguing that the warnings provided by the police department were not sufficient as they did not communicate his right to have an attorney present during questioning. The Florida Supreme Court held that *Miranda* requires that a suspect must be expressly advised of both the right to talk to a lawyer *before* questioning and the right to consult a lawyer at any time *during* questioning. The Florida court deemed the warning given to Powell misleading because it did not specify that Powell could consult with a lawyer during questioning. The U.S. Supreme Court then granted certiorari.

ISSUE

Was the police department's standard *Miranda*-type warning flawed because it did not specifically inform suspects that they also possess the right to have an attorney physically present during questioning?

HOLDING

No. The police department's effort to warn incoming arrestees of their *Miranda* rights was not constitutionally flawed simply because it failed to specifically inform them that they have the right to have an attorney physically present during questioning.

RATIONALE

Justice Ginsburg wrote the opinion for a 7–2 Court, holding that informing a suspect that he has a right to an attorney prior to questioning and that he may invoke any right during the interview satisfies the requirements of *Miranda*. The opinion noted that the Court has never required that the *Miranda* warnings adhere to specific wording but rather that they reasonably communicate the rights to a suspect. In determining whether police warnings were satisfactory, reviewing courts are not required to "examine [them] as if construing a will or defining the terms of an easement. The inquiry is simply whether the warnings reasonably 'convey to a suspect his rights as required by *Miranda*'" (citing *Duckworth v. Eagan*, 492 U. S. 195 (1989)). The warnings Powell received satisfy this standard. By informing Powell that he had the right to

FLORIDA v. POWELL (cont.)

talk to a lawyer before answering any questions, the police officers communicated that he could consult with a lawyer before answering any particular question. And the statement that Powell had the right to use any of his rights at any time during the interview made clear that he could exercise his right to an attorney while the interrogation was under way. In combination, the two warnings reasonably conveyed the right to have an attorney present not only at the outset of interrogation but at all times.

CASE EXCERPT

"The four warnings *Miranda* requires are invariable, but this Court has not dictated the words in which the essential information must be conveyed. In determining whether police officers adequately conveyed the four warnings, we have said, reviewing courts are not required to examine the words employed as if construing a will or defining the terms of an easement. The inquiry is simply whether the warnings reasonably 'conve[y] to [a suspect] his rights as required by *Miranda*.'"

CASE SIGNIFICANCE

This case reaffirms the Court's earlier ruling in *Duckworth v. Eagan*, which held that the *Miranda* rights need not be presented or recited exactly as they appeared in the original case. This is important for law enforcement purposes on the basis that it frees officers, and in this case agencies, from the burden of having to enumerate the *Miranda* rights exactly as they were articulated in the language of the original decision. Here, the agency provided incoming arrestees with a version of the warning that, the Court held, was close enough to convey its prophylactic meaning and spirit. There is no indication from the Court, however, as to exactly how far the warnings may deviate from the original language. Such questions are answered on a case-by-case basis, but officers and agencies would be well advised to tailor the language they use for such purposes as closely as possible to the original text of the *Miranda* opinion just to be on the safe side.

MARYLAND v. SHATZER

559 U.S.—(2010)

FACTS

Shatzer was interviewed, while incarcerated for an unrelated offense, by a police officer regarding allegations that he had sexually abused his 3-year-old son. He first signed a *Miranda* waiver but then declined to be interrogated without an attorney present, and the interrogation was terminated. Two and a half years following that aborted interview another officer returned to interview Shatzer regarding new information about the alleged abuse of his son. The officer again explained to Shatzer his *Miranda* rights and received a signed waiver. During this interview Shatzer made incriminating statements. Shatzer later sought to suppress his statements pursuant to *Edwards v. Arizona*, which held that once a suspect invokes the *Miranda* right to an attorney any subsequent attempts at custodial interrogation by the police are inherently involuntary. Maryland courts suppressed Shatzer's statements.

ISSUE

Does the rule established by *Edwards* apply to situations where there is a "long" break (such as two and a half years, as occurred in this case) such that police are forever prohibited from reestablishing contact with a suspect for purposes of conducting an interrogation on separate offenses?

HOLDING

No. The *Edwards* rule does not apply where there has elapsed a significant amount of time (more than 14 days).

RATIONALE

Writing for a unanimous Court, Justice Scalia reversed the Maryland courts. The Supreme Court held that there was a break in custody for the purposes of *Miranda* and thus *Edwards* did not apply. The Court then went a step further and created a bright line rule for determining when a break in custody has occurred. The Court created an arbitrary period of 14 days in which *Edwards'* prophylactic rule expires after a break in custody.

CASE EXCERPT

"The only logical endpoint of *Edwards* disability is termination of *Miranda* custody and any of its lingering effects. Without that limitation—and barring some purely arbitrary time-limit—every *Edwards* prohibition of custodial interrogation of a particular suspect would be eternal. The prohibition applies, of course, when the subsequent interrogation pertains to a different crime, when it is conducted by a different law enforcement authority, and even when the suspect has met with an attorney after the first interrogation. And it not only prevents questioning *ex ante;* it would render invalid *ex post,* confessions invited and obtained from suspects who (unbeknownst to the interrogators) have acquired *Edwards* immunity previously in connection with any offense in any jurisdiction. In a country that harbors a large number of repeat offenders, this consequence is disastrous."

CASE SIGNIFICANCE

This case creates an exception to the *Edwards* rule that holds that once a suspect has invoked the right to remain silent, no subsequent questioning regarding any offense may take place. Here, respondent Shatzer was incarcerated on other charges and an arguably significant amount of time (two and a half years) had elapsed between his first properly warned interview and the subsequent contact reinitiated by the police. The Court reasoned that enough time had elapsed between the two interviews for purposes of satisfying the prophylactic goals of the *Edwards* rule. Furthermore, the Court held that a break of only 14 days is necessary for the police to reinitiate contact.

BERGHUIS v. THOMPKINS

560 U.S.—(2010)

FACTS

In 2000, two victims were shot outside a mall in Michigan. One of the victims died. The other victim survived and later testified in court. Thompkins fled from the crime scene and was found approximately one year later in Ohio. After his arrest, two police officers traveled from Michigan to Ohio to interrogate him during his wait for transfer to Michigan. The interrogation began in the early afternoon and continued for approximately three hours. Thompkins was read his *Miranda* rights, refused to sign the *Miranda* form, and remained silent throughout most of the interrogation. Near the end of the interrogation he answered "yes" when one of the officers asked if he prayed to God to forgive him for the shooting. At trial, Thompkins claimed that someone else had been the shooter and made a motion to suppress his incriminating statement, claiming that he had invoked his Fifth Amendment right to remain silent. His motion was denied, and he was convicted. On appeal, he argued his Fifth Amendment rights were violated because the police continued to interrogate him when he wished to remain silent.

ISSUE

Does a suspect have to clearly state that he or she wants to remain silent in order to invoke his or her *Miranda* rights?

HOLDING

Yes. A suspect must verbally indicate a desire to remain silent in order to invoke the protections afforded by *Miranda.*

RATIONALE

Writing for a 5–4 majority, Justice Kennedy upheld Thompkins' conviction. The Court held that Thompkins did not invoke his right to remain silent, and thus the police were entitled to continue to interrogate him. Justice Kennedy stated that a defendant must invoke the right to remain silent in an unambiguous manner. The Court further held that a waiver of the right to remain silent can be implied based on a defendant's understanding of the right and failure to invoke the right.

CASE EXCERPT

"Thompkins did not say that he wanted to remain silent or that he did not want to talk with the police. Had he made either of these simple, unambiguous statements, he would have invoked his 'right to cut off questioning.' Here he did neither, so he did not invoke his right to remain silent."

CASE SIGNIFICANCE

This case clarifies the requirements necessary for a suspect to invoke the *Miranda* protections. Specifically, the court ruled that a suspect cannot simply sit mute and later assert that he had invoked the right to remain silent. Rather, one must clearly and unequivocally state something to the effect of "I wish to remain silent." Here, Thompkins failed to do so. Had he merely uttered this simple statement, the full force of the *Miranda* protections would have applied.

J.D.B. v. NORTH CAROLINA

564 U.S.—(2011)

FACTS

In Chapel Hill, North Carolina, two homes were burglarized. In a neighboring yard police found and questioned J.D.B., a 13-year-old male. J.D.B. was released after the initial questioning but was questioned a second time after police received a report that a digital

J.D.B. v. NORTH CAROLINA *(cont.)*

camera matching the description of one of the stolen items had been seen in his possession. Following up on this report, a police investigator was sent to J.D.B.'s school to remove him from class and to question him. In a closed conference room on school grounds, the investigator, the school's uniformed resource officer, and two school administrators questioned J.D.B. for nearly an hour. The police investigator had informed the administration at the school of his intentions to question J.D.B., but both the administration and the investigator neglected to notify J.D.B.'s grandmother, his legal guardian. Before questioning began, no *Miranda* warnings were read to J.D.B. and no opportunity to speak to his grandmother was offered. Furthermore, neither the investigator, the uniformed resource officer, nor the school administrators informed J.D.B. that he had the right to leave at any time. The investigator threatened to send J.D.B. to a secure detention facility, and in response J.D.B. confessed. At this point in the interview the investigator informed J.D.B. that he had the right to not answer any further questions and could leave at any time. At his adjudication hearing J.D.B.'s public defender filed a motion to suppress J.D.B.'s confession, arguing that he was in custody at the time of the interrogation and had not been properly given his *Miranda* warnings. The court denied the motion and subsequently found J.D.B. delinquent. On appeal, the state court affirmed, rejecting the claim that J.D.B. was in custody at the time of the interrogation and that his confession should be excluded.

ISSUE

Was J.D.B. in custody for purposes of Fifth Amendment analysis?

HOLDING

Yes. Given J.D.B.'s age (13), he was in custody and therefore entitled to the protections afforded by *Miranda* and its progeny.

RATIONALE

In a 5–4 decision, the Supreme Court rejected the lower court's reasoning, in an opinion written by Justice Sotomayor. Justice Sotomayor noted that the *Miranda* warnings do not need to be read if a person is not in custody—which the court has defined as when a reasonable person would feel free to leave or decline to answer an officer's questions. She explained that it is "common sense" that youths are not adults and that the

reasonable person standard need be applied to the reasonableness of an objective person of the same age as the youth in question. She explained that a youth is far more likely to feel compelled to answer the questions of a police officer than an adult would. The Court concluded that if the suspect's age is known to the officer at the time of questioning, or would have been apparent to a reasonable officer, its inclusion in the custody analysis is consistent with the objective nature of that test. The Court did not specify an age at which police must consider the youth of the suspect in determining his or her ability to understand his or her rights, but the practical effect of this decision is that police officers are now more likely to give warnings to any suspect who does not appear to be close to age 18.

CASE EXCERPT

"A child's age is far more than a chronological fact. It is a fact that 'generates commonsense conclusions about behavior and perception.' Such conclusions apply broadly to children as a class. And, they are self-evident to anyone who was a child once himself, including any police officer or judge...Time and again, this Court has drawn these commonsense conclusions for itself. We have observed that children generally are less mature and responsible than adults, that they often lack the experience, perspective, and judgment to recognize and avoid choices that could be detrimental to them, that they are more vulnerable or susceptible to outside pressures than adults, and so on. Addressing the specific context of police interrogation, we have observed that events that would leave a man cold and unimpressed can overawe and overwhelm a lad in his early teens. Describing no one child in particular, these observations restate what any parent knows—indeed, what any person knows—about children generally."

CASE SIGNIFICANCE

Here the Supreme Court deals with the questions of age and custody. Specifically, the Court evaluated the question of whether or not J.D.B. was in custody in light of his age (13 years old at the time). Given the difference in both a young child's sensibilities and sensitivities to the demands of custodial interrogation, it was determined that J.D.B. was entitled to the protections afforded by *Miranda* and its progeny of cases. Because the Court did not specify a particular age at which such sensibilities and sensitivities become more naturally immune to the rigors of custodial interrogation, investigators must err on the side of caution and inform all youthful suspects of their rights under *Miranda* during focused questioning.

DISCUSSION QUESTIONS

1. Why is it a good idea for police officers to always read the *Miranda* warnings from a printed card or other prepared source rather than just "winging" it from memory? How might this affect the admissibility of a suspect's statement at trial? How might it influence juror behavior?

2. How would you explain to a group of skeptical officers that the *Miranda* warnings actually promote a professional image of the police?

3. Why is it important for law enforcement agencies to develop internal procedures for communicating information regarding a suspect's prior invocation of the right to remain silent?

4. What practical measures can be taken to document that a suspect has been properly Mirandized in the field?

5. What special considerations arise when informing a suspect with diminished mental capacity (e.g., mental retardation or intoxication) of his or her *Miranda* rights?

CHAPTER NINETEEN

WHAT CONSTITUTES INTERROGATION?

BREWER V. WILLIAMS, *430 U.S. 387 (1977)*
RHODE ISLAND V. INNIS, *446 U.S. 291 (1980)*

ARIZONA V. MAURO, *481 U.S. 520 (1987)*

INTRODUCTION

As a practical matter, one of the most confusing aspects of the *Miranda* decision involves determining exactly when and under what circumstances an officer must read a suspect his or her rights. This confusion is exacerbated by a pervasive belief among members of the general public that the police must inform suspects of their rights anytime the most innocuous of questions is put forth. Contrary to this misguided perception, however, officers are not required to read the *Miranda* warnings every time an individual is questioned but, instead, must do so only during a custodial interrogation.

The task at hand thus becomes one of defining exactly what constitutes a custodial interrogation. As implied, two conditions must be met—the person must be in custody and he or she must be subjected to interrogation. "Custody" occurs when an individual is significantly deprived of his or her freedom to leave. "Interrogation" occurs when officers ask probative questions about an individual's involvement in a particular crime. Where these two conditions are met—the individual is not free to leave and he or she is being questioned about a specific crime—then, and only then, must the warnings be given.

A word of caution is appropriate at this point, especially where broad interpretation is given to the above definition of custodial interrogation. For example, it might reasonably be argued that the *Miranda* warnings must be given during traffic stops, insofar as the motorist is compelled to remain on the scene and answer questions about his or her involvement in a criminal traffic offense.

Eventually, the Supreme Court resolved this issue in *Berkemer v. McCarty*, 468 U.S. 420 (1984), by ruling that the roadside questioning of a motorist detained pursuant to a lawful traffic stop does not constitute a custodial interrogation. Consequently, officers are not required to inform traffic violators of their *Miranda* rights.

In spite of this clarification, problematic situations arise for police officers almost daily. For example, an officer dispatched to the scene of a domestic violence call notes that a physical assault has clearly taken place. Must the *Miranda* warning be given before any questions are asked of a suspected assailant, or is it permissible for the officer to ask general questions in order to first find out what occurred? While there exists no universal protocol for these and other types of conceivable situations the police frequently encounter, the safest bet is to warn suspects in order to prevent a subsequent claim that their rights were violated. To this important end, the cases included in this chapter illustrate problematic situations where officers conducted custodial interrogations (or the functional equivalent thereof) that were later scrutinized for constitutional appropriateness by the Supreme Court.

BREWER v. WILLIAMS
430 U.S. 387 (1977)

FACTS

Williams surrendered to police in Davenport, Iowa, on charges stemming from the abduction and murder of a

10-year-old Des Moines girl. While awaiting transport from Davenport to Des Moines, he was twice advised by two separate attorneys to refrain from speaking with officers about the alleged offense. Furthermore, Williams was arraigned before a judge in Davenport who informed him of his *Miranda* rights. Before leaving the courtroom, Williams consulted with yet a third attorney, who reiterated what the other two had already told him. When Des Moines detectives arrived, they too informed Williams of his *Miranda* rights. Thus, not only had Williams been twice informed of his *Miranda* rights by state agents, but he was also advised by three separate attorneys to remain silent if asked any questions about the alleged crime. While driving back to Des Moines, one of the detectives remarked to Williams that they should probably stop and locate the young girl's body so that her parents could provide her with a "Christian burial." Williams conceded and directed the transporting detectives to her body. He was eventually tried for first-degree murder and the state's supreme court allowed the conviction to stand. A federal district court granted Williams' petition for habeas corpus review on grounds that the evidence in question had been wrongly admitted at trial. The Eighth Circuit Court of Appeals affirmed the petition, and the U.S. Supreme Court granted certiorari.

ISSUE

Did the officer's appeal for information regarding the whereabouts of the young girl's body violate Williams' Sixth Amendment right to counsel?

HOLDING

Yes. Officers are prohibited from appealing to a suspect's moral or religious beliefs for purposes of soliciting incriminating statements in the absence of legal representation.

RATIONALE

The officer's appeal for information regarding the whereabouts of the young girl's body violated Williams' Sixth Amendment right to counsel on at least two grounds. First, judicial proceedings had formally been initiated against Williams, thereby triggering his right to counsel during any custodial interrogations. Second, the officer's statement regarding the need for a "Christian burial" was tantamount to a custodial interrogation. Consequently, a 5–4 majority of the Court ruled that the officer consciously and knowingly set out to violate Williams' Sixth Amendment right to counsel

as well as his Fifth Amendment privilege against self-incrimination.

CASE EXCERPT

"There can be no serious doubt that Detective Leaming deliberately and designedly set out to elicit information from Williams just as surely as—and perhaps more effectively than—if he had formally interrogated him. Detective Leaming was fully aware before departing for Des Moines that Williams was being represented in Davenport by Kelly and in Des Moines by McKnight. Yet he purposely sought during Williams' isolation from his lawyers to obtain as much incriminating information as possible. Indeed, Detective Leaming conceded as much when he testified at Williams' trial:

Q: In fact, Captain, whether he was a mental patient or not, you were trying to get all the information you could before he got to his lawyer, weren't you?
A: I was sure hoping to find out where that little girl was, yes, sir......
Q: Well, I'll put it this way: You was [sic] hoping to get all the information you could before Williams got back to McKnight, weren't you?
A: Yes, sir.

CASE SIGNIFICANCE

This decision is important in two regards. First, it served to remind officers that once formal proceedings have been initiated against a suspect, he or she is protected by the Sixth Amendment right to counsel so that no questioning about the offense may be undertaken unless an attorney is physically present. Second, the decision clarified the conditions that amount to custodial interrogation. Thus, although there was no direct questioning of Williams, the officer's reference to a "Christian burial" nonetheless created a coercive environment violative of his right to counsel.

RHODE ISLAND v. INNIS

446 U.S. 291 (1980)

FACTS

Police arrested Innis after he was identified by a robbery victim. He was advised no less than three times of his *Miranda* rights by the patrol officer and two supervisory personnel on the scene. A prior robbery victim had been killed with a sawed-off shotgun. While

RHODE ISLAND v. INNIS *(cont.)*

en route to the jail, one of the transporting officers expressed concern to another that children from a nearby school for the handicapped might find the weapon and accidentally harm themselves.

Overhearing this comment and apparently sharing similar concern, Innis told the officers to turn the car around so that he could show them where the weapon was hidden. Upon arriving back at the scene of his arrest, Innis was again informed of his *Miranda* rights. Indicating that he understood these rights, he nonetheless led officers to a nearby field where the gun was recovered. Innis was subsequently convicted of kidnapping, robbery, and murder. On appeal, the Rhode Island Supreme Court set aside the conviction on grounds that the transporting officers had interrogated Innis without the benefit of counsel while transporting him to the jail. The U.S. Supreme Court then granted certiorari.

ISSUE
Did the conversation overheard by Innis that led him to disclose the shotgun's location constitute an interrogation for purposes of Sixth Amendment analysis?

HOLDING
No. The conversation between the two officers did not constitute an interrogation or its functional equivalent as the suspect was not directly involved in the exchange. Therefore, no Sixth Amendment right was either implicated or violated.

RATIONALE
The U.S. Supreme Court reversed the Rhode Island Supreme Court's ruling that the transporting officers had interrogated Innis and thereby violated his Sixth Amendment right to counsel. In reaching this decision, the Court first reviewed the various procedural safeguards established by its decision in *Miranda v. Arizona*. Specifically, it was noted that the term "interrogation" refers not only to instances of express questioning, but also to any words or actions undertaken by the police that are reasonably likely to elicit an incriminating response from the suspect. Given this definition, which places greater emphasis upon the perception of the suspect rather than the intent of the police, a majority of the justices concluded that the conversation that had transpired between the officers did not constitute

an interrogation insofar as there had been no direct questioning of Innis. Furthermore, the conversation fell short of an interrogation on grounds that at no time did the officers attempt to elicit a response from Innis. Finally, the majority also observed that there was no indication that the two officers were specifically aware of and intentionally sought to exploit Innis' concern for the safety of nearby handicapped children.

CASE EXCERPT
"The case thus boils down to whether, in the context of a brief conversation, the officers should have known that the respondent would suddenly be moved to make a self-incriminating response. Given the fact that the entire conversation appears to have consisted of no more than a few offhand remarks, we cannot say that the officers should have known that it was reasonably likely that Innis would so respond. This is not a case where the police carried on a lengthy harangue in the presence of the suspect. Nor does the record support the respondent's contention that, under the circumstances, the officers' comments were particularly 'evocative.' It is our view, therefore, that the respondent was not subjected by the police to words or actions that the police should have known were reasonably likely to elicit an incriminating response from him."

CASE SIGNIFICANCE
This case is important in that it helped clarify those police behaviors that constitute an interrogation and those that do not. Recall that in the earlier matter of *Brewer v. Williams* the Supreme Court ruled that an officer's direct appeal to a suspect for information regarding the whereabouts of a murder victim's body so that the parents could provide her with a "Christian burial" constituted an interrogation for purposes of Sixth Amendment analysis. In the present matter, however, the Court concluded that the behavior of the two officers did not constitute an interrogation for purposes of Sixth Amendment analysis on the grounds that they did not directly engage the suspect in conversation—they were speaking only among themselves and did not ask him any questions. Although the distinction between these two cases may seem clear, the use of such tactics to obtain information remains risky given that the situation will be assessed not from the perspective of the officers but, instead, from that of the suspect. If the case can be

made that a defendant believed he or she was being actively interrogated by the police, then most courts will rule in favor of the defendant's Sixth Amendment interest.

ARIZONA v. MAURO
481 U.S. 520 (1987)

FACTS
Seeking information about the murder of his son, officers informed Mauro of his *Miranda* rights, whereupon he declined to make any statements until an attorney was present. Officers promptly terminated the interview. Later, however, they allowed Mauro's wife to meet with him. Also present in the room during this meeting was an officer who openly laid a tape recorder on the desk between the two. During their conversation, Mauro made incriminating statements to his wife. These statements were later introduced at trial and Mauro was convicted. The Arizona Supreme Court reversed the conviction, finding that the tape-recorded conversation violated Mauro's right to avoid self-incrimination under the Fifth Amendment. The U.S. Supreme Court then granted certiorari.

ISSUE
Does the tape recording of a conversation between a suspect and his or her spouse that occurs in the presence of a police officer violate the Fifth Amendment privilege against self-incrimination?

HOLDING
No. The self-incrimination privilege of the Fifth Amendment does not forbid the introduction of incriminating statements made by a suspect to his or her spouse in the presence of a police officer, especially in instances where the suspect was not subjected to any compelling influences, psychological ploys, or direct questioning generally characteristic of custodial interrogation or its functional equivalent.

RATIONALE
By a 5–4 vote, the Court ruled that Mauro's incriminating statements were admissible on several grounds. First, the attending officer did not ask Mauro any questions about the alleged crime. Second, Mauro chose to speak openly with his wife, knowing full well that a tape recorder was being used. Third, the police did not orchestrate the meeting between Mauro and his

wife—she approached them and asked for the meeting with her husband. Finally, there existed no evidence to suggest that Mauro was coerced to speak to his wife or to make incriminating statements against his will during their meeting. In contrast, the dissenting justices argued that the incriminating statements were obtained through use of a powerful psychological ploy set into motion at a time when it was reasonably likely to produce such evidence.

CASE EXCERPT
"There is no evidence that the officers sent Mrs. Mauro in to see her husband for the purpose of eliciting incriminating statements. As the trial court found, the officers tried to discourage her from talking to her husband, but finally yielded to her insistent demands. Nor was Detective Manson's presence improper. His testimony, that the trial court found credible, indicated a number of legitimate reasons—not related to securing incriminating statements—for having a police officer present. Finally, the weakness of Mauro's claim that he was interrogated is underscored by examining the situation from his perspective. We doubt that a suspect, told by officers that his wife will be allowed to speak to him, would feel that he was being coerced to incriminate himself in any way."

CASE SIGNIFICANCE
This case eroded the rights of criminals insofar as it allows authorities to tape record verbal exchanges between a suspect and others so long as no compelling influence, psychological ploy, or direct questioning is involved. Consistent with the facts of the present case, officers may sit in on or even record the conversation between a suspect and visitor so long as such measures are openly undertaken. The suspect cannot be coerced or tricked into giving the information under false pretenses. So long as the environment in which the information is disclosed does not constitute the functional equivalent of an interrogation, such tactics for obtaining information are constitutionally permissible.

DISCUSSION QUESTIONS

1. Why do so many members of the public think that the police must read the *Miranda* warnings, even in situations where it is not legally required?
2. How should officers respond when confronted by an individual who demands to be given the

Miranda warnings, even though they may not be legally necessary?

3. Must an arrestee be informed of his or her *Miranda* rights before being asked routine questions during the booking process? Why or why not?

4. What were the major differences in the facts and circumstances surrounding the *Brewer* case as opposed to the *Innis* case? In other words, why did the Supreme Court decide that Brewer's confession was not admissible but that Innis's confession was?

5. Why is it arguably a bad idea for the police to engage a suspect in casual conversation about even the most nonincriminating matters?

CHAPTER TWENTY

CIVIL LIABILITY

MONROE v. PAPE, *365 U.S. 167 (1961)*

MONELL v. DEPARTMENT OF SOCIAL SERVICES OF NEW YORK, *436 U.S. 658 (1978)*

OWEN v. CITY OF INDEPENDENCE, *445 U.S. 622 (1980)*

MALLEY v. BRIGGS, *475 U.S. 335 (1986)*

CITY OF CANTON v. HARRIS, *489 U.S. 378 (1989)*

WILL v. MICHIGAN DEPARTMENT OF STATE POLICE, *491 U.S. 58 (1989)*

BOARD OF THE COUNTY COMMISSIONERS OF BRYAN COUNTY v. BROWN, *520 U.S. 397 (1997)*

MCMILLIAN v. MONROE COUNTY, *520 U.S. 781 (1997)*

COUNTY OF SACRAMENTO v. LEWIS, *523 U.S. 833 (1998)*

SAUCIER v. KATZ, *533 U.S. 194 (2001)*

TOWN OF CASTLE ROCK, COLORADO v. GONZALES, *545 U.S. 748 (2005)*

PEARSON v. CALLAHAN, *555 U.S.—(2009)*

INTRODUCTION

42 U.S.C. Section 1983 (hereafter referred to as Section 1983) provides a remedy in federal court for the "deprivation of any rights...secured by the Constitution and laws" of the United States. As such, it has been addressed by the Supreme Court on many occasions. Almost every case in this chapter deals with this important piece of legislation. Section 1983 states that "Every person who, under color of any statute, ordinance, regulation, custom, or usage, of any State or Territory, subjects, or causes to be subjected, any citizen of the United States or other persons within the jurisdiction thereof to the deprivation of any rights, privileges, or immunities secured by the Constitution and laws, shall be liable to the party injured in an action at law, suit in equity, or other proper proceeding for redress."

Section 1983 was originally enacted as part of the Ku Klux Klan Act of April 20, 1871 (also known as Section 1 of the Civil Rights Act of 1871). The Act was designed to address atrocities being committed by Klan members in the wake of the Civil War, but it did not target Klan members as such. Instead, Section 1983 imposed liability on state representatives who failed to enforce state laws against illegal Klan activities. But the statute was rarely used and remained effectively dormant for some 90 years after it was signed into law.

Section 1983 enjoyed a resurgence in *Monroe v. Pape.* In that case, a group of police officers allegedly entered the home of James Monroe without warning, then forced the occupants to stand naked in the living room while the house was searched and ransacked. Monroe brought a Section 1983 action against the police officers and the city of Chicago. The case eventually reached the U.S. Supreme Court, where eight justices held that the alleged misuse of authority could support a Section 1983 action against the police officers—that is, the Supreme Court held that Section 1983 could be used as a vehicle to sue the police.

One of the requirements for a successful Section 1983 lawsuit is that the defendant, the person being sued, must have acted "under color of law." The Supreme Court has stated that someone acts under color of law when he or she acts in an official capacity (*Lugar v. Edmondson Oil Co.,* 457 U.S. 922, 937 (1982)).

For example, a police officer who is on duty acts under color of law. By contrast, someone acting in a private capacity (e.g., an ordinary citizen) cannot be said to have acted under color of law. To complicate matters, certain officials who act under color of law can nevertheless not be sued. In *Will v. Michigan Department of State Police,* for example, the Supreme Court held that neither states nor state officials, acting in their official capacity, can be held liable under Section 1983.

What happens when it is unclear whether the defendant named in a lawsuit is a party who can be sued? The Supreme Court confronted this question in *McMillian v. Monroe County.* The specific question before the Court was whether a sheriff is a representative of the state or of the county. As a representative of the state, the sheriff could not be sued in his or her official capacity, but as a representative of the county, he or she could. The Court held that it is necessary to consult individual state constitutions, laws, and/or regulations to make this determination.

The second requirement for a successful Section 1983 lawsuit is that a violation of constitutional rights take place. In determining whether constitutional rights have been violated, the plaintiff(s) must establish that the defendant's (or defendants') conduct violated a specific constitutional provision, such as the Fourth Amendment.

Recently, the courts have begun to require that constitutional rights violations alleged under Section 1983 be committed with a certain level of culpability. That is, plaintiffs generally have to prove that the defendant(s) intended for the violation to occur. There is a very clear reason for this: Not all constitutional rights violations are (or should be) actionable under Section 1983, only the most egregious of civil rights violations. The level of culpability required for a constitutional rights violation varies depending on the type of unconstitutional conduct alleged by the plaintiff.

Typically, in Section 1983 cases, the plaintiff's lawsuit will target an individual officer, that officer's supervisor, the city or municipality for which the officer works, or a combination thereof. While the individual officer responsible for inflicting harm should arguably be held liable, plaintiffs are often attracted to "bigger fish" where there are larger rewards. Governmental entities, in particular, have deep pockets and are attractive targets for civil litigation. Individual officers can be sued, of course, because they are most directly responsible for constitutional rights violations, when they occur. The following paragraphs therefore discuss

cases involving individuals as well as municipal or county liability.

Cities and counties can be held liable under Section 1983 if they adopt and implement policies or adopt customs that become responsible for constitutional rights violations (see *Monell v. Department of Social Services of New York*). In general, a Section 1983 claim against a county or municipality will fail if a common practice is engaged in by lower-ranking officials who have no authority to make "policy" in the traditional sense of the term. For example, if a group of police officers regularly use excessive force but do so on their own, with no authorization from the city or county, then the city or county could not be held liable for their actions.

In another city/county liability case, *City of Canton v. Harris,* the Supreme Court held that counties (and, by extension, cities) can be held liable for inadequately training their law enforcement officers. The facts of the case in *Canton* were that Harris was arrested and brought to the police station in a patrol wagon. On arrival, the officers found Harris lying on the floor of the wagon. She was asked if she needed medical attention, but she responded incoherently. After she was brought into the station, she slumped to the floor on two occasions. Eventually she was left lying on the floor; no medical attention was summoned for her. Harris later sued, seeking to hold the city liable for a violation of her Fourteenth Amendment right, under the due process clause, to receive medical attention while in police custody. However, the Court held that "only where a municipality's failure to train its employees in a relevant respect evidences a 'deliberate indifference' to the rights of its inhabitants can such a shortcoming be properly thought of as a city 'policy or custom' that is actionable under [Section] 1983" (*City of Canton v. Harris*).

In *Board of the County Commissioners of Bryan County v. Brown* the Supreme Court revisited the city/county liability issue. In particular, the question before the Court was whether a single hiring decision by a municipality's policymaker could give rise to an inadequate hiring claim under Section 1983. In that case Brown's claim was fueled by the injuries she suffered at the hands of Bryan County Reserve Deputy Stacy Burns during a high-speed pursuit, and by the fact that Burns had two previous misdemeanor convictions for assault and battery, both of which were overlooked during the preemployment screening process. Brown seemed to have a good case, but the Court's decision in *Bryan County* set the bar for a claim against a municipality for inadequate hiring rather high. Specifically, the Court held that "[e]ven assuming without deciding that proof of a single instance of inadequate screening could ever trigger municipal liability, Moore's failure to scrutinize Burns' record cannot constitute 'deliberate indifference' to respondent's federally protected right to be free from the use of excessive force" (*Board of the County Commissioners of Bryan County v. Brown*).

For a finding of individual liability, Section 1983 requires a plaintiff to demonstrate that his or her constitutional rights were violated by someone acting under color of state law. The constitutional rights most frequently claimed in Section 1983 lawsuits include those stemming from the Fourth, Eighth, and Fourteenth Amendments to the Constitution. We focus here on Fourteenth Amendment cases, as some of the others are discussed in a different context in other chapters (e.g., *Tennessee v. Garner* in Chapter Six).

The Fourteenth Amendment contains two primary components, both of which are actionable under Section 1983. These are the so-called "substantive" and "procedural" components. The essence of substantive due process is protection from arbitrary and unreasonable action on the part of state officials. A "shocks the conscience" standard has been used in cases involving allegations of Fourteenth Amendment substantive due process (*County of Sacramento v. Lewis*). There, the Supreme Court held that police officers will not be held liable for substantive due process violations unless their conduct shocks the conscience.

A different standard has been applied in procedural due process cases. At the risk of simplification, a procedural due process violation is one that violates a significant life, liberty, or property interest. To clarify, one court distinguished between procedural and substantive due process in the following way: "substantive due process prohibits the government's abuse of power or its use for the purpose of oppression, and procedural due process prohibits arbitrary and unfair deprivations of protected life, liberty, or property interests without procedural safeguards" (*Howard v. Grinage*, 82 F.3d 1343 (6th Cir. 1996)).

Police officers enjoy qualified immunity, a defense to Section 1983 civil liability. Basically, qualified immunity shields individual police officers from liability for reasonably mistaken beliefs. One of the best examples of a reasonably mistaken belief was in the case of *Malley v. Briggs*. In *Malley* plaintiffs filed a Section 1983 suit alleging that a police officer applied for, and

obtained, a warrant that failed to establish probable cause. Rather than focus on the probable cause issue, the Supreme Court stated that the "question in this case is whether a reasonably well-trained officer in petitioner's position would have known that his affidavit failed to establish probable cause and that he should not have applied for the warrant." The Court went on to note that "[o]nly where the warrant application is so lacking in indicia of probable cause as to render official belief in its existence unreasonable will the shield of immunity be lost."

Importantly, the qualified immunity defense needs to viewed separately from the constitutional rights violation claimed by the plaintiff, as recently decided by the Supreme Court in *Saucier v. Katz*. There, the Court held that questions of whether excessive force is used and whether qualified immunity should be granted are to be kept separate and are not be fused into a single inquiry.

The term "qualified immunity" suggests that such immunity is not absolute. However, municipalities and counties *cannot* claim absolute immunity, or even qualified immunity. Such was the Supreme Court's decision in *Owen v. City of Independence*.

MONROE v. PAPE
365 U.S. 167 (1961)

FACTS

A group of police officers allegedly entered the home of James Monroe without warning, then forced the occupants to stand naked in the living room while the house was searched and ransacked. Monroe brought a Section 1983 action against the police officers and the city of Chicago, and the U.S. Supreme Court granted certiorari.

ISSUE

Can plaintiffs sue individual police officers for misconduct under 42 U.S.C. Section 1983?

HOLDING

Yes. 42 U.S.C. Section 1983 provides a cause of action against police officers for misuse of authority.

RATIONALE

Section 1983 provides that any "person" who "under color of" state law deprives another of "any rights, privileges, or immunities secured by the Constitution and laws shall be liable in an action at law, suit in equity, or

MONROE v. PAPE *(cont.)*

other proper proceeding for redress." This provision, enacted as part of the Ku Klux Klan Act of 1871, can serve as a cause of action against police officers who misuse their authority.

CASE EXCERPT

"Although the legislation was enacted because of the conditions that existed in the South at that time, it is cast in general language and is as applicable to Illinois as it is to the States whose names were mentioned over and again in the debates. It is no answer that the State has a law which if enforced would give relief. The federal remedy is supplementary to the state remedy, and the latter need not be first sought and refused before the federal one is invoked. Hence the fact that Illinois by its constitution and laws outlaws unreasonable searches and seizures is no barrier to the present suit in the federal court."

CASE SIGNIFICANCE

This case has been described as the "fountainhead" of Section 1983 litigation. It effectively opened the door to Section 1983 litigation against law enforcement officials. Prior to *Pape,* Section 1983 was not used against law enforcement authorities who misused their authority.

MONELL v. DEPARTMENT OF SOCIAL SERVICES OF NEW YORK
436 U.S. 658 (1978)

FACTS

Female employees of the Department of Social Services filed a lawsuit against the Department and the city of New York (among other officials) under 42 U.S.C. Section 1983. They claimed that the city maintained a policy that compelled pregnant employees to take unpaid leaves of absence before such leaves were required for medical reasons. They further claimed that municipalities are considered "persons" for purposes of Section 1983. The U.S. Supreme Court granted certiorari.

ISSUE

Are municipalities considered persons within the meaning of 42 U.S.C. Section 1983?

HOLDING

Yes. Municipalities are considered persons within the meaning of 42 U.S.C. Section 1983, but they can be held liable only for constitutional violations that are sanctioned by policy or custom.

RATIONALE

"*Monroe v. Pape* is overruled insofar as it holds that local governments are wholly immune from suit under Section 1983. Local governing bodies (and local officials sued in their official capacities) can, therefore, be sued directly under Section 1983 for monetary, declaratory, and injunctive relief in those situations where, as here, the action that is alleged to be unconstitutional implements or executes a policy statement, ordinance, regulation, or decision officially adopted or promulgated by those whose edicts or acts may fairly be said to represent official policy. In addition, local governments, like every other Section 1983 'person,' may be sued for constitutional deprivations visited pursuant to governmental 'custom' even though such custom has not received formal approval through the government's official decisionmaking channels."

CASE EXCERPT

"A local government may not be sued under 1983 for an injury inflicted solely by its employees or agents. Instead, it is when execution of a government's policy or custom, whether made by its lawmakers or by those whose edicts or acts may fairly be said to represent official policy, inflicts the injury that the government as an entity is responsible under 1983."

CASE SIGNIFICANCE

This case is significant because it opened the door to Section 1983 litigation against municipalities and, by extension, other units of local government. Prior to *Monell,* cities were not considered "persons" within the meaning of Section 1983. Of key importance in *Monell* is the Court's requirement that a policy or custom be in place before a city can be held liable for constitutional rights violations committed by its employees. Without this requirement, most cities and counties would have long ago gone bankrupt because of constitutional rights violations committed by their subordinates without their knowledge.

OWEN v. CITY OF INDEPENDENCE
445 U.S. 622 (1980)

FACTS

Amidst allegations that its police department was acting improperly, the city council of Independence,

Missouri, discharged the police chief, giving no reason for the dismissal, and only sending the chief a notice that his position was terminated. The discharged chief brought an action under 42 U.S.C Section 1983 for violation of federally protected rights. Specifically, he claimed that he had been discharged without reason and without a hearing, in violation of his substantive and procedural due process rights under the Fourteenth Amendment. The district court and the court of appeals both found in favor of the defendants, deciding that even though the plaintiff's rights were violated, the defendants enjoyed qualified immunity because they acted in good faith. The U.S. Supreme Court then granted certiorari.

ISSUE

Are municipalities entitled to qualified immunity in Section 1983 actions?

HOLDING

No. Municipalities sued under 42 U.S.C. Section 1983 do not enjoy qualified immunity. "A municipality has no immunity from liability under Section 1983 flowing from its constitutional violations and may not assert the good faith of its officers as a defense to such liability."

RATIONALE

"We believe that today's decision, together with prior precedents in this area, properly allocates these costs among the three principals in the scenario of the Section 1983 cause of action: the victim of the constitutional deprivation; the officer whose conduct caused the injury; and the public, as represented by the municipal entity. The innocent individual who is harmed by an abuse of governmental authority is assured that he will be compensated for his injury. The offending official, so long as he conducts himself in good faith, may go about his business secure in the knowledge that a qualified immunity will protect him from personal liability for damages that are more appropriately chargeable to the populace as a whole. And the public will be forced to bear only the costs of injury inflicted by the 'execution of a government's policy or custom, whether made by its lawmakers or by those whose edicts or acts may fairly be said to represent official policy.'"

CASE EXCERPT

"We can discern no 'tradition so well grounded in history and reason' that would warrant the conclusion that in enacting the Civil Rights Act, the 42d Congress *sub silentio* extended to municipalities a qualified immunity based on the good faith of their officers. Absent any clearer indication that Congress intended so to limit the reach of a statute expressly designed to provide a 'broad remedy for violations of federally protected civil rights,' we are unwilling to suppose that injuries occasioned by a municipality's unconstitutional conduct were not also meant to be fully redressable through its sweep."

CASE SIGNIFICANCE

This case is important because it established that municipalities (and, by extension, counties) cannot assert immunity from liability. Only individual officials working for the city or county have this benefit. Importantly, this does not mean that cities and counties can be sued successfully very often. For a plaintiff to succeed with a Section 1983 lawsuit against a county or municipality, he or she must show that a policy or custom was responsible for some injury. Or, if the plaintiff alleges that the city or county failed to train its officers, he or she must show that the defendant acted with deliberate indifference to the plaintiffs' federally protected rights.

MALLEY v. BRIGGS
475 U.S. 335 (1986)

FACTS

A court-authorized wiretap intercepted a conversation between Driscoll and "Dr. Shogun." Based on information revealed in the conversation, police concluded that a marijuana party was taking place at Briggs' home. Arrest warrants were issued for Briggs and Driscoll, as well as 20 other people. Briggs was arrested, arraigned, and released. Extensive news coverage followed because Briggs was a prominent member of the community. The grand jury refused to return an indictment against Briggs, so all charges were dropped. He filed a Section 1983 lawsuit against Malley, the officer who was responsible for the wiretap, and the U.S. Supreme Court granted certiorari.

ISSUE

Is absolute immunity granted to police officers in Section 1983 actions?

HOLDING

No. Police officers do not enjoy absolute immunity in Section 1983 actions. Instead, they enjoy qualified immunity.

MALLEY v. BRIGGS *(cont.)*

RATIONALE

"Although we have previously held that police officers sued under Section 1983 for false arrest are qualifiedly immune, petitioner urges that he should be absolutely immune because his function in seeking an arrest warrant is similar to that of a complaining witness. The difficulty with this submission is that complaining witnesses were not absolutely immune at common law. In 1871, the generally accepted rule was that one who procured the issuance of an arrest warrant by submitting a complaint could be held liable if the complaint was made maliciously and without probable cause.... Accordingly, we held that the same standard of objective reasonableness that we applied in the context of a suppression hearing in *Leon* [*United States v. Leon,* 468 U.S. 897 (1984)] defines the qualified immunity accorded an officer whose request for a warrant allegedly caused an unconstitutional arrest. Only where the warrant application is so lacking in indicia of probable cause as to render official belief in its existence unreasonable will the shield of immunity be lost."

CASE EXCERPT

"As an alternative ground for claiming absolute immunity, petitioner draws an analogy between an officer requesting a warrant and a prosecutor who asks a grand jury to indict a suspect. Like the prosecutor, petitioner argues, the officer must exercise a discretionary judgment based on the evidence before him, and like the prosecutor, the officer may not exercise his best judgment if the threat of retaliatory lawsuits hangs over him. Thus, petitioner urges us to read 1983 as giving the officer the same absolute immunity enjoyed by the prosecutor. Even were we to overlook the fact that petitioner is inviting us to expand what was a qualified immunity at common law into an absolute immunity, we would find his analogy between himself and a prosecutor untenable. We have interpreted 1983 to give absolute immunity to functions 'intimately associated with the judicial phase of the criminal process.'"

CASE SIGNIFICANCE

This case is important because it no longer provided police officers absolute immunity from liability under Section 1983. Prosecutors, judges, legislators, and some other parties do still enjoy absolute immunity, however. Officers still enjoy absolute immunity from giving perjured testimony, just not in other areas of

their duties. Indeed, the bulk of police work takes place out of a courtroom, so this decision is one that benefits defendants and other individuals who find themselves subjected to police authority.

CITY OF CANTON v. HARRIS
489 U.S. 378 (1989)

FACTS

Harris was arrested by officers of the Canton Police Department and brought to the police station. When she arrived at the station Harris was found lying on the floor of the police wagon. When officers asked if she needed medical attention, she responded incoherently. After she was taken into the police station she slumped to the ground two more times. Officers finally left her on the floor to prevent her from falling again. She never received any medical attention at the stationhouse. Approximately one hour later she was released and taken to the hospital in an ambulance provided by her family. She was hospitalized for a week due to several emotional problems. She received outpatient treatment for nearly a year after that. She sued the city under Section 1983, claiming it failed to train its officers adequately.

ISSUE

Can a city be held liable under Section 1983 for constitutional violations resulting from failing to train its officers?

HOLDING

Yes. Cities can be held liable under Section 1983 for failure to train, but only if such failure amounts to "deliberate indifference."

RATIONALE

"In *Monell v. New York City Department of Social Services,* we decided that a municipality can be found liable under Section 1983 only where the municipality itself causes the constitutional violation at issue. *Respondeat superior* or vicarious liability will not attach under Section 1983.... [A] municipality can be liable under Section 1983 only where its policies are the 'moving force [behind] the constitutional violation.' Only where a municipality's failure to train its employees in a relevant respect evidences a 'deliberate indifference' to the rights of its inhabitants can such a shortcoming be properly thought of as a city 'policy or custom' that is actionable under Section

1983....The issue in a case like this one, however, is whether that training program is adequate; and if it is not, the question becomes whether such inadequate training can justifiably be said to represent 'city police.'...But it may happen that in light of the duties assigned to specific officers or employees that need for more or different training is so obvious, and the inadequacy so likely to result in the violation of constitutional rights, that the policymakers of the city can reasonably be said to have been deliberately indifferent to that need."

CASE EXCERPT

"In resolving the issue of a city's liability, the focus must be on adequacy of the training program in relation to the tasks the particular officers must perform. That a particular officer may be unsatisfactorily trained will not alone suffice to fasten liability on the city, for the officer's shortcomings may have resulted from factors other than a faulty training program. It may be, for example, that an otherwise sound program has occasionally been negligently administered. Neither will it suffice to prove that an injury or accident could have been avoided if an officer had had better or more training, sufficient to equip him to avoid the particular injury-causing conduct. Such a claim could be made about almost any encounter resulting in injury, yet not condemn the adequacy of the program to enable officers to respond properly to the usual and recurring situations with which they must deal. And plainly, adequately trained officers occasionally make mistakes; the fact that they do says little about the training program or the legal basis for holding the city liable."

CASE SIGNIFICANCE

This decision and one similar to it (*Board of the County Commissioners of Bryan County v. Brown,* discussed below) permit liability against cities and counties for failure to train, but only if deliberate indifference is shown. Importantly, if a plaintiff does not allege failure to train but, instead, argues that a city/county policy is responsible for the injury he or she suffered, a showing of deliberate indifference is not needed. That is, whether a city/county acts with deliberate indifference or simply no intent or culpability at all, it can be held liable for policies and customs that result in injuries of a constitutional nature. *Canton* is one of several recent decisions where the Supreme Court has forced plaintiffs to show that the defendant acted with a certain amount of culpability before a finding of liability will be returned.

WILL v. MICHIGAN DEPARTMENT OF STATE POLICE
491 U.S. 58 (1989)

FACTS

An employee filed a claim in Michigan Circuit Court against the Michigan Department of State Police and the Michigan Director of State Police in his official capacity, claiming that both parties denied promotion for an improper reason, in violation of 42 U.S.C. Section 1983. The Circuit Court remanded the case to the Michigan Civil Service Commission for a hearing, then the employee filed suit in the Michigan Court of Claims, raising the same Section 1983 claim as in his initial lawsuit. The circuit court held that (1) the employee established a constitutional violation, (2) the state police and the director of state police were "persons" for Section 1983 purposes, and (3) although the circuit court action was prohibited by state law, the court of claims action could go forward. The Michigan Court of Appeals held that a state is not a "person" under Section 1983 and vacated the lower court's judgment. It then remanded the case for a determination as to whether the director of state police may enjoy immunity from suit. Finally, the Michigan Supreme Court held that neither the state nor a state official acting in his or her official capacity is a "person" under Section 1983. The U.S. Supreme Court then granted certiorari.

ISSUE

Are states and state employees acting in their official capacities considered "persons" within the meaning of 42 U.S.C. Section 1983?

HOLDING

No. Neither states nor state officials acting in their official capacity are "persons" within the meaning of Section 1983.

RATIONALE

"Our conclusion that a State is not a 'person' within the meaning of Section 1983 is reinforced by Congress's purpose in enacting the statute. Congress enacted Section 1 of the Civil Rights Act of 1871...the precursor to Section 1983, shortly after the end of the Civil War 'in response to the widespread deprivations of civil rights in the Southern States and the inability or unwillingness of authorities in those States to protect those rights or punish wrongdoers.'...Although

WILL v. MICHIGAN DEPARTMENT OF STATE POLICE (cont.)

Congress did not establish federal courts as the exclusive forum to remedy these deprivations, ... it is plain that 'Congress assigned to the federal courts a paramount role' in this endeavor."

CASE EXCERPT

"If a State is a 'person' within the meaning of 1983, the section is to be read as saying that 'every person, including a State, who, under color of any statute, ordinance, regulation, custom, or usage, of any State or Territory or the District of Columbia, subjects.... That would be a decidedly awkward way of expressing an intent to subject the States to liability. At the very least, reading the statute in this way is not so clearly indicated that it provides reason to depart from the often-expressed understanding that "in common usage, the term 'person' does not include the sovereign, [and] statutes employing the [word] are ordinarily construed to exclude it... Section 1983 provides a federal forum to remedy many deprivations of civil liberties, but it does not provide a federal forum for litigants who seek a remedy against a State for alleged deprivations of civil liberties. The Eleventh Amendment bars such suits unless the State has waived its immunity, or unless Congress has exercised its undoubted power under 5 of the Fourteenth Amendment to override that immunity."

CASE SIGNIFICANCE

This case applies only to state officials. In plain terms, the case prohibited lawsuits against states as well as state officials acting in their official capacities. States enjoy immunity and "a suit against a state official in his or her official capacity is not a suit against the official but rather is a suit against the official's office.... As such, it is no different from a suit against the State itself." Local units of government such as cities and counties can still be sued under Section 1983. Also, nothing prohibits plaintiffs from suing state officials in their individual capacities for damages.

BOARD OF THE COUNTY COMMISSIONERS OF BRYAN COUNTY v. BROWN

520 U.S. 397 (1997)

FACTS

Brown was injured when Burns, an unarmed Oklahoma county deputy, pulled her from a truck that had been stopped after a high-speed pursuit. The passenger filed a lawsuit, claiming that the county, on the basis of the county sheriff's prior decision to hire the deputy, ought to be liable. The plaintiff claimed that Moore, the elected sheriff, had failed to adequately screen the deputy's background because he had a history of misdemeanor offenses, including assault and battery. The U.S. Supreme Court granted certiorari.

ISSUE

Can a county be held liable under Section 1983 for a sheriff's single hiring decision?

HOLDING

No. A county cannot be held liable under 42 U.S.C. 1983 for a single hiring decision made by one of its employees.

RATIONALE

"Even assuming without deciding that proof of a single instance of inadequate screening could ever trigger municipal liability, Moore's failure to scrutinize Burns' record cannot constitute deliberate indifference to respondent's federally protected right to be free from the use of excessive force. To test the link between Moore's action and Brown's injury, it must be asked whether a full review of Burns' record reveals that Moore should have concluded that Burns' use of excessive force would be a plainly obvious consequence of his decision to hire Burns. Respondent's showing on this point was inadequate because the primary infractions on which she relies to prove Burns' propensity for violence arose from a single college fight. A full review of Burns' record might well have led Moore to conclude that Burns was an extremely poor deputy candidate, but he would not necessarily have reached that decision because Burns' use of excessive force would have been a plainly obvious consequence of the decision to hire him. The District Court therefore erred in submitting the inadequate screening theory to the jury."

CASE EXCERPT

"Sheriff Moore's hiring decision was itself legal, and Sheriff Moore did not authorize Burns to use excessive force. Respondent's claim, rather, is that a single facially lawful hiring decision can launch a series of events that ultimately cause a violation of federal rights. Where a plaintiff claims that the municipality has not directly inflicted an injury, but nonetheless has caused an employee to do so, rigorous standards of culpability and causation must be applied to ensure that the municipality is not held liable solely for the actions of its employee."

CASE SIGNIFICANCE

This case reduced the potential scope of earlier decisions. In *City of Canton v. Harris,* the Court held that counties can be held liable for inadequate training that amounts to deliberate indifference. Here, the Court held that single hiring decisions are not enough to hold counties liable for constitutional rights violations. So, counties can take a measure of comfort in the fact that their hiring decisions—assuming there is not a pattern of poor hiring—will be shielded from liability. However, once officers or deputies are hired, the city or county must adequately train them. Failure to adequately train—that is, failure that amounts to deliberate indifference to people's federally protected rights—can serve as a basis for Section 1983 civil liability.

MCMILLIAN v. MONROE COUNTY

520 U.S. 781 (1997)

FACTS

McMillian was convicted of murder and sentenced to death. His conviction was later overturned after a finding that investigators had suppressed exculpatory evidence, which amounts to a due process violation. He brought suit against the investigators, the sheriff, and Monroe County under 42 U.S.C. Section 1983. The case was based on the assumption that the sheriff was acting as a representative of the county when he and other investigators alleged suppressed the exculpatory evidence in question. The U.S. Supreme Court granted certiorari.

ISSUE

Is a sheriff a representative of the county?

HOLDING

No. Whether a sheriff is a representative of the county or of the state is determined by the state's constitution, laws, or regulations (in Alabama, the sheriff is not a representative of the county).

RATIONALE

"In determining a local government's Section 1983 liability, a court's task is to identify those who speak with final authority for the local governmental actor concerning the action alleged to have cause the violation at issue (*Jett v. Dallas Independent School District,* 491 U.S. 701, 703).... In deciding this dispute, the question is not whether...sheriffs act as county or state officials in all of their official actions, but whom they represent in a particular area or on a particular issue."

CASE EXCERPT

"Our inquiry is guided by two principles. First, the question is not whether Sheriff Tate acts for Alabama or Monroe County in some categorical, 'all or nothing' manner. Our cases on the liability of local governments under Section 1983 instruct us to ask whether governmental officials are final policymakers for the local government in a particular area, or on a particular issue. Thus, we are not seeking to make a characterization of Alabama sheriffs that will hold true for every type of official action they engage in. We simply ask whether Sheriff Tate represents the State or the county when he acts in a law enforcement capacity. Second, our inquiry is dependent on an analysis of state law. This is not to say that state law can answer the question for us by, for example, simply labeling as a state official an official who clearly makes county policy. But our understanding of the actual function of a governmental official, in a particular area, will necessarily be dependent on the definition of the official's functions under relevant state law."

CASE SIGNIFICANCE

This case is important because it suggested that some sheriffs can be sued and others cannot. Where sheriffs represent counties, they can be sued. So can counties. However, where sheriffs represent the state, they cannot be sued in their official capacity, although they can be sued in their individual capacity.

COUNTY OF SACRAMENTO v. LEWIS

523 U.S. 833 (1998)

FACTS

On his way to a call to break up a fight, a police officer observed a motorcycle approaching at high speed. The officer turned on his lights, yelled for the motorcycle to stop, and unsuccessfully attempted to block the motorcycle by moving his cruiser close to that of a county sheriff's deputy. The deputy switched on his lights and siren and began chasing the motorcycle. During

COUNTY OF SACRAMENTO v. LEWIS *(cont.)*

the chase, the motorcycle tipped over. The deputy was unable to bring his cruiser to a halt before hitting and killing the motorcycle's passenger. Representatives of the passenger's estate brought a Section 1983 action, alleging a substantive due process violation under the Fourteenth Amendment to the U.S. Constitution. The district court, granting summary judgment in favor of the deputy, suggested he was entitled to qualified immunity. The Court of Appeals for the Ninth Circuit reversed, suggesting that a "deliberate indifference" standard be applied to Fourteenth Amendment substantive due process claims, and the U.S. Supreme Court granted certiorari.

ISSUE

Is "deliberate indifference" the appropriate standard for judging Fourteenth Amendment substantive due process claims arising under 42 U.S.C. Section 1983?

HOLDING

No. A police officer will not be held liable for a substantive due process violation unless his or her conduct "shocks the conscience."

RATIONALE

"A police officer does not violate substantive due process by causing death through deliberate or reckless indifference to life in a high-speed automobile chase aimed at apprehending a suspected offender.... Lewis' allegations are insufficient to state a substantive due process violation. Protection against governmental arbitrariness is the core of due process, including substantive due process, but only the most egregious executive action can be said to be 'arbitrary' in the constitutional sense...; the cognizable level of executive abuse of power is that which shocks the conscience.... In the circumstances of a high-speed chase aimed at apprehending a suspected offender, where unforeseen circumstances demand an instant judgment on the part of an officer who feels the pulls of competing obligations, only a purpose to cause harm unrelated to the legitimate object of arrest will satisfy the shocks-the-conscience test. Such chases with no intent to harm suspects physically or to worsen their legal plight do not give rise to substantive due process liability."

CASE EXCERPT

"Smith was faced with a course of lawless behavior for which the police were not to blame. They had done nothing to cause Willard's high-speed driving in the first place, nothing to excuse his flouting of the commonly understood law enforcement authority to control traffic, and nothing (beyond a refusal to call off the chase) to encourage him to race through traffic at breakneck speed forcing other drivers out of their travel lanes. Willard's outrageous behavior was practically instantaneous, and so was Smith's instinctive response. While prudence would have repressed the reaction, the officer's instinct was to do his job as a law enforcement officer, not to induce Willard's lawlessness, or to terrorize, cause harm, or kill. Prudence, that is, was subject to countervailing enforcement considerations, and while Smith exaggerated their demands, there is no reason to believe that they were tainted by an improper or malicious motive on his part."

CASE SIGNIFICANCE

Historically, to successfully state a claim under Section 1983, a plaintiff must show that he or she suffered a constitutional rights violation by a person acting under color of state law. Recently, however, the Supreme Court has begun to impose a culpability requirement on Section 1983 claims. The significance of this case is that for a plaintiff to succeed with a substantive due process claim, in addition to showing a constitutional violation by an official acting under color of law, the plaintiff must also prove that the official's conduct shocked the conscience. This is an exceedingly high standard, making it fairly difficult for people to succeed with Section 1983 substantive due process claims.

SAUCIER v. KATZ
533 U.S. 194 (2001)

FACTS

Katz, an animal-rights protestor, was taken into custody when he attempted to disrupt Vice President Gore's speech at a military base. Katz filed a *Bivens* action (the vehicle for Section 1983 lawsuits against federal officials) against Saucier, alleging that Saucier had violated his Fourth Amendment rights by using excessive force when arresting him. The District Court ruled that Saucier was not entitled to summary judgment on the claim of excessive force. The Court of Appeals for the Ninth Circuit affirmed, using a two-part qualified immunity inquiry. First, it found that the law governing Saucier's conduct at the time of the arrest was clear, so it moved to the second inquiry: whether a reasonable officer could have believed, given that the law was clear at the time of arrest, that his conduct was unlawful. The court concluded that the qualified immunity inquiry and the Fourth Amendment excessive force inquiry were the same and concluded that qualified immunity was inappropriate; the U.S. Supreme Court then granted certiorari.

ISSUE
Are the qualified immunity inquiry and the Fourth Amendment excessive force inquiry the same?

HOLDING
No. The questions of whether excessive force was used and whether qualified immunity should be granted are to be kept separate, not fused into a single inquiry. The first inquiry should be whether a federal constitutional right would have been violated on the facts alleged. The second inquiry, assuming such a violation could be made out, requires determining whether the constitutional right was clearly established.

RATIONALE
"A qualified immunity ruling requires an analysis not susceptible of fusion with the question whether unreasonable force was used in making the arrest. The Ninth Circuit's approach cannot be reconciled with *Anderson v. Creighton*, 483 U.S. 637 (1987). A qualified immunity defense must be considered in proper sequence. A ruling should be made early in the proceedings so that the cost and expenses of trial are avoided where the defense is dispositive. Such immunity is an entitlement not to stand trial, not a defense from liability.... The initial inquiry is whether a constitutional right would have been violated on the facts alleged, for if no right would have been violated, there is no need for further inquiry into immunity. However, if a violation could be made out on a favorable view of the parties' submissions, the next, sequential step is whether the right was clearly established. This inquiry must be undertaken in light of the case's specific context, not as a broad general proposition. The relevant, dispositive inquiry is whether it would be clear to a reasonable officer that the conduct was unlawful in the situation he confronted.... The Ninth Circuit's approach—to deny summary judgment if a material issue of fact remains on the excessive force

claim—could undermine the goal of qualified immunity to avoid excessive disruption of government and permit the resolution of many insubstantial claims on summary judgment."

CASE EXCERPT
"Petitioner did not know the full extent of the threat respondent posed or how many other persons there might be who, in concert with respondent, posed a threat to the security of the Vice President. There were other potential protestors in the crowd, and at least one other individual was arrested and placed into the van with respondent. In carrying out the detention, as it has been assumed the officers had the right to do, petitioner was required to recognize the necessity to protect the Vice President by securing respondent and restoring order to the scene. It cannot be said there was a clearly established rule that would prohibit using the force petitioner did to place respondent into the van to accomplish these objectives."

CASE SIGNIFICANCE
This case addressed a somewhat narrow and controversial issue in police civil liability law: qualified immunity. The Fourth Amendment prohibits unreasonable searches and seizures. "Reasonableness" is determined by reference to what a reasonable police officer would have done under the circumstances. However, the courts also use a reasonableness test when determining whether qualified immunity should be extended to a defendant police officer. Just like the Fourth Amendment reasonableness analysis, qualified immunity considers how a reasonable officer would behave. The Ninth Circuit thought these two inquiries should be fused into one to avoid confusion. The Supreme Court disagreed and held that two separate reasonableness tests should be conducted. First, to determine whether a Fourth Amendment violation has taken place, courts must consider whether a reasonable officer would have acted in the same way under the circumstances. Then, courts must move to the qualified immunity analysis, which requires determining whether a reasonable officer would believe the law surrounding the conduct in question was clear. In other words, if the law was unclear, and such a determination is reasonable, qualified immunity will be granted. Therefore, qualified immunity serves as a defense to officers who act on reasonably mistaken beliefs, even if their actions violate the Fourth Amendment.

TOWN OF CASTLE ROCK, COLORADO v. GONZALES

545 U.S. 748 (2005)

FACTS

Respondent filed this suit under 42 U. S. C. §1983 alleging that petitioner violated the Fourteenth Amendment's due process clause when its police officers, acting pursuant to official policy or custom, failed to respond to her repeated reports over several hours that her estranged husband had taken their three children in violation of her restraining order against him. Ultimately, the husband murdered the children. The District Court granted the town's motion to dismiss, but an en banc majority of the Tenth Circuit reversed, finding that respondent had alleged a cognizable procedural due process claim because a Colorado statute established the state legislature's clear intent to require police to enforce retraining orders, and thus its intent that the order's recipient have an entitlement to its enforcement.

ISSUE

Under Colorado law, did Gonzales have a property interest in having a protective order enforced by the police?

HOLDING

No. Respondent, Gonzales, did not have a protected property interest in the enforcement of the restraining order under Colorado law.

RATIONALE

Respondent's alleged interest stems only from a State's *statutory* scheme—from a restraining order that was authorized by and tracked precisely the statute on which the Court of Appeals relied. She does not assert that she has any common-law or contractual entitlement to enforcement. If she was given a statutory entitlement, we would expect to see some indication of that in the statute itself. Although Colorado's statute spoke of "protected person[s]" such as respondent, it did so in connection with matters other than a right to enforcement. It said that a "protected person shall be provided with a copy of [a restraining] order" when it is issued, §18-6-803.5(3)(a); that a law enforcement agency "shall make all reasonable efforts to contact the protected party upon the arrest of the restrained person," §18-6-803.5(3)(d); and that the

agency "shall give [to the protected person] a copy" of the report it submits to the court that issued the order, §18-6-803.5(3)(e). Perhaps most importantly, the statute spoke directly to the protected person's power to "initiate contempt proceedings against the restrained person if the order [was] issued in a civil action or request the prosecuting attorney to initiate contempt proceedings if the order [was] issued in a criminal action" §18-6-803.5(7). The protected person's express power to "initiate" civil contempt proceedings contrasts tellingly with the mere ability to "request" initiation of criminal contempt proceedings—and even more dramatically with the complete silence about any power to "request" (much less demand) that an arrest be made.

CASE EXCERPT

"Even if we were to think otherwise concerning the creation of an entitlement by Colorado, it is by no means clear that an individual entitlement to enforcement of a restraining order could constitute a 'property' interest for purposes of the Due Process Clause. Such a right would not, of course, resemble any traditional conception of property."

CASE SIGNIFICANCE

In this case, the police were not deemed liable due to the manner in which the Court interpreted the narrow language and specific wording of the Colorado law regarding the enforcement of restraining orders. Had the law been worded differently, the police would have likely been held liable for the deaths of the children. This case is important because it points out to state legislatures and police departments the very narrow margin of error that exists surrounding the duty to protect individuals named in such protective orders. Police departments need to ensure that they have a thorough understanding of their duty to protect under their own state laws and that, as a matter of policy and practice, such orders are given the attention they deserve.

PEARSON v. CALLAHAN

555 U.S.—(2009)

FACTS

The Central Utah Narcotics Task Force is charged with investigating illegal drug use and sales. In 2002, Brian Bartholomew, who became an informant for the task force after having been charged with the unlawful possession of methamphetamine, informed Officer Jeffrey Whatcott that respondent Afton Callahan had arranged to sell Bartholomew methamphetamine later that day. That evening, Bartholomew arrived at respondent's residence at about 8 p.m. Once there, Bartholomew went inside and confirmed that respondent had methamphetamine available for sale. Bartholomew then told respondent that he needed to obtain money to make his purchase and left. Bartholomew met with members of the task force at about 9 p.m. and told them that he would be able to buy a gram of methamphetamine for $100. After concluding that Bartholomew was capable of completing the planned purchase, the officers searched him, determined that he had no controlled substances on his person, gave him a marked $100 bill and a concealed electronic transmitter to monitor his conversations, and agreed on a signal that he would give after completing the purchase.

The officers drove Bartholomew to respondent's trailer home, and respondent's daughter let him inside. Respondent then retrieved a large bag containing methamphetamine from his freezer and sold Bartholomew a gram of methamphetamine, which he put into a small plastic bag. Bartholomew gave the arrest signal to the officers who were monitoring the conversation, and they entered the trailer through a porch door. In the enclosed porch, the officers encountered Bartholomew, respondent, and two other persons, and they saw respondent drop a plastic bag, which they later determined contained methamphetamine. The officers then conducted a protective sweep of the premises. In addition to the large bag of methamphetamine, the officers recovered the marked bill from respondent and a small bag containing methamphetamine from Bartholomew, and they found drug syringes in the residence. As a result, respondent was charged with the unlawful possession and distribution of methamphetamine.

ISSUE

Should the two-prong requirements of *Saucier* be rigidly enforced?

HOLDING

No. The *Saucier* procedure should not be regarded as an inflexible requirement, and petitioners are entitled to qualified immunity on the ground that it was not clearly established at the time of the search that their conduct was unconstitutional.

RATIONALE

The Supreme Court, in a unanimous decision authored by Justice Alito, held that while *Saucier's* two-part test for qualified immunity is sound, there is no requirement that a court making a qualified immunity determination find a constitutional violation *prior* to determining whether a constitutional right was clearly established. Instead, courts have the discretion to decide which of the two parts of the test should be examined first, in the interests of judicial economy. Compelling parties to litigate constitutional issues first, when it is clear that the alleged right was not clearly established at the time of the violation, was a waste of the court's time. The Court also held that the officers in this case were entitled to qualified immunity, as at the time of their search, several federal circuit courts had endorsed the applicability of the consent once removed doctrine to informants, and the officers were entitled to rely on that law.

CASE EXCERPT

"On reconsidering the procedure required in *Saucier*, we conclude that, while the sequence set forth there is often appropriate, it should no longer be regarded as mandatory. The judges of the district courts and the courts of appeals should be permitted to exercise their sound discretion in deciding which of the two prongs of the qualified immunity analysis should be addressed first in light of the circumstances in the particular case at hand."

CASE SIGNIFICANCE

Typically, under *Saucier*, courts are first required to ask whether a federal constitutional right would have been violated based on the alleged facts of the case. Secondarily, it should then ask whether there was an established constitutional right that was clearly established. This order of determination is no longer set in stone, so to speak. Instead, lower courts now have the discretion to first ask if there was a clearly established constitutional right before making a determination as to the first question—whether there was a violation of that right.

DISCUSSION QUESTIONS

1. Are civil lawsuits against the police an effective remedy when constitutional rights are violated?

2. When would it be more advantageous for a person to pursue civil litigation rather than some other remedy?

3. If civil litigation is not an option, aggrieved parties can file complaints with police departments' citizen complaint divisions. Is this procedure effective?

4. Clearly, we live in a litigious society where people are quick to sue one another. What is your opinion of this state of affairs?

5. Are jury verdicts against the police out of control? If not, where else in the world of civil litigation are they out of control?

GLOSSARY

42 U.S.C. Section 1983: A federal statute providing for civil litigation against law enforcement officials acting in their official capacity. The statute states: "Every person who, under color of any statute, ordinance, regulation, custom, or usage, of any State or Territory, subjects, or causes to be subjected, any citizen of the United States or other persons within the jurisdiction thereof to the deprivation of any rights, privileges, or immunities secured by the Constitution and laws, shall be liable to the party injured in an action at law, suit in equity, or other proper proceeding for redress."

absolute immunity: An official who cannot be sued under any circumstances enjoys absolute immunity.

apparent authority: When the police reasonably believe a third party has authority to grant consent.

appellant: The person who appeals.

appellee: The person who is appealed against. The appellee is sometimes called the "respondent."

armspan rule: The requirement that a search incident to arrest be limited to the area "within [the] immediate control" of the person arrested—that is, "the area from within which he might have obtained either a weapon or something that could have been used as evidence against him."

arrest: The taking of a person into custody for the commission of an offense as the prelude to prosecuting him or her for it.

arrest warrant: Judicial authorization to arrest a particular person. If no name is available, a "John Doe" arrest warrant can be issued.

articulate/articulable: To express, formulate, or present one's thoughts in clear and effective fashion.

checkpoints: A law enforcement practice of briefly stopping people at fixed locations, such as on highways or in airports.

civil asset forfeiture: A legal method for the government to take possession of property used to facilitate or obtained by a criminal act.

civil litigation: A lawsuit.

closely regulated business: A business subject to strict licensing and monitoring requirements (e.g., a firearms dealership).

color of law: When a law enforcement officer acts in his or her official capacity, he or she is said to have acted under color of law.

common authority: Mutual use of property by persons generally having joint access or control for most purposes.

concurring opinion: A different reason for the court's decision offered by another judge or justice.

consent search: A search based on a voluntary waiver of one's Fourth Amendment rights.

203

culpability: Intent.

custodial interrogation: Questioning initiated by law enforcement officers after a person has been taken into custody or deprived of his or her freedom in any significant way.

deadly force: Physical force that is reasonably likely to cause death. A gun is an instrument of deadly force.

defendant: The person charged with a crime.

dissent: Much like an opinion, but written in opposition to the court's opinion.

distinguish: When a previous decision does not apply to the current facts, a court will hand down a "new" decision. A distinguished case is one where *stare decisis* does not or cannot apply.

district courts: Federal trial courts. There are 94 federal district courts in the United States as of this writing.

drug-courier profiling: The act of looking for individuals who fit the characteristics of people who transport illegal narcotics.

due process: A concern with people's rights and liberties; a perspective that gives significant weight to human freedom. The due process perspective closely resembles a liberal political orientation.

***Edwards* rule:** A decision stating that once a suspect expresses a desire to deal with the police only through counsel, he or she may not be subjected to further interrogation until such time as the request is fulfilled or the accused initiates further communication with the authorities.

Eighth Amendment: "Excessive bail shall not be required, nor excessive fines imposed, nor cruel and unusual punishments inflicted."

exclusionary rule: The rule that evidence obtained in violation of the Constitution cannot be used in a criminal trial to prove guilt.

exigent circumstances: Emergencies.

Fifth Amendment: "No person shall be held to answer for a capital, or otherwise infamous crime, unless on a presentment or indictment of a Grand Jury, except in cases arising in the land or naval forces, or in the Militia, when in actual service in time of War or public danger; nor shall any person be subject for the same offense to be twice put in jeopardy of life or limb; nor shall be compelled in any criminal case to be a witness against himself, nor be deprived of life, liberty, or property, without due process of law; nor shall private property be taken for public use, without just compensation."

Fourteenth Amendment: "All persons born or naturalized in the United States, and subject to the jurisdiction thereof, are citizens of the United States and of the State wherein they reside. No State shall make or enforce any law which shall abridge the privileges or immunities of citizens of the United States, nor shall any State deprive any person of life, liberty, or property, without due process of law; nor deny to any person within its jurisdiction the equal protection of the laws."

Fourth Amendment: "The right of the people to be secure in their persons, houses, papers, and effects, against unreasonable searches and seizures, shall not be violated, and no Warrants shall issue, but upon probable cause, supported by Oath or affirmation and particularly describing the place to be searched, and the persons or things to be seized."

frisk: A pat down of the outer clothing to locate weapons or other dangerous instruments.

"fruit of the poisonous tree" doctrine: The exclusionary rule applies not only to evidence obtained as a direct result of a Constitutional rights violation, but also to evidence indirectly derived from the Constitutional rights violation.

"good-faith" exception: If an honest and "good-faith" mistake is made during a search or seizure, any subsequently obtained evidence will be considered admissible at trial.

habeas corpus: A judicial order used to determine whether or not a prisoner is being restrained of his or her liberty without due process.

harmless error doctrine: A judicial rule stating that the admission of illegally obtained evidence by a trial court need not automatically require reversal of a conviction where it can be established that the error in question caused no real harm.

hot pursuit: An emergency situation in which police chase a fleeing suspect.

house: Any structure that a person uses as a residence (and frequently a business) on either a temporary or long-term basis.

immediate area/span of control: That area within a suspect's ready reach where a weapon, evidence of criminal activity, or implements of escape may be located.

immediately apparent: The requirement that the police have probable cause (more than 50 percent certainty) to seize evidence under the plain view doctrine.

incident to arrest: Events or actions taken after an arrest has been made.

independent source: An exception to the "fruit of the poisonous tree" doctrine that provides that evidence provided by a neutral third party (or other source) in no way connected with the police will be admissible.

indigence: A state of impoverishment. An indigent defendant is one who lacks funds or the ability to hire legal defense.

inevitable discovery: An exception to the "fruit of the poisonous tree" doctrine that provides that evidence that would inevitably have been discovered will be admissible even if it was obtained in an unconstitutional fashion.

inspection: A "search" to ensure compliance with some set of rules or regulations. Inspections are not intended for detecting evidence of criminal activity.

jailhouse informant: An individual who assists authorities by providing incriminating evidence against another prisoner.

justification: A term used synonymously with "cause." It is usually part of a question: Did the police have *justification* to search?

"knock and announce" requirement: The common law requirement that police officers first knock and announce their presence before serving search or arrest warrants.

lawful access: The requirement that the police be lawfully in the place where evidence is to be seized under the plain view doctrine.

neutral and detached magistrate: A judge or magistrate who is (1) objective and not working with anyone in the executive branch of government and (2) not receiving financial compensation for the issuance of warrants.

nondeadly force: Physical force that is *not* reasonably likely to cause death. Pepper spray is an instrument of nondeadly force.

objective reasonableness: The proper course of action as viewed by a "reasonable person."

opinion: The "voice" of the court containing the reasoning for a decision.

papers and effects: Personal items such as business records, letters, diaries, and memos.

particularity (in a search vs. arrest warrant): Particularity refers to the person to be arrested, the location to be searched, and/or the items to be seized. Particularity in a search warrant requires that the warrant specify the place to be searched *and* the items to be seized. Particularity in an arrest warrant is satisfied with the arrestee's complete name or a sufficiently detailed description of the suspect.

photo lineup: A photographic collage of individual "mug shots" generally assembled for purposes of identifying a particular criminal suspect from an array of other individuals.

"plain view" doctrine: A Court-created doctrine that permits warrantless seizure of evidence by the police when (1) the police are lawfully in the area where the evidence is located and (2) the items are "immediately apparent" as subject to seizure.

police–probation partnerships: The most common form consists of the pairing of police officers with probation officers for the purpose of conducting spot checks on probationers.

precedent: A rule of case law (i.e., a decision by a court) that is binding on all lower courts as well as the court issuing the decision.

prima facie: On the face of, at first glance.

pro se representation: Representing oneself in a legal proceeding.

probable cause (in a search vs. arrest warrant): Probable cause is, simply, more than 50 percent certainty. The officer applying for a search warrant must show probable cause that the items to be seized are connected with criminal activity *and* probable cause that the items to be seized are in the location to be searched. The probable cause showing in an arrest warrant requires that the officer applying for the warrant show probable cause that the person to be arrested committed the crime.

procedural due process: Protection from arbitrary and unfair deprivations of protected life, liberty, or property interests without procedural safeguards.

prosecutor: A representative of the government charged with presenting evidence against the defendant.

protective sweep: A cursory visual inspection of those places in which a person might be hiding.

"purged taint" exception: An exception to the "fruit of the poisonous tree" doctrine that provides that unconstitutionally obtained evidence may be admissible if the "taint" of the unconstitutional act has been significantly reduced, such as by a significant time lapse.

qualified immunity: A judicially created defense that does not appear in the language of Section 1983, or in any other statute. Qualified immunity can serve as more than an affirmative defense, and in some cases affords immunity from suit.

reasonable expectation of privacy: An individual's expectation of privacy that society is prepared to recognize as reasonable. The reasonable expectation of privacy is commonly contrasted with a *subjective* expectation of privacy, one that an individual believes is reasonable.

reasonable suspicion: A standard of justification that falls below probable cause but above an unarticulated hunch. It is the standard of justification necessary for stops and frisks.

reasonableness clause: The reasonableness clause consists of the following text from the Fourth Amendment: "The right of the people to be secure in their persons, houses, papers, and effects, against unreasonable searches and seizures, shall not be violated."

remand: When a case is remanded it is sent back to the trial court for further action consistent with the appellate court's decision.

return (of warrant): The act of a law enforcement officer delivering back to a presiding court official a judicial order that he has executed along with a brief account of his or her doings under the order.

reverse: To nullify a trial verdict. A reversal is not the same as an acquittal.

school disciplinary search: A search of students' lockers or personal effects for evidence of rule violations.

search: A governmental infringement on a reasonable expectation of privacy.

search incident to arrest: A search conducted in close temporal proximity to an arrest, usually directly afterward.

search warrant: Judicial authorization to look for evidence of criminal activity.

seizure (of a person vs. of evidence): To interfere with a person's movement to the extent that he or she is not free to leave and/or to interfere with his or her possessory interest in property.

Sixth Amendment: "In all criminal prosecutions, the accused shall enjoy the right to a speedy and public trial, by an impartial jury of the State and district wherein the crime shall have been committed, which district shall have been previously ascertained by law, and to be informed of the nature and cause of the accusation; to be confronted with the witnesses against him; to have compulsory process for obtaining witnesses in his favor, and to have the Assistance of Counsel for his defense."

sovereign immunity: The rule that states and state officials acting in their official capacities cannot be sued in federal court.

standardized field sobriety test: Any number of widely accepted tasks used by law enforcement personnel to make a preliminary determination that an individual is intoxicated (e.g., horizontal gaze nystagmus).

stare decisis: A Latin term meaning to abide by or adhere to decided cases.

statutes: Legal codes, such as the penal code.

stop: A stop occurs when the police question or communicate with a person and a reasonable person would believe that he or she is not free to leave.

stop and frisk: The detention of an individual for investigative purposes. The ensuing frisk or "pat down" is limited to the individual's outer clothing for purposes of confirming the presence of a weapon that may be used to harm an officer or another person.

subjective reasonableness: The proper course of action as viewed by the individual engaged in an act.

substantive due process: Protection from arbitrary and unreasonable action on the part of state officials.

Title III of the Omnibus Crime Control and Safe Streets Act of 1968: Federal legislation that sets forth specific requirements for electronic surveillance activities.

totality of circumstances: All of the facts and circumstances surrounding a case.

U.S. Supreme Court ("the Court"): The highest court in the United States. Appeals from state supreme courts or U.S. courts of appeals may be appealed here if they raise a federal constitutional question.

vacate: To set aside a lower court's verdict.

vehicle inventories: To take note of and document the contents of an automobile, usually after an arrest of a suspect and/or impoundment of the vehicle.

warrant clause: The warrant clause consists of the following text from the Fourth Amendment: "and no Warrants shall issue, but upon probable cause, supported by Oath or affirmation and particularly describing the place to be searched, and the persons or things to be seized."

Warren Court: The Supreme Court under Chief Justice Earl Warren. The Warren Court handed down many due process–oriented decisions.

wingspan: That area within a suspect's immediate control where he or she may gain control of a weapon, evidence, or the implements of escape.

writ of certiorari: An order by the Supreme Court requiring the lower court to send the case and a record of its proceedings up for review.

INDEX

9 780199 957910